...aira/Chashiba Katase
English translation copyright © 2016 Kyo Shirodaira/Chashiba Katase

All rights reserved.

Published in the United States by Kodansha Comics,
an imprint of Kodansha USA Publishing, LLC, New York.

Publication rights for this English edition arranged through Kodansha Ltd.,
Tokyo.

First published in Japan in 2015 by Kodansha Ltd., Tokyo, as *Kyokou Suiri*
volume 2.

ISBN 978-1-63236-380-0

Printed in the United States of America.

www.kodanshacomics.com

9 8 7 6 5 4 3 2 1

Translation: Alethea Nibley & Athena Nibley
Lettering: Lys Blakeslee
Editing: Ajani Oloye
Kodansha Comics edition cover design: Phil Balsman

Yamada-kun AND THE Seven Witches

"A very funny manga with a lot of heart and character."
—Adventures in Poor Taste

SWAPPED WITH A KISS?!

Class troublemaker Ryu Yamada is already having a bad day when he stumbles down a staircase along with star student Urara Shiraishi. When he wakes up, he realizes they have switched bodies—and that Ryu has the power to trade places with anyone just by kissing them. Ryu and Urara take full advantage of the situation to improve their lives, but with such an oddly amazing power, just how long will they be able to keep their secret under wraps?

Available now in print and digitally!

Maria
THE VIRGIN WITCH

PURITY AND POWER

As a war to determine the rightful ruler of medieval France ravages the land, the witch Maria decides she will not stand idly by as men kill each other in the name of God and glory. Using her powerful magic, she summons various beasts and demons —even going as far as using a succubus to seduce soldiers into submission under the veil of night— all to stop the needless slaughter. However, after the Archangel Michael puts an end to her meddling, he curses her to lose her powers if she ever gives up her virginity. Will she forgo the forbidden fruit of adulthood in order to bring an end to the merciless machine of war?

Available now in print and digitally!

KODANSHA COMICS

INUYASHIKI

A superhero like none you've ever seen, from the creator of "Gantz"!

ICHIRO INUYASHIKI IS DOWN ON HIS LUCK. HE LOOKS MUCH OLDER THAN HIS 58 YEARS, HIS CHILDREN DESPISE HIM, AND HIS WIFE THINKS HE'S A USELESS COWARD. SO WHEN HE'S DIAGNOSED WITH STOMACH CANCER AND GIVEN THREE MONTHS TO LIVE, IT SEEMS THE ONLY ONE WHO'LL MISS HIM IS HIS DOG.

THEN A BLINDING LIGHT FILLS THE SKY, AND THE OLD MAN IS KILLED... ONLY TO WAKE UP LATER IN A BODY HE ALMOST RECOGNIZES AS HIS OWN. CAN IT BE THAT ICHIRO INUYASHIKI IS NO LONGER HUMAN?

COMES IN EXTRA-LARGE EDITIONS WITH COLOR PAGES!

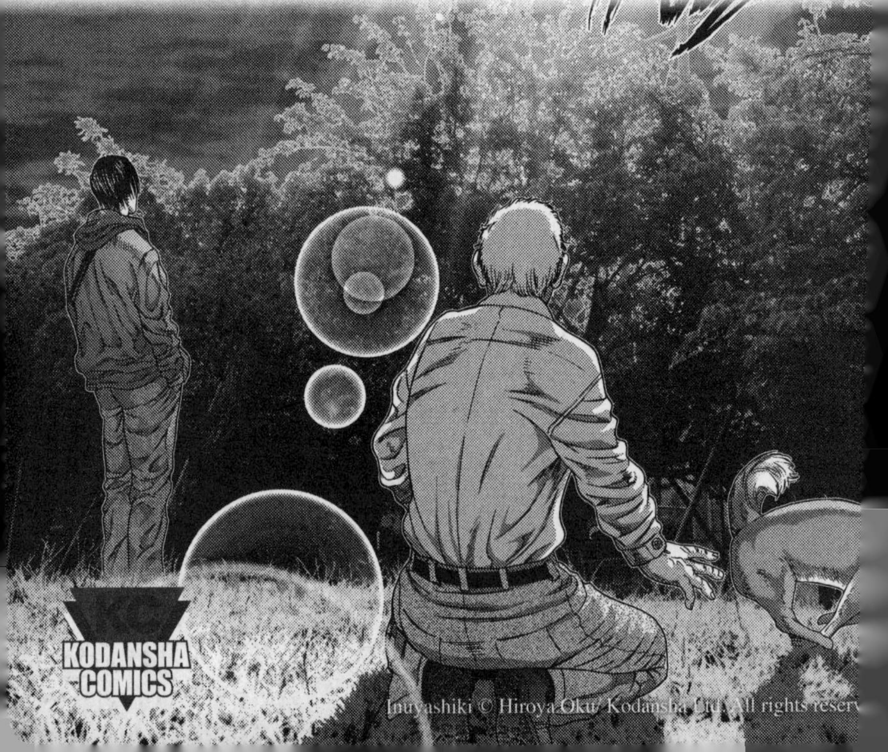
KODANSHA COMICS

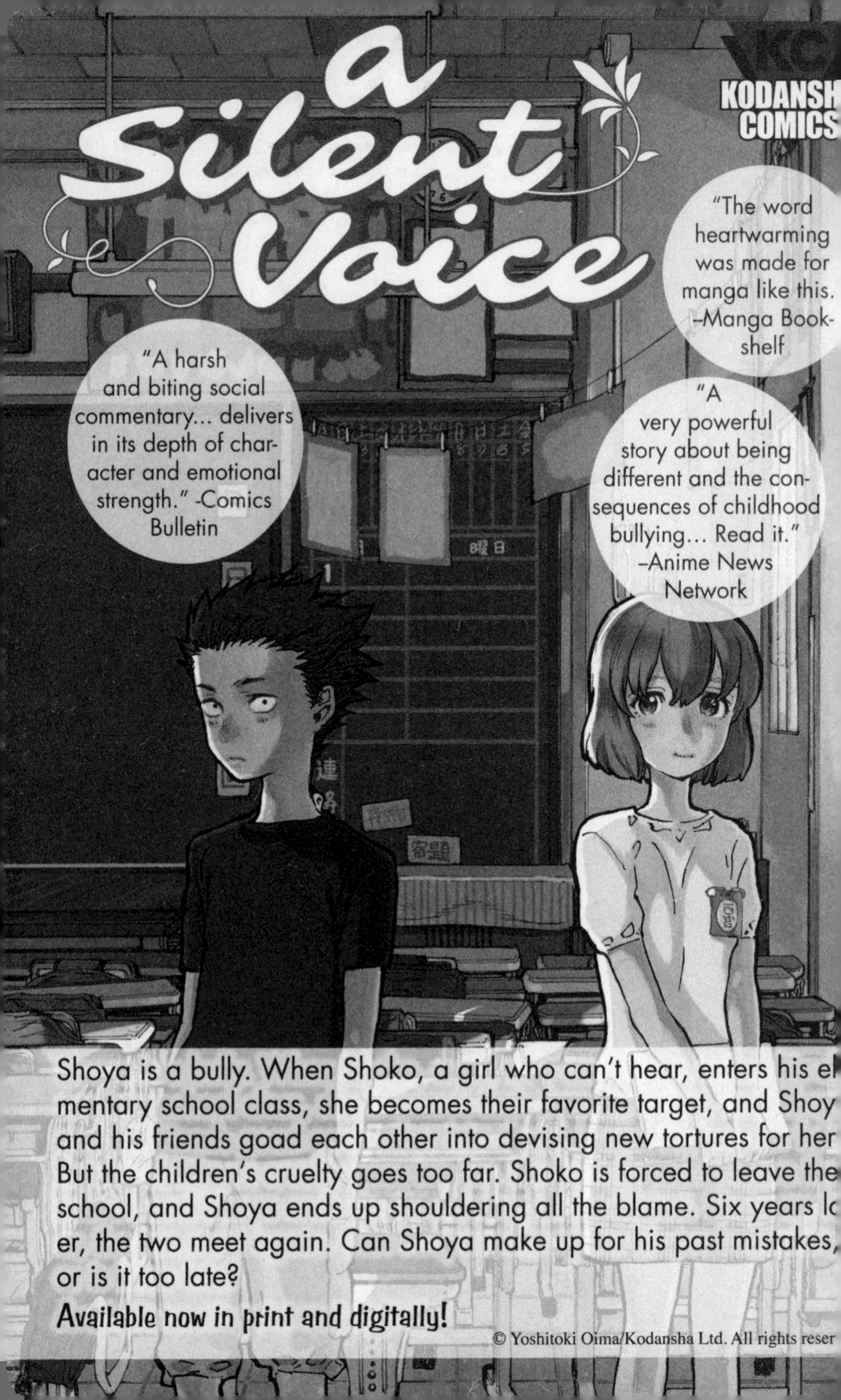
a Silent Voice
KODANSHA COMICS
"A harsh and biting social commentary... delivers in its depth of character and emotional strength." -Comics Bulletin
"The word heartwarming was made for manga like this." –Manga Bookshelf
"A very powerful story about being different and the consequences of childhood bullying... Read it." –Anime News Network
Shoya is a bully. When Shoko, a girl who can't hear, enters his elementary school class, she becomes their favorite target, and Shoya and his friends goad each other into devising new tortures for her. But the children's cruelty goes too far. Shoko is forced to leave the school, and Shoya ends up shouldering all the blame. Six years later, the two meet again. Can Shoya make up for his past mistakes, or is it too late?
Available now in print and digitally!
© Yoshitoki Oima/Kodansha Ltd. All rights reserved.

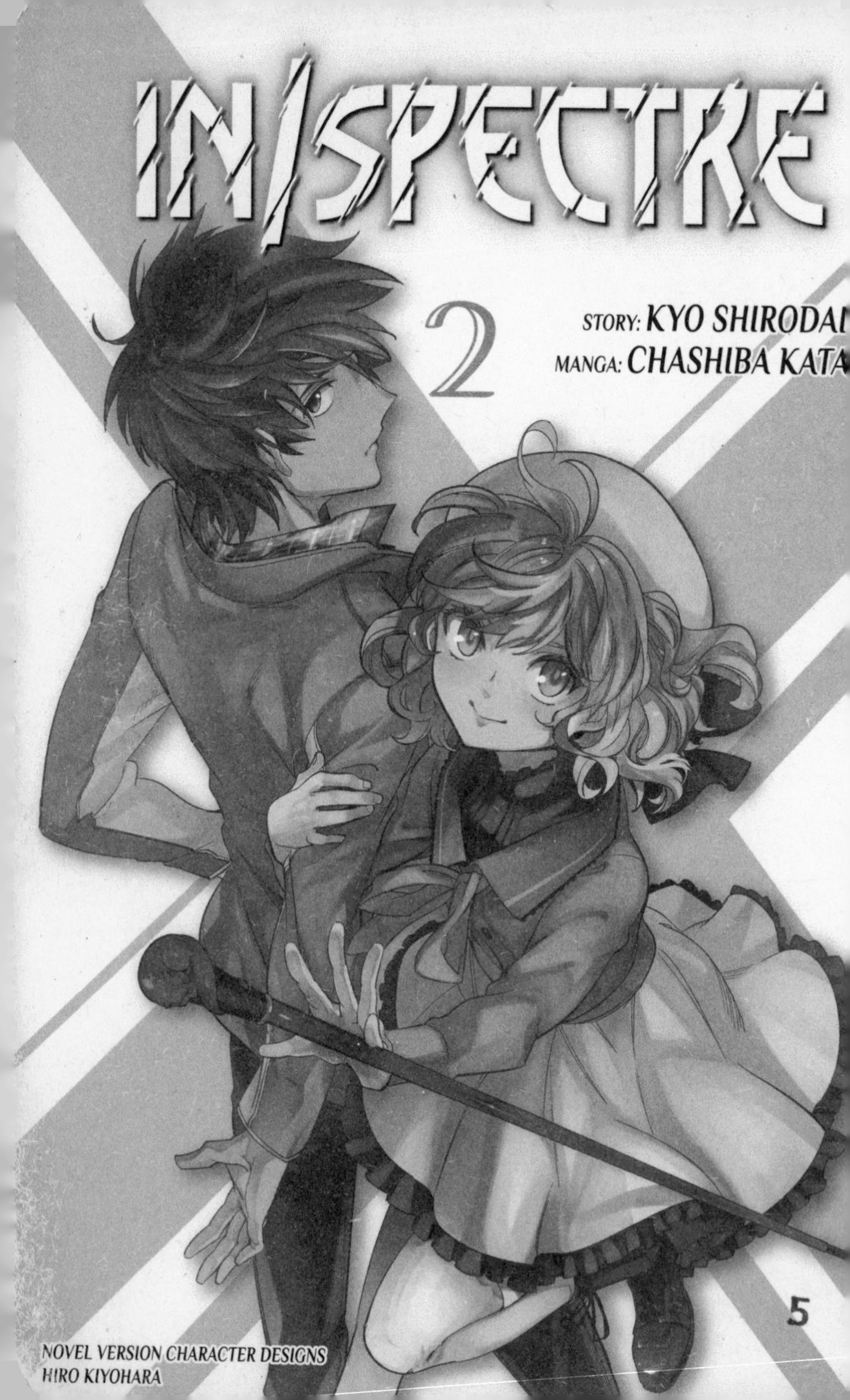
IN/SPECTRE
2
STORY: KYO SHIRODAI
MANGA: CHASHIBA KATA
5
NOVEL VERSION CHARACTER DESIGNS
HIRO KIYOHARA

CONTENTS

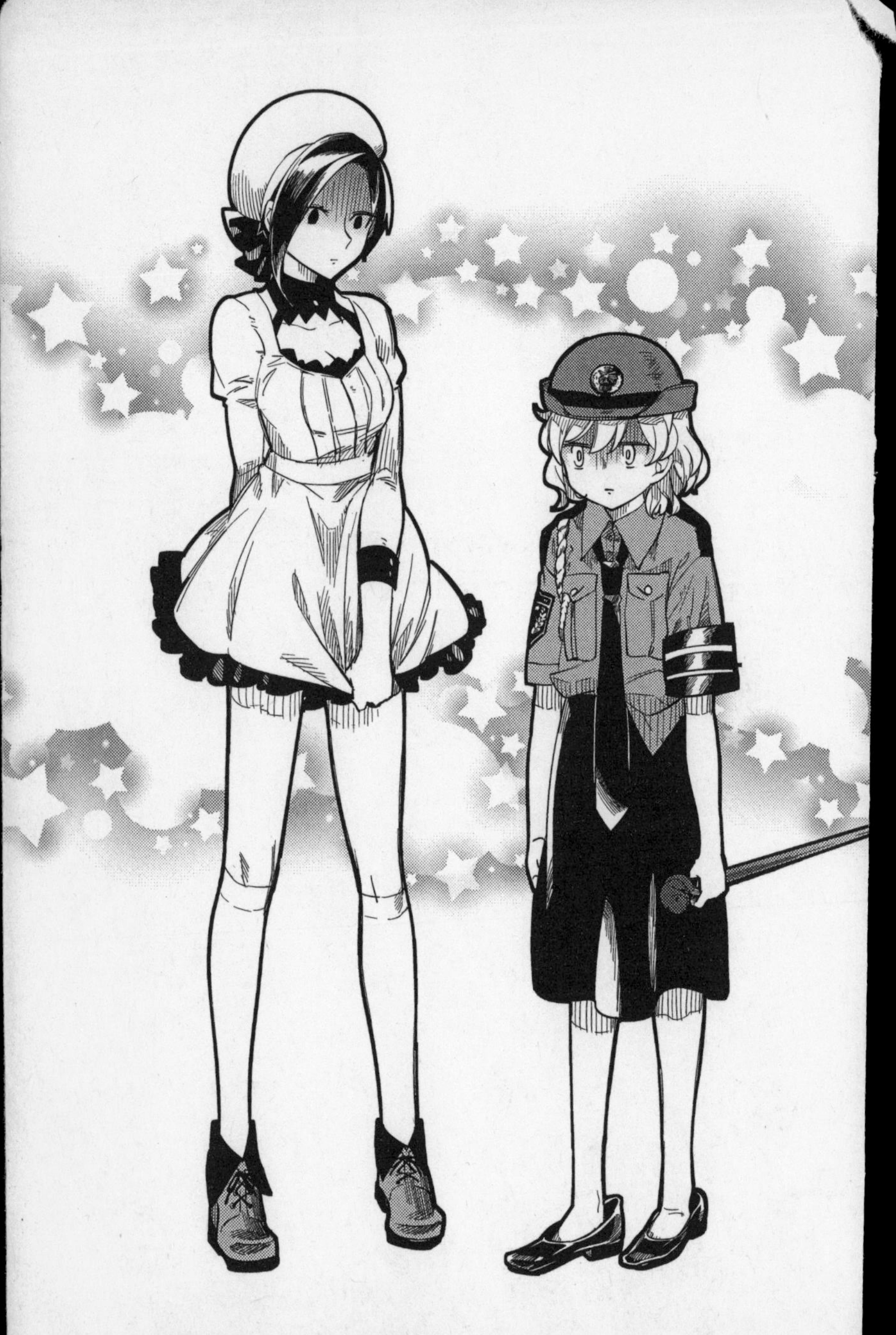

CHAPTER 3: "IDOL DIES BY STEEL BEAM"

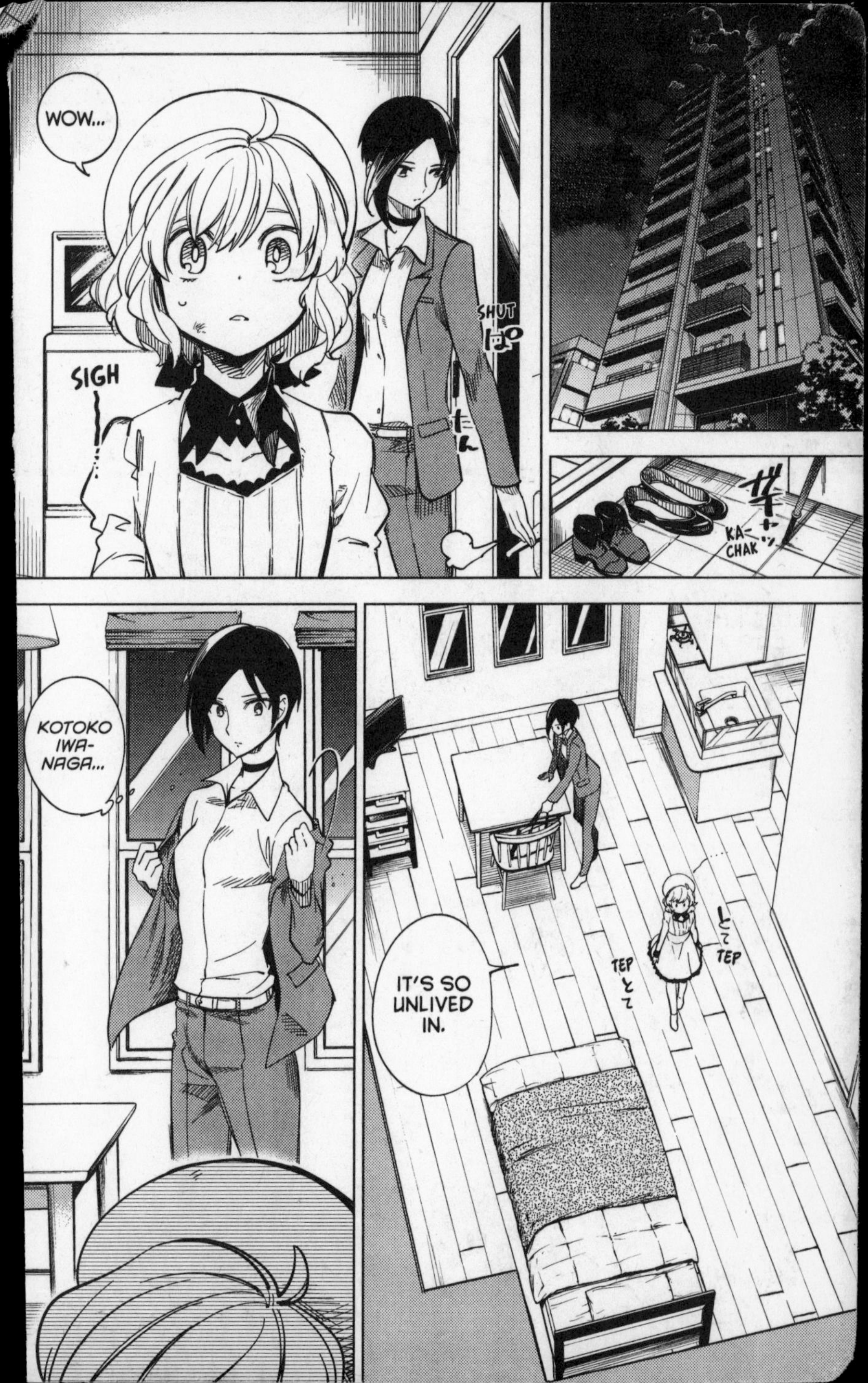
KA-CHAK
WOW...
SHUT
SIGH
IT'S SO UNLIVED IN.
TEP
TEP
KOTOKO IWA-NAGA...

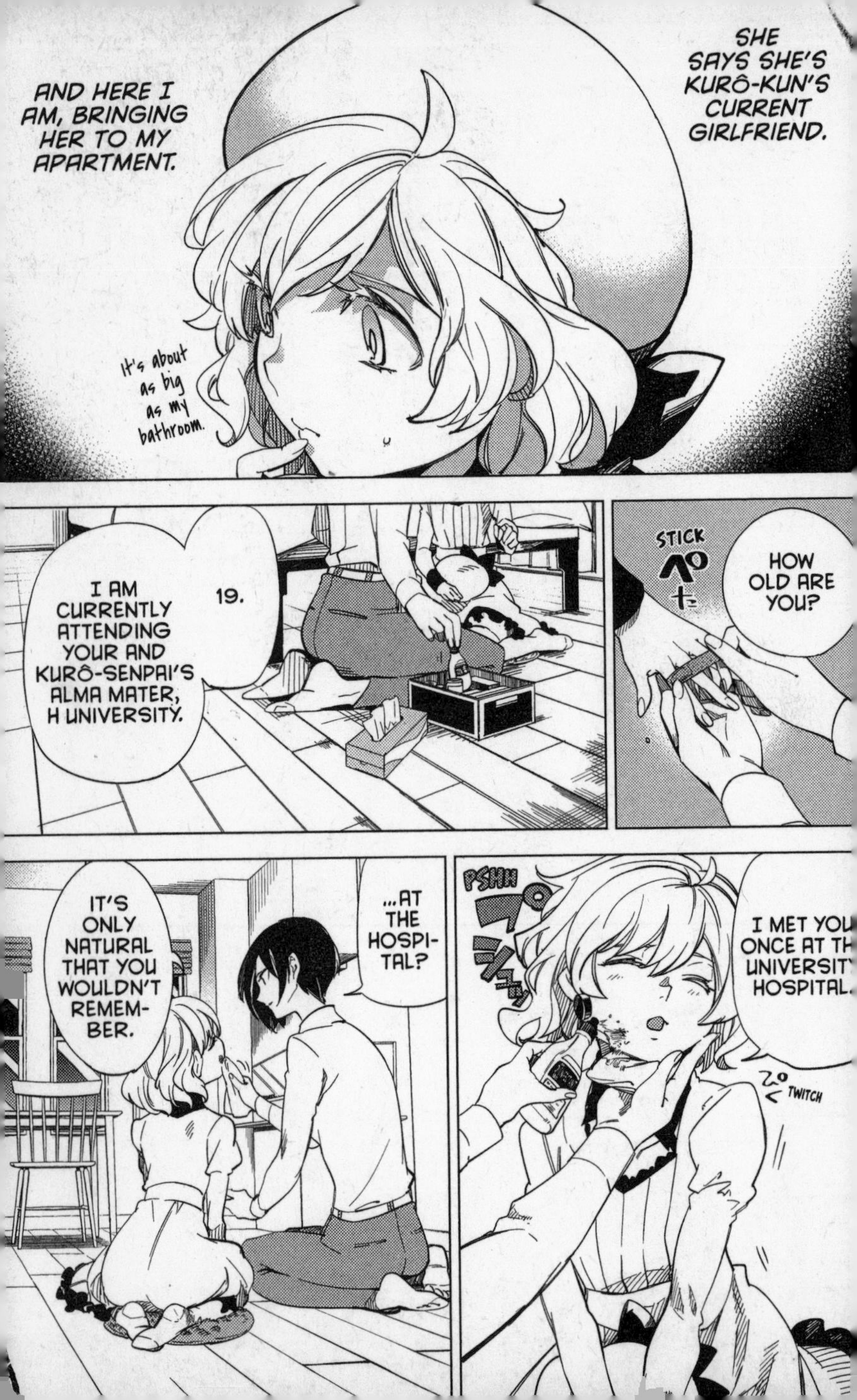
SHE SAYS SHE'S KURÔ-KUN'S CURRENT GIRLFRIEND.
AND HERE I AM, BRINGING HER TO MY APARTMENT.
It's about as big as my bathroom.
STICK
HOW OLD ARE YOU?
19.
I AM CURRENTLY ATTENDING YOUR AND KURÔ-SENPAI'S ALMA MATER, H UNIVERSITY.
PSHH
I MET YOU ONCE AT TH UNIVERSIT HOSPITAL.
TWITCH
...AT THE HOSPI-TAL?
IT'S ONLY NATURAL THAT YOU WOULDN'T REMEM-BER.

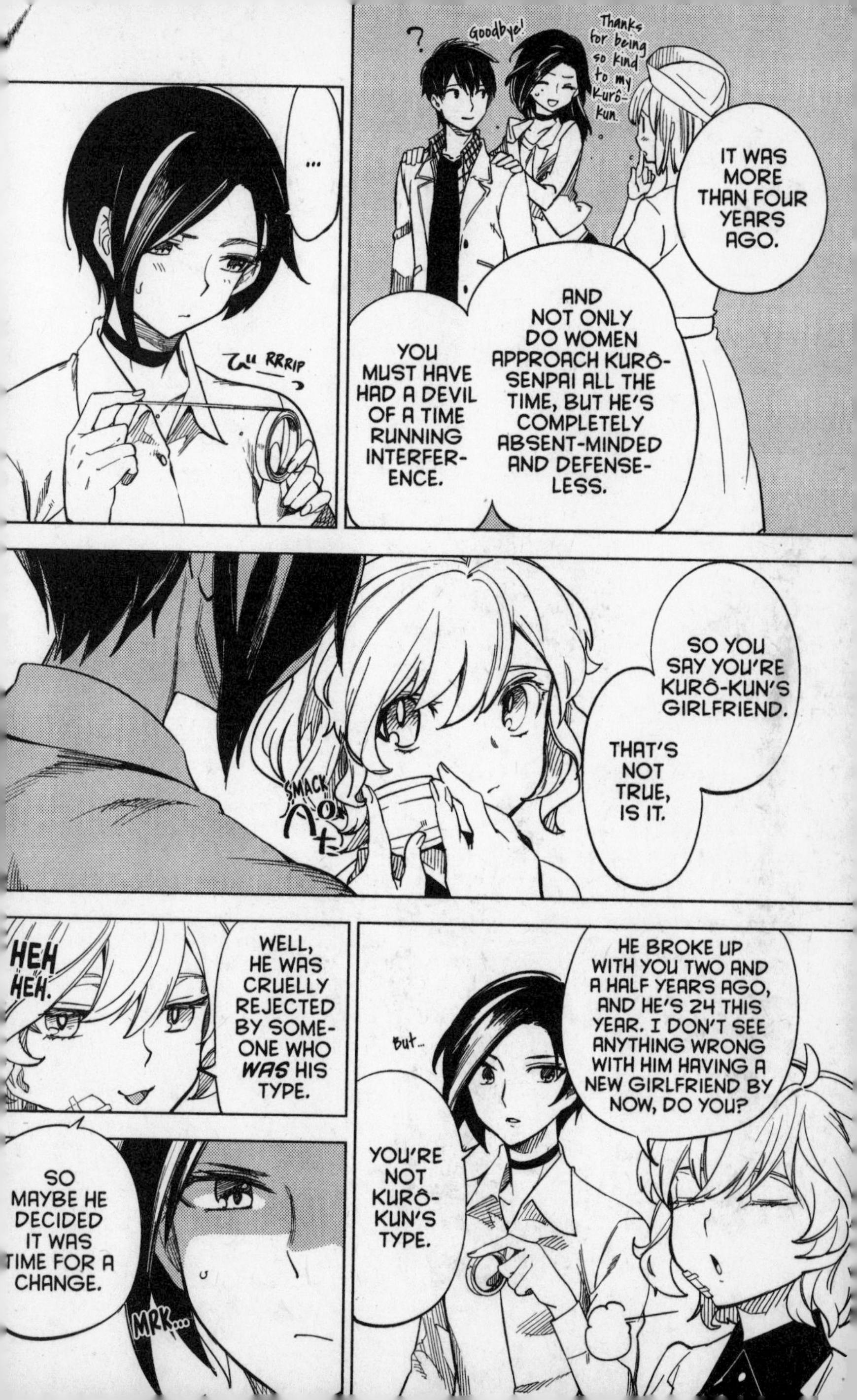
Thanks for being so kind to my Kurô-kun.
Goodbye!
?
IT WAS MORE THAN FOUR YEARS AGO.
AND NOT ONLY DO WOMEN APPROACH KURÔ-SENPAI ALL THE TIME, BUT HE'S COMPLETELY ABSENT-MINDED AND DEFENSE-LESS.
YOU MUST HAVE HAD A DEVIL OF A TIME RUNNING INTERFER-ENCE.
...
RRRIP
SO YOU SAY YOU'RE KURÔ-KUN'S GIRLFRIEND.
THAT'S NOT TRUE, IS IT.
SMACK
HE BROKE UP WITH YOU TWO AND A HALF YEARS AGO, AND HE'S 24 THIS YEAR. I DON'T SEE ANYTHING WRONG WITH HIM HAVING A NEW GIRLFRIEND BY NOW, DO YOU?
But...
YOU'RE NOT KURÔ-KUN'S TYPE.
HEH HEH.
WELL, HE WAS CRUELLY REJECTED BY SOME-ONE WHO WAS HIS TYPE.
SO MAYBE HE DECIDED IT WAS TIME FOR A CHANGE.
MRK...

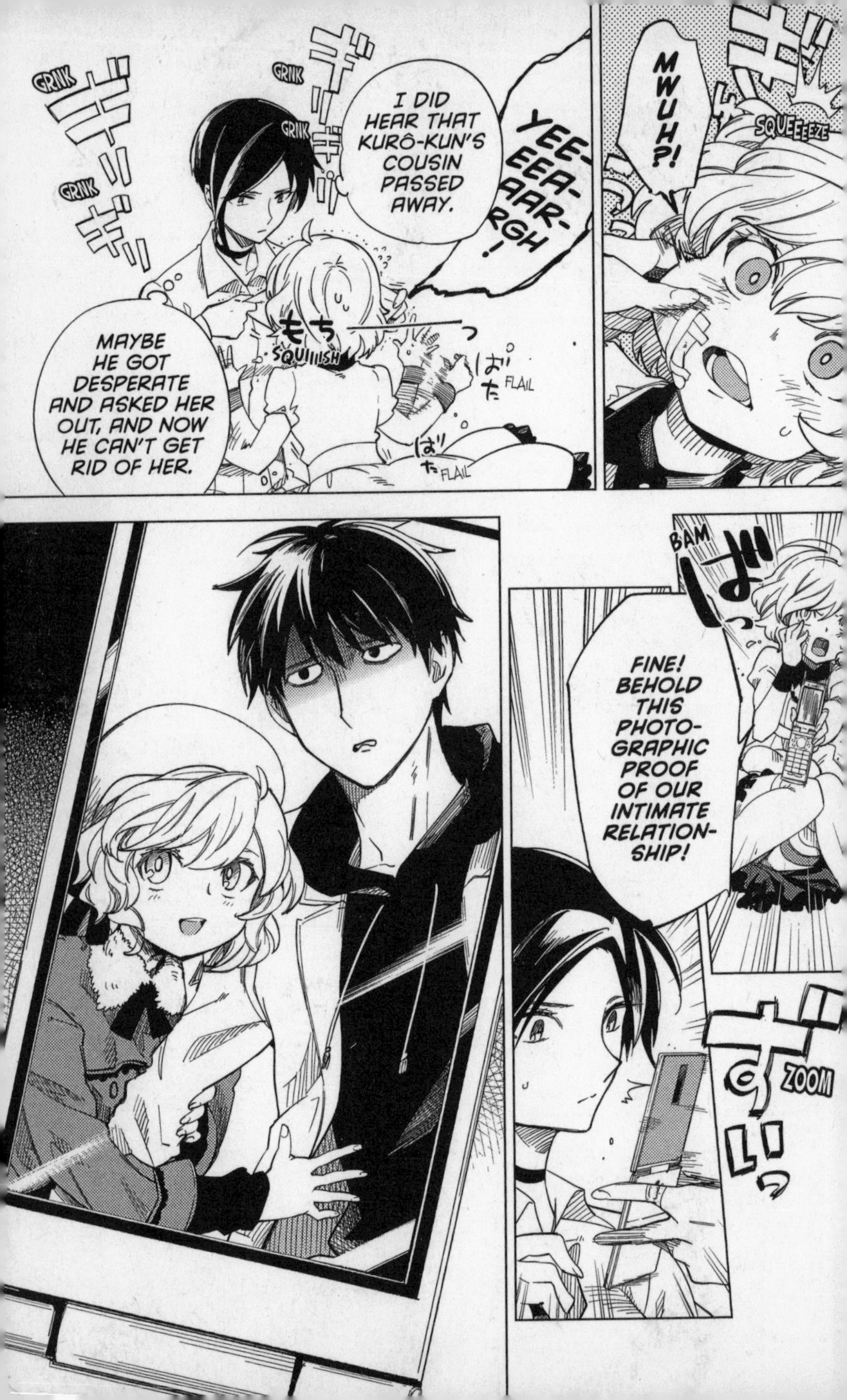

MWUH?!
SQUEEEEZE
YEE-EEA-AAR-RGH!
GRNK
GRNK
I DID HEAR THAT KURÔ-KUN'S COUSIN PASSED AWAY.
GRNK
GRNK
SQUIIISH
FLAIL
FLAIL
MAYBE HE GOT DESPERATE AND ASKED HER OUT, AND NOW HE CAN'T GET RID OF HER.
BAM
FINE! BEHOLD THIS PHOTOGRAPHIC PROOF OF OUR INTIMATE RELATIONSHIP!
ZOOM

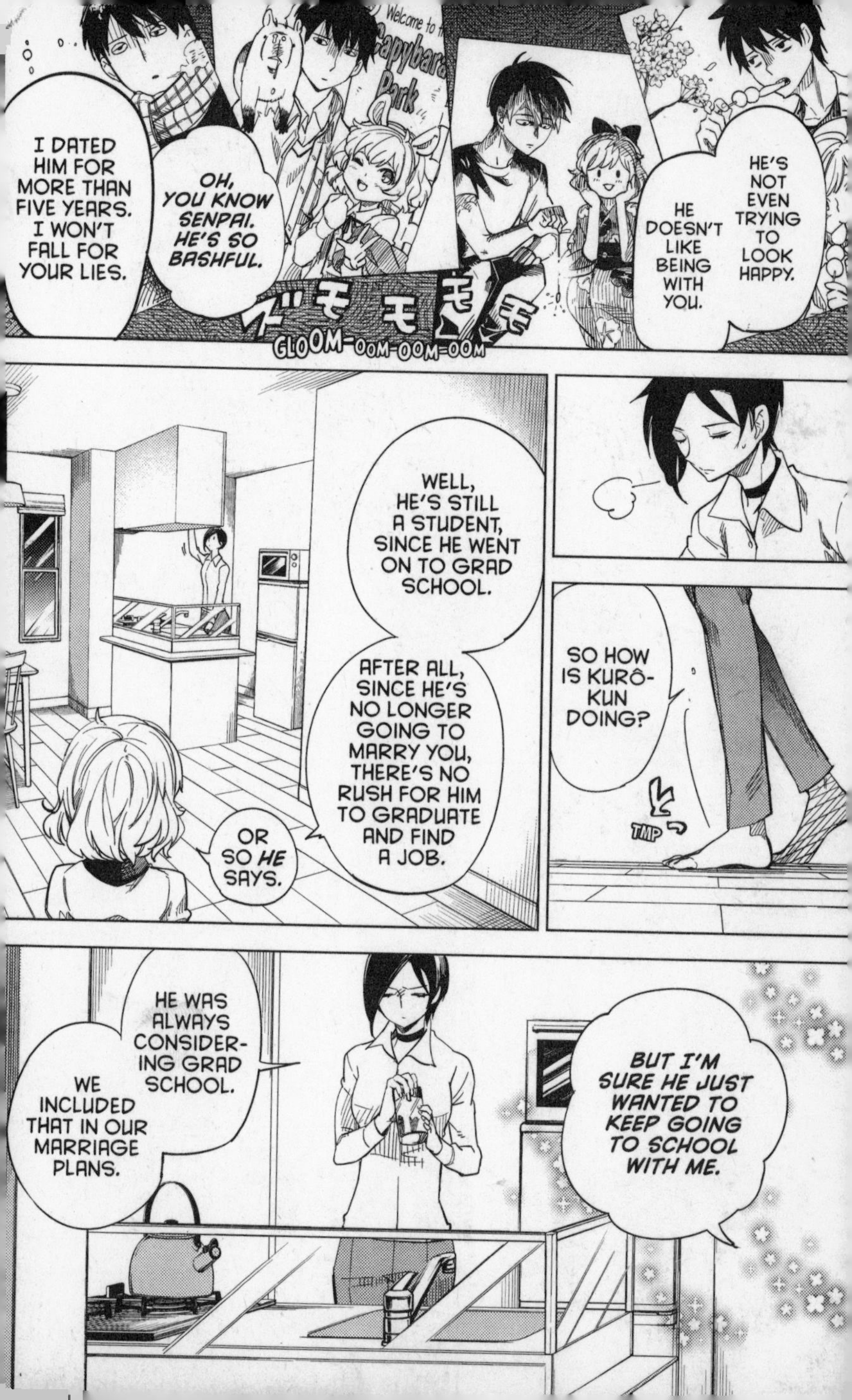
HE'S NOT EVEN TRYING TO LOOK HAPPY.
HE DOESN'T LIKE BEING WITH YOU.
OH, YOU KNOW SENPAI. HE'S SO BASHFUL.
I DATED HIM FOR MORE THAN FIVE YEARS. I WON'T FALL FOR YOUR LIES.
GLOOM-OOM-OOM-OOM
SO HOW IS KURÔ-KUN DOING?
TMP
WELL, HE'S STILL A STUDENT, SINCE HE WENT ON TO GRAD SCHOOL.
AFTER ALL, SINCE HE'S NO LONGER GOING TO MARRY YOU, THERE'S NO RUSH FOR HIM TO GRADUATE AND FIND A JOB.
OR SO *HE* SAYS.
HE WAS ALWAYS CONSIDERING GRAD SCHOOL.
WE INCLUDED THAT IN OUR MARRIAGE PLANS.
BUT I'M SURE HE JUST WANTED TO KEEP GOING TO SCHOOL WITH ME.

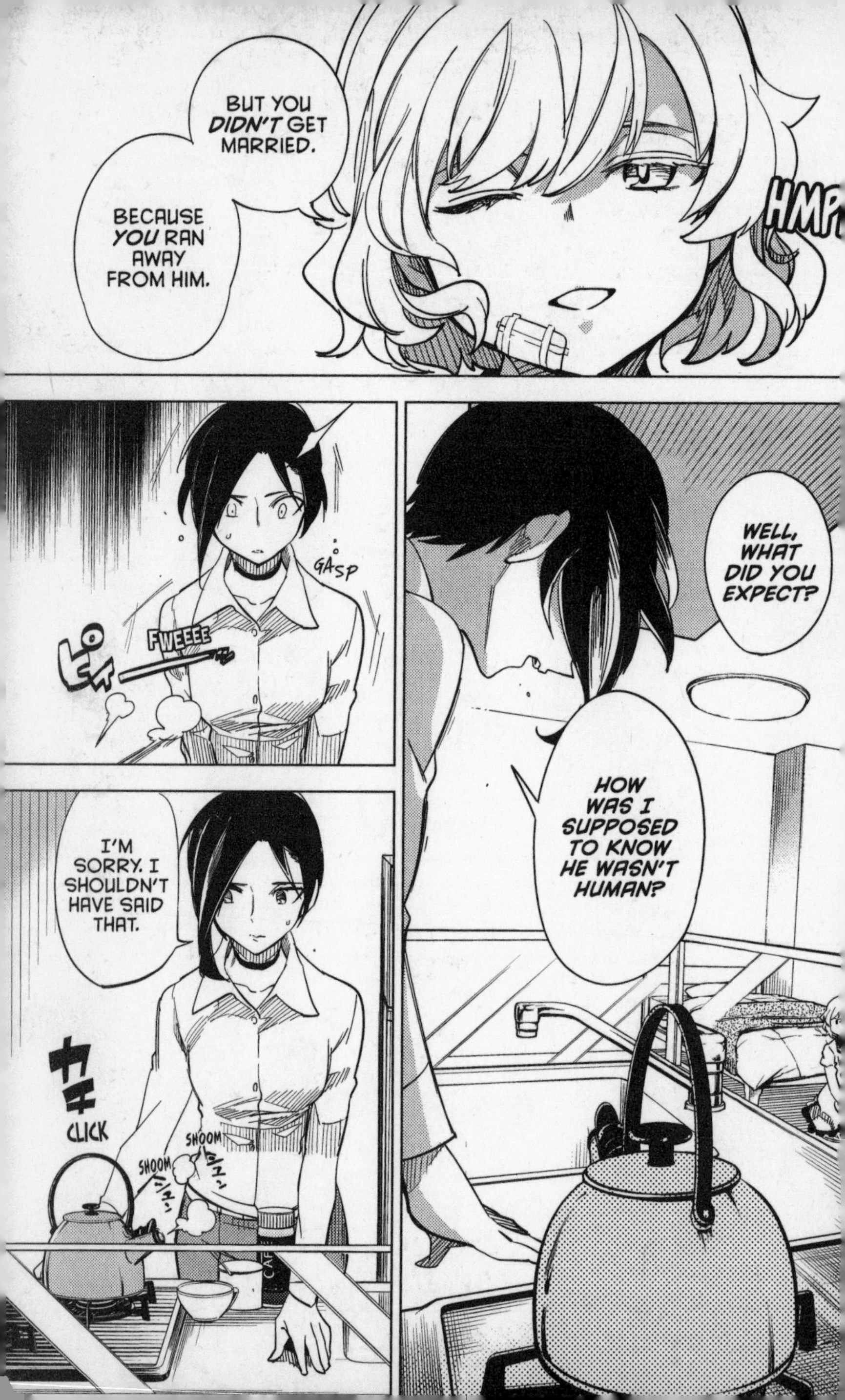
HMP
BUT YOU *DIDN'T* GET MARRIED.
BECAUSE *YOU* RAN AWAY FROM HIM.
WELL, WHAT DID YOU EXPECT?
HOW WAS I SUPPOSED TO KNOW HE WASN'T HUMAN?
GASP
FWEEEE
I'M SORRY. I SHOULDN'T HAVE SAID THAT.
CLICK
SHOOM
SHOOM

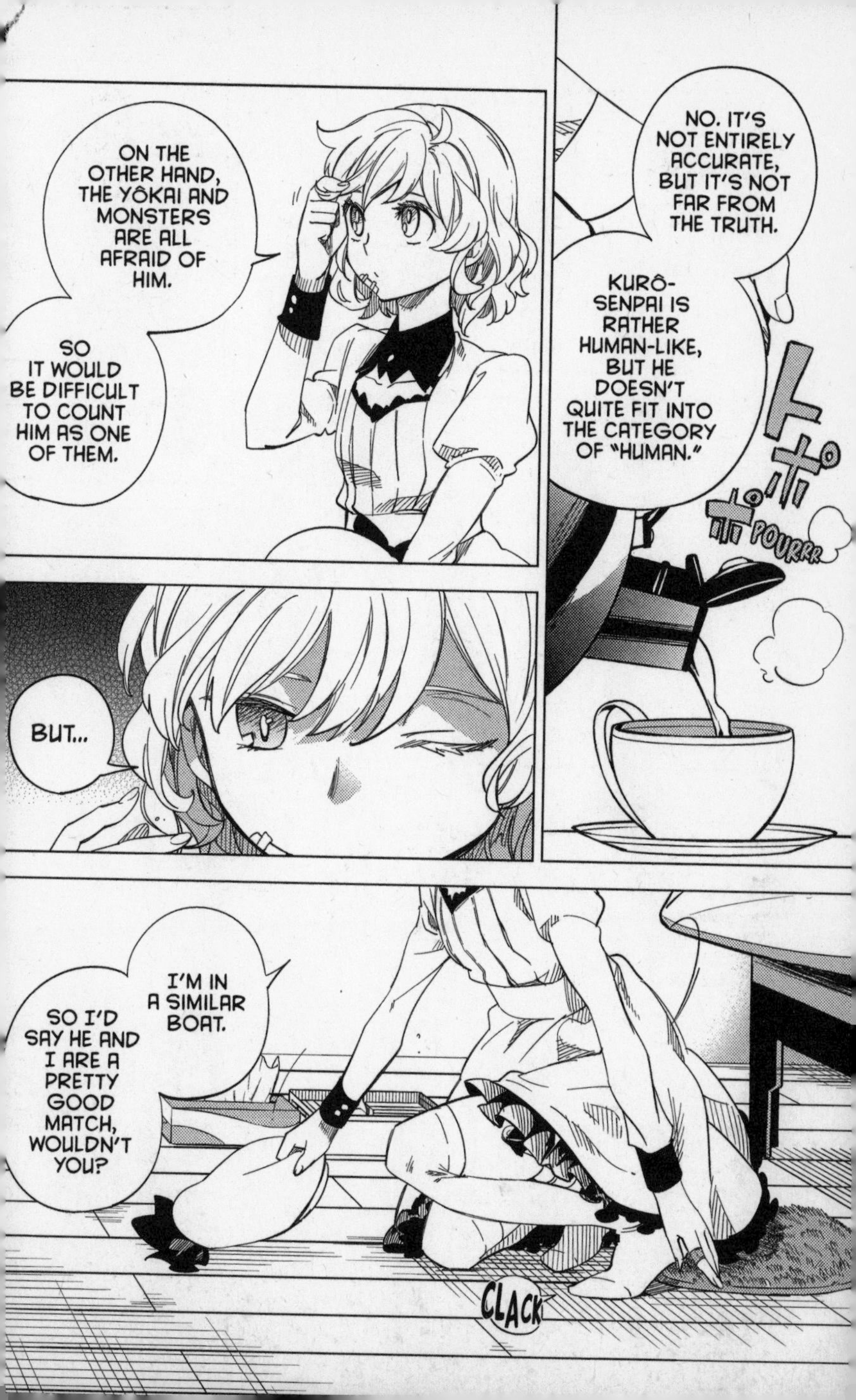
NO. IT'S NOT ENTIRELY ACCURATE, BUT IT'S NOT FAR FROM THE TRUTH.
KURÔ-SENPAI IS RATHER HUMAN-LIKE, BUT HE DOESN'T QUITE FIT INTO THE CATEGORY OF "HUMAN."
トポポ
POURRR
ON THE OTHER HAND, THE YÔKAI AND MONSTERS ARE ALL AFRAID OF HIM.
SO IT WOULD BE DIFFICULT TO COUNT HIM AS ONE OF THEM.
BUT...
I'M IN A SIMILAR BOAT.
SO I'D SAY HE AND I ARE A PRETTY GOOD MATCH, WOULDN'T YOU?
CLACK

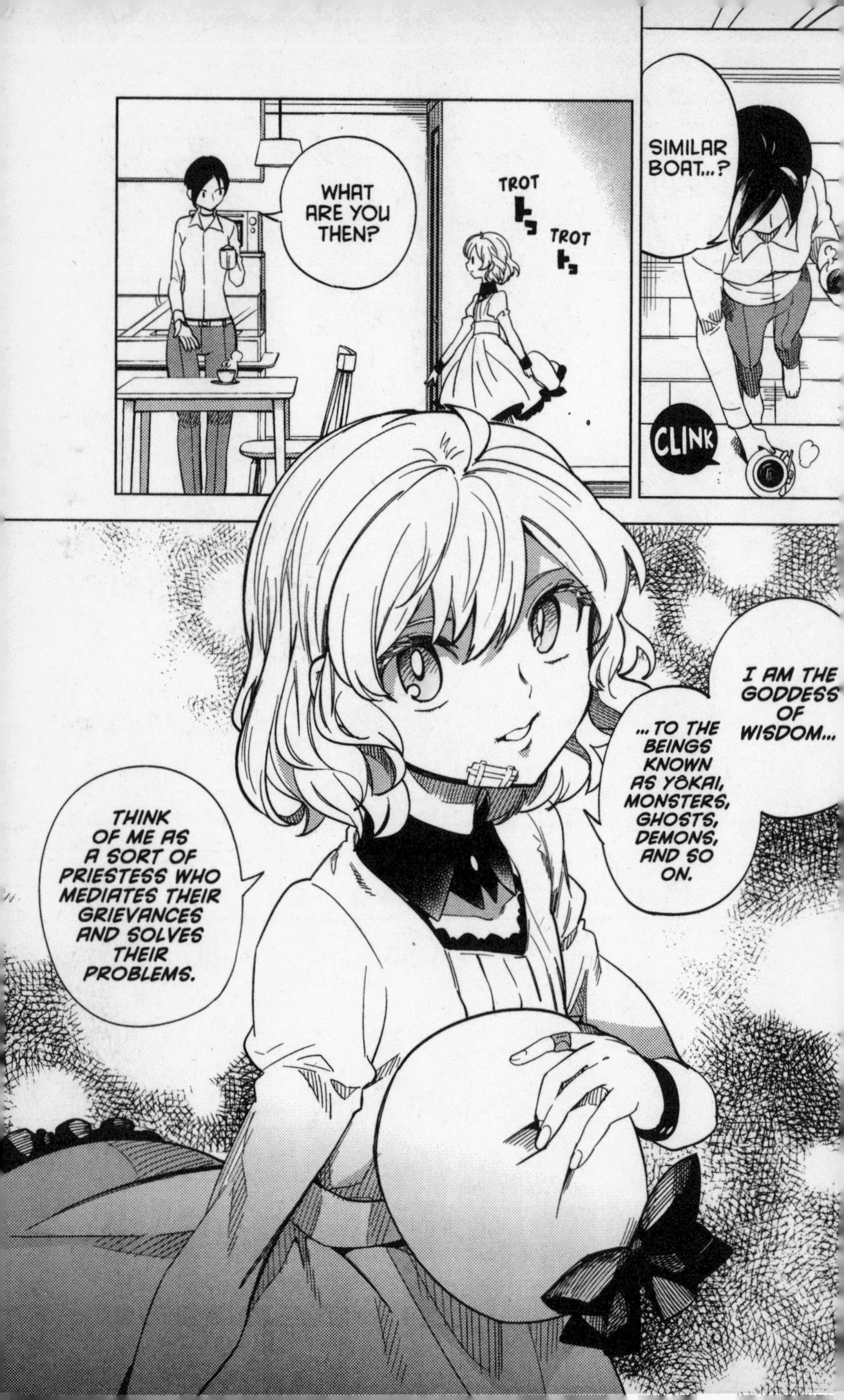
SIMILAR BOAT...?
CLINK
WHAT ARE YOU THEN?
TROT
TROT
I AM THE GODDESS OF WISDOM...
...TO THE BEINGS KNOWN AS YÔKAI, MONSTERS, GHOSTS, DEMONS, AND SO ON.
THINK OF ME AS A SORT OF PRIESTESS WHO MEDIATES THEIR GRIEVANCES AND SOLVES THEIR PROBLEMS.

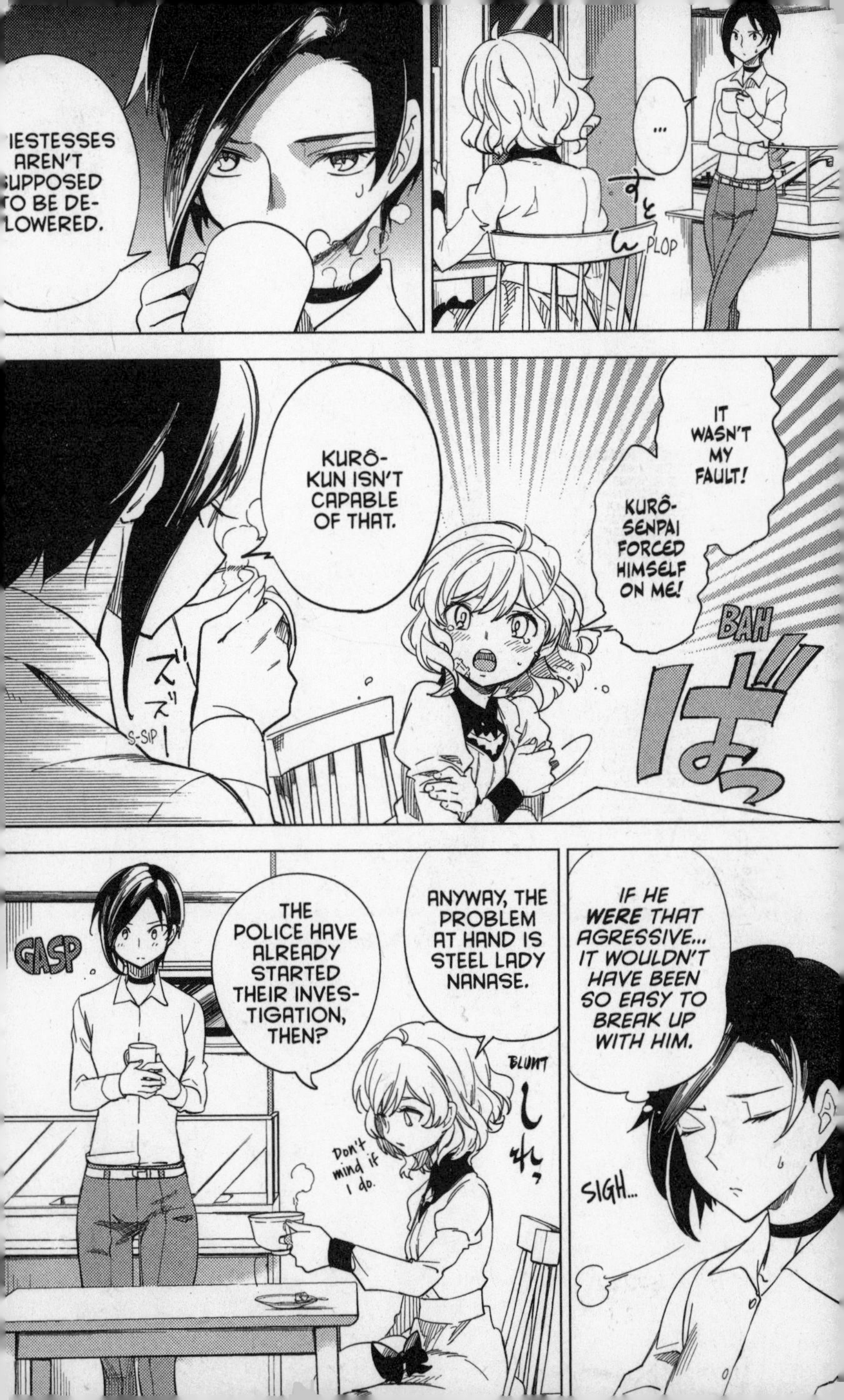
...
すとん
PLOP
IESTESSES AREN'T UPPOSED TO BE DE-LOWERED.
IT WASN'T MY FAULT!
KURÔ-SENPAI FORCED HIMSELF ON ME!
BAH
ばっ
KURÔ-KUN ISN'T CAPABLE OF THAT.
ズズー
S-SIP
IF HE WERE THAT AGRESSIVE... IT WOULDN'T HAVE BEEN SO EASY TO BREAK UP WITH HIM.
SIGH...
ANYWAY, THE PROBLEM AT HAND IS STEEL LADY NANASE.
BLUNT
しれっ
Don't mind if I do.
THE POLICE HAVE ALREADY STARTED THEIR INVESTIGATION, THEN?
GASP

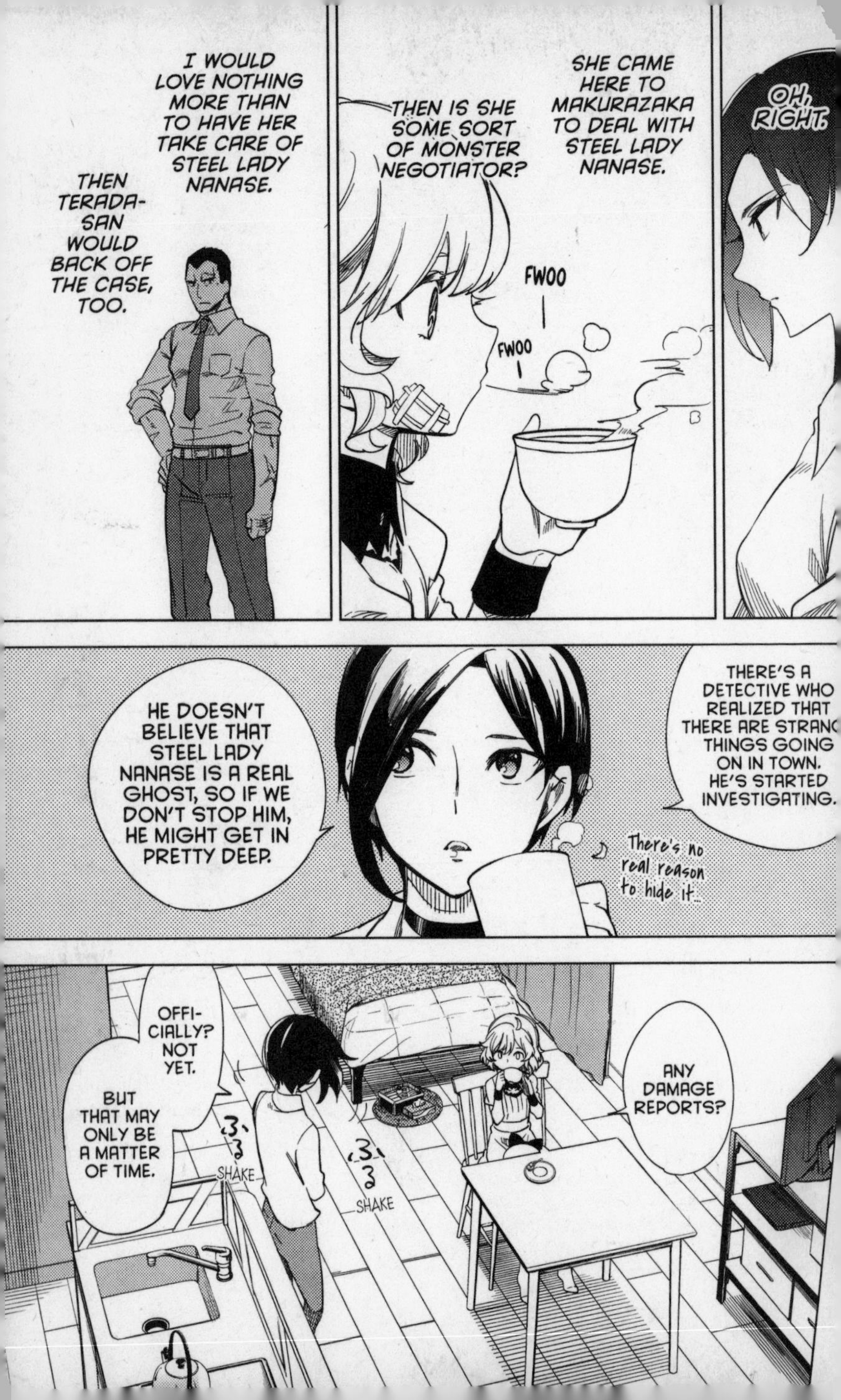
OH, RIGHT.
SHE CAME HERE TO MAKURAZAKA TO DEAL WITH STEEL LADY NANASE.
THEN IS SHE SOME SORT OF MONSTER NEGOTIATOR?
FWOO
FWOO
I WOULD LOVE NOTHING MORE THAN TO HAVE HER TAKE CARE OF STEEL LADY NANASE.
THEN TERADA-SAN WOULD BACK OFF THE CASE, TOO.
THERE'S A DETECTIVE WHO REALIZED THAT THERE ARE STRANG THINGS GOING ON IN TOWN. HE'S STARTED INVESTIGATING.
There's no real reason to hide it...
HE DOESN'T BELIEVE THAT STEEL LADY NANASE IS A REAL GHOST, SO IF WE DON'T STOP HIM, HE MIGHT GET IN PRETTY DEEP.
ANY DAMAGE REPORTS?
OFFI-CIALLY? NOT YET.
BUT THAT MAY ONLY BE A MATTER OF TIME.
SHAKE
SHAKE

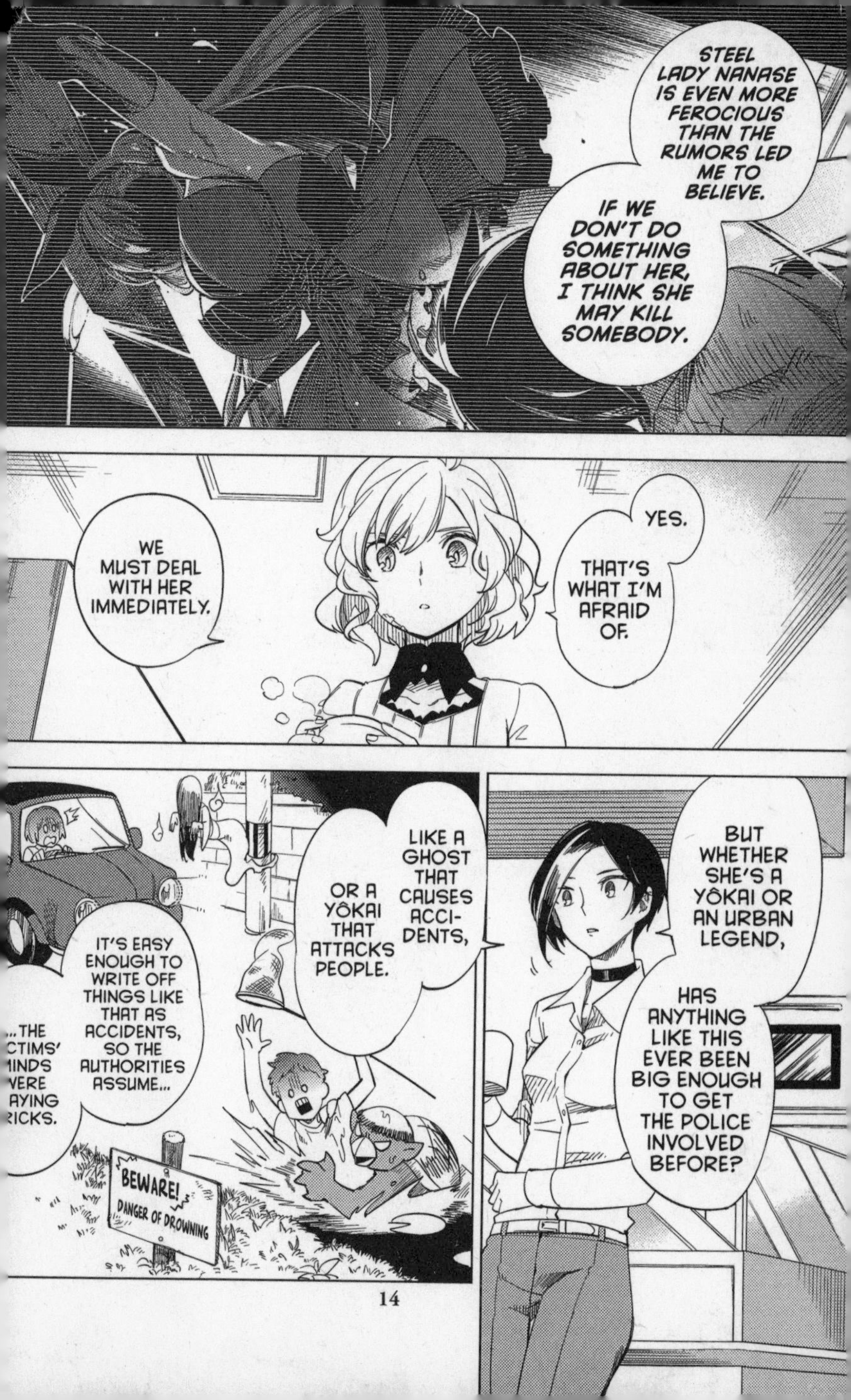
STEEL LADY NANASE IS EVEN MORE FEROCIOUS THAN THE RUMORS LED ME TO BELIEVE.
IF WE DON'T DO SOMETHING ABOUT HER, I THINK SHE MAY KILL SOMEBODY.
YES.
THAT'S WHAT I'M AFRAID OF.
WE MUST DEAL WITH HER IMMEDIATELY.
BUT WHETHER SHE'S A YÔKAI OR AN URBAN LEGEND,
HAS ANYTHING LIKE THIS EVER BEEN BIG ENOUGH TO GET THE POLICE INVOLVED BEFORE?
LIKE A GHOST THAT CAUSES ACCI-DENTS,
OR A YÔKAI THAT ATTACKS PEOPLE.
IT'S EASY ENOUGH TO WRITE OFF THINGS LIKE THAT AS ACCIDENTS, SO THE AUTHORITIES ASSUME...
...THE CTIMS' MINDS WERE AYING RICKS.
BEWARE!
DANGER OF DROWNING

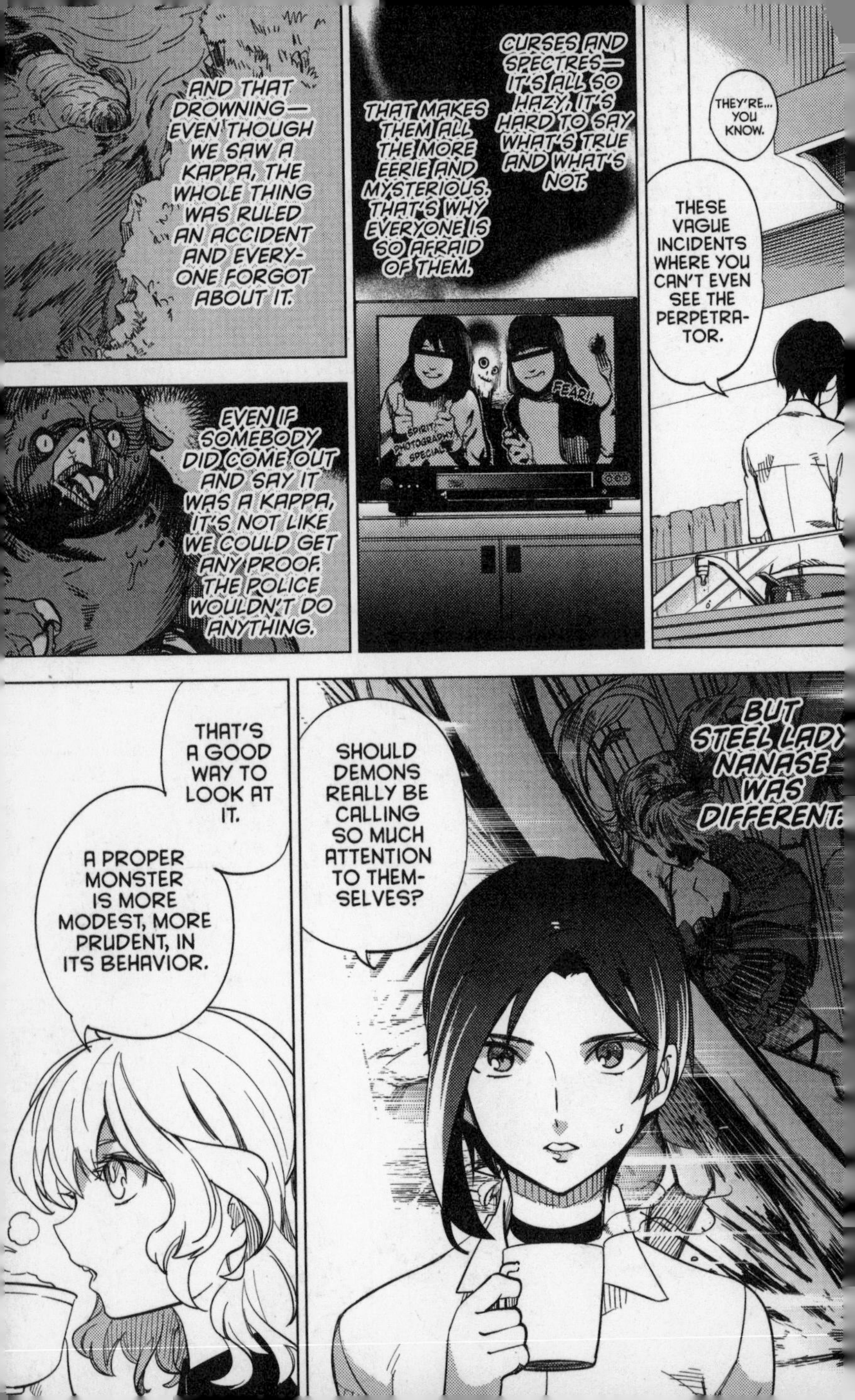
THEY'RE... YOU KNOW.
THESE VAGUE INCIDENTS WHERE YOU CAN'T EVEN SEE THE PERPETRATOR.
CURSES AND SPECTRES— IT'S ALL SO HAZY, IT'S HARD TO SAY WHAT'S TRUE AND WHAT'S NOT.
THAT MAKES THEM ALL THE MORE EERIE AND MYSTERIOUS. THAT'S WHY EVERYONE IS SO AFRAID OF THEM.
SPIRIT PHOTOGRAPHY SPECIAL
FEAR!!
AND THAT DROWNING— EVEN THOUGH WE SAW A KAPPA, THE WHOLE THING WAS RULED AN ACCIDENT AND EVERY-ONE FORGOT ABOUT IT.
EVEN IF SOMEBODY DID COME OUT AND SAY IT WAS A KAPPA, IT'S NOT LIKE WE COULD GET ANY PROOF. THE POLICE WOULDN'T DO ANYTHING.
BUT STEEL LADY NANASE WAS DIFFERENT.
SHOULD DEMONS REALLY BE CALLING SO MUCH ATTENTION TO THEM-SELVES?
THAT'S A GOOD WAY TO LOOK AT IT.
A PROPER MONSTER IS MORE MODEST, MORE PRUDENT, IN ITS BEHAVIOR.

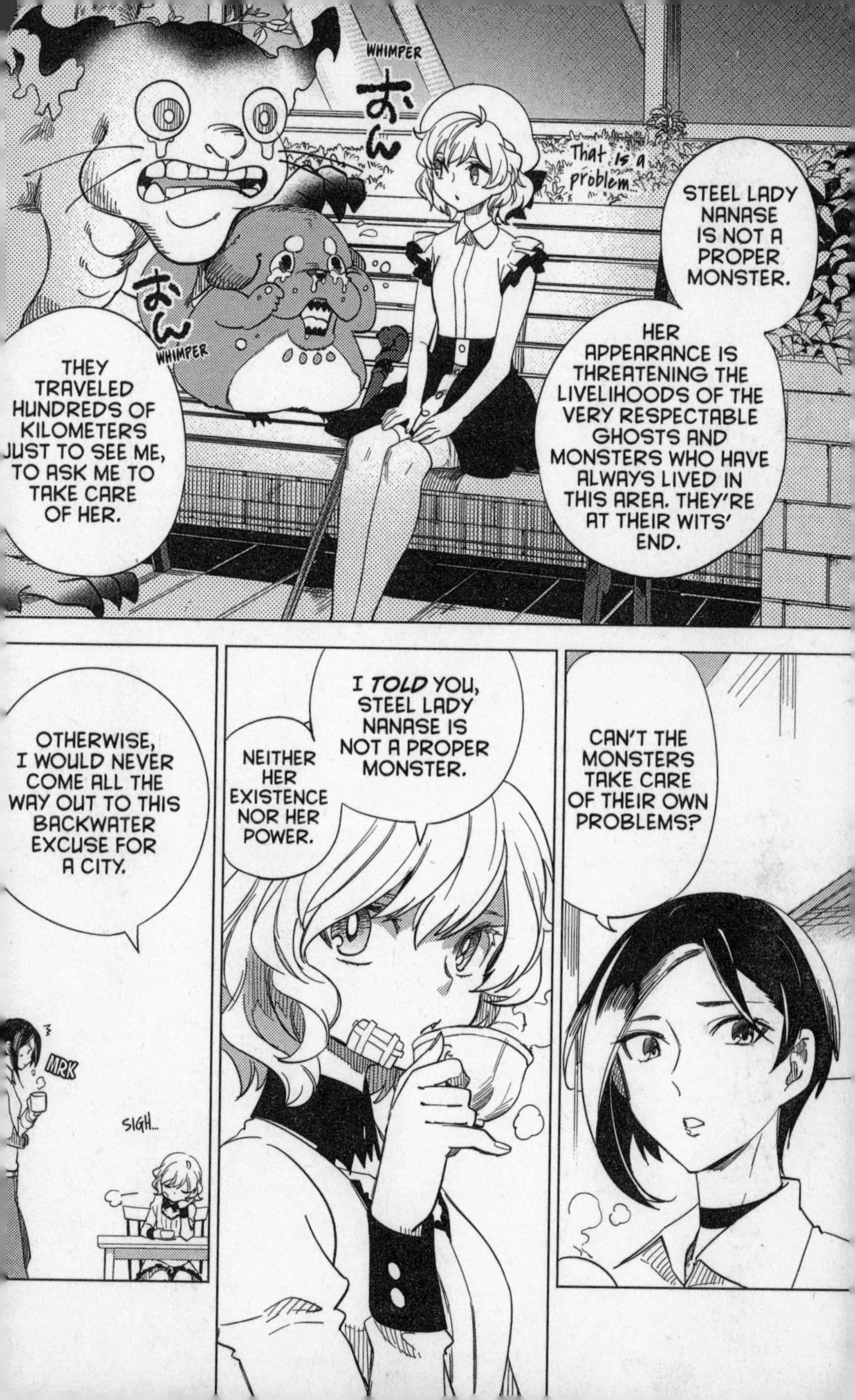
STEEL LADY NANASE IS NOT A PROPER MONSTER.
That is a problem...
WHIMPER
おん
HER APPEARANCE IS THREATENING THE LIVELIHOODS OF THE VERY RESPECTABLE GHOSTS AND MONSTERS WHO HAVE ALWAYS LIVED IN THIS AREA. THEY'RE AT THEIR WITS' END.
おん
WHIMPER
THEY TRAVELED HUNDREDS OF KILOMETERS JUST TO SEE ME, TO ASK ME TO TAKE CARE OF HER.
CAN'T THE MONSTERS TAKE CARE OF THEIR OWN PROBLEMS?
I *TOLD* YOU, STEEL LADY NANASE IS NOT A PROPER MONSTER.
NEITHER HER EXISTENCE NOR HER POWER.
OTHERWISE, I WOULD NEVER COME ALL THE WAY OUT TO THIS BACKWATER EXCUSE FOR A CITY.
MRK
SIGH...

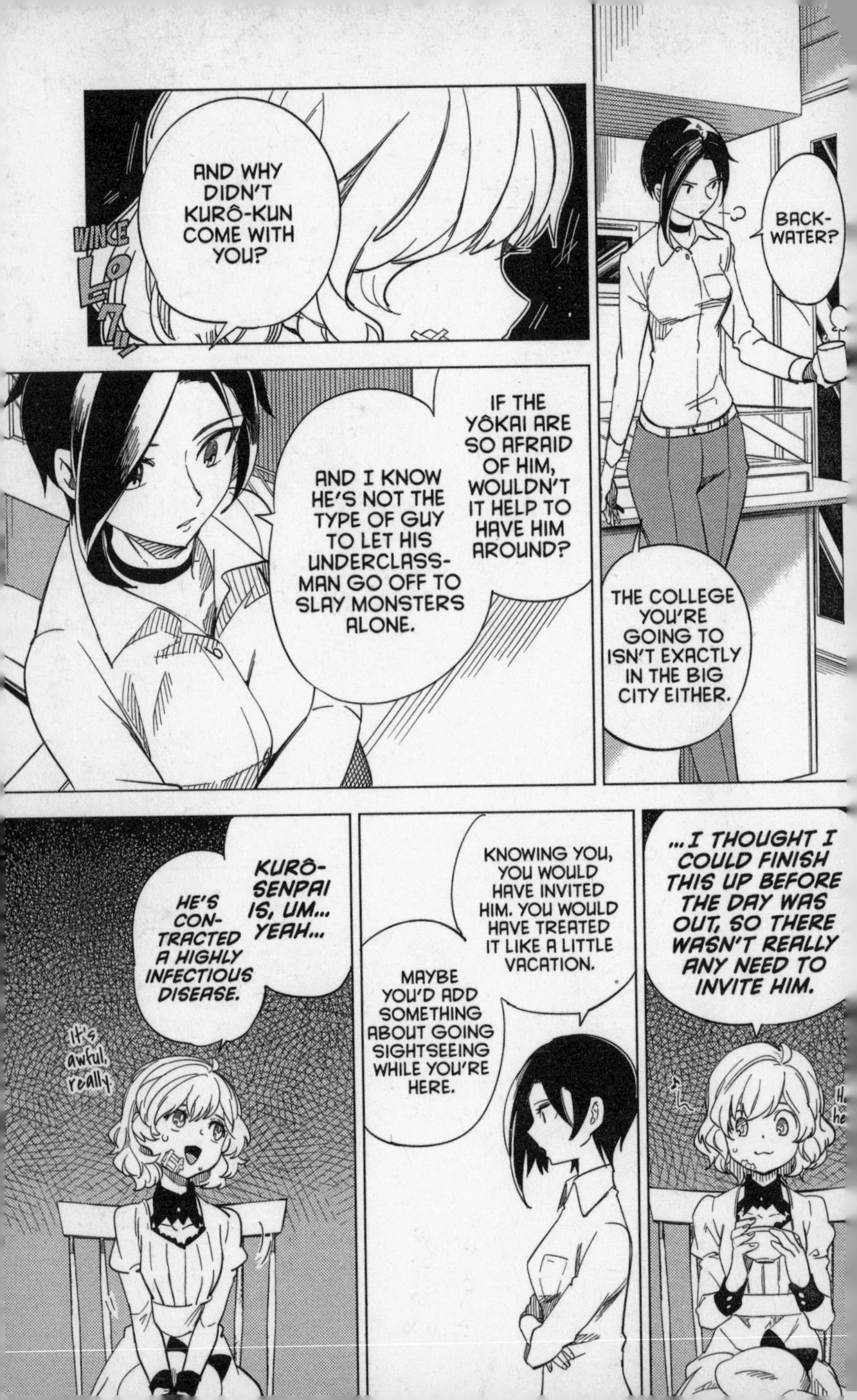
BACK-WATER?
THE COLLEGE YOU'RE GOING TO ISN'T EXACTLY IN THE BIG CITY EITHER.
WINCE
AND WHY DIDN'T KURÔ-KUN COME WITH YOU?
IF THE YÔKAI ARE SO AFRAID OF HIM, WOULDN'T IT HELP TO HAVE HIM AROUND?
AND I KNOW HE'S NOT THE TYPE OF GUY TO LET HIS UNDERCLASS-MAN GO OFF TO SLAY MONSTERS ALONE.
...I THOUGHT I COULD FINISH THIS UP BEFORE THE DAY WAS OUT, SO THERE WASN'T REALLY ANY NEED TO INVITE HIM.
KNOWING YOU, YOU WOULD HAVE INVITED HIM. YOU WOULD HAVE TREATED IT LIKE A LITTLE VACATION.
MAYBE YOU'D ADD SOMETHING ABOUT GOING SIGHTSEEING WHILE YOU'RE HERE.
KURÔ-SENPAI IS, UM... YEAH...
HE'S CON-TRACTED A HIGHLY INFECTIOUS DISEASE.
It's awful, really.

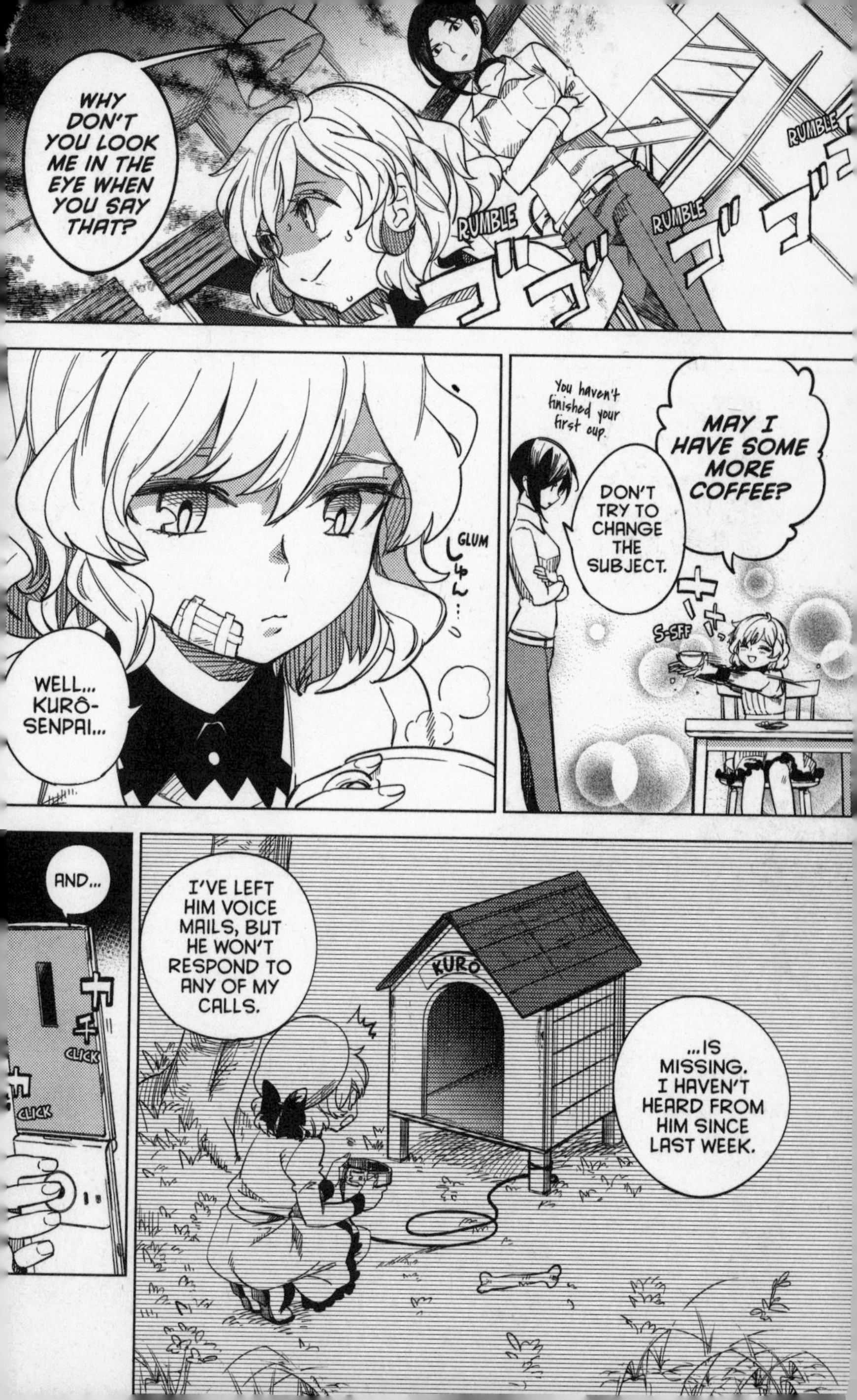
WHY DON'T YOU LOOK ME IN THE EYE WHEN YOU SAY THAT?
RUMBLE
RUMBLE
RUMBLE
MAY I HAVE SOME MORE COFFEE?
You haven't finished your first cup.
DON'T TRY TO CHANGE THE SUBJECT.
S-SFF
GLUM
WELL... KURÔ-SENPAI...
...IS MISSING. I HAVEN'T HEARD FROM HIM SINCE LAST WEEK.
I'VE LEFT HIM VOICE MAILS, BUT HE WON'T RESPOND TO ANY OF MY CALLS.
KURO
AND...
CLICK
CLICK

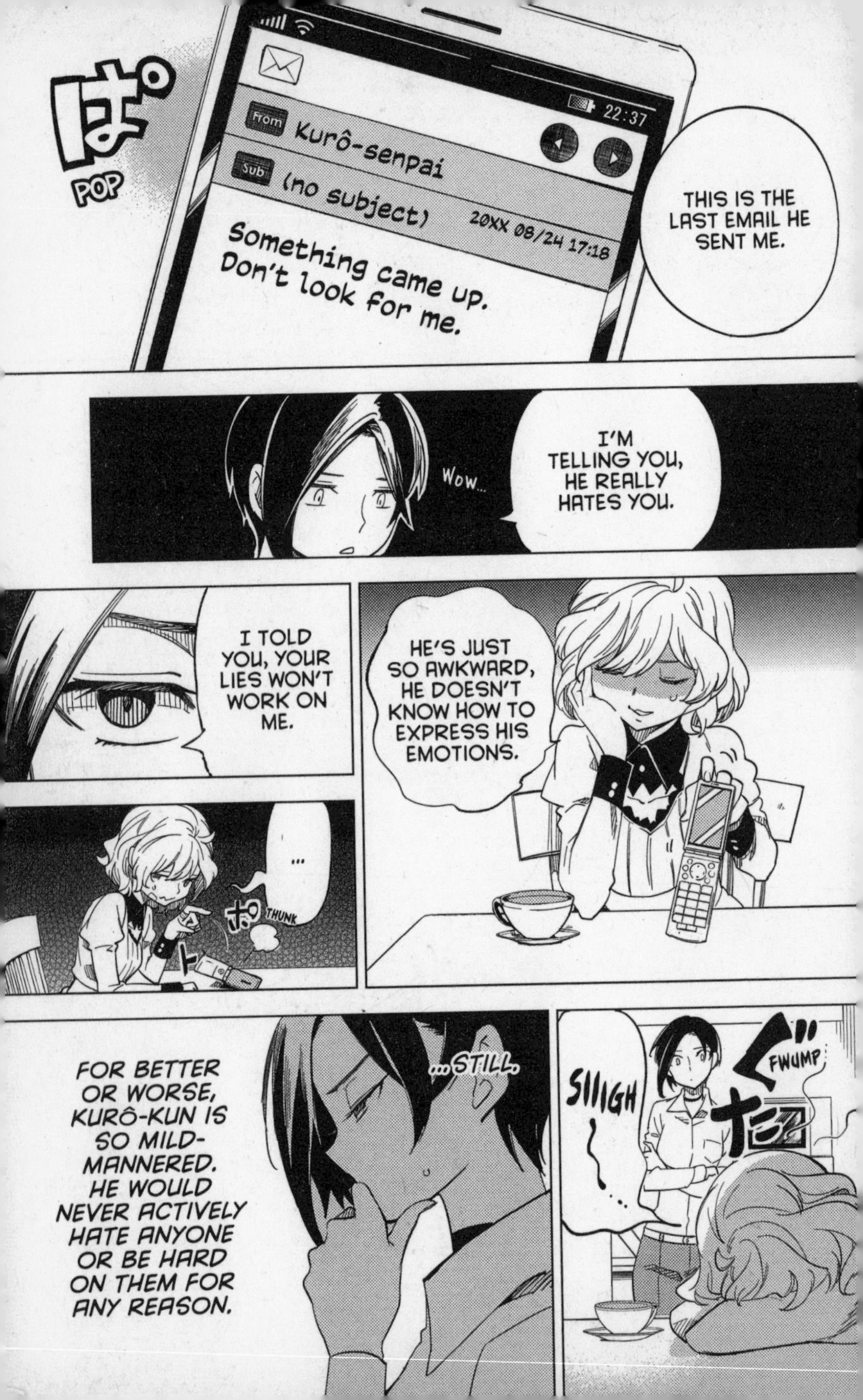
22:37
From Kurô-senpai
Sub (no subject)
20XX 08/24 17:18
Something came up. Don't look for me.
THIS IS THE LAST EMAIL HE SENT ME.
ぽ
POP
I'M TELLING YOU, HE REALLY HATES YOU.
WOW...
HE'S JUST SO AWKWARD, HE DOESN'T KNOW HOW TO EXPRESS HIS EMOTIONS.
I TOLD YOU, YOUR LIES WON'T WORK ON ME.
...
THUNK
FWUMP
SIIIGH
...
...STILL.
FOR BETTER OR WORSE, KURÔ-KUN IS SO MILD-MANNERED. HE WOULD NEVER ACTIVELY HATE ANYONE OR BE HARD ON THEM FOR ANY REASON.

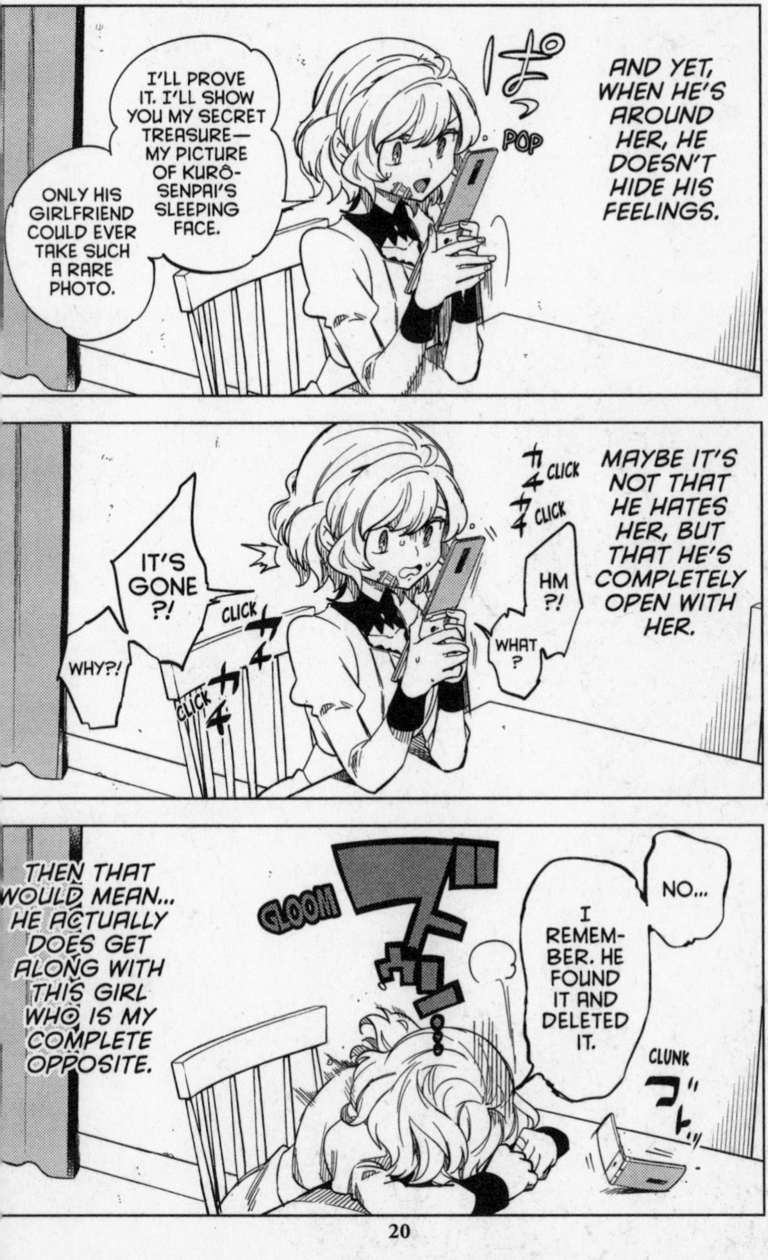
AND YET, WHEN HE'S AROUND HER, HE DOESN'T HIDE HIS FEELINGS.
POP
I'LL PROVE IT. I'LL SHOW YOU MY SECRET TREASURE— MY PICTURE OF KURÔ-SENPAI'S SLEEPING FACE.
ONLY HIS GIRLFRIEND COULD EVER TAKE SUCH A RARE PHOTO.
MAYBE IT'S NOT THAT HE HATES HER, BUT THAT HE'S COMPLETELY OPEN WITH HER.
CLICK
CLICK
HM ?!
WHAT ?
CLICK
IT'S GONE ?!
CLICK
WHY?!
CLUNK
NO...
I REMEMBER. HE FOUND IT AND DELETED IT.
GLOOM
THEN THAT WOULD MEAN... HE ACTUALLY DOES GET ALONG WITH THIS GIRL WHO IS MY COMPLETE OPPOSITE.

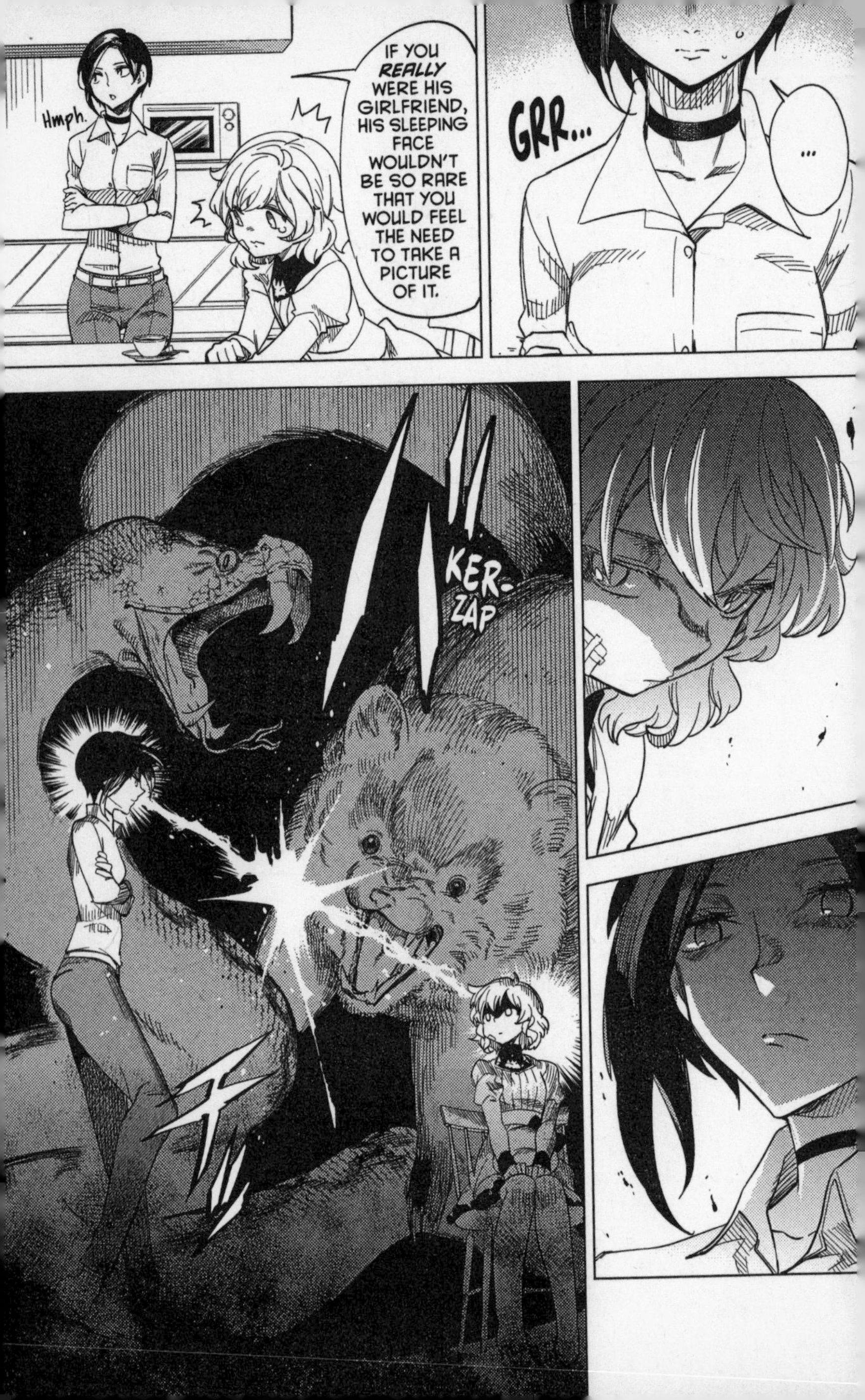
GRR...
...
IF YOU REALLY WERE HIS GIRLFRIEND, HIS SLEEPING FACE WOULDN'T BE SO RARE THAT YOU WOULD FEEL THE NEED TO TAKE A PICTURE OF IT.
Hmph.
KER-ZAP

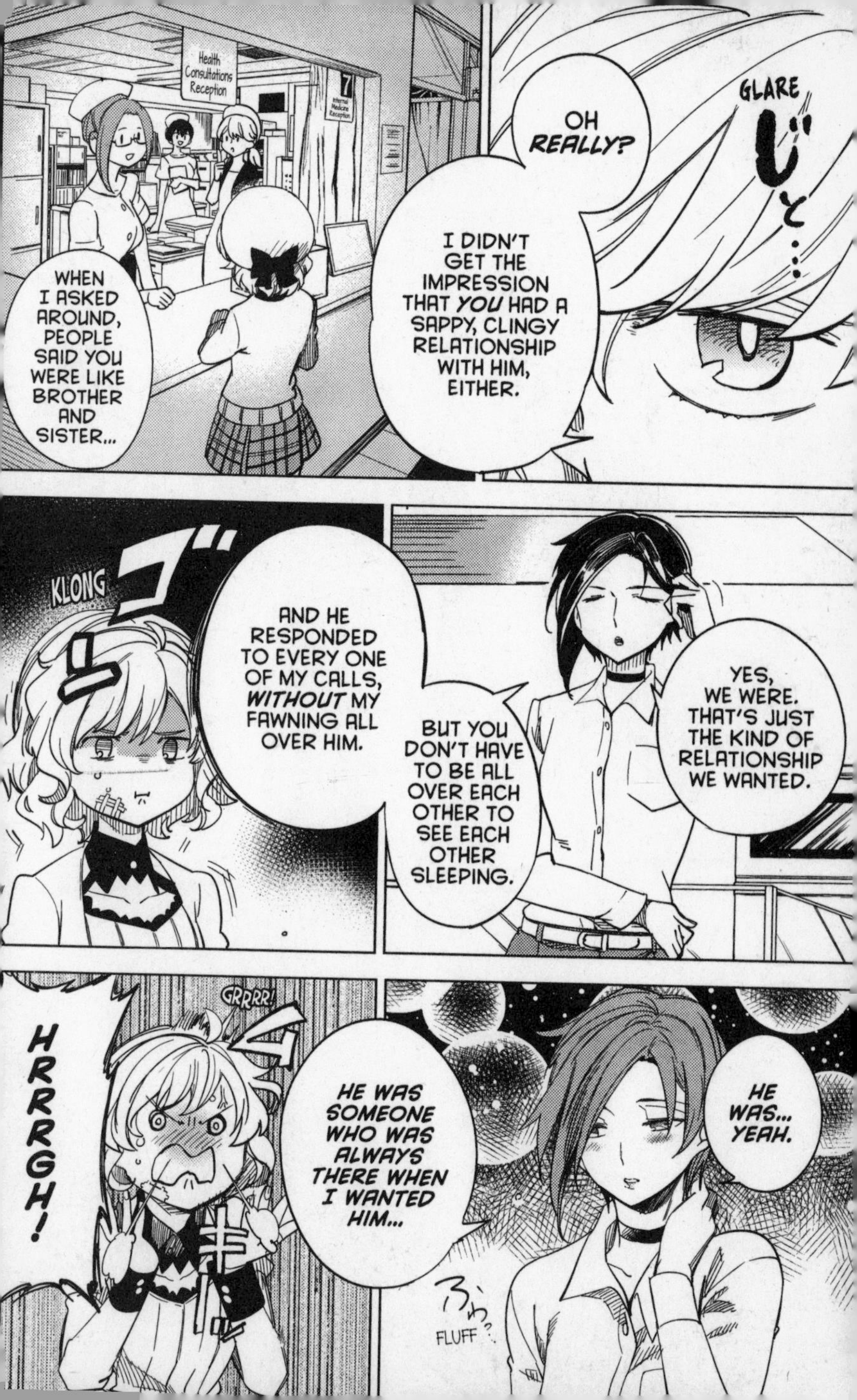
GLARE
じと…
OH *REALLY?*
I DIDN'T GET THE IMPRESSION THAT *YOU* HAD A SAPPY, CLINGY RELATIONSHIP WITH HIM, EITHER.
Health Consultations Reception
7
Internal Medicine Reception
WHEN I ASKED AROUND, PEOPLE SAID YOU WERE LIKE BROTHER AND SISTER...
YES, WE WERE. THAT'S JUST THE KIND OF RELATIONSHIP WE WANTED.
BUT YOU DON'T HAVE TO BE ALL OVER EACH OTHER TO SEE EACH OTHER SLEEPING.
AND HE RESPONDED TO EVERY ONE OF MY CALLS, *WITHOUT* MY FAWNING ALL OVER HIM.
KLONG
ゴ
HE WAS... YEAH.
ふわ
FLUFF
HE WAS SOMEONE WHO WAS ALWAYS THERE WHEN I WANTED HIM...
GRRRR!
HRRRGH!

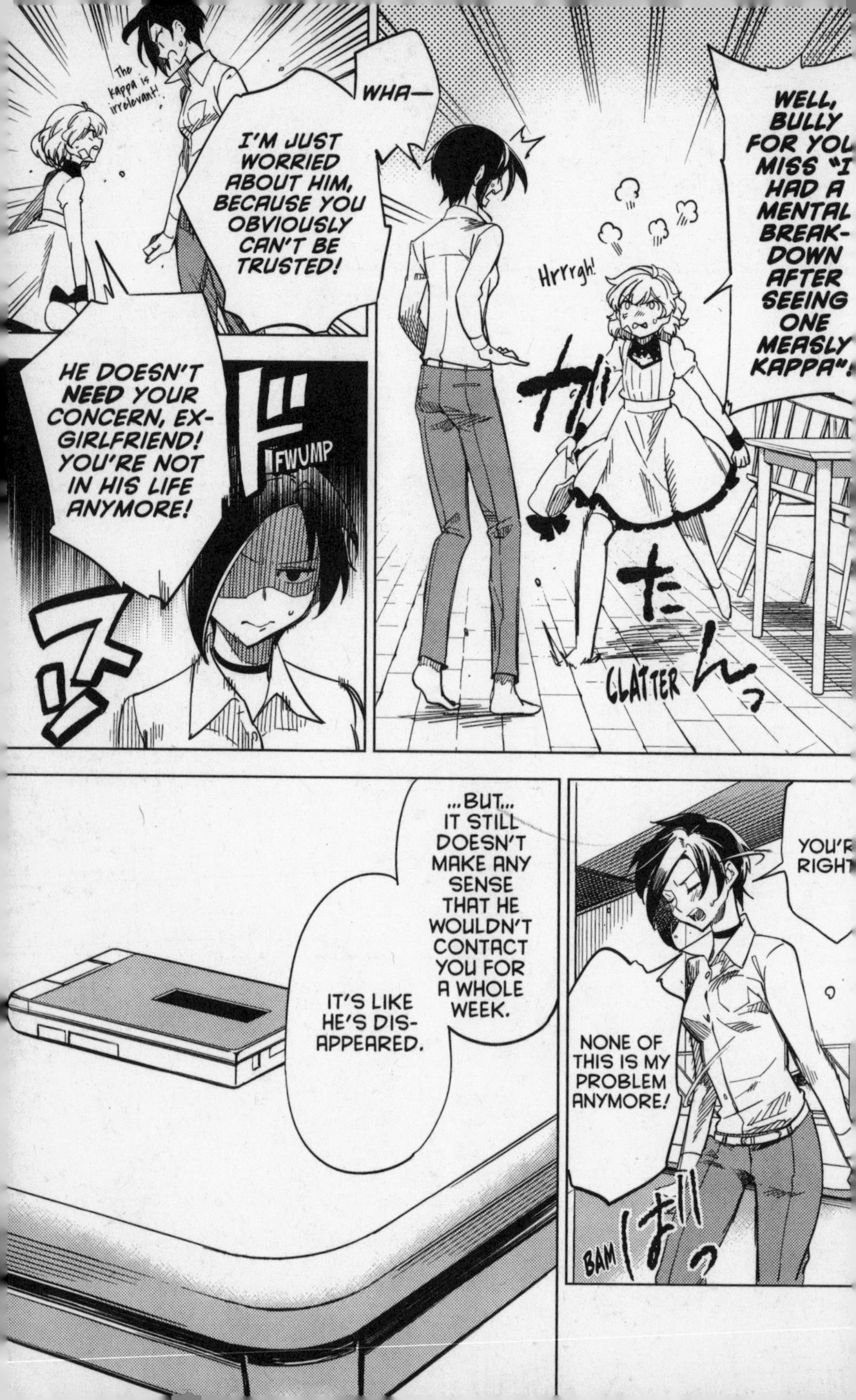
WELL, BULLY FOR YOU MISS "I HAD A MENTAL BREAK-DOWN AFTER SEEING ONE MEASLY KAPPA"!
WHA—
Hrrrgh!
たんっ
CLATTER
The kappa is irrelevant!
I'M JUST WORRIED ABOUT HIM, BECAUSE YOU OBVIOUSLY CAN'T BE TRUSTED!
HE DOESN'T NEED YOUR CONCERN, EX-GIRLFRIEND! YOU'RE NOT IN HIS LIFE ANYMORE!
ド
FWUMP
YOU'R RIGHT
NONE OF THIS IS MY PROBLEM ANYMORE!
BAM
ばっ
...BUT... IT STILL DOESN'T MAKE ANY SENSE THAT HE WOULDN'T CONTACT YOU FOR A WHOLE WEEK.
IT'S LIKE HE'S DIS-APPEARED.

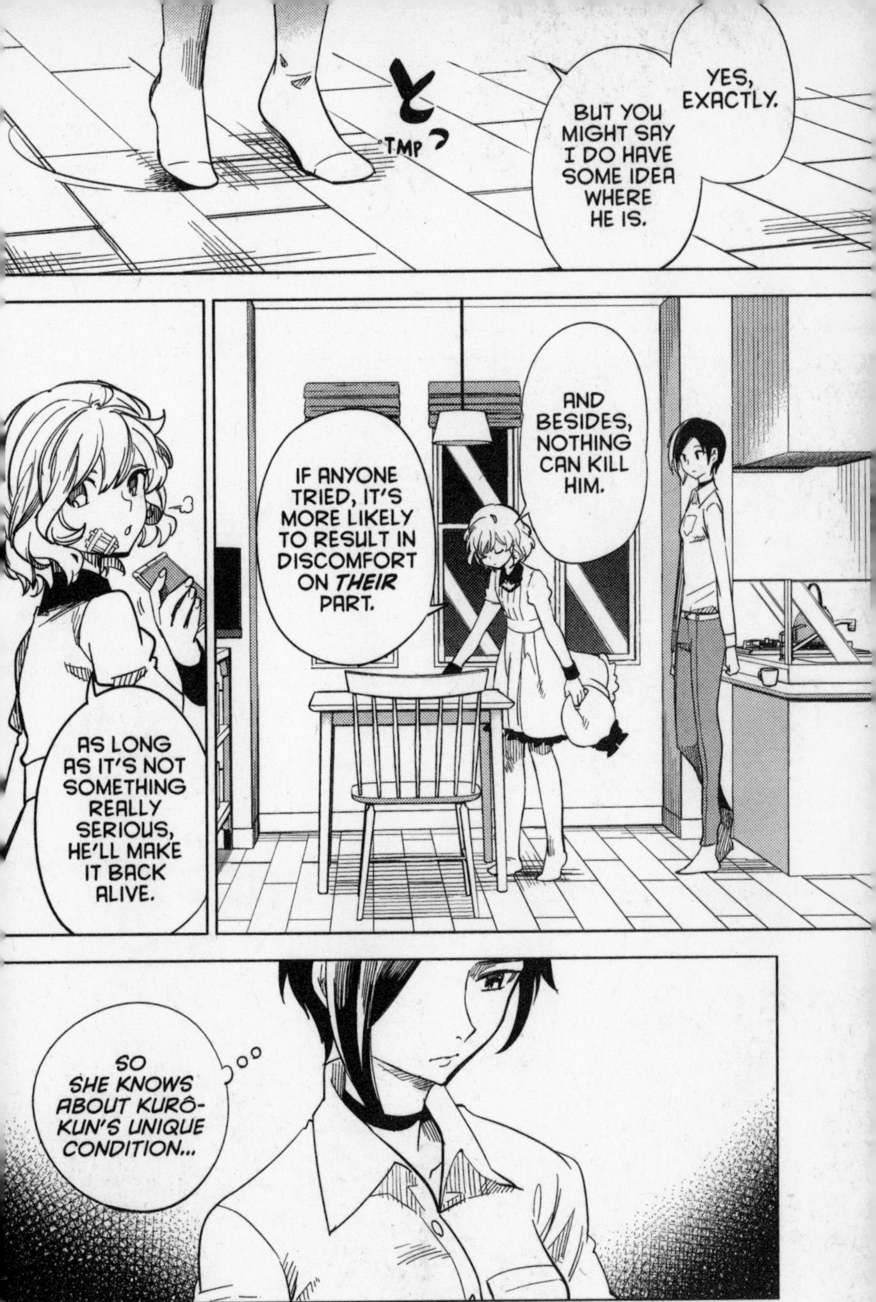
YES, EXACTLY.
BUT YOU MIGHT SAY I DO HAVE SOME IDEA WHERE HE IS.
と TMP
AND BESIDES, NOTHING CAN KILL HIM.
IF ANYONE TRIED, IT'S MORE LIKELY TO RESULT IN DISCOMFORT ON *THEIR* PART.
AS LONG AS IT'S NOT SOMETHING REALLY SERIOUS, HE'LL MAKE IT BACK ALIVE.
SO SHE KNOWS ABOUT KURÔ-KUN'S UNIQUE CONDITION...

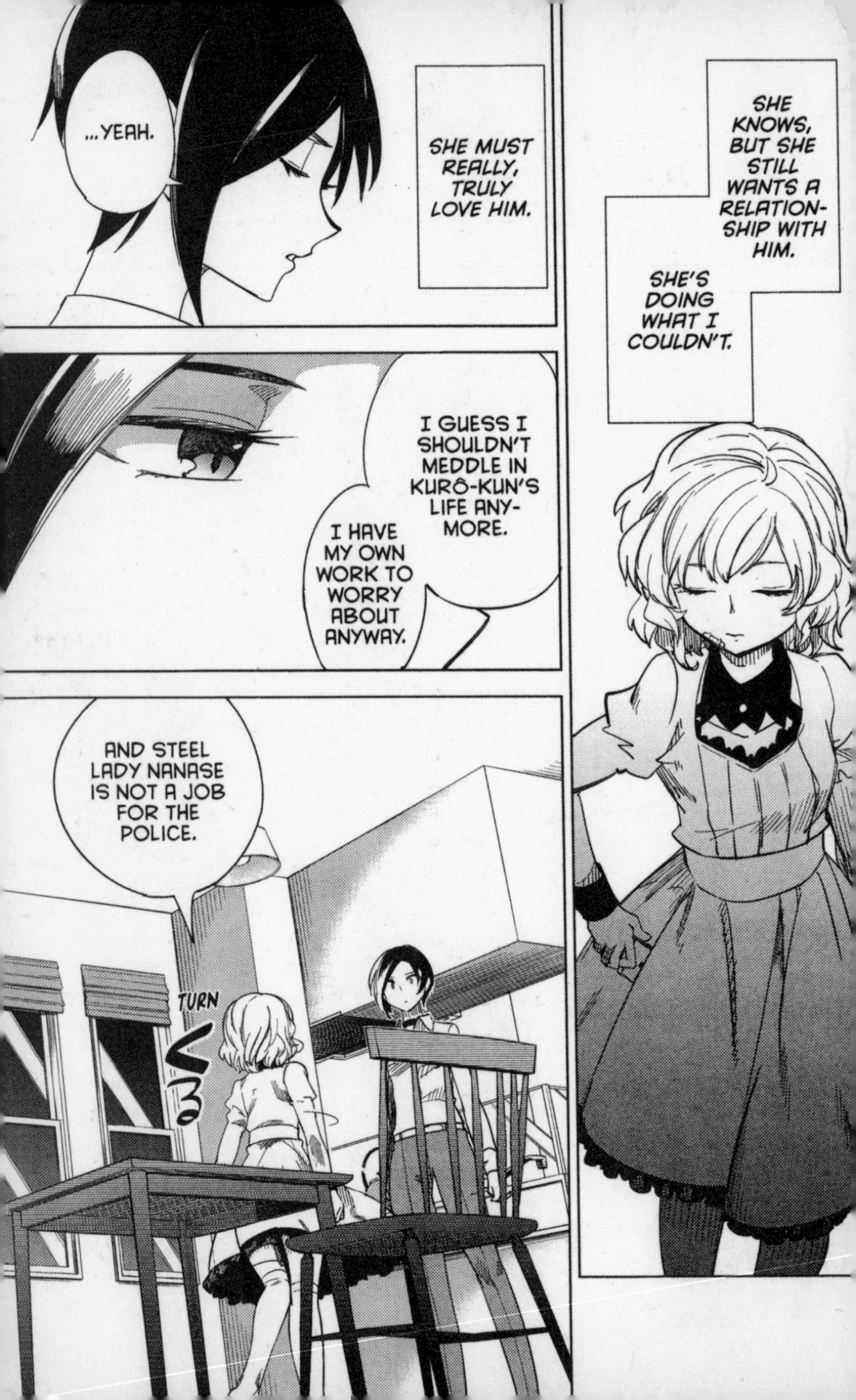
SHE KNOWS, BUT SHE STILL WANTS A RELATIONSHIP WITH HIM.
SHE'S DOING WHAT I COULDN'T.
SHE MUST REALLY, TRULY LOVE HIM.
...YEAH.
I GUESS I SHOULDN'T MEDDLE IN KURÔ-KUN'S LIFE ANYMORE.
I HAVE MY OWN WORK TO WORRY ABOUT ANYWAY.
AND STEEL LADY NANASE IS NOT A JOB FOR THE POLICE.
TURN

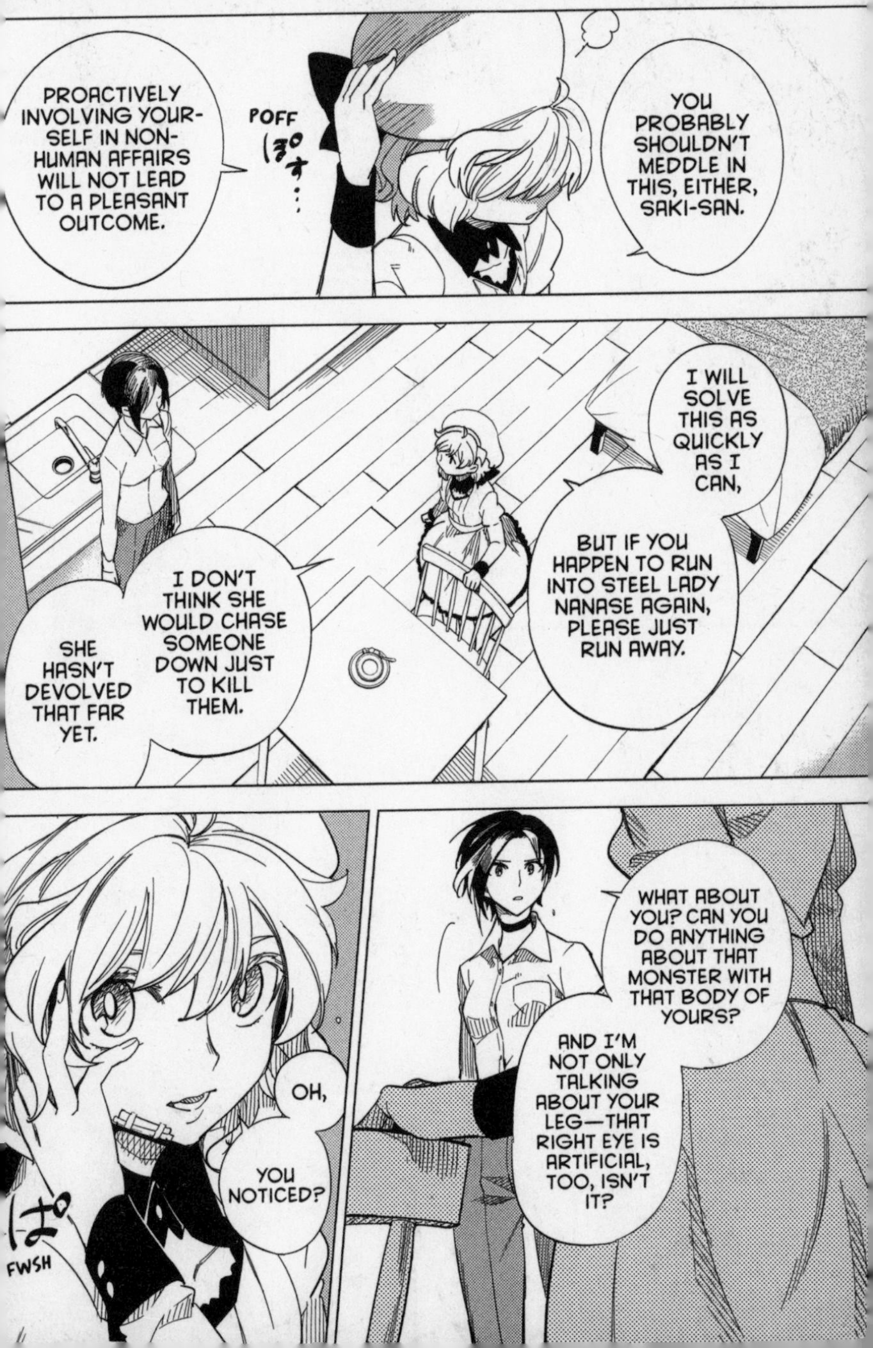
YOU PROBABLY SHOULDN'T MEDDLE IN THIS, EITHER, SAKI-SAN.
POFF
PROACTIVELY INVOLVING YOUR-SELF IN NON-HUMAN AFFAIRS WILL NOT LEAD TO A PLEASANT OUTCOME.
I WILL SOLVE THIS AS QUICKLY AS I CAN,
BUT IF YOU HAPPEN TO RUN INTO STEEL LADY NANASE AGAIN, PLEASE JUST RUN AWAY.
I DON'T THINK SHE WOULD CHASE SOMEONE DOWN JUST TO KILL THEM.
SHE HASN'T DEVOLVED THAT FAR YET.
WHAT ABOUT YOU? CAN YOU DO ANYTHING ABOUT THAT MONSTER WITH THAT BODY OF YOURS?
AND I'M NOT ONLY TALKING ABOUT YOUR LEG—THAT RIGHT EYE IS ARTIFICIAL, TOO, ISN'T IT?
OH,
YOU NOTICED?
ぱ
FWSH

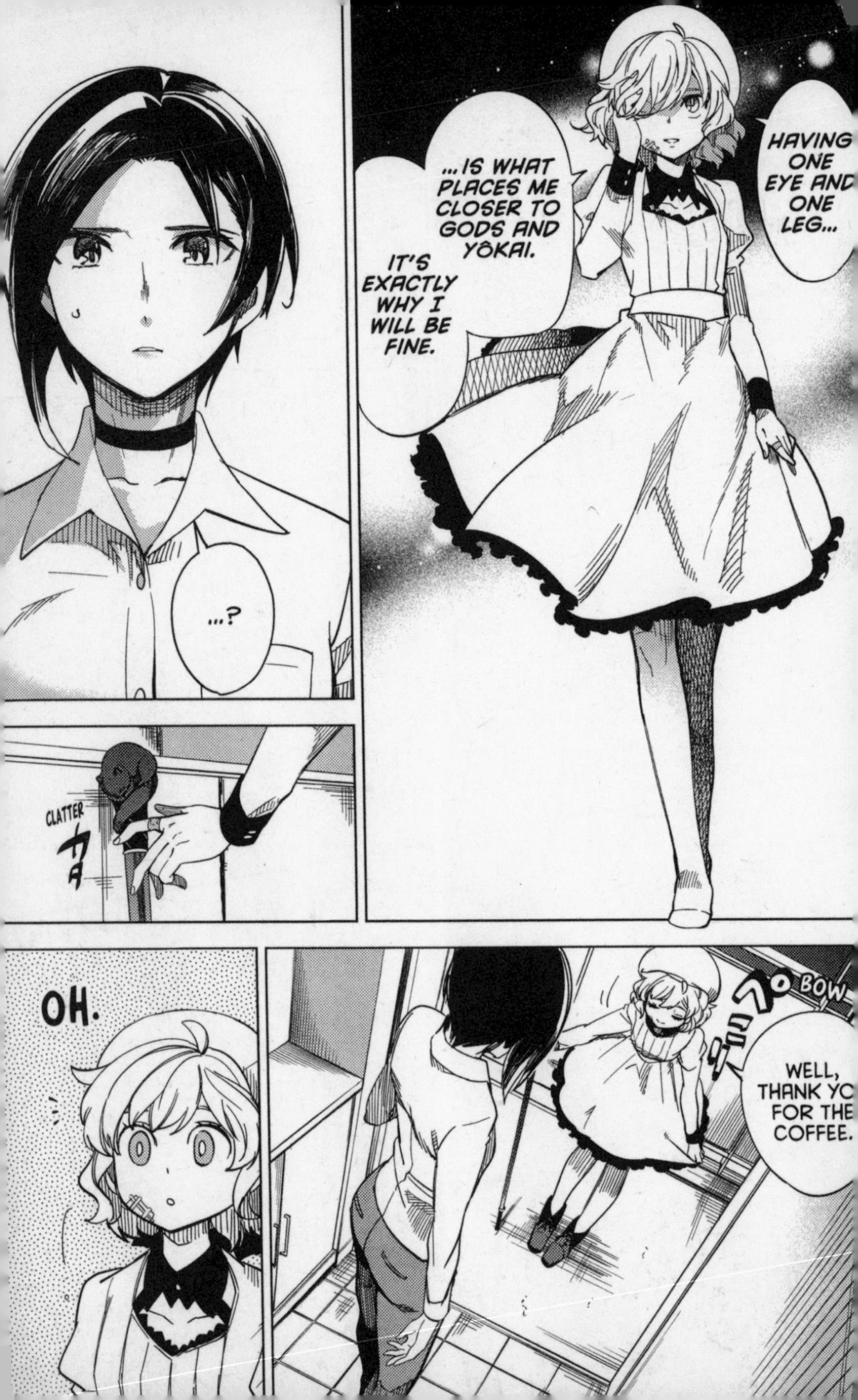
HAVING ONE EYE AND ONE LEG...
...IS WHAT PLACES ME CLOSER TO GODS AND YÔKAI.
IT'S EXACTLY WHY I WILL BE FINE.
...?
CLATTER
BOW
WELL, THANK YO FOR THE COFFEE.
OH.

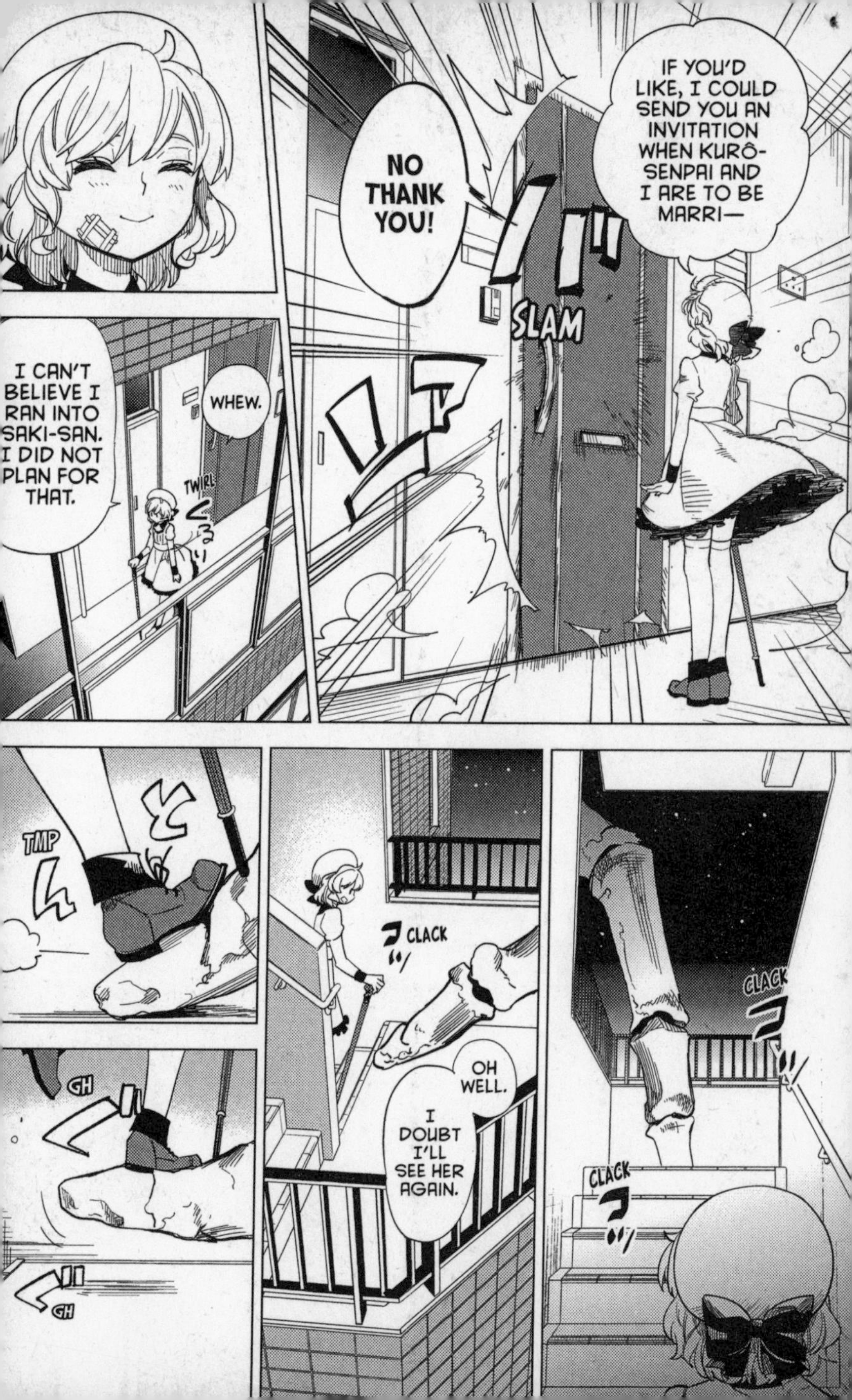
IF YOU'D LIKE, I COULD SEND YOU AN INVITATION WHEN KURÔ-SENPAI AND I ARE TO BE MARRI—
NO THANK YOU!
SLAM
WHEW.
I CAN'T BELIEVE I RAN INTO SAKI-SAN. I DID NOT PLAN FOR THAT.
TWIRL
CLACK
CLACK
CLACK
OH WELL.
I DOUBT I'LL SEE HER AGAIN.
TMP
GH
GH

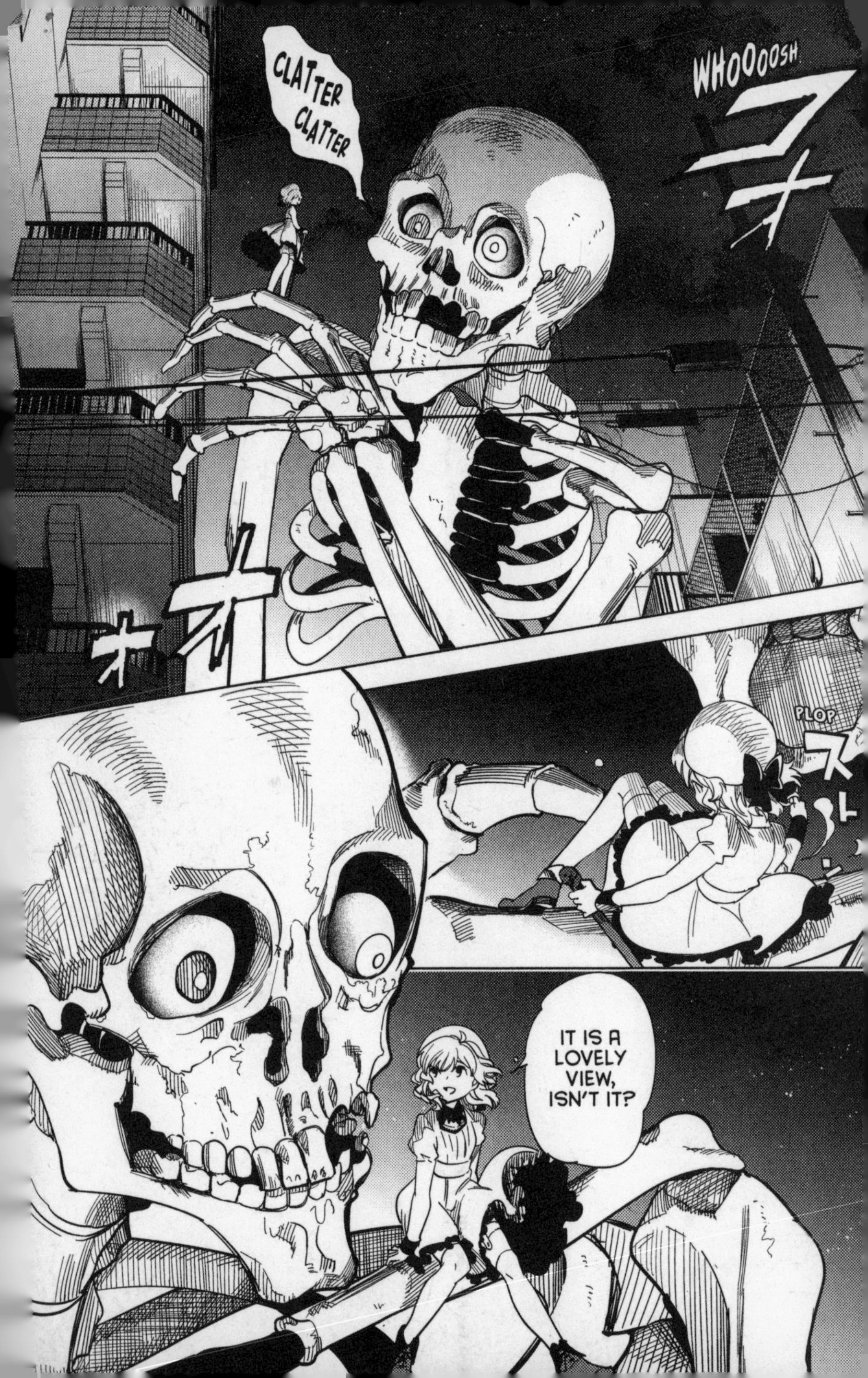
WHOOOOSH
CLATTER CLATTER
PLOP
IT IS A LOVELY VIEW, ISN'T IT?

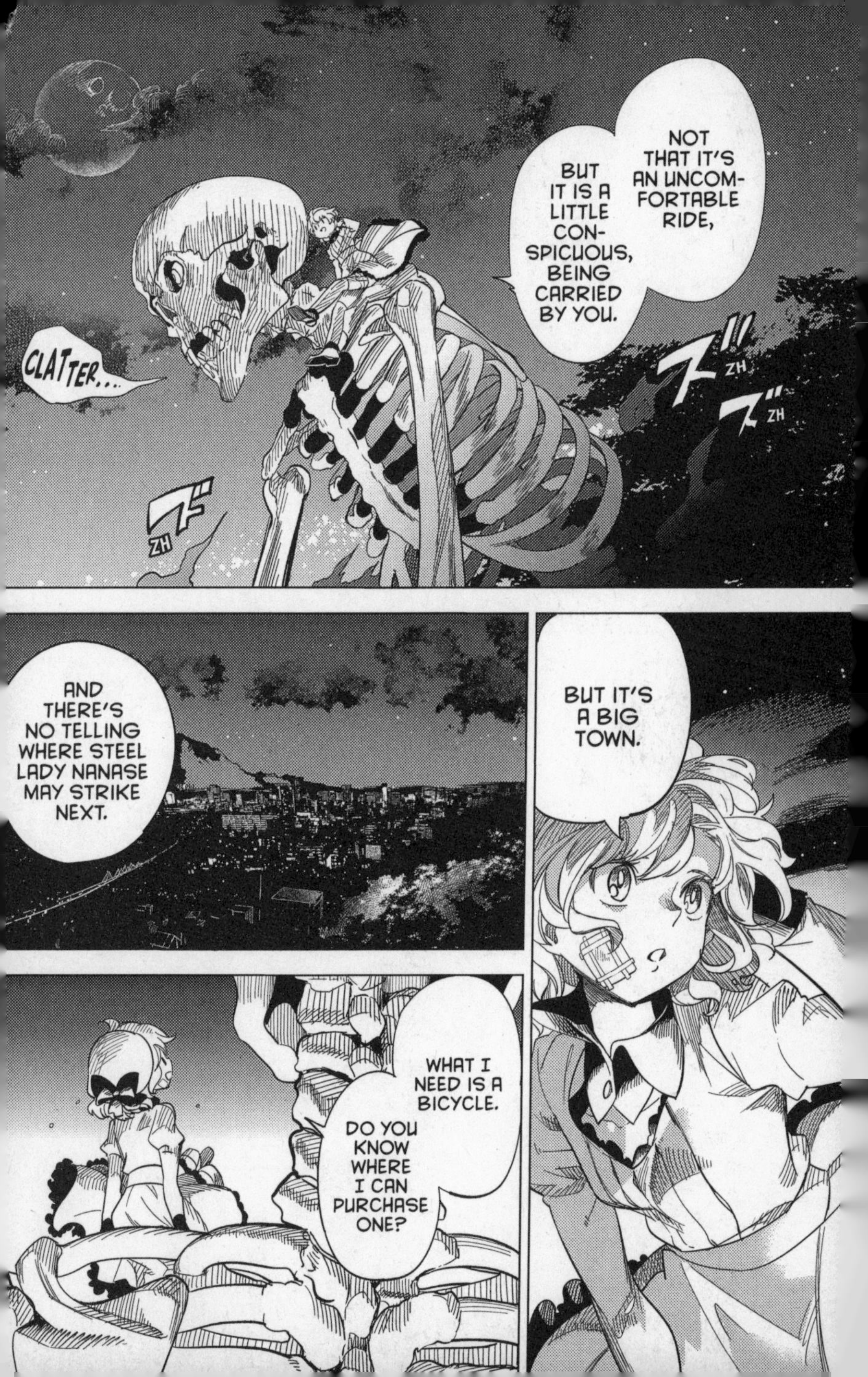
NOT THAT IT'S AN UNCOM-FORTABLE RIDE,
BUT IT IS A LITTLE CON-SPICUOUS, BEING CARRIED BY YOU.
ZH
ZH
CLATTER...
ZH
BUT IT'S A BIG TOWN.
AND THERE'S NO TELLING WHERE STEEL LADY NANASE MAY STRIKE NEXT.
WHAT I NEED IS A BICYCLE.
DO YOU KNOW WHERE I CAN PURCHASE ONE?

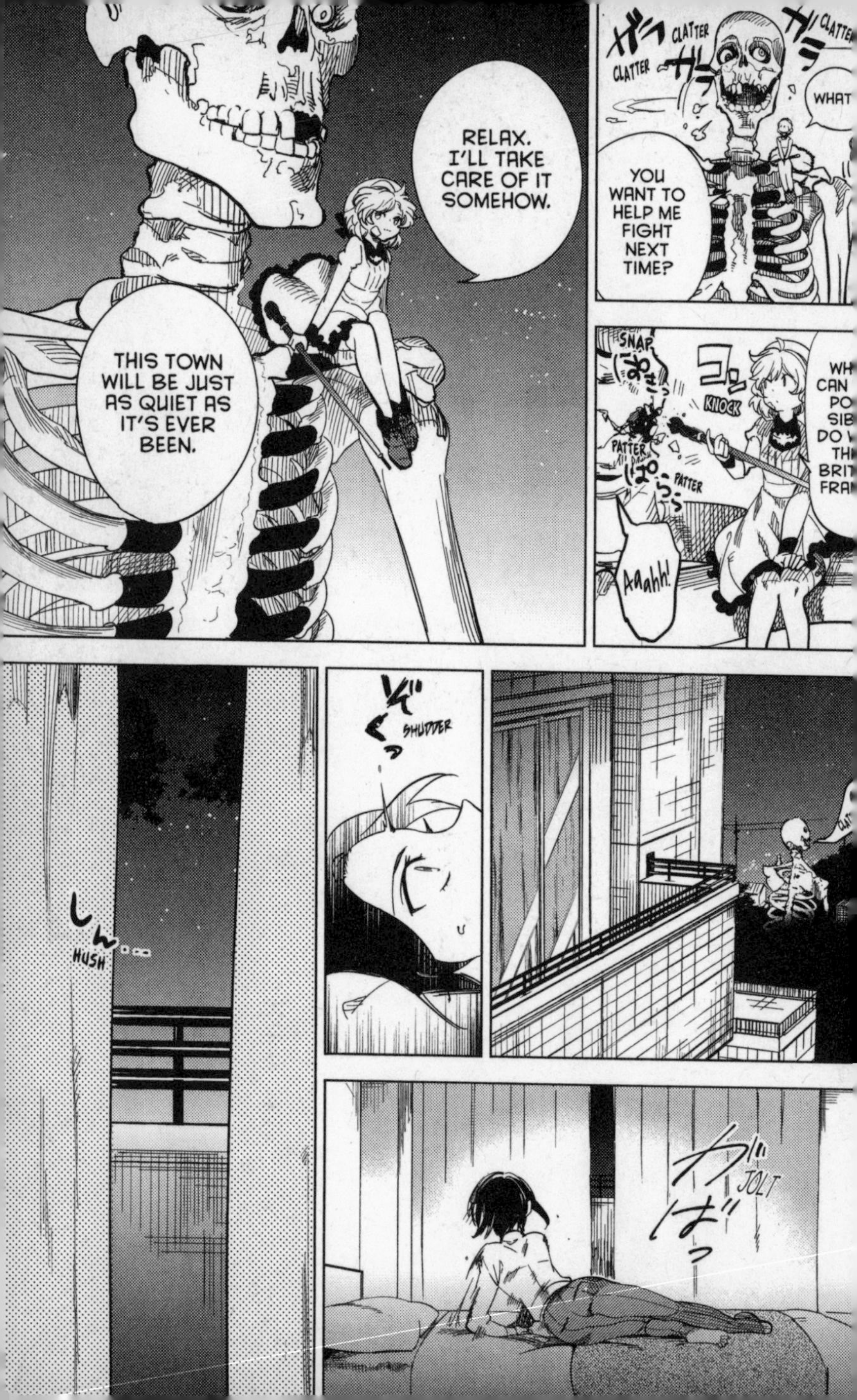

CLATTER
CLATTER
CLATTER
WHAT
YOU WANT TO HELP ME FIGHT NEXT TIME?
SNAP
KNOCK
PATTER
PATTER
Aaahh!
RELAX. I'LL TAKE CARE OF IT SOMEHOW.
THIS TOWN WILL BE JUST AS QUIET AS IT'S EVER BEEN.
SHUDDER
JOLT
HUSH

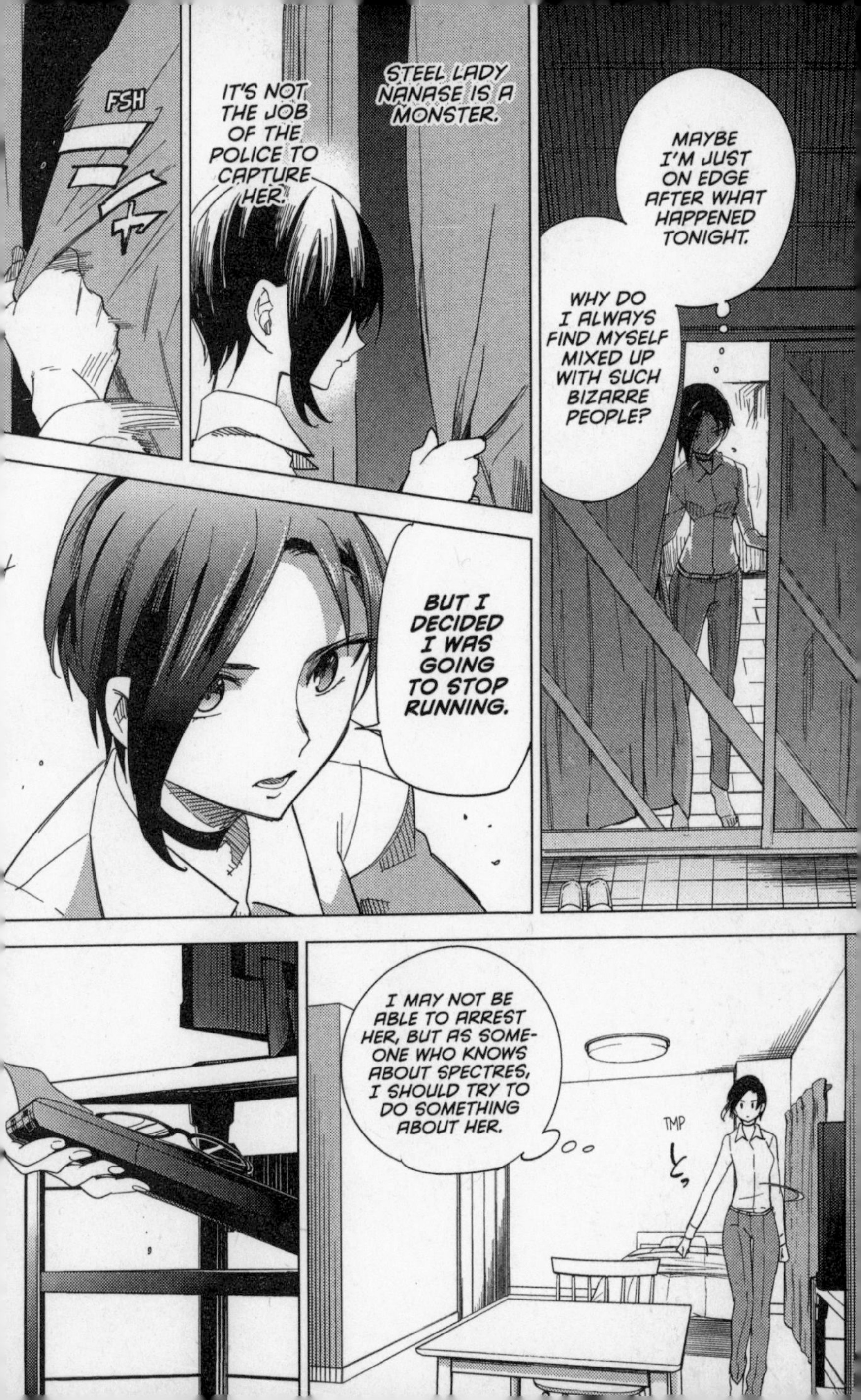
MAYBE I'M JUST ON EDGE AFTER WHAT HAPPENED TONIGHT.
WHY DO I ALWAYS FIND MYSELF MIXED UP WITH SUCH BIZARRE PEOPLE?
STEEL LADY NANASE IS A MONSTER.
IT'S NOT THE JOB OF THE POLICE TO CAPTURE HER.
FSH
BUT I DECIDED I WAS GOING TO STOP RUNNING.
I MAY NOT BE ABLE TO ARREST HER, BUT AS SOMEONE WHO KNOWS ABOUT SPECTRES, I SHOULD TRY TO DO SOMETHING ABOUT HER.
TMP

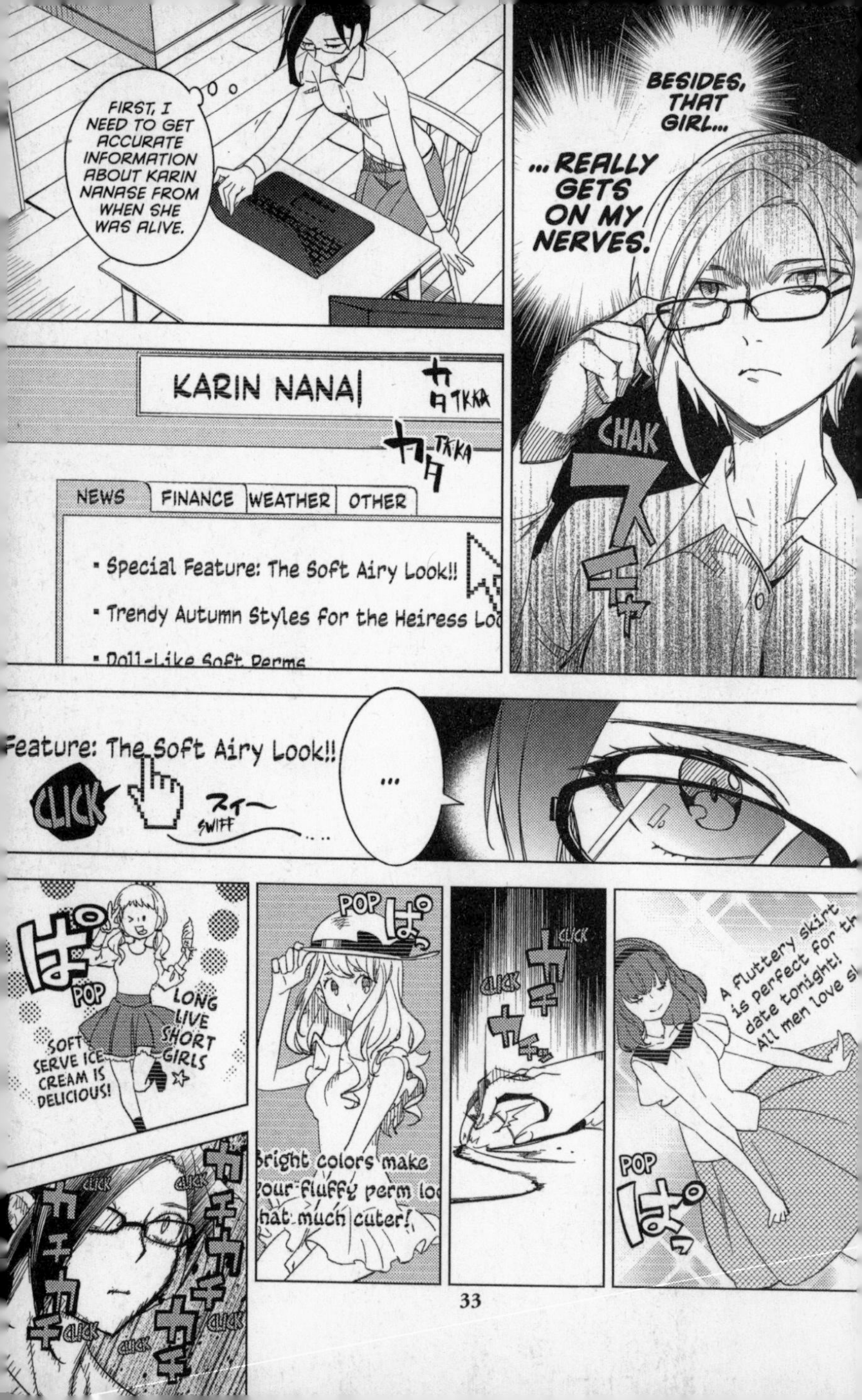
BESIDES, THAT GIRL...
...REALLY GETS ON MY NERVES.
CHAK
FIRST, I NEED TO GET ACCURATE INFORMATION ABOUT KARIN NANASE FROM WHEN SHE WAS ALIVE.
KARIN NANA|
TKKA
TKKA
NEWS
FINANCE
WEATHER
OTHER
• Special Feature: The Soft Airy Look!!
• Trendy Autumn Styles for the Heiress Lo
...
Feature: The Soft Airy Look!!
CLICK
SWIFF
A fluttery skirt is perfect for th date tonight! All men love s
POP
CLICK
CLICK
POP
Bright colors make your fluffy perm lo hat much cuter!
POP
LONG LIVE SHORT GIRLS
SOFT SERVE ICE CREAM IS DELICIOUS!
CLICK
CLICK
CLICK
CLICK
CLICK

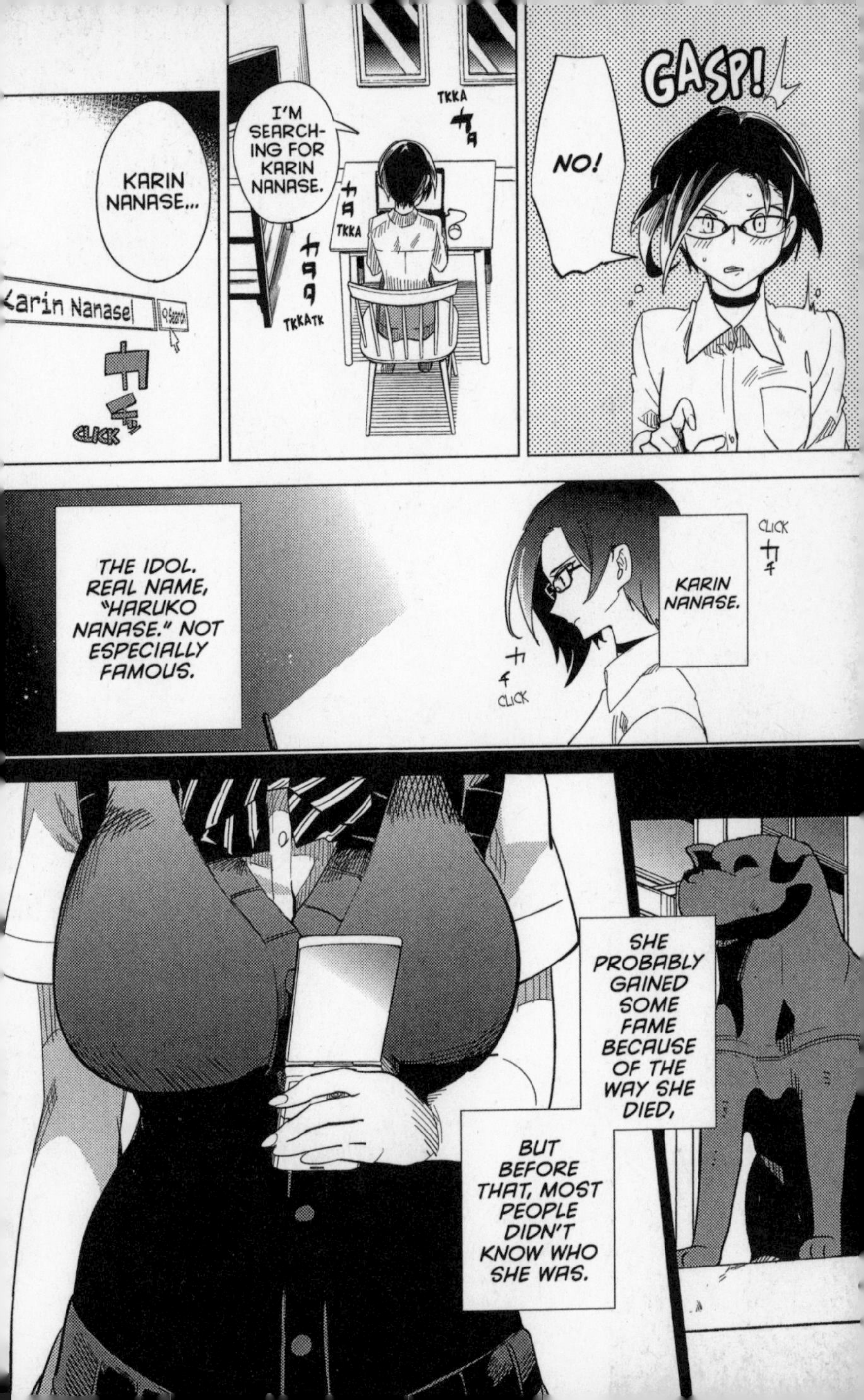
GASP!
NO!
TKKA
I'M SEARCHING FOR KARIN NANASE.
TKKA
TKKATK
KARIN NANASE...
Karin Nanase
Search
CLICK
CLICK
KARIN NANASE.
THE IDOL. REAL NAME, "HARUKO NANASE." NOT ESPECIALLY FAMOUS.
CLICK
SHE PROBABLY GAINED SOME FAME BECAUSE OF THE WAY SHE DIED,
BUT BEFORE THAT, MOST PEOPLE DIDN'T KNOW WHO SHE WAS.

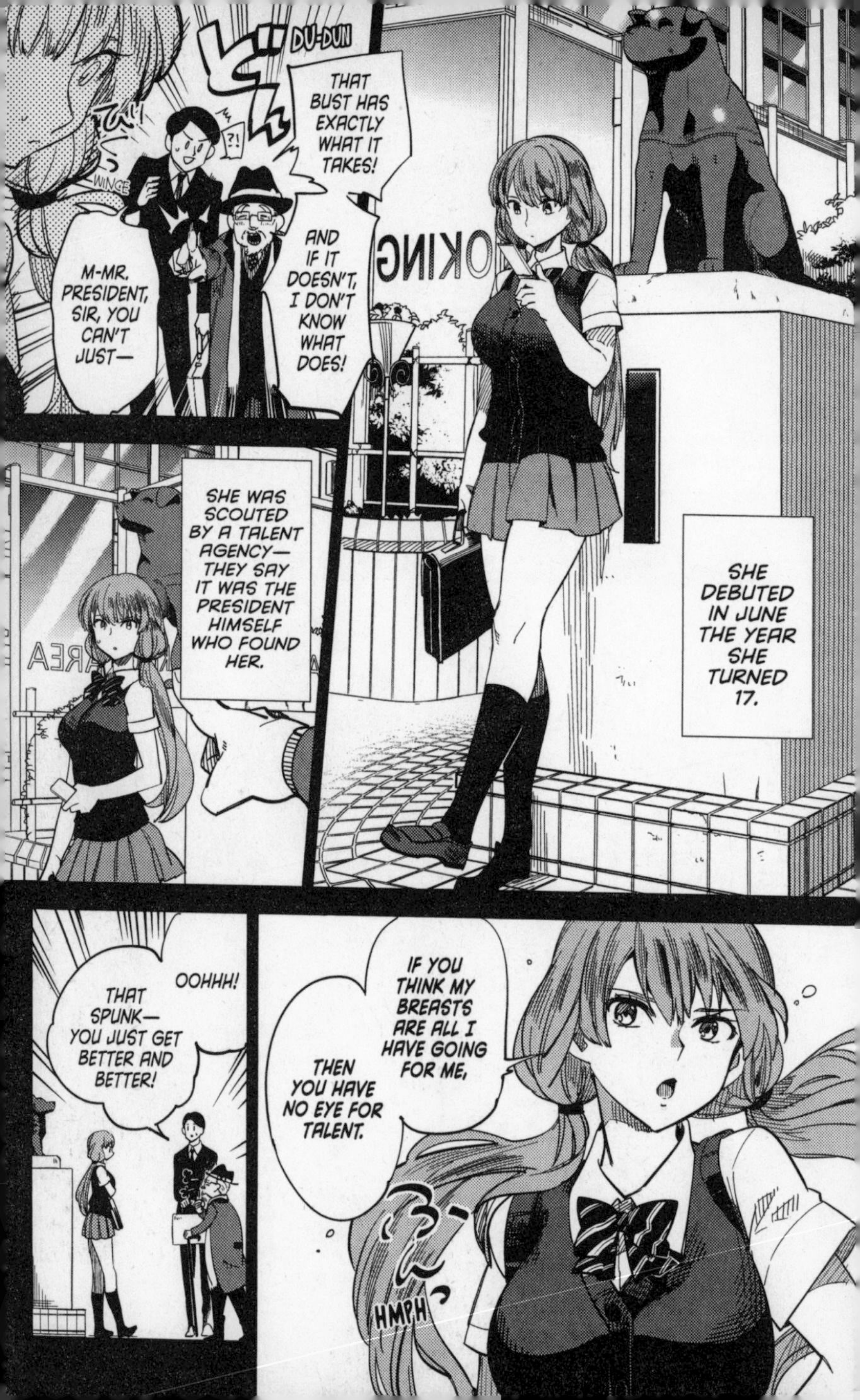
SHE DEBUTED IN JUNE THE YEAR SHE TURNED 17.
DU-DUN
THAT BUST HAS EXACTLY WHAT IT TAKES!
AND IF IT DOESN'T, I DON'T KNOW WHAT DOES!
WINCE
?!
M-MR. PRESIDENT, SIR, YOU CAN'T JUST—
SHE WAS SCOUTED BY A TALENT AGENCY—THEY SAY IT WAS THE PRESIDENT HIMSELF WHO FOUND HER.
IF YOU THINK MY BREASTS ARE ALL I HAVE GOING FOR ME,
THEN YOU HAVE NO EYE FOR TALENT.
HMPH
OOHHH!
THAT SPUNK—YOU JUST GET BETTER AND BETTER!

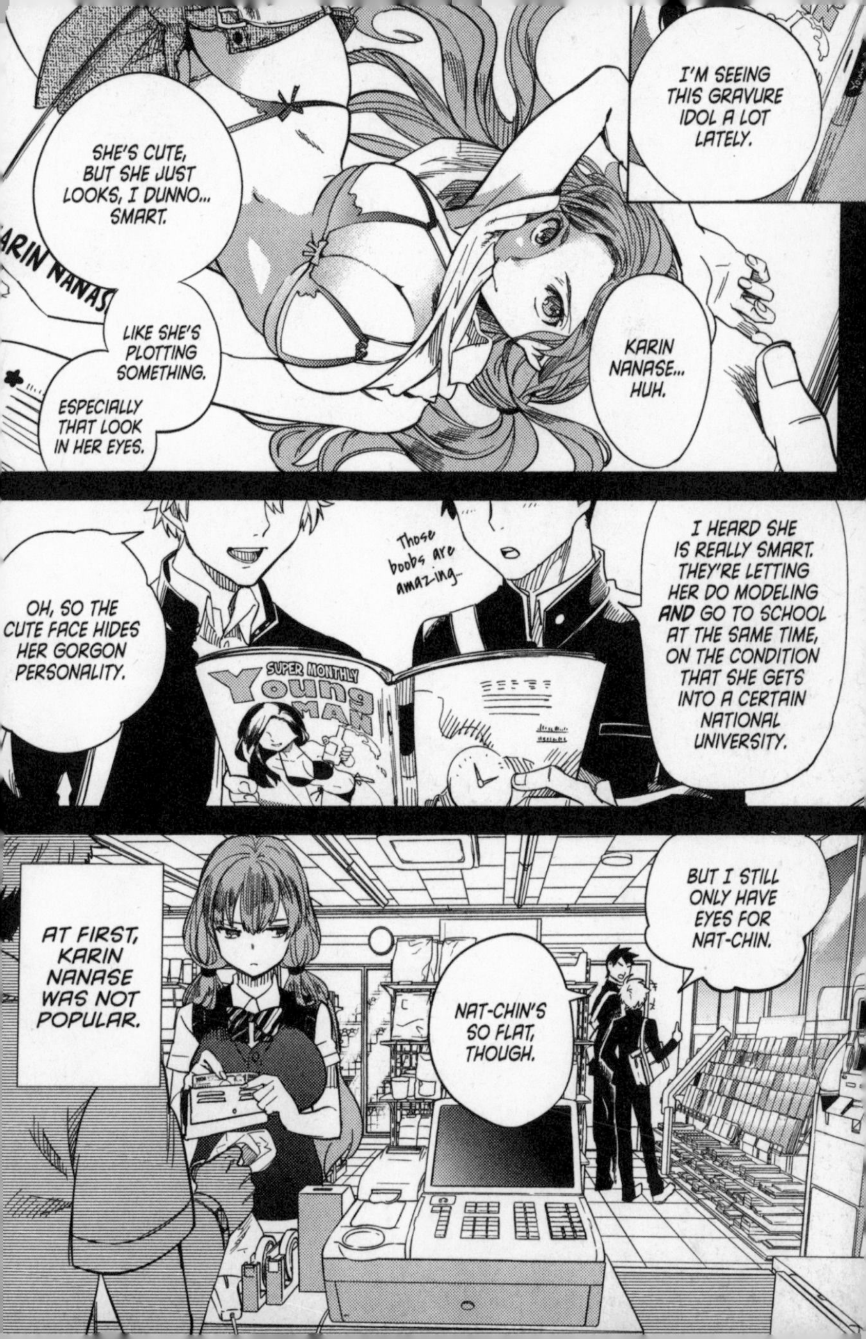
I'M SEEING THIS GRAVURE IDOL A LOT LATELY.
KARIN NANASE... HUH.
KARIN NANASE
SHE'S CUTE, BUT SHE JUST LOOKS, I DUNNO... SMART.
LIKE SHE'S PLOTTING SOMETHING.
ESPECIALLY THAT LOOK IN HER EYES.
I HEARD SHE IS REALLY SMART. THEY'RE LETTING HER DO MODELING AND GO TO SCHOOL AT THE SAME TIME, ON THE CONDITION THAT SHE GETS INTO A CERTAIN NATIONAL UNIVERSITY.
Those boobs are amazing...
SUPER MONTHLY Young MAN
OH, SO THE CUTE FACE HIDES HER GORGON PERSONALITY.
BUT I STILL ONLY HAVE EYES FOR NAT-CHIN.
NAT-CHIN'S SO FLAT, THOUGH.
AT FIRST, KARIN NANASE WAS NOT POPULAR.

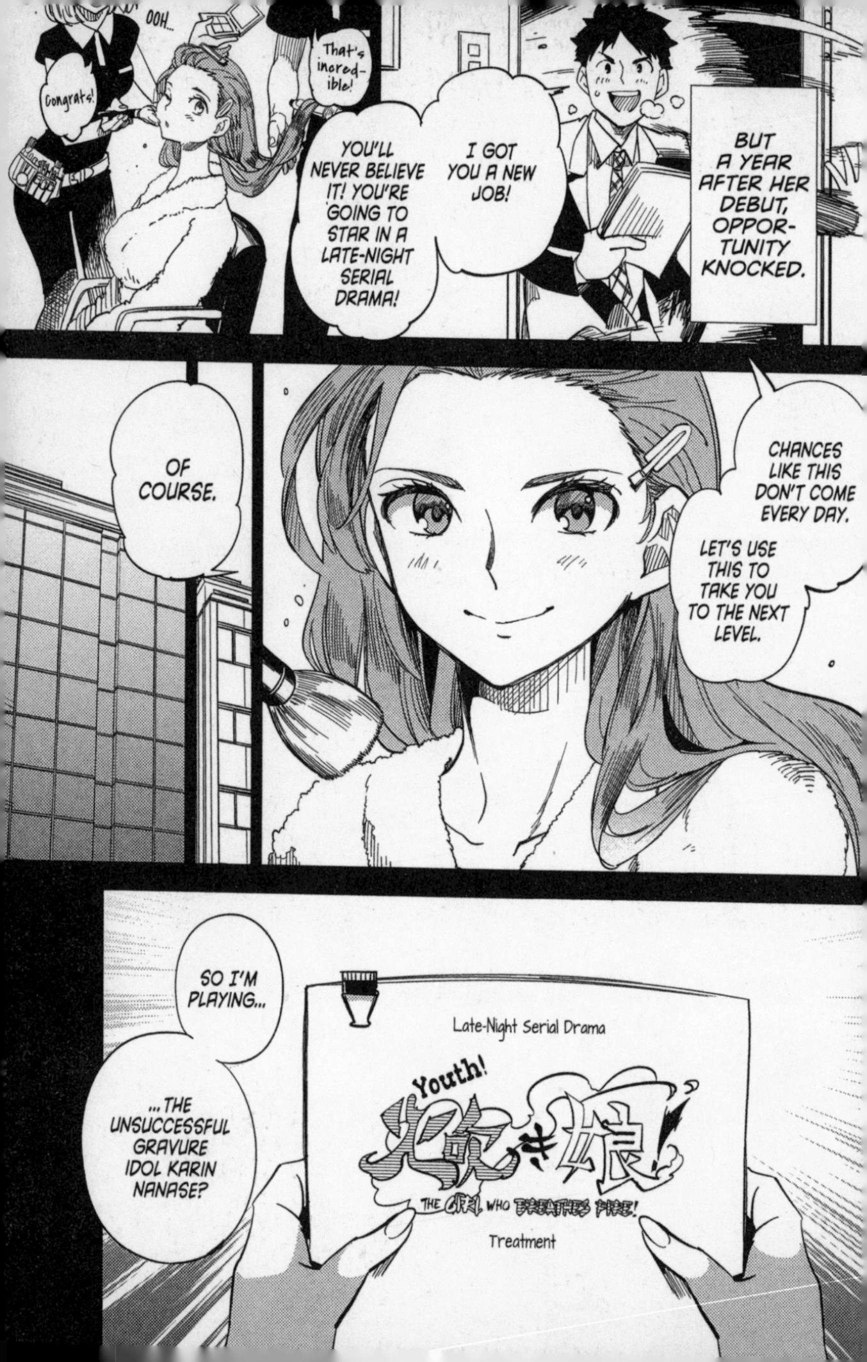
BUT A YEAR AFTER HER DEBUT, OPPORTUNITY KNOCKED.
I GOT YOU A NEW JOB!
YOU'LL NEVER BELIEVE IT! YOU'RE GOING TO STAR IN A LATE-NIGHT SERIAL DRAMA!
That's incred-ible!
OOH...
Congrats!
CHANCES LIKE THIS DON'T COME EVERY DAY.
LET'S USE THIS TO TAKE YOU TO THE NEXT LEVEL.
OF COURSE.
SO I'M PLAYING...
...THE UNSUCCESSFUL GRAVURE IDOL KARIN NANASE?
Late-Night Serial Drama
Youth!
THE GIRL WHO BREATHES FIRE!
Treatment

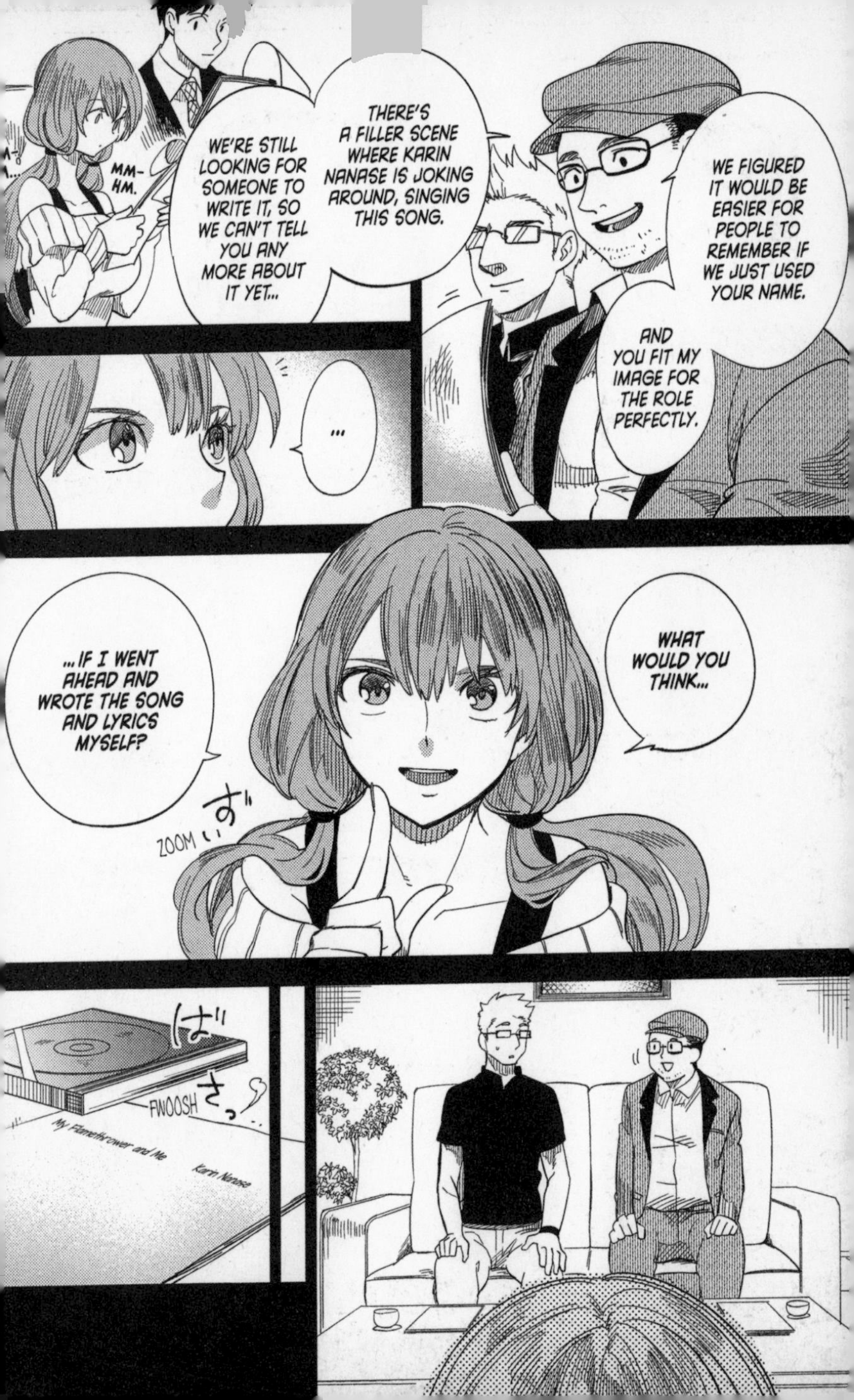
THERE'S A FILLER SCENE WHERE KARIN NANASE IS JOKING AROUND, SINGING THIS SONG.
WE FIGURED IT WOULD BE EASIER FOR PEOPLE TO REMEMBER IF WE JUST USED YOUR NAME.
AND YOU FIT MY IMAGE FOR THE ROLE PERFECTLY.
WE'RE STILL LOOKING FOR SOMEONE TO WRITE IT, SO WE CAN'T TELL YOU ANY MORE ABOUT IT YET...
MM-HM.
...
WHAT WOULD YOU THINK...
...IF I WENT AHEAD AND WROTE THE SONG AND LYRICS MYSELF?
ZOOM
FWOOSH
My Flamethrower and Me
Karin Nanase

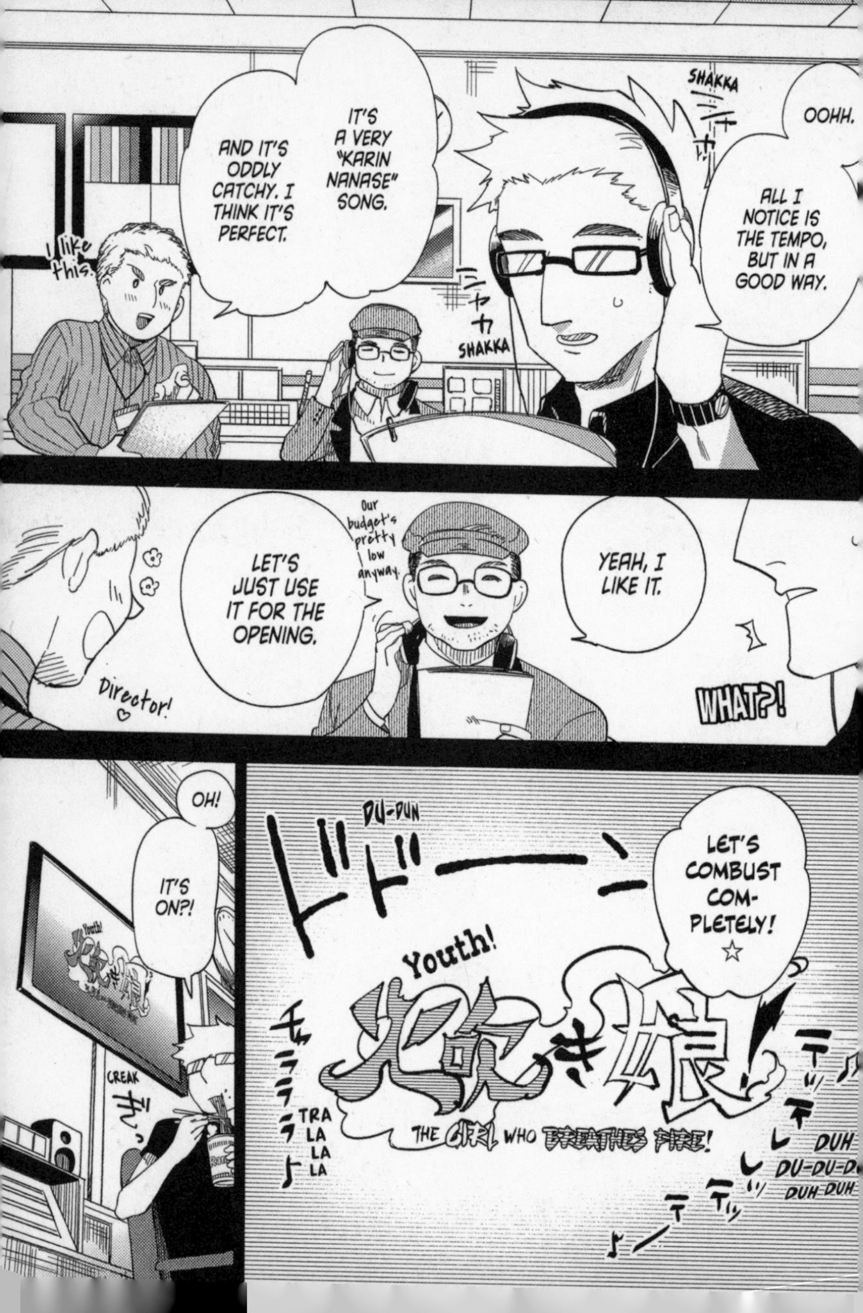
OOHH.
ALL I NOTICE IS THE TEMPO, BUT IN A GOOD WAY.
SHAKKA
IT'S A VERY "KARIN NANASE" SONG.
AND IT'S ODDLY CATCHY. I THINK IT'S PERFECT.
I like this.
SHAKKA
WHAT?!
YEAH, I LIKE IT.
Our budget's pretty low anyway.
LET'S JUST USE IT FOR THE OPENING.
Director! ♡
LET'S COMBUST COM-PLETELY! ☆
DU-DUN
Youth!
THE GIRL WHO BREATHES FIRE!
DUH DU-DU-DU DUH-DUH
TRA LA LA LA
OH!
IT'S ON?!
CREAK

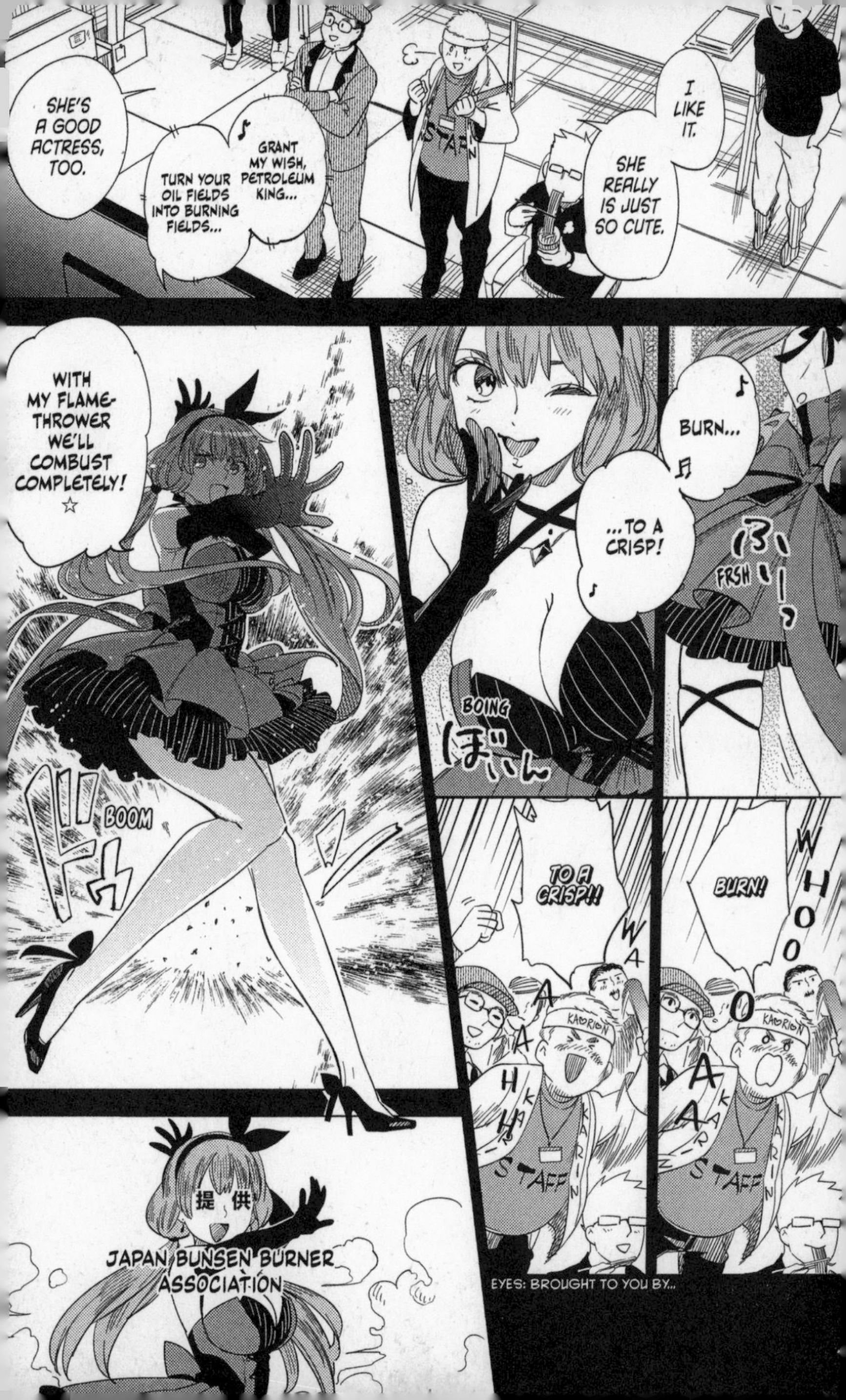
I LIKE IT.
SHE REALLY IS JUST SO CUTE.
GRANT MY WISH, PETROLEUM KING...
TURN YOUR OIL FIELDS INTO BURNING FIELDS...
SHE'S A GOOD ACTRESS, TOO.
BURN...
FRSH
...TO A CRISP!
BOING
BURN!
WHOOOO
OAAA
TO A CRISP!!
WAAAHH
EYES: BROUGHT TO YOU BY...
WITH MY FLAME-THROWER WE'LL COMBUST COMPLETELY! ☆
BOOM
提供
JAPAN BUNSEN BURNER ASSOCIATION

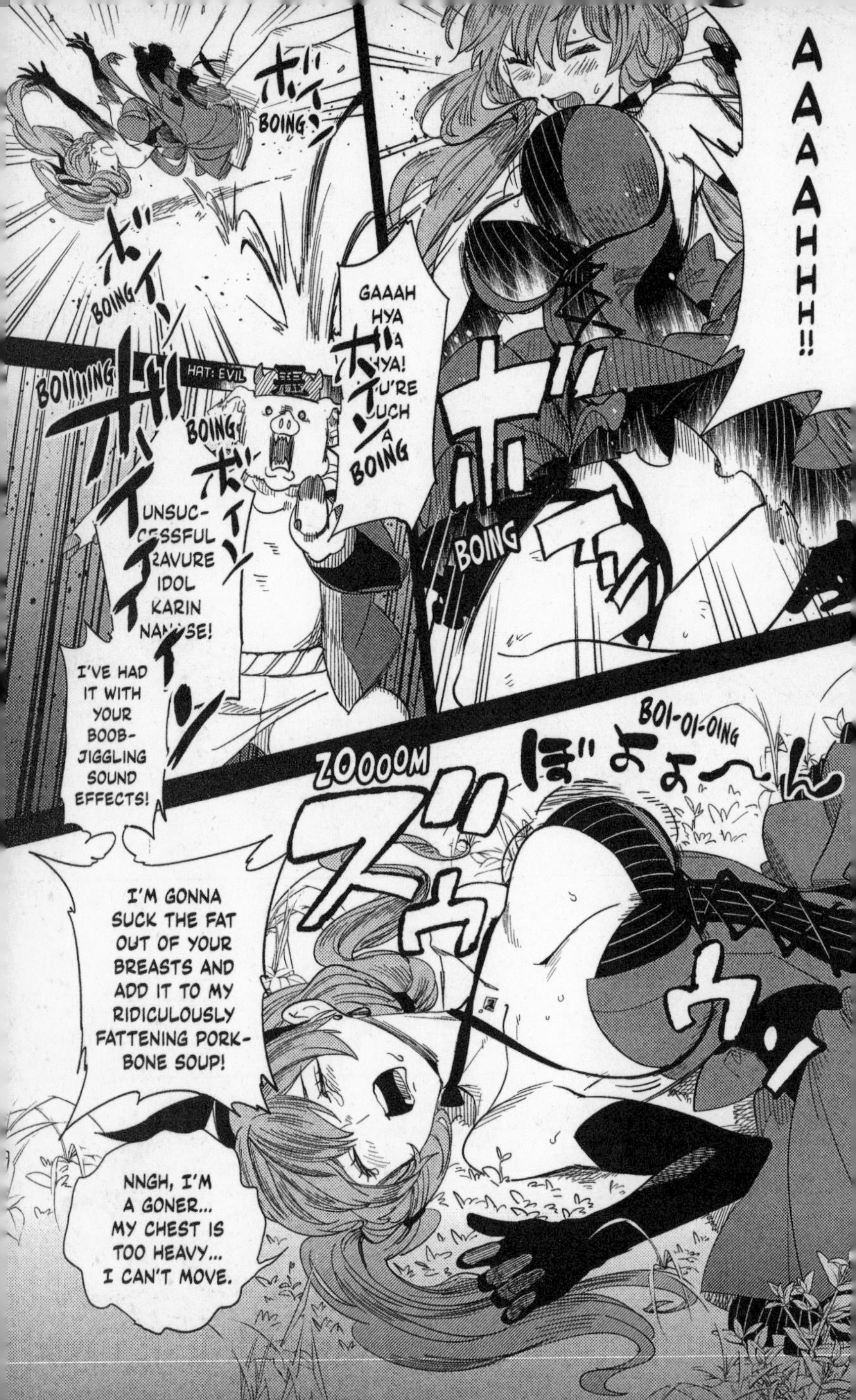
AAAAHHH!!
BOING
BOING
BOIIIING
HAT: EVIL
BOING
GAAAH HYA HA HYA! YOU'RE SUCH A BOING
UNSUCCESSFUL GRAVURE IDOL KARIN NANASE!
I'VE HAD IT WITH YOUR BOOB-JIGGLING SOUND EFFECTS!
BOING
BOI-OI-OING
ZOOOOM
I'M GONNA SUCK THE FAT OUT OF YOUR BREASTS AND ADD IT TO MY RIDICULOUSLY FATTENING PORK-BONE SOUP!
NNGH, I'M A GONER... MY CHEST IS TOO HEAVY... I CAN'T MOVE.

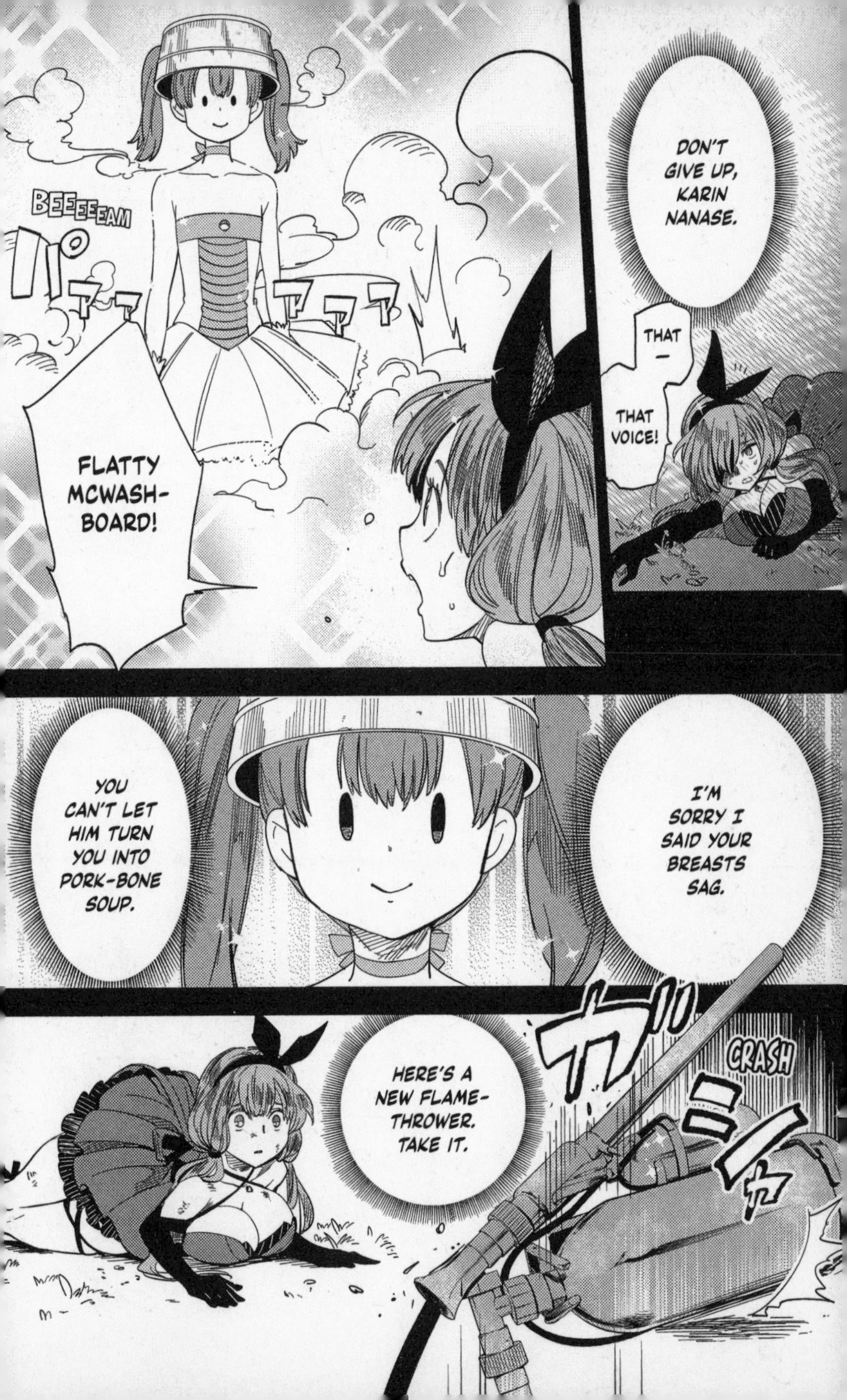
DON'T GIVE UP, KARIN NANASE.
THAT—
THAT VOICE!
BEEEEEAM
FLATTY MCWASH-BOARD!
I'M SORRY I SAID YOUR BREASTS SAG.
YOU CAN'T LET HIM TURN YOU INTO PORK-BONE SOUP.
CRASH
HERE'S A NEW FLAME-THROWER. TAKE IT.

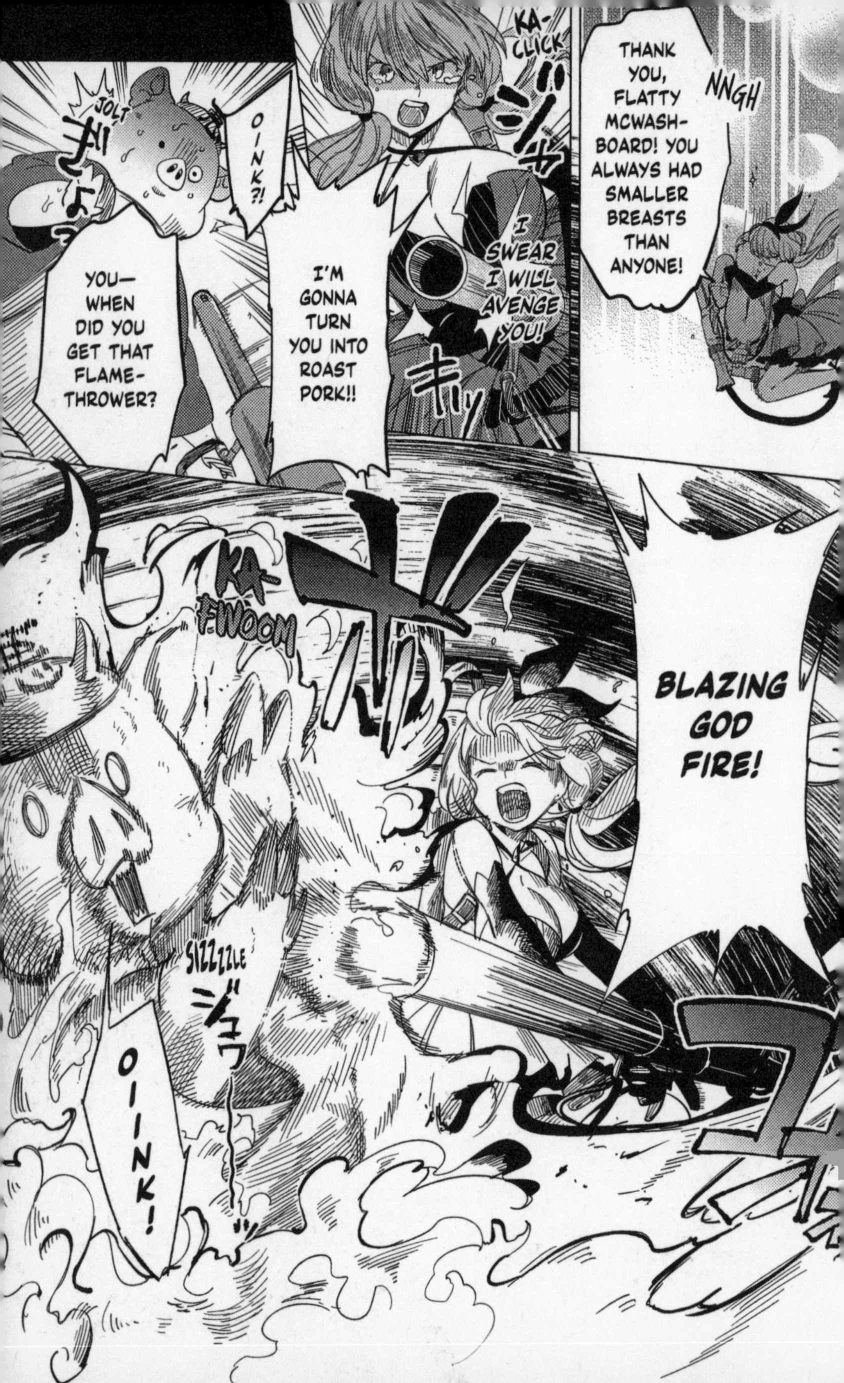
THANK YOU, FLATTY MCWASH-BOARD! YOU ALWAYS HAD SMALLER BREASTS THAN ANYONE!
NNGH
KA-CLICK
I SWEAR I WILL AVENGE YOU!
I'M GONNA TURN YOU INTO ROAST PORK!!
OINK?!
JOLT
YOU—WHEN DID YOU GET THAT FLAME-THROWER?
BLAZING GOD FIRE!
KA-FWOOM
SIZZZZLE
OIINK!

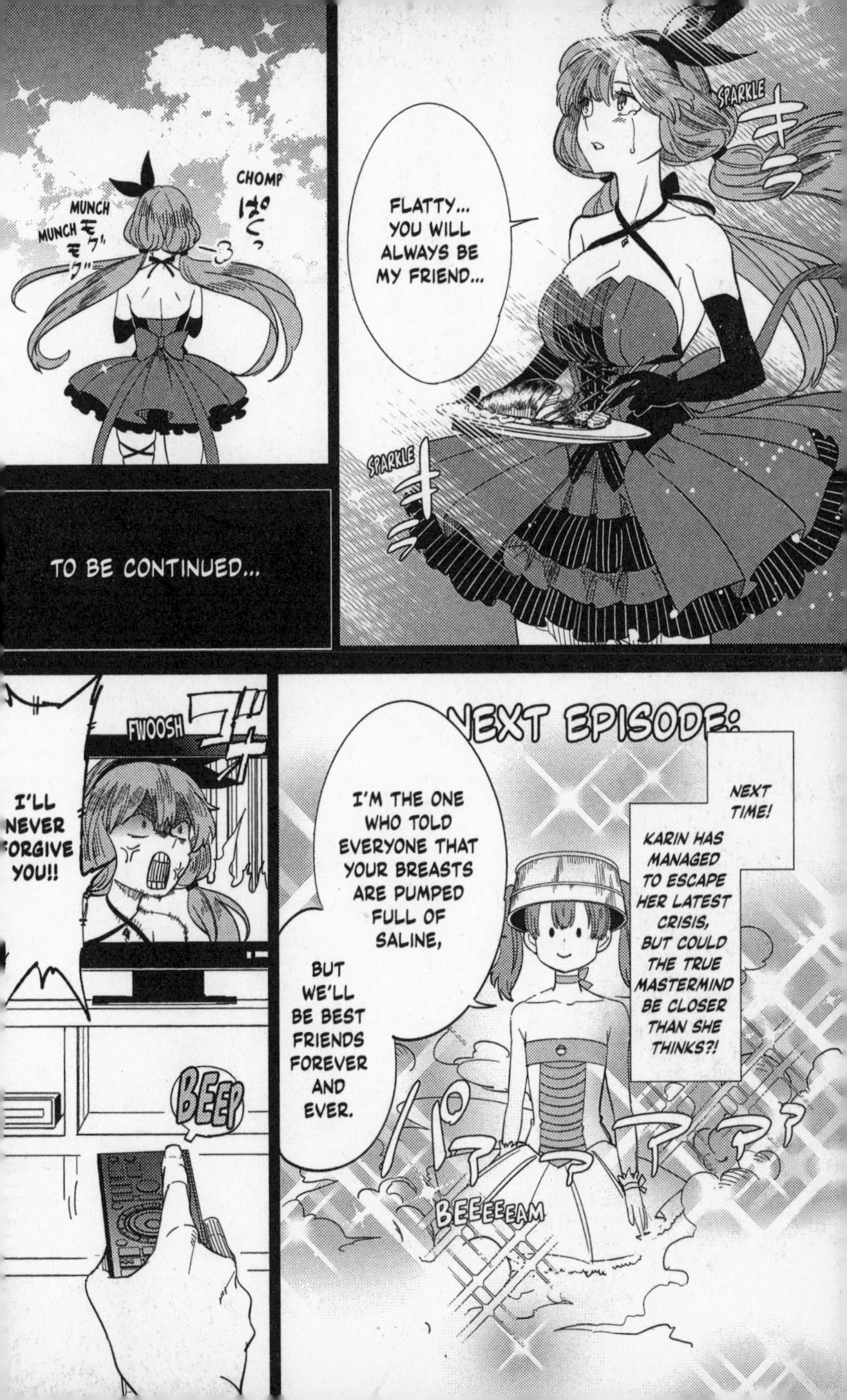
SPARKLE
FLATTY... YOU WILL ALWAYS BE MY FRIEND...
SPARKLE
CHOMP
MUNCH MUNCH
TO BE CONTINUED...
NEXT EPISODE:
NEXT TIME!
KARIN HAS MANAGED TO ESCAPE HER LATEST CRISIS, BUT COULD THE TRUE MASTERMIND BE CLOSER THAN SHE THINKS?!
I'M THE ONE WHO TOLD EVERYONE THAT YOUR BREASTS ARE PUMPED FULL OF SALINE,
BUT WE'LL BE BEST FRIENDS FOREVER AND EVER.
BEEEEEAM
FWOOSH
I'LL NEVER FORGIVE YOU!!
BEEP

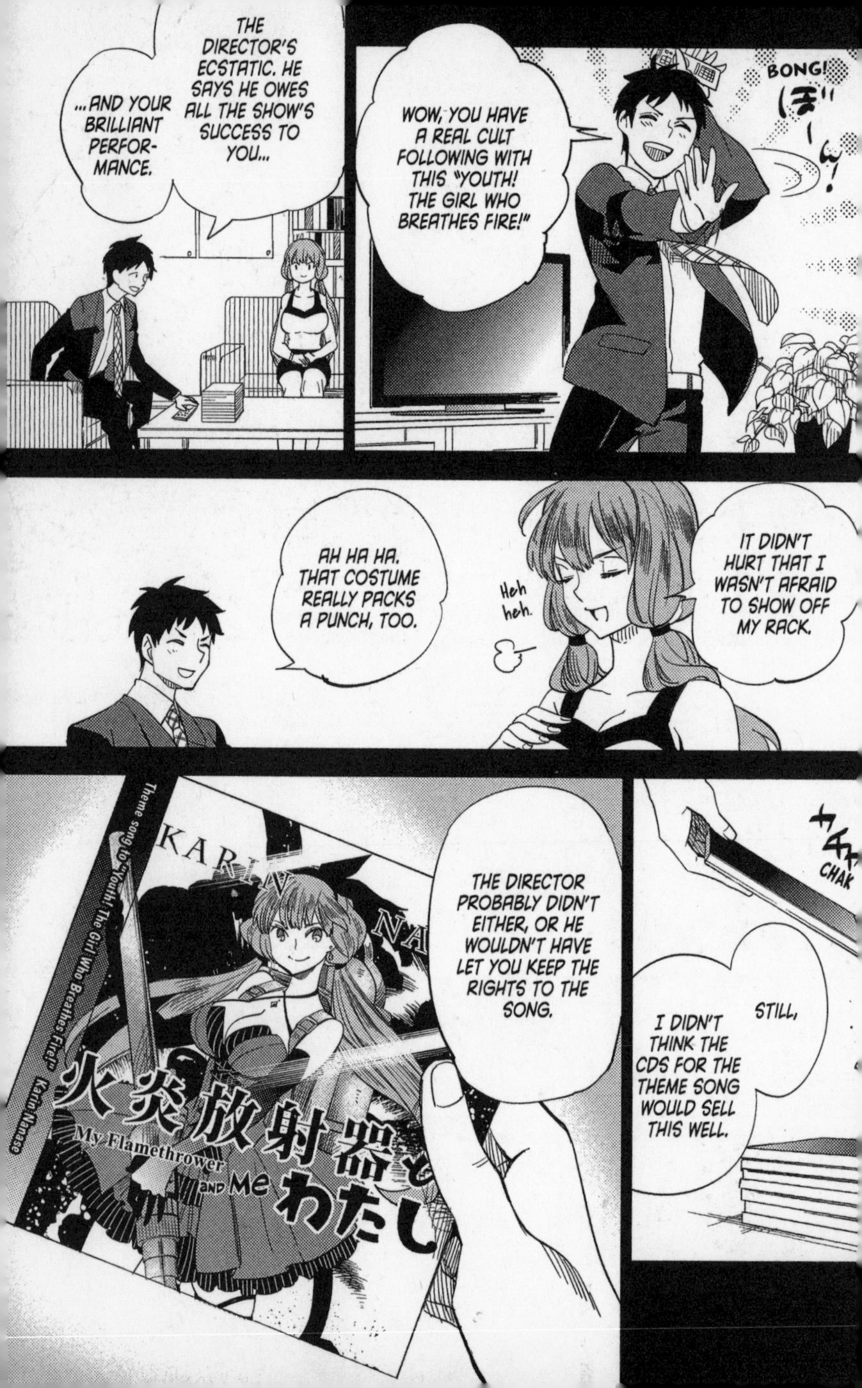
BONG!
ぼーん!
WOW, YOU HAVE A REAL CULT FOLLOWING WITH THIS "YOUTH! THE GIRL WHO BREATHES FIRE!"
THE DIRECTOR'S ECSTATIC. HE SAYS HE OWES ALL THE SHOW'S SUCCESS TO YOU...
...AND YOUR BRILLIANT PERFORMANCE.
IT DIDN'T HURT THAT I WASN'T AFRAID TO SHOW OFF MY RACK.
Heh heh.
AH HA HA. THAT COSTUME REALLY PACKS A PUNCH, TOO.
CHAK
STILL,
I DIDN'T THINK THE CDS FOR THE THEME SONG WOULD SELL THIS WELL.
THE DIRECTOR PROBABLY DIDN'T EITHER, OR HE WOULDN'T HAVE LET YOU KEEP THE RIGHTS TO THE SONG.
Theme song to "Youth! The Girl Who Breathes Fire!"
火炎放射器とわたし
My Flamethrower and Me
Karin Nanase

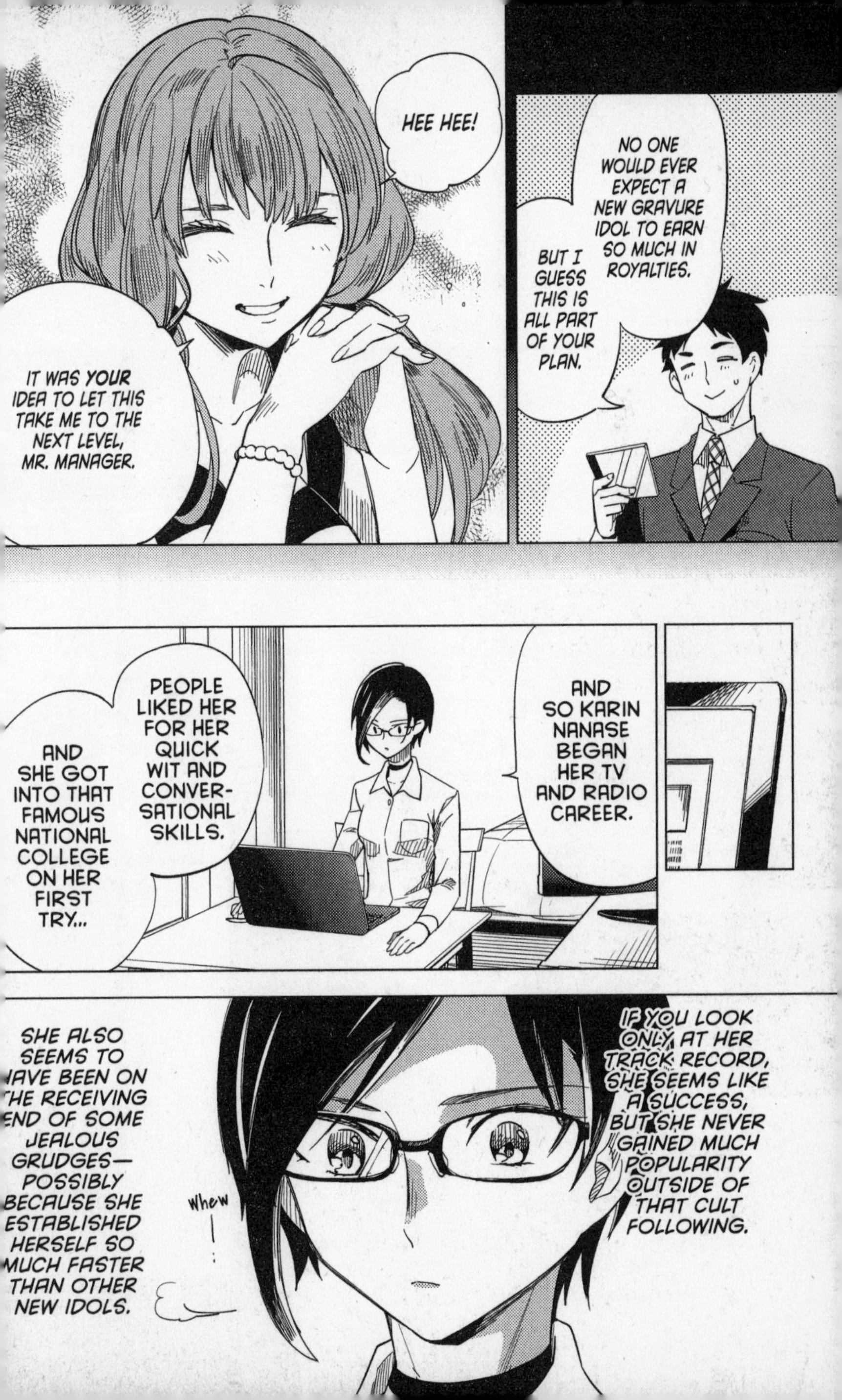
NO ONE WOULD EVER EXPECT A NEW GRAVURE IDOL TO EARN SO MUCH IN ROYALTIES.
BUT I GUESS THIS IS ALL PART OF YOUR PLAN.
HEE HEE!
IT WAS *YOUR* IDEA TO LET THIS TAKE ME TO THE NEXT LEVEL, MR. MANAGER.
AND SO KARIN NANASE BEGAN HER TV AND RADIO CAREER.
PEOPLE LIKED HER FOR HER QUICK WIT AND CONVERSATIONAL SKILLS.
AND SHE GOT INTO THAT FAMOUS NATIONAL COLLEGE ON HER FIRST TRY...
IF YOU LOOK ONLY AT HER TRACK RECORD, SHE SEEMS LIKE A SUCCESS, BUT SHE NEVER GAINED MUCH POPULARITY OUTSIDE OF THAT CULT FOLLOWING.
Whew
SHE ALSO SEEMS TO HAVE BEEN ON THE RECEIVING END OF SOME JEALOUS GRUDGES—POSSIBLY BECAUSE SHE ESTABLISHED HERSELF SO MUCH FASTER THAN OTHER NEW IDOLS.

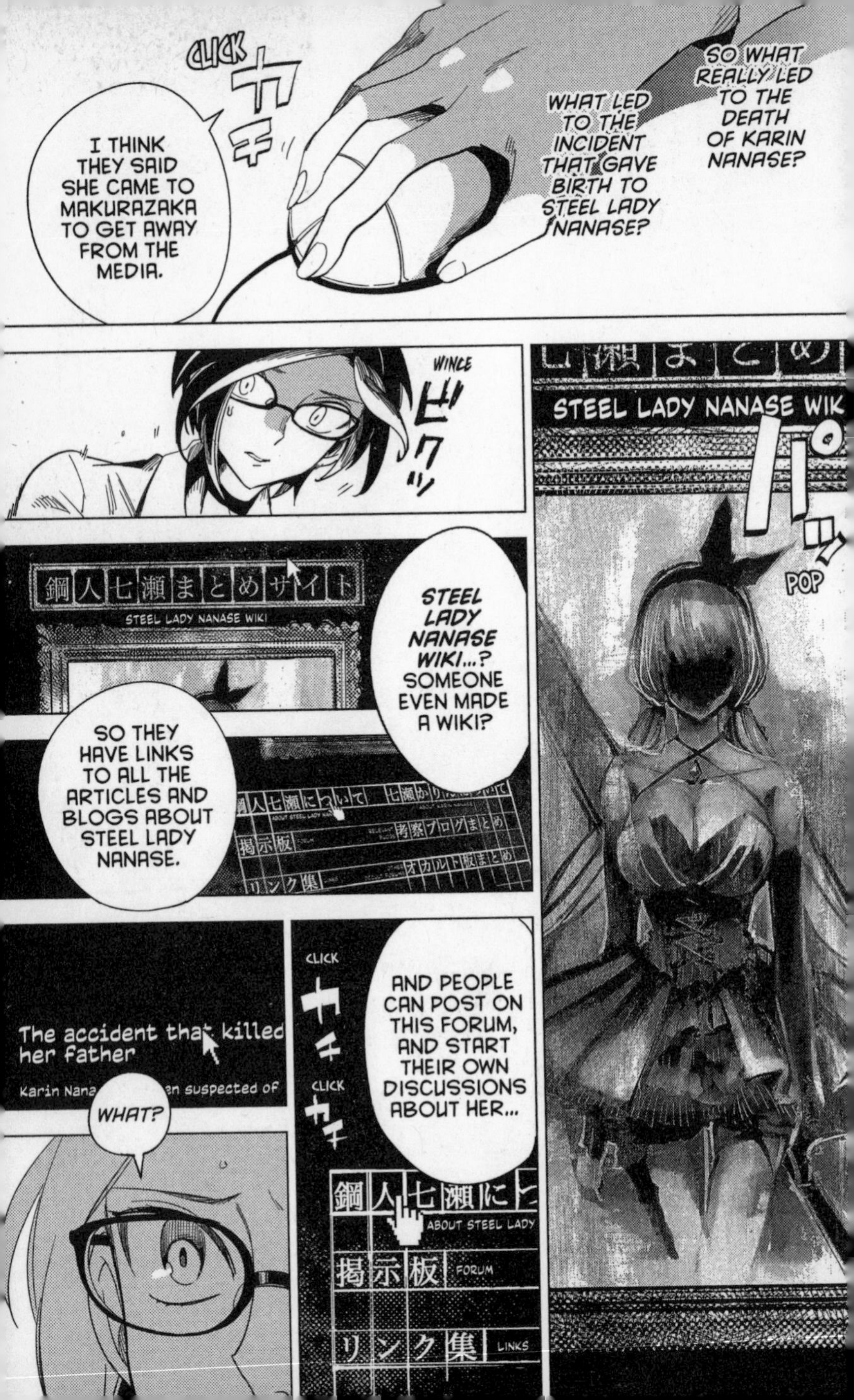
SO WHAT REALLY LED TO THE DEATH OF KARIN NANASE?
WHAT LED TO THE INCIDENT THAT GAVE BIRTH TO STEEL LADY NANASE?
CLICK
I THINK THEY SAID SHE CAME TO MAKURAZAKA TO GET AWAY FROM THE MEDIA.
STEEL LADY NANASE WIK
POP
WINCE
鋼人七瀬まとめサイト
STEEL LADY NANASE WIKI
STEEL LADY NANASE WIKI...? SOMEONE EVEN MADE A WIKI?
SO THEY HAVE LINKS TO ALL THE ARTICLES AND BLOGS ABOUT STEEL LADY NANASE.
鋼人七瀬について
七瀬かりんについて
考察ブログまとめ
掲示板
オカルト板まとめ
リンク集
CLICK
CLICK
AND PEOPLE CAN POST ON THIS FORUM, AND START THEIR OWN DISCUSSIONS ABOUT HER...
鋼人七瀬にと
ABOUT STEEL LADY
掲示板
FORUM
リンク集
LINKS
The accident that killed her father
Karin Nana en suspected of
WHAT?

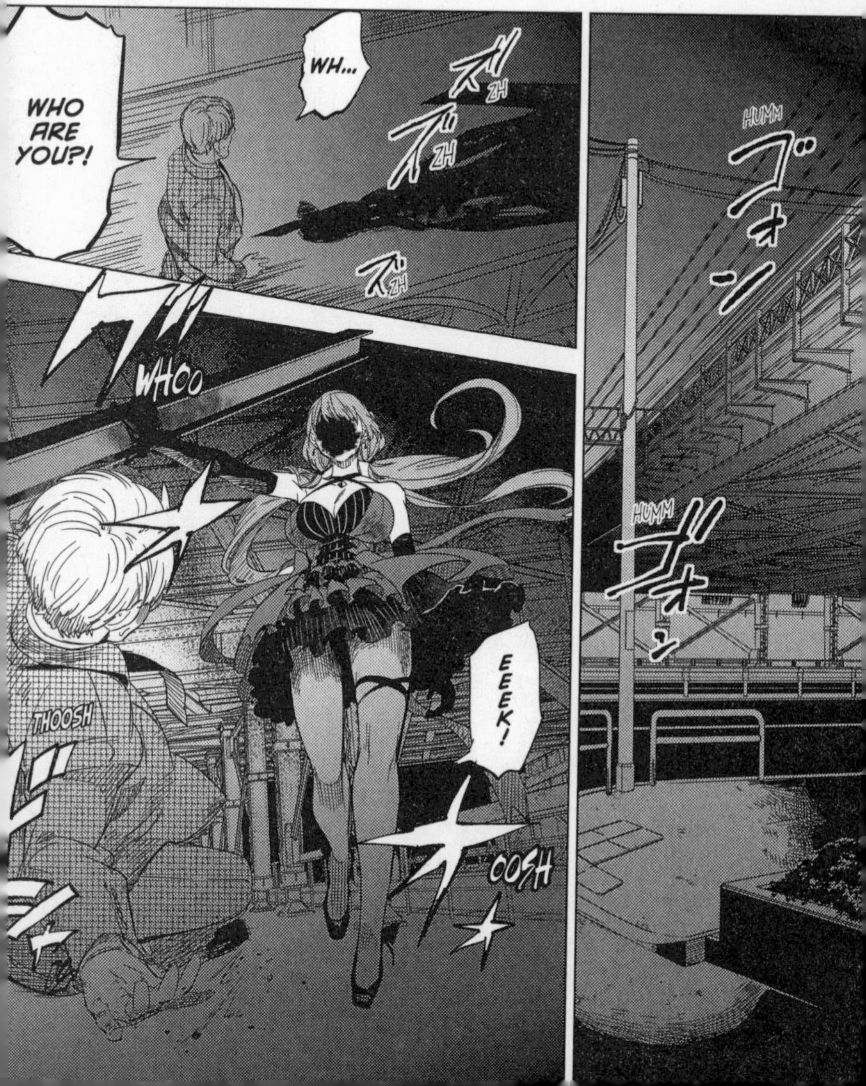
HUMM
ゴォーン
HUMM
ZH
ZH
ZH
WH...
WHO ARE YOU?!
WHOO
EEEK!
OOSH
THOOSH

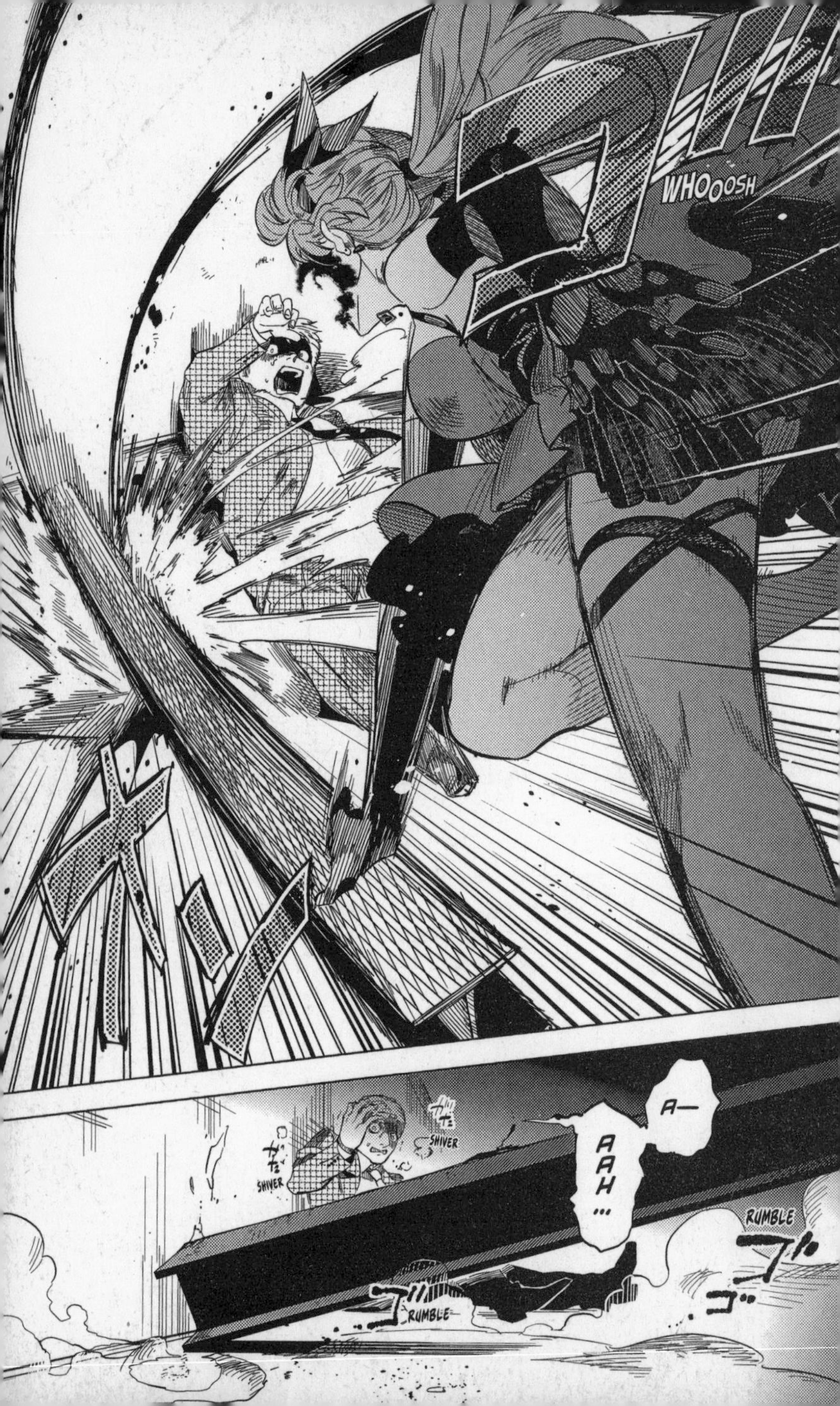
WHOOOSH
A—
AAH...
SHIVER
RUMBLE
SHIVER
RUMBLE

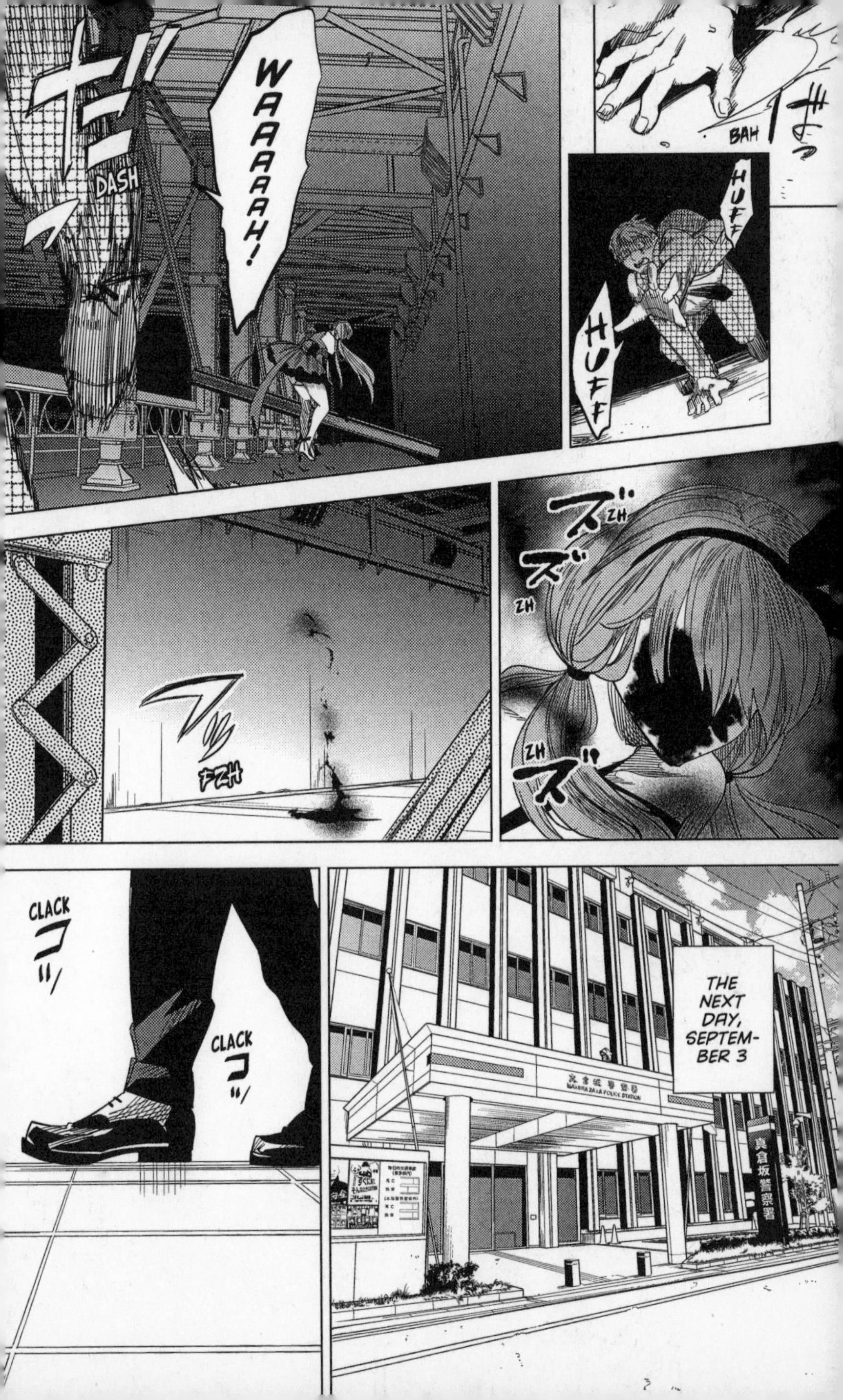
BAH
HUFF
HUFF
WAAAAAAH!
DASH
ZH
ZH
ZH
FZH
THE NEXT DAY, SEPTEMBER 3
真倉坂警察署
CLACK
CLACK

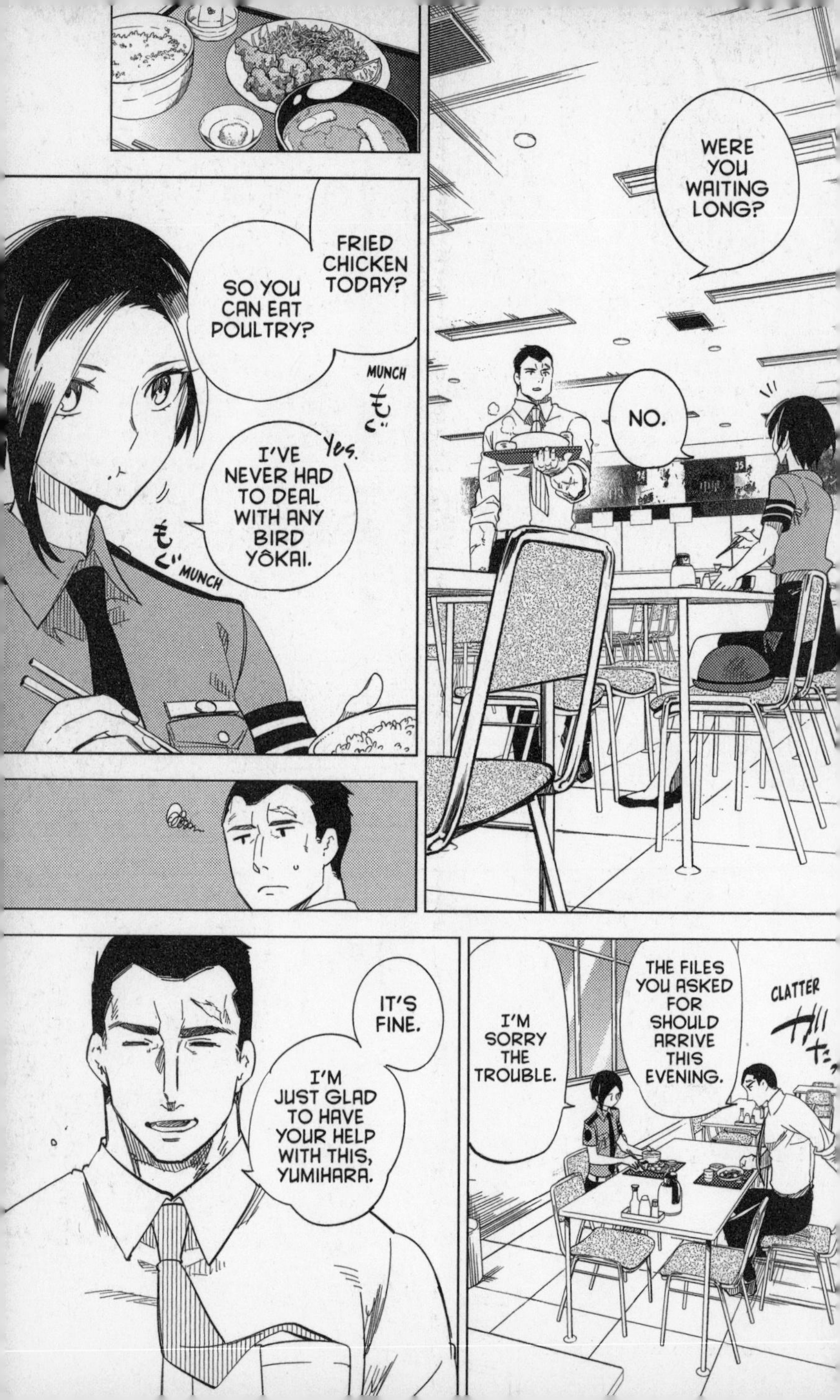

WERE YOU WAITING LONG?
NO.
FRIED CHICKEN TODAY?
SO YOU CAN EAT POULTRY?
MUNCH
もぐ
Yes.
I'VE NEVER HAD TO DEAL WITH ANY BIRD YÔKAI.
もぐ
MUNCH
CLATTER
THE FILES YOU ASKED FOR SHOULD ARRIVE THIS EVENING.
I'M SORRY THE TROUBLE.
IT'S FINE.
I'M JUST GLAD TO HAVE YOUR HELP WITH THIS, YUMIHARA.

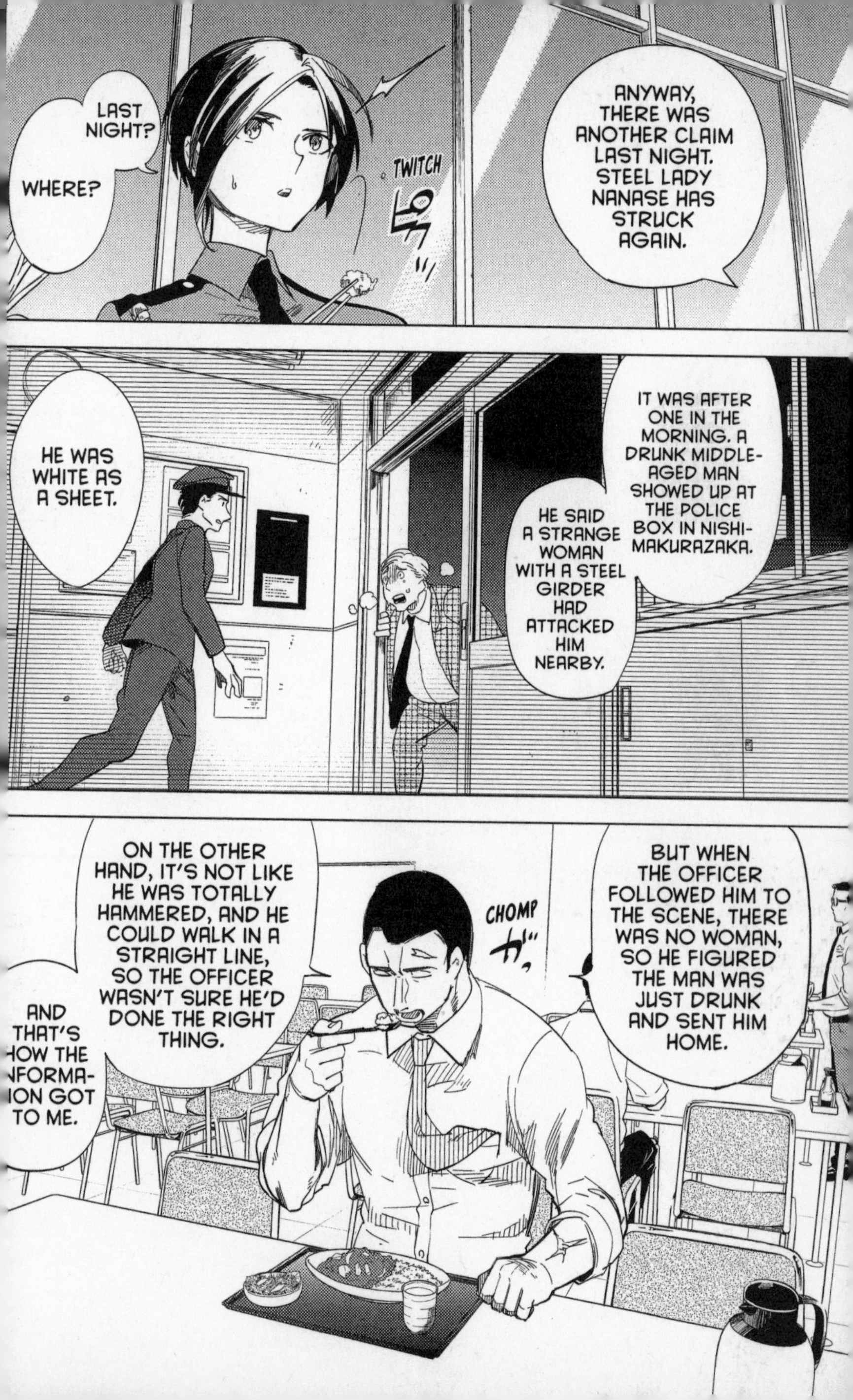
ANYWAY, THERE WAS ANOTHER CLAIM LAST NIGHT. STEEL LADY NANASE HAS STRUCK AGAIN.
TWITCH
LAST NIGHT?
WHERE?
IT WAS AFTER ONE IN THE MORNING. A DRUNK MIDDLE-AGED MAN SHOWED UP AT THE POLICE BOX IN NISHI-MAKURAZAKA.
HE SAID A STRANGE WOMAN WITH A STEEL GIRDER HAD ATTACKED HIM NEARBY.
HE WAS WHITE AS A SHEET.
BUT WHEN THE OFFICER FOLLOWED HIM TO THE SCENE, THERE WAS NO WOMAN, SO HE FIGURED THE MAN WAS JUST DRUNK AND SENT HIM HOME.
CHOMP
ON THE OTHER HAND, IT'S NOT LIKE HE WAS TOTALLY HAMMERED, AND HE COULD WALK IN A STRAIGHT LINE, SO THE OFFICER WASN'T SURE HE'D DONE THE RIGHT THING.
AND THAT'S HOW THE NFORMA- ION GOT TO ME.

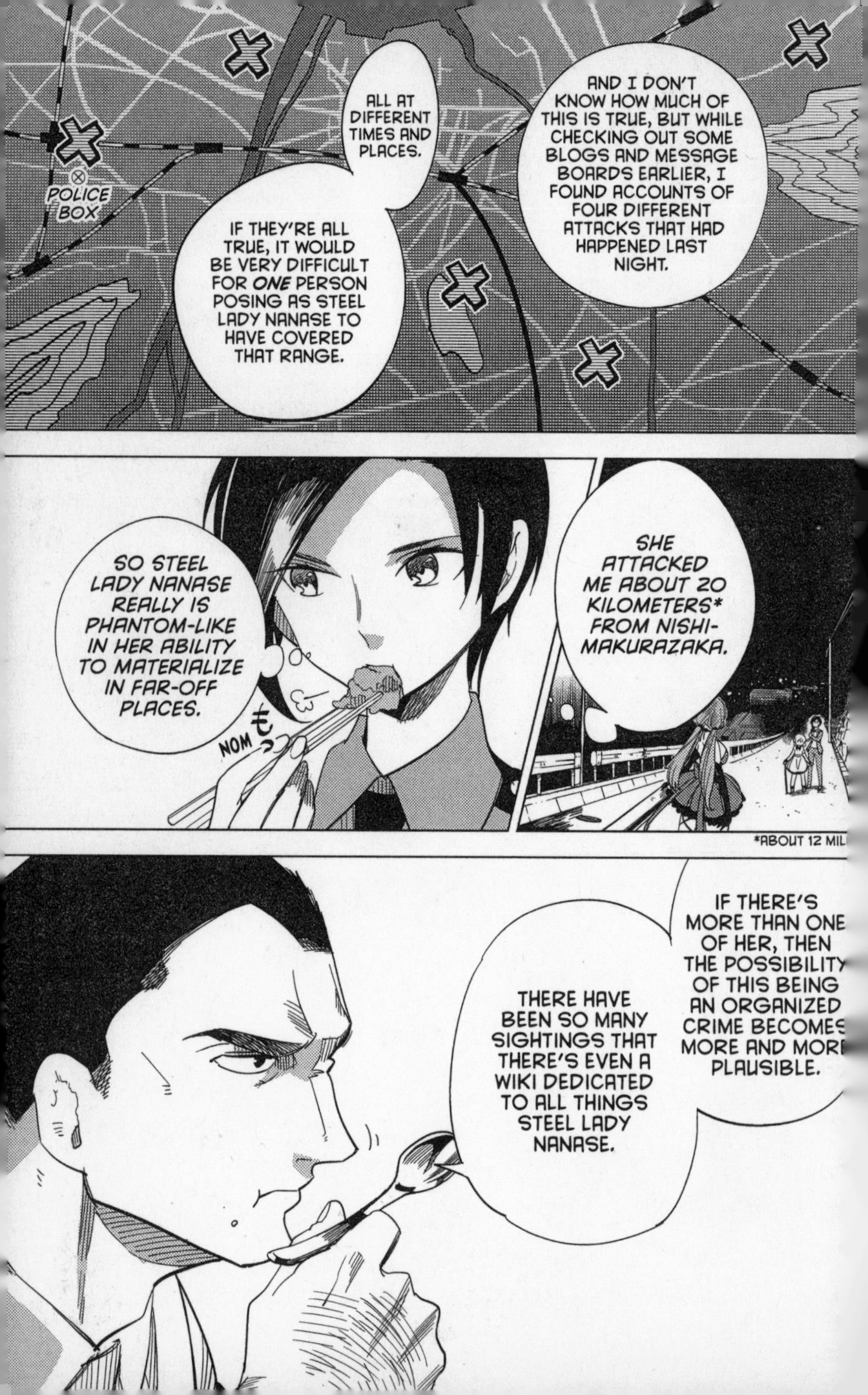
AND I DON'T KNOW HOW MUCH OF THIS IS TRUE, BUT WHILE CHECKING OUT SOME BLOGS AND MESSAGE BOARDS EARLIER, I FOUND ACCOUNTS OF FOUR DIFFERENT ATTACKS THAT HAD HAPPENED LAST NIGHT.
ALL AT DIFFERENT TIMES AND PLACES.
IF THEY'RE ALL TRUE, IT WOULD BE VERY DIFFICULT FOR *ONE* PERSON POSING AS STEEL LADY NANASE TO HAVE COVERED THAT RANGE.
POLICE BOX
SHE ATTACKED ME ABOUT 20 KILOMETERS FROM NISHI-MAKURAZAKA.*
SO STEEL LADY NANASE REALLY IS PHANTOM-LIKE IN HER ABILITY TO MATERIALIZE IN FAR-OFF PLACES.
NOM もっ
*ABOUT 12 MIL
IF THERE'S MORE THAN ONE OF HER, THEN THE POSSIBILITY OF THIS BEING AN ORGANIZED CRIME BECOMES MORE AND MORE PLAUSIBLE.
THERE HAVE BEEN SO MANY SIGHTINGS THAT THERE'S EVEN A WIKI DEDICATED TO ALL THINGS STEEL LADY NANASE.

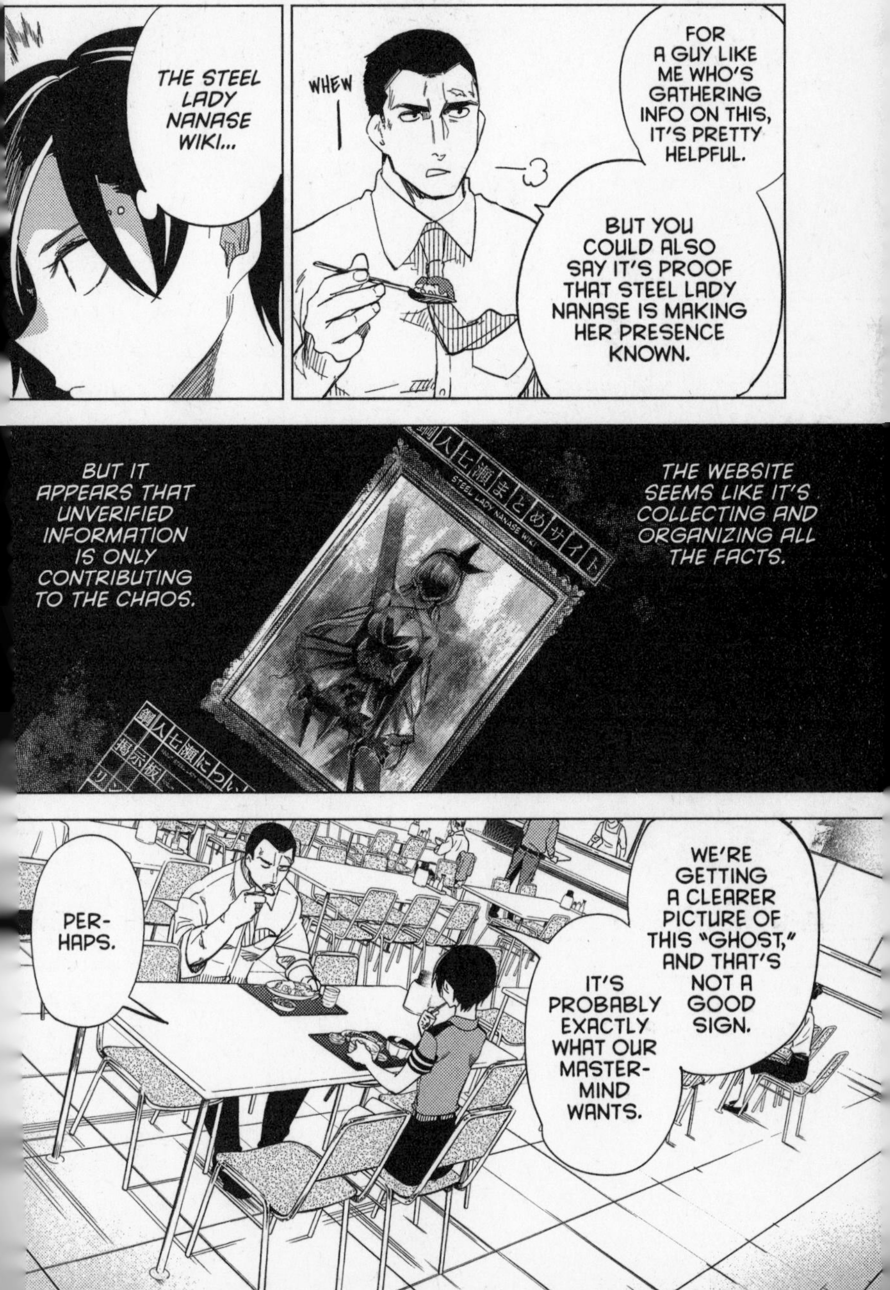
FOR A GUY LIKE ME WHO'S GATHERING INFO ON THIS, IT'S PRETTY HELPFUL.
WHEW
BUT YOU COULD ALSO SAY IT'S PROOF THAT STEEL LADY NANASE IS MAKING HER PRESENCE KNOWN.
THE STEEL LADY NANASE WIKI...
THE WEBSITE SEEMS LIKE IT'S COLLECTING AND ORGANIZING ALL THE FACTS.
鋼人七瀬まとめサイト
STEEL LADY NANASE WIKI
BUT IT APPEARS THAT UNVERIFIED INFORMATION IS ONLY CONTRIBUTING TO THE CHAOS.
WE'RE GETTING A CLEARER PICTURE OF THIS "GHOST," AND THAT'S NOT A GOOD SIGN.
IT'S PROBABLY EXACTLY WHAT OUR MASTER-MIND WANTS.
PER-HAPS.

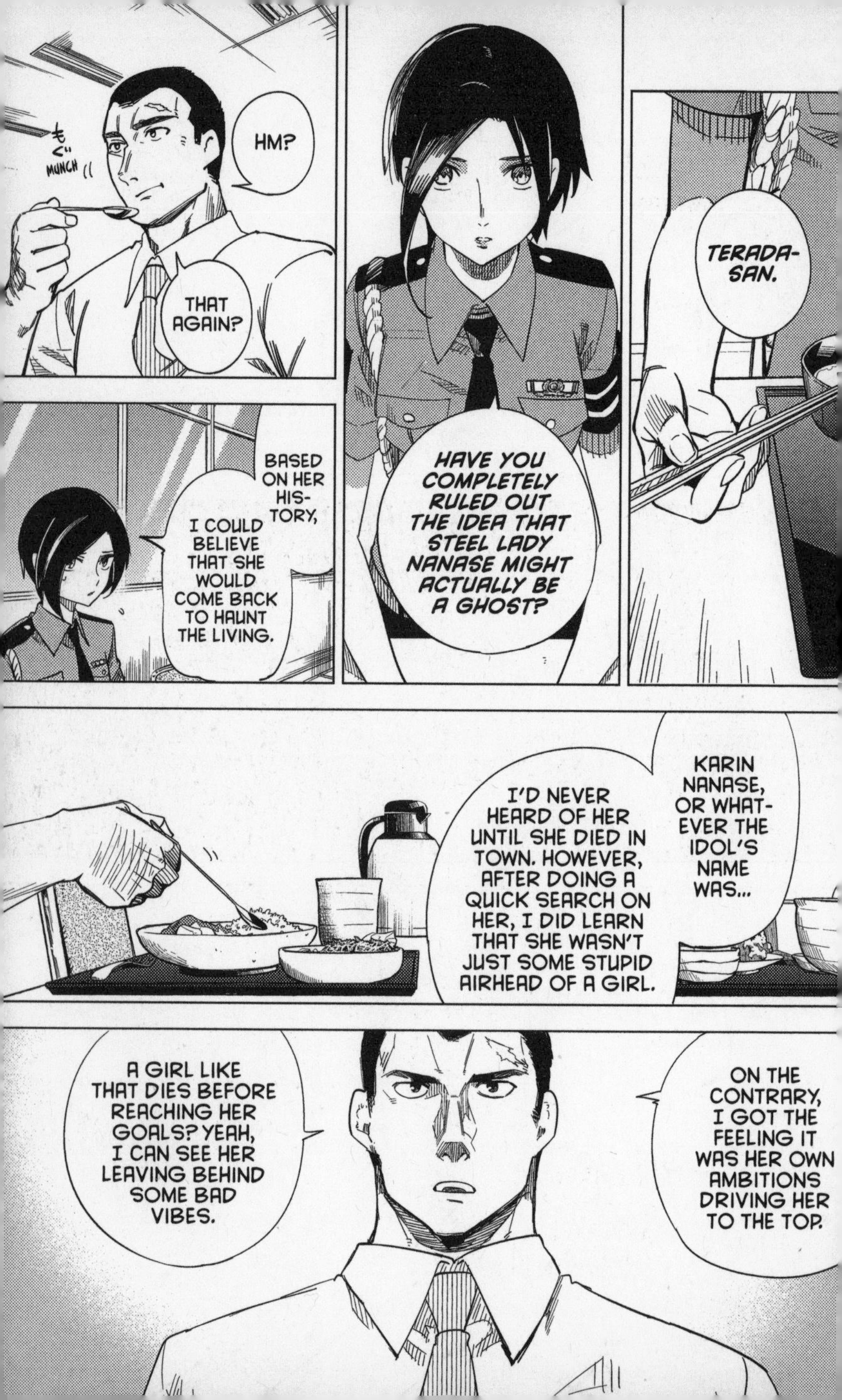
TERADA-SAN.
HAVE YOU COMPLETELY RULED OUT THE IDEA THAT STEEL LADY NANASE MIGHT ACTUALLY BE A GHOST?
もぐ
MUNCH
HM?
THAT AGAIN?
BASED ON HER HISTORY,
I COULD BELIEVE THAT SHE WOULD COME BACK TO HAUNT THE LIVING.
KARIN NANASE, OR WHATEVER THE IDOL'S NAME WAS...
I'D NEVER HEARD OF HER UNTIL SHE DIED IN TOWN. HOWEVER, AFTER DOING A QUICK SEARCH ON HER, I DID LEARN THAT SHE WASN'T JUST SOME STUPID AIRHEAD OF A GIRL.
ON THE CONTRARY, I GOT THE FEELING IT WAS HER OWN AMBITIONS DRIVING HER TO THE TOP.
A GIRL LIKE THAT DIES BEFORE REACHING HER GOALS? YEAH, I CAN SEE HER LEAVING BEHIND SOME BAD VIBES.

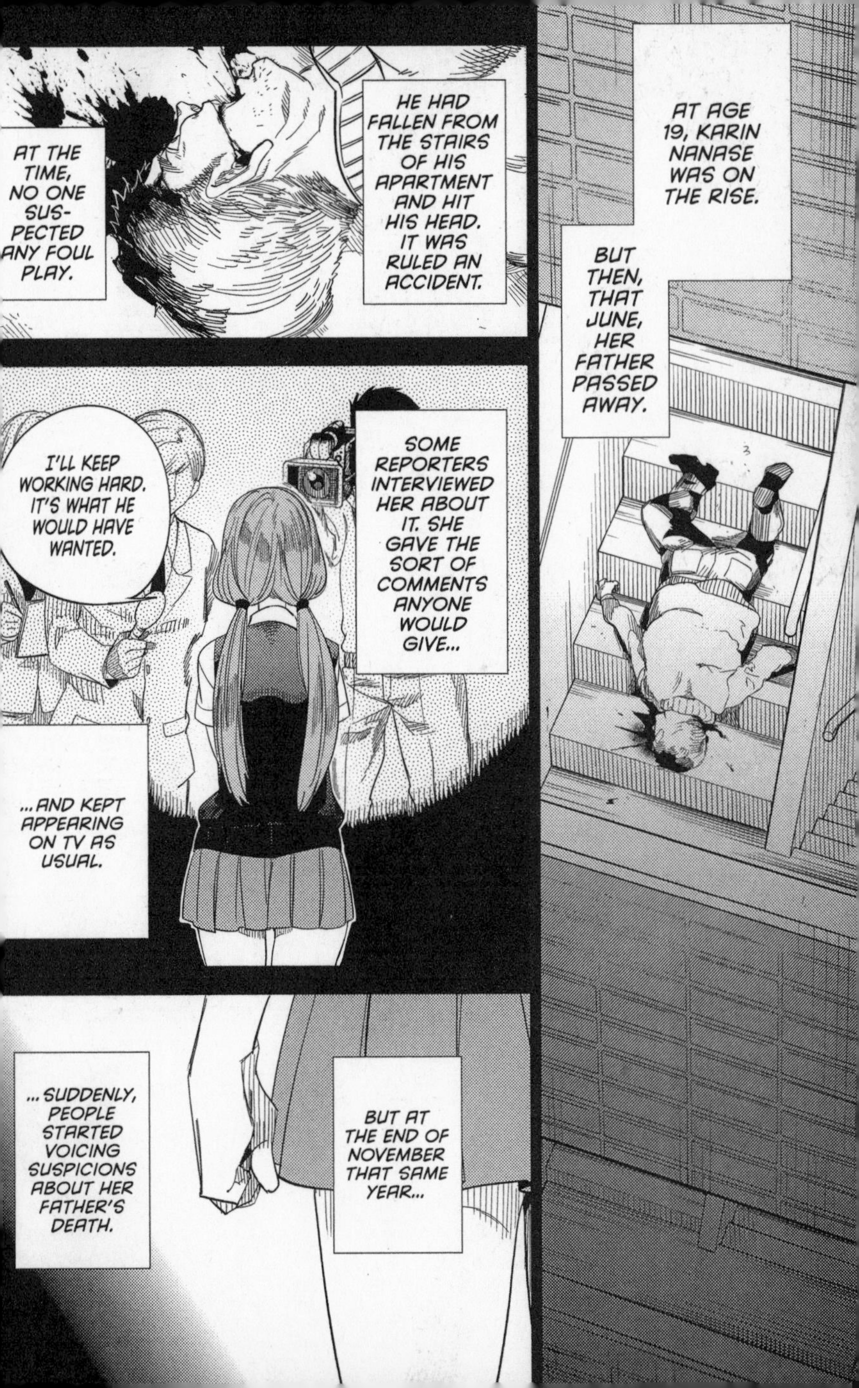
AT AGE 19, KARIN NANASE WAS ON THE RISE.
BUT THEN, THAT JUNE, HER FATHER PASSED AWAY.
HE HAD FALLEN FROM THE STAIRS OF HIS APARTMENT AND HIT HIS HEAD. IT WAS RULED AN ACCIDENT.
AT THE TIME, NO ONE SUS-PECTED ANY FOUL PLAY.
SOME REPORTERS INTERVIEWED HER ABOUT IT. SHE GAVE THE SORT OF COMMENTS ANYONE WOULD GIVE...
I'LL KEEP WORKING HARD. IT'S WHAT HE WOULD HAVE WANTED.
...AND KEPT APPEARING ON TV AS USUAL.
BUT AT THE END OF NOVEMBER THAT SAME YEAR...
...SUDDENLY, PEOPLE STARTED VOICING SUSPICIONS ABOUT HER FATHER'S DEATH.

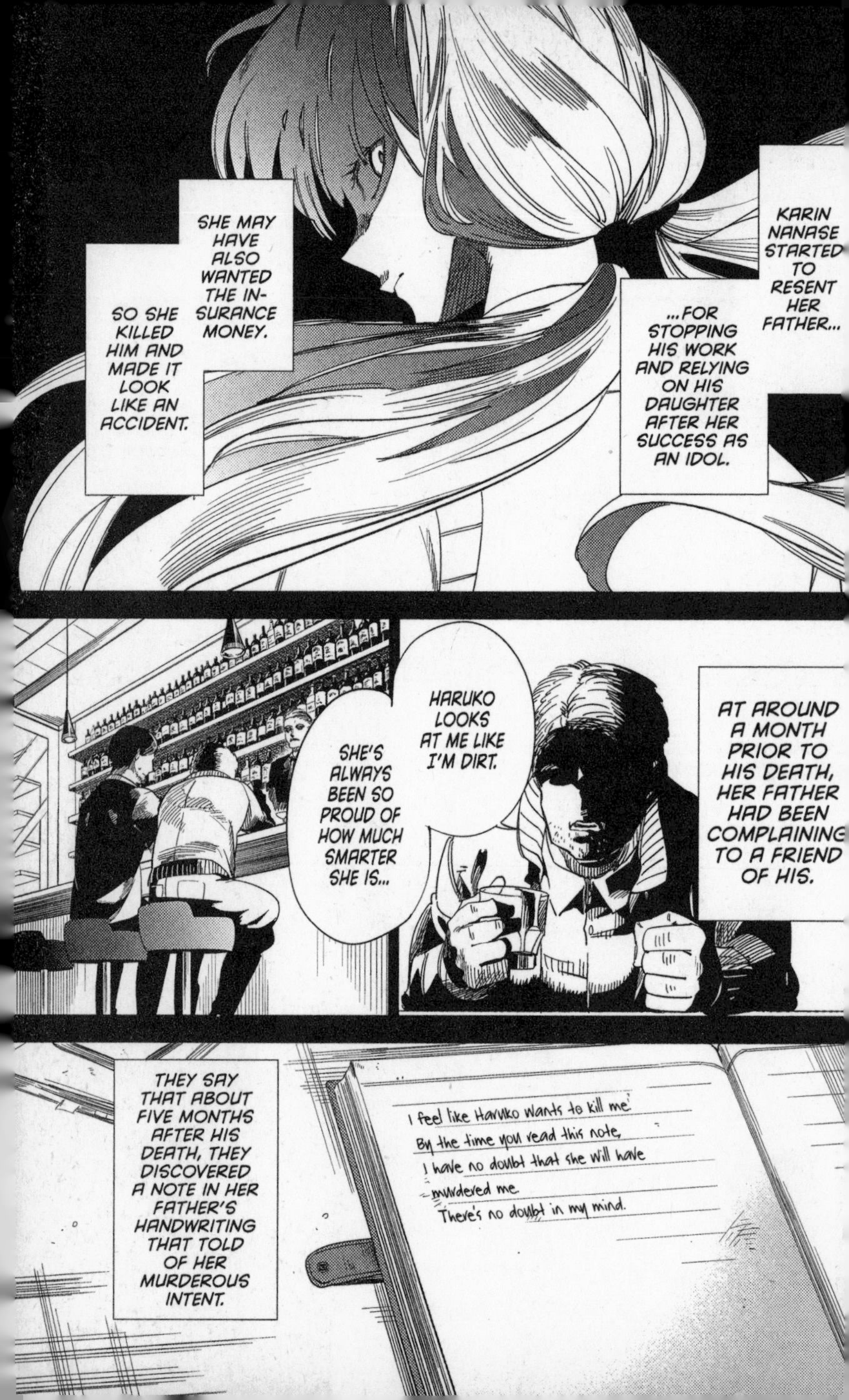
KARIN NANASE STARTED TO RESENT HER FATHER...
...FOR STOPPING HIS WORK AND RELYING ON HIS DAUGHTER AFTER HER SUCCESS AS AN IDOL.
SHE MAY HAVE ALSO WANTED THE IN-SURANCE MONEY.
SO SHE KILLED HIM AND MADE IT LOOK LIKE AN ACCIDENT.
AT AROUND A MONTH PRIOR TO HIS DEATH, HER FATHER HAD BEEN COMPLAINING TO A FRIEND OF HIS.
HARUKO LOOKS AT ME LIKE I'M DIRT.
SHE'S ALWAYS BEEN SO PROUD OF HOW MUCH SMARTER SHE IS...
THEY SAY THAT ABOUT FIVE MONTHS AFTER HIS DEATH, THEY DISCOVERED A NOTE IN HER FATHER'S HANDWRITING THAT TOLD OF HER MURDEROUS INTENT.
I feel like Haruko wants to kill me.
By the time you read this note,
I have no doubt that she will have
murdered me.
There's no doubt in my mind.

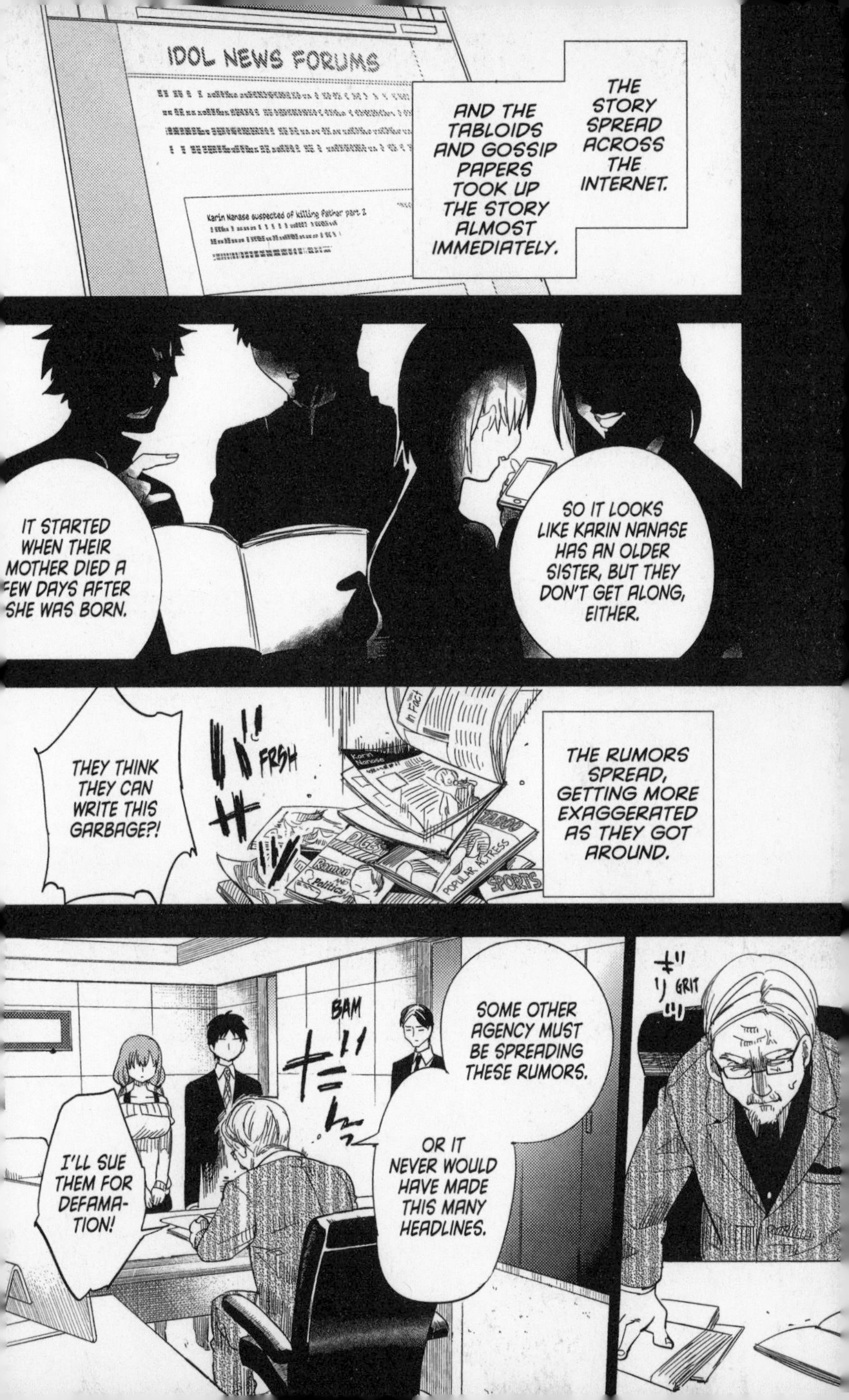
THE STORY SPREAD ACROSS THE INTERNET.
AND THE TABLOIDS AND GOSSIP PAPERS TOOK UP THE STORY ALMOST IMMEDIATELY.
IDOL NEWS FORUMS
Karin Nanase suspected of killing father part 2
SO IT LOOKS LIKE KARIN NANASE HAS AN OLDER SISTER, BUT THEY DON'T GET ALONG, EITHER.
IT STARTED WHEN THEIR MOTHER DIED A FEW DAYS AFTER SHE WAS BORN.
THE RUMORS SPREAD, GETTING MORE EXAGGERATED AS THEY GOT AROUND.
In Fact
Karin Nanase
POPULAR ACTRESS
SPORTS
Ramen and Politics
FRSH
THEY THINK THEY CAN WRITE THIS GARBAGE?!
GRIT
SOME OTHER AGENCY MUST BE SPREADING THESE RUMORS.
OR IT NEVER WOULD HAVE MADE THIS MANY HEADLINES.
BAM
I'LL SUE THEM FOR DEFAMATION!

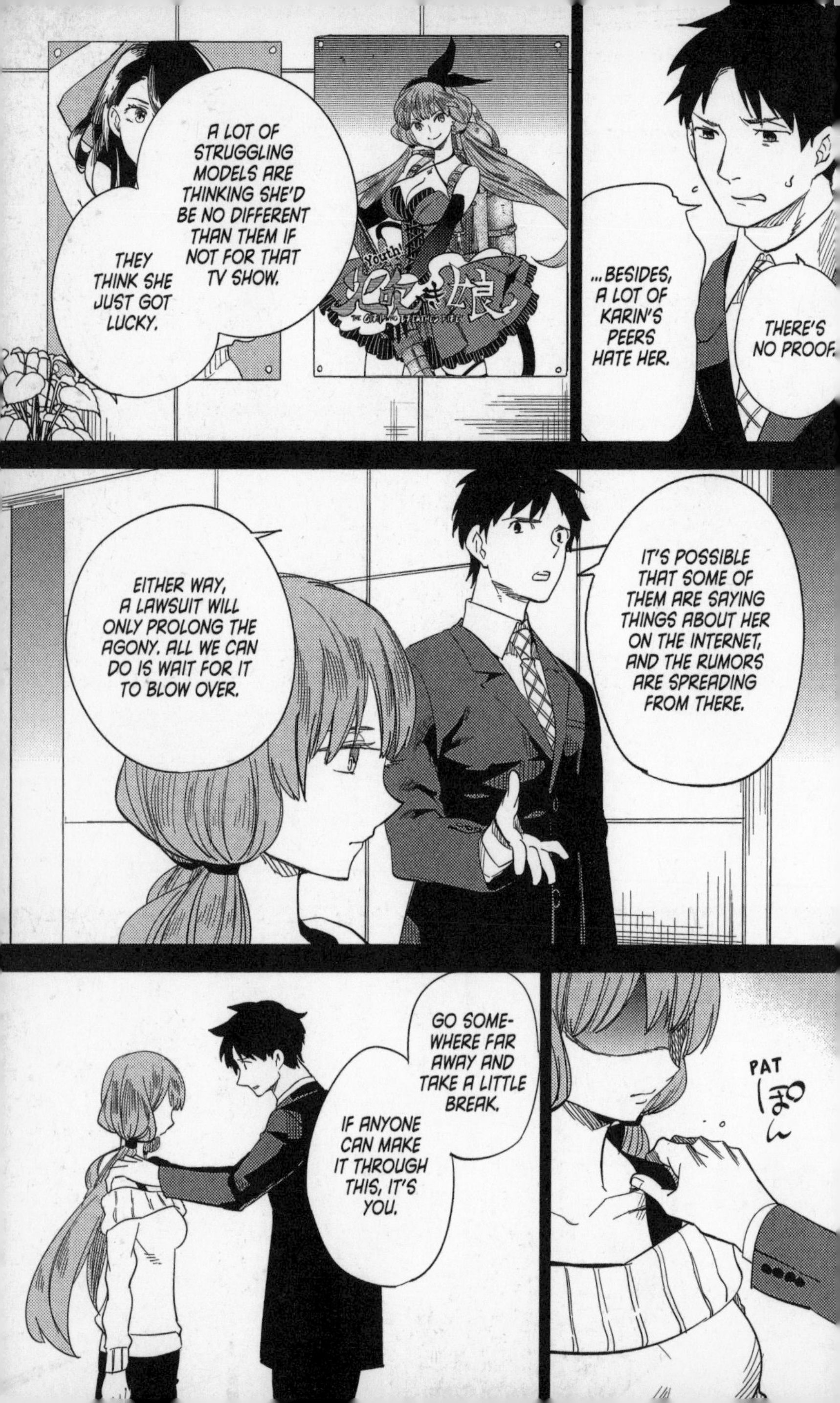
THERE'S NO PROOF.
...BESIDES, A LOT OF KARIN'S PEERS HATE HER.
A LOT OF STRUGGLING MODELS ARE THINKING SHE'D BE NO DIFFERENT THAN THEM IF NOT FOR THAT TV SHOW.
THEY THINK SHE JUST GOT LUCKY.
Youth!
IT'S POSSIBLE THAT SOME OF THEM ARE SAYING THINGS ABOUT HER ON THE INTERNET, AND THE RUMORS ARE SPREADING FROM THERE.
EITHER WAY, A LAWSUIT WILL ONLY PROLONG THE AGONY. ALL WE CAN DO IS WAIT FOR IT TO BLOW OVER.
PAT
ぽん
GO SOME-WHERE FAR AWAY AND TAKE A LITTLE BREAK.
IF ANYONE CAN MAKE IT THROUGH THIS, IT'S YOU.

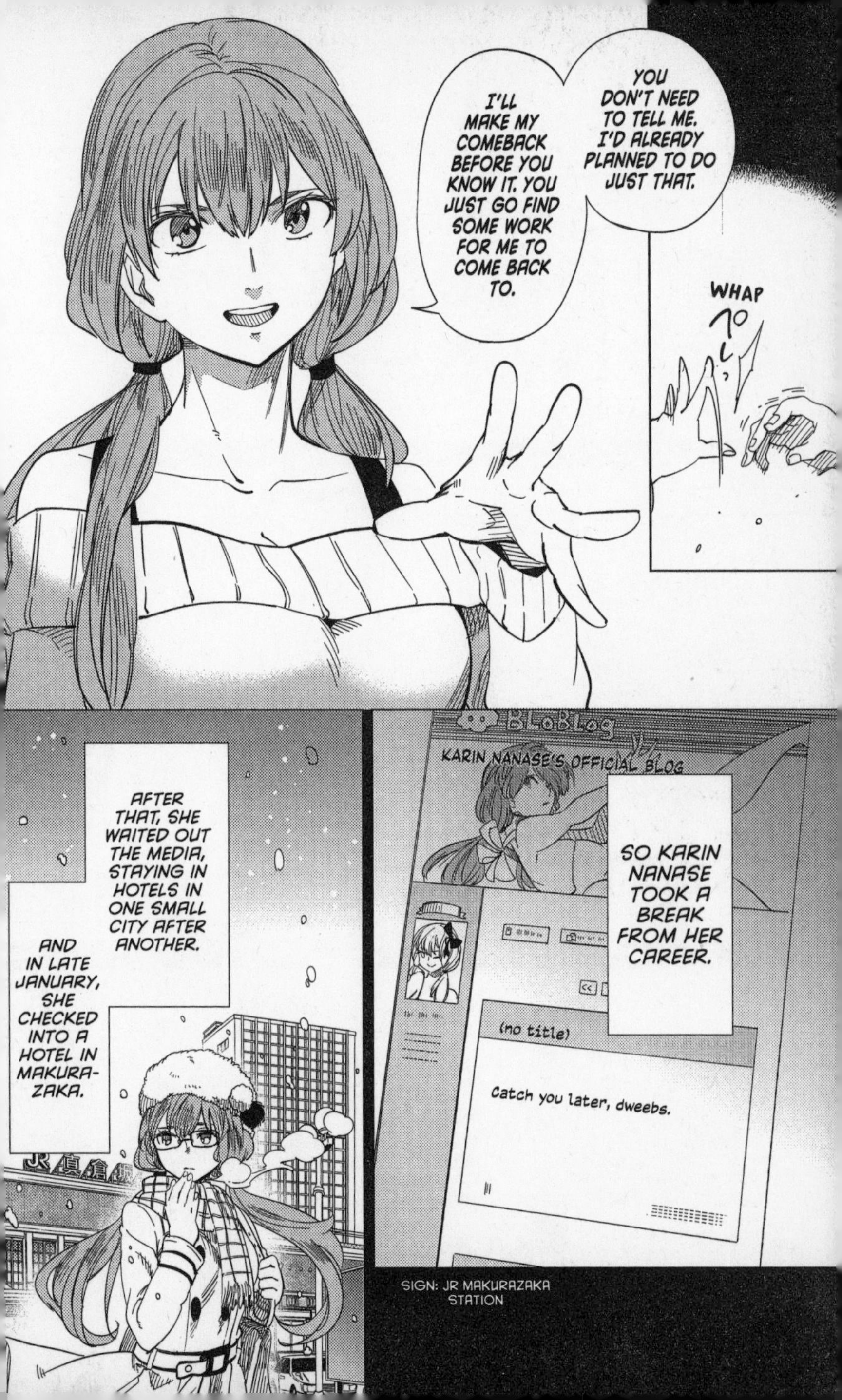
YOU DON'T NEED TO TELL ME. I'D ALREADY PLANNED TO DO JUST THAT.
I'LL MAKE MY COMEBACK BEFORE YOU KNOW IT. YOU JUST GO FIND SOME WORK FOR ME TO COME BACK TO.
WHAP
BLoBLog
KARIN NANASE'S OFFICIAL BLOG
SO KARIN NANASE TOOK A BREAK FROM HER CAREER.
(no title)
Catch you later, dweebs.
AFTER THAT, SHE WAITED OUT THE MEDIA, STAYING IN HOTELS IN ONE SMALL CITY AFTER ANOTHER.
AND IN LATE JANUARY, SHE CHECKED INTO A HOTEL IN MAKURA-ZAKA.
SIGN: JR MAKURAZAKA STATION

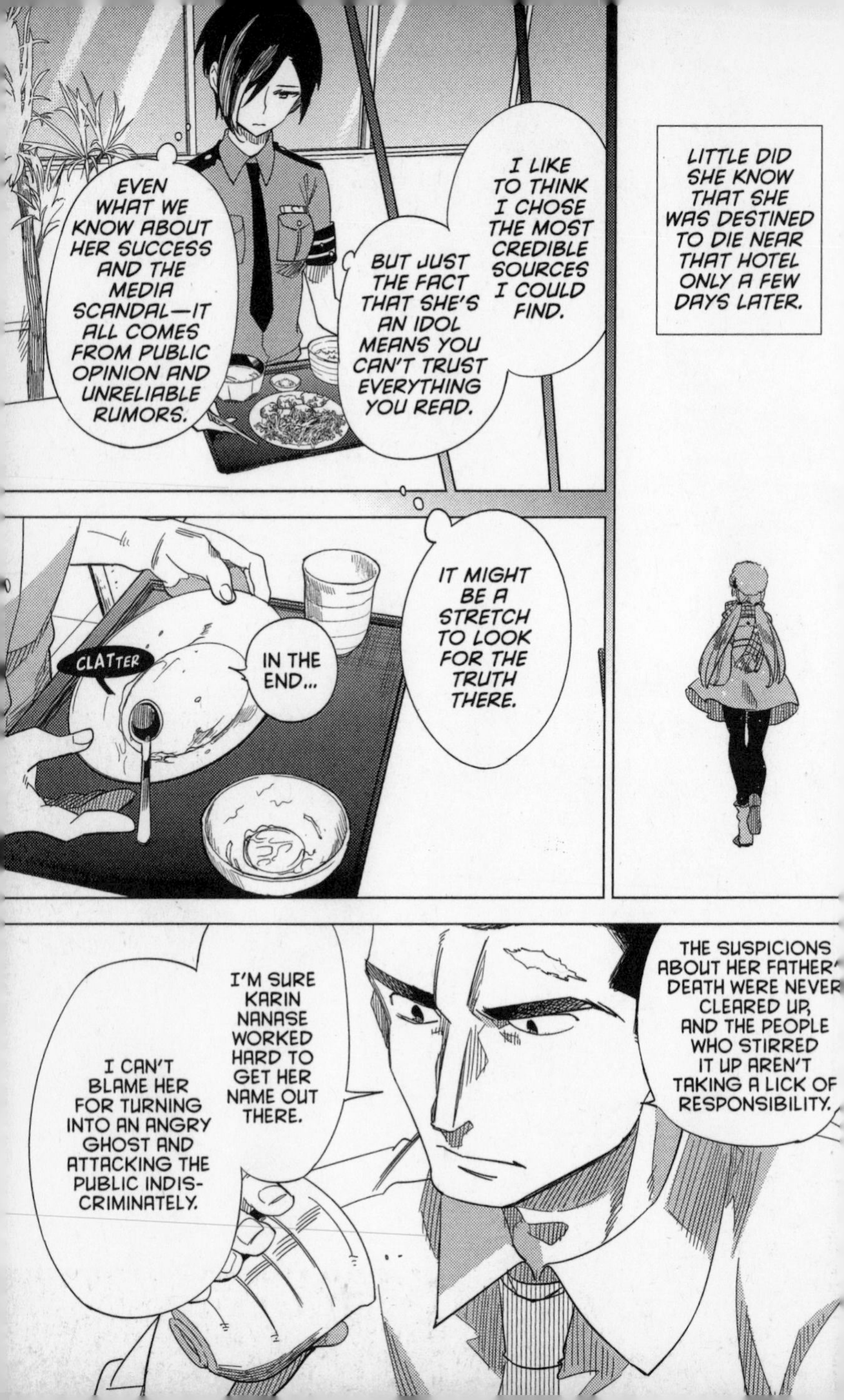
LITTLE DID SHE KNOW THAT SHE WAS DESTINED TO DIE NEAR THAT HOTEL ONLY A FEW DAYS LATER.
I LIKE TO THINK I CHOSE THE MOST CREDIBLE SOURCES I COULD FIND.
BUT JUST THE FACT THAT SHE'S AN IDOL MEANS YOU CAN'T TRUST EVERYTHING YOU READ.
EVEN WHAT WE KNOW ABOUT HER SUCCESS AND THE MEDIA SCANDAL—IT ALL COMES FROM PUBLIC OPINION AND UNRELIABLE RUMORS.
IT MIGHT BE A STRETCH TO LOOK FOR THE TRUTH THERE.
IN THE END...
CLATTER
THE SUSPICIONS ABOUT HER FATHER' DEATH WERE NEVER CLEARED UP, AND THE PEOPLE WHO STIRRED IT UP AREN'T TAKING A LICK OF RESPONSIBILITY.
I'M SURE KARIN NANASE WORKED HARD TO GET HER NAME OUT THERE.
I CAN'T BLAME HER FOR TURNING INTO AN ANGRY GHOST AND ATTACKING THE PUBLIC INDIS-CRIMINATELY.

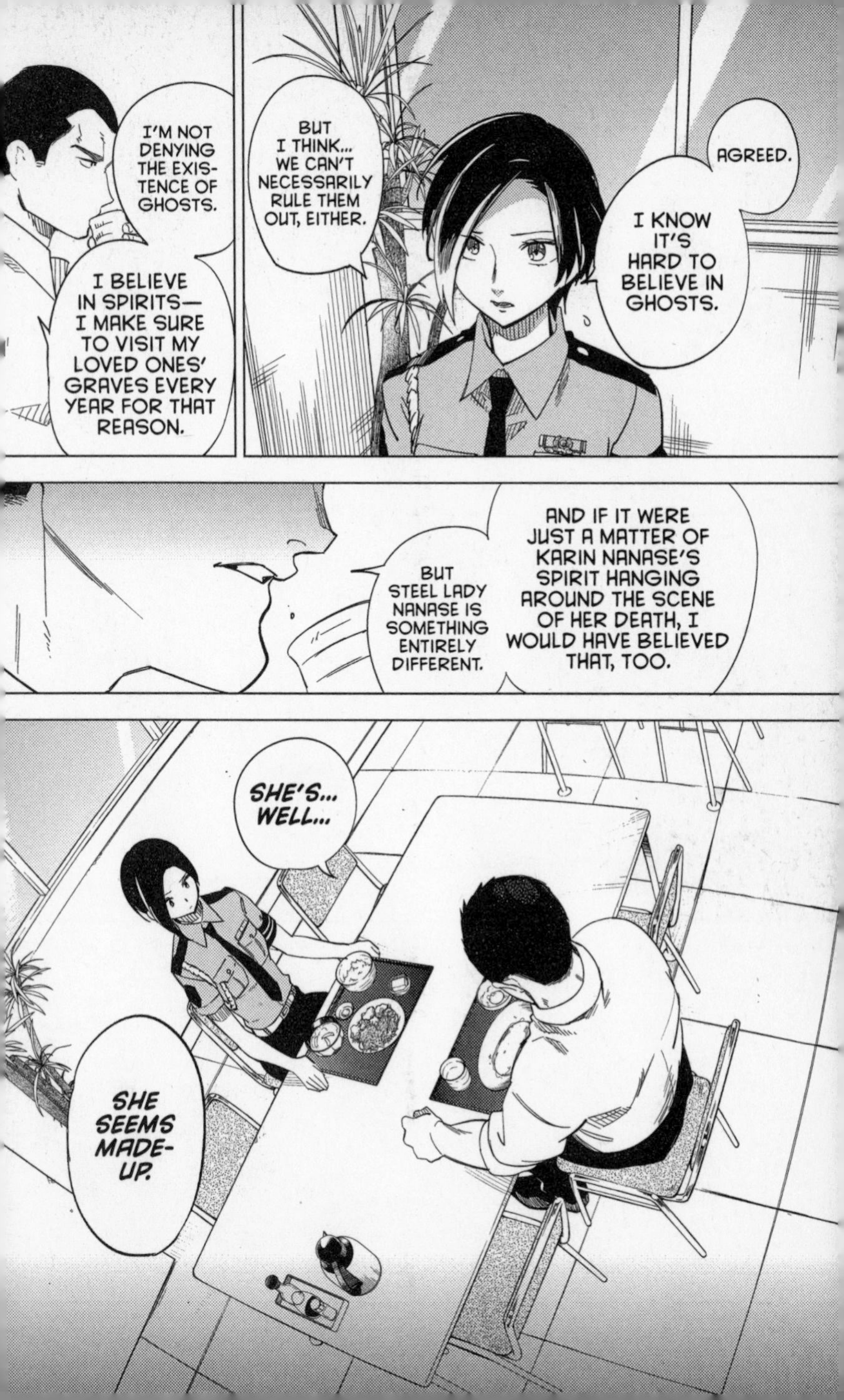
AGREED.
I KNOW IT'S HARD TO BELIEVE IN GHOSTS.
BUT I THINK... WE CAN'T NECESSARILY RULE THEM OUT, EITHER.
I'M NOT DENYING THE EXISTENCE OF GHOSTS.
I BELIEVE IN SPIRITS—I MAKE SURE TO VISIT MY LOVED ONES' GRAVES EVERY YEAR FOR THAT REASON.
AND IF IT WERE JUST A MATTER OF KARIN NANASE'S SPIRIT HANGING AROUND THE SCENE OF HER DEATH, I WOULD HAVE BELIEVED THAT, TOO.
BUT STEEL LADY NANASE IS SOMETHING ENTIRELY DIFFERENT.
SHE'S... WELL...
SHE SEEMS MADE-UP.

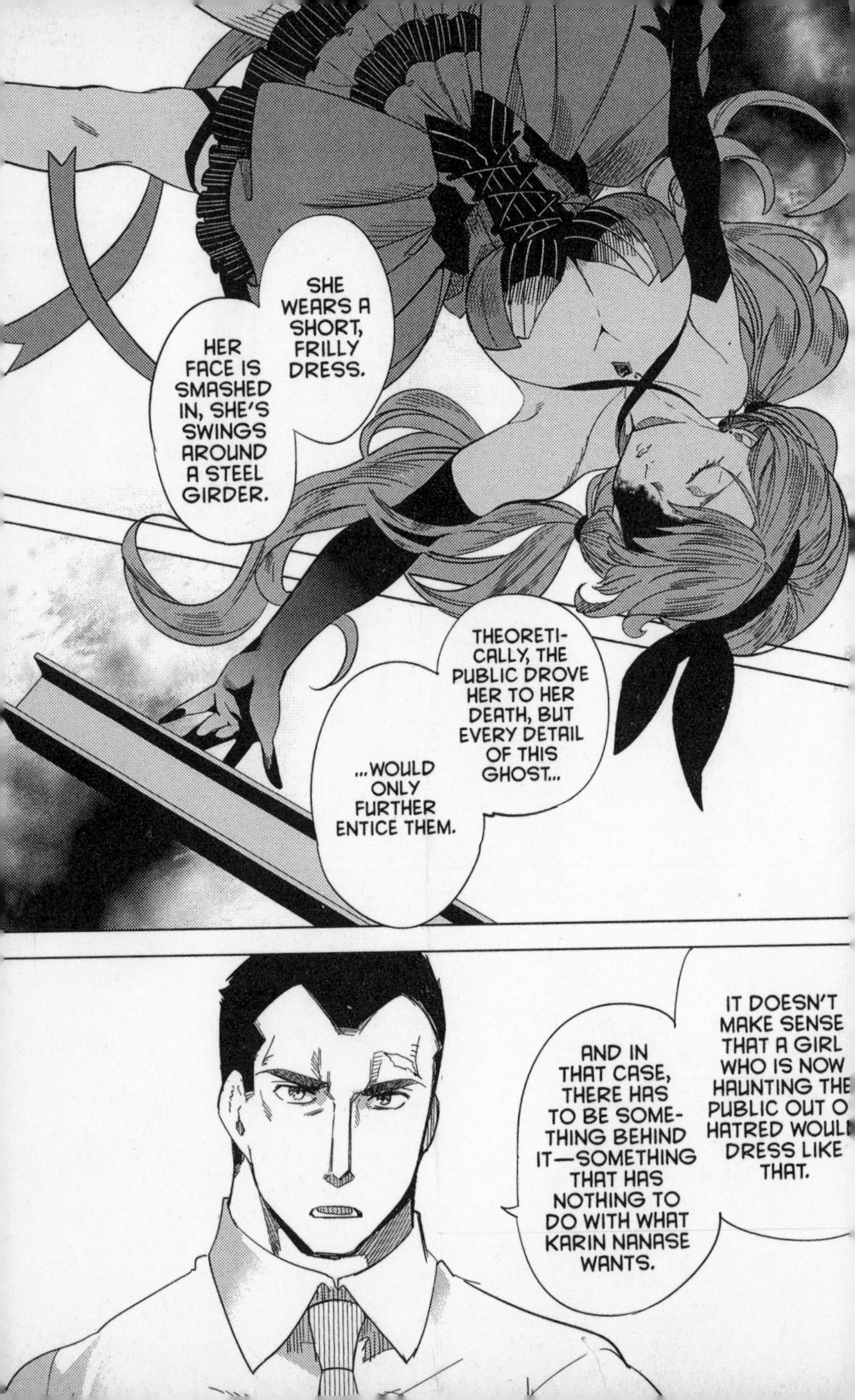
SHE WEARS A SHORT, FRILLY DRESS.
HER FACE IS SMASHED IN, SHE'S SWINGS AROUND A STEEL GIRDER.
THEORETICALLY, THE PUBLIC DROVE HER TO HER DEATH, BUT EVERY DETAIL OF THIS GHOST...
...WOULD ONLY FURTHER ENTICE THEM.
IT DOESN'T MAKE SENSE THAT A GIRL WHO IS NOW HAUNTING THE PUBLIC OUT O HATRED WOUL DRESS LIKE THAT.
AND IN THAT CASE, THERE HAS TO BE SOMETHING BEHIND IT—SOMETHING THAT HAS NOTHING TO DO WITH WHAT KARIN NANASE WANTS.

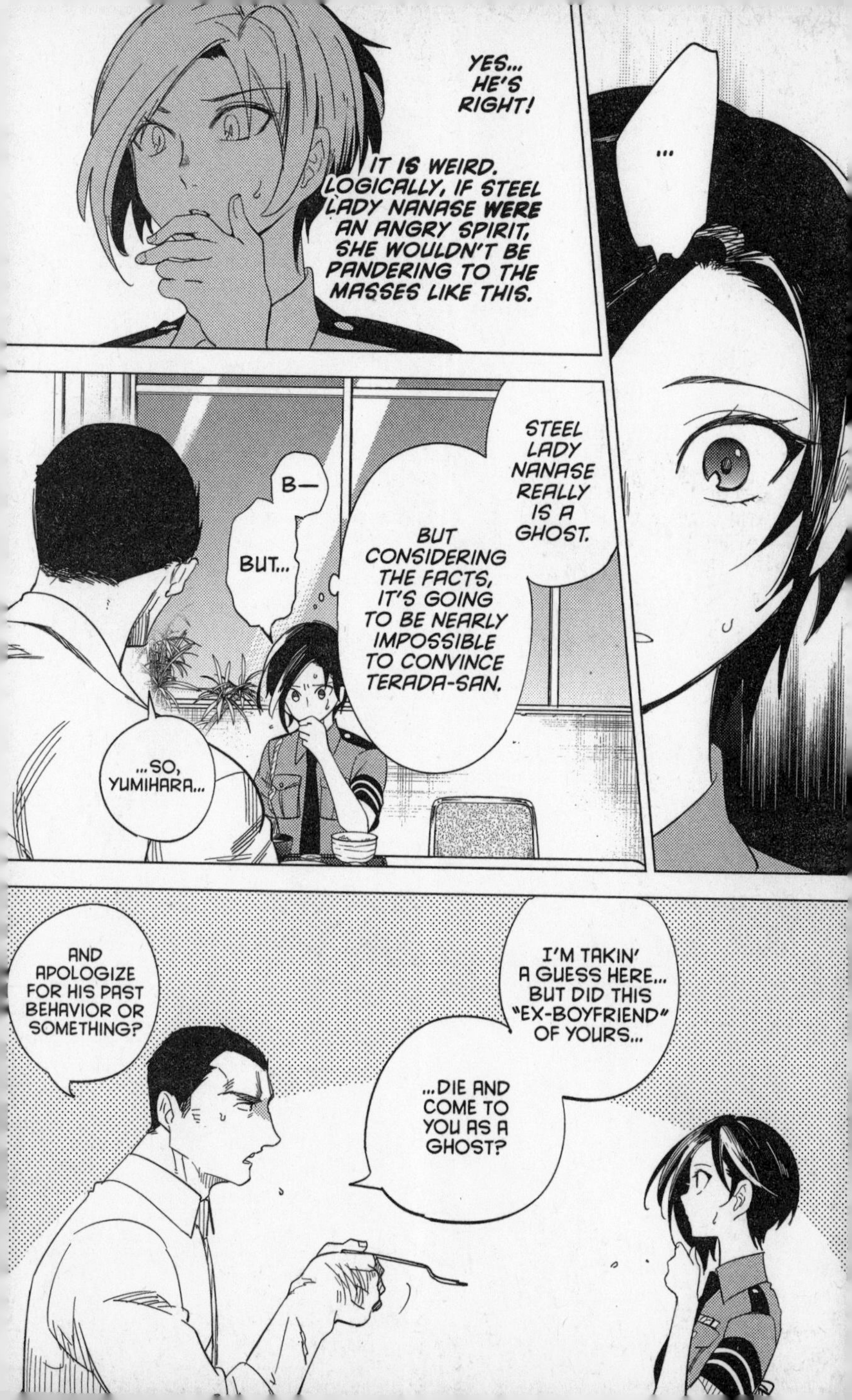
...
YES... HE'S RIGHT!
IT IS WEIRD. LOGICALLY, IF STEEL LADY NANASE WERE AN ANGRY SPIRIT, SHE WOULDN'T BE PANDERING TO THE MASSES LIKE THIS.
STEEL LADY NANASE REALLY IS A GHOST.
BUT CONSIDERING THE FACTS, IT'S GOING TO BE NEARLY IMPOSSIBLE TO CONVINCE TERADA-SAN.
B— BUT...
...SO, YUMIHARA...
I'M TAKIN' A GUESS HERE... BUT DID THIS "EX-BOYFRIEND" OF YOURS...
...DIE AND COME TO YOU AS A GHOST?
AND APOLOGIZE FOR HIS PAST BEHAVIOR OR SOMETHING?

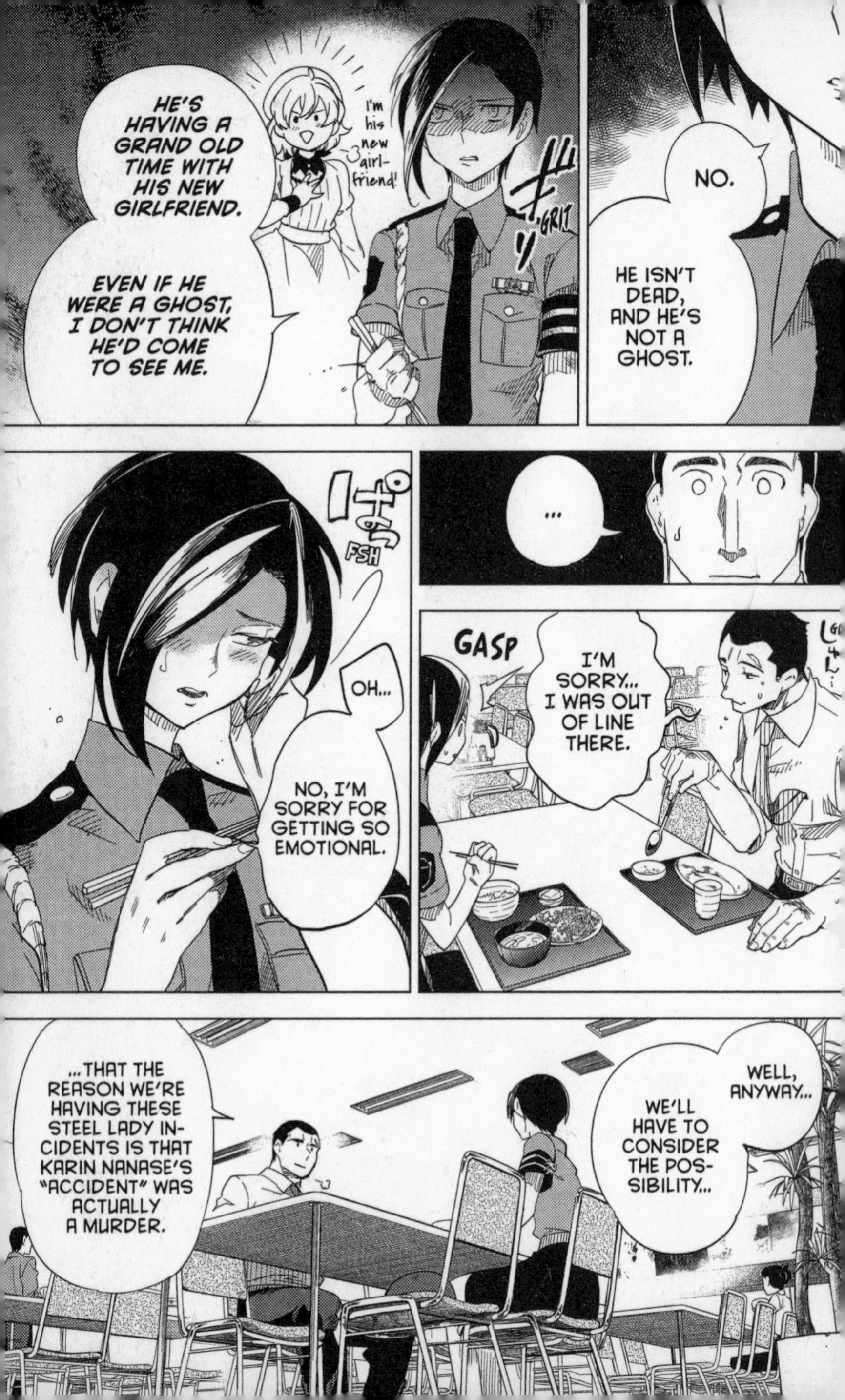
NO.
HE ISN'T DEAD, AND HE'S NOT A GHOST.
HE'S HAVING A GRAND OLD TIME WITH HIS NEW GIRLFRIEND.
I'm his new girlfriend!
GRIT
EVEN IF HE WERE A GHOST, I DON'T THINK HE'D COME TO SEE ME.
...
GASP
I'M SORRY... I WAS OUT OF LINE THERE.
FSH
OH...
NO, I'M SORRY FOR GETTING SO EMOTIONAL.
WELL, ANYWAY...
WE'LL HAVE TO CONSIDER THE POSSIBILITY...
...THAT THE REASON WE'RE HAVING THESE STEEL LADY INCIDENTS IS THAT KARIN NANASE'S "ACCIDENT" WAS ACTUALLY A MURDER.

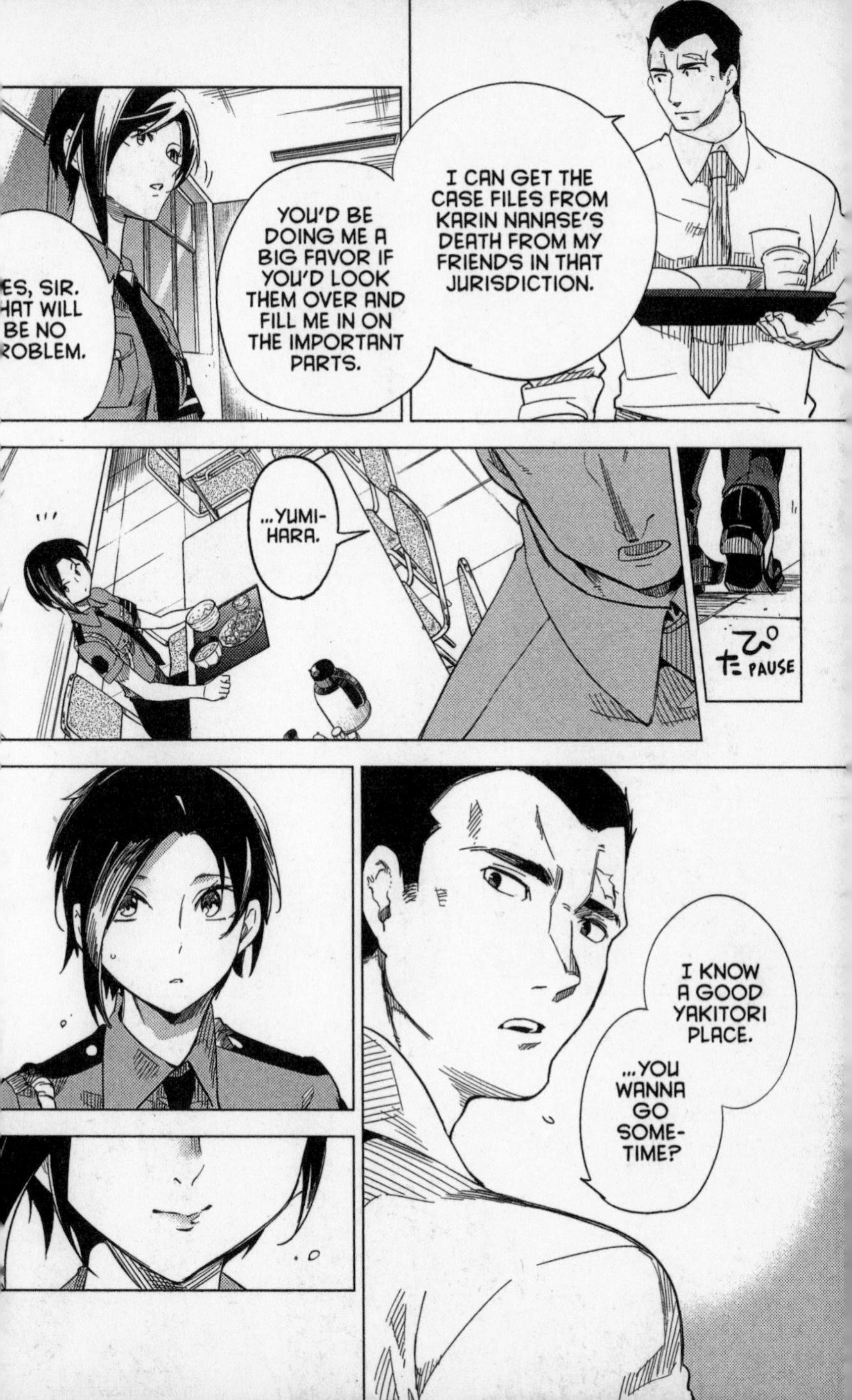
I CAN GET THE CASE FILES FROM KARIN NANASE'S DEATH FROM MY FRIENDS IN THAT JURISDICTION.
YOU'D BE DOING ME A BIG FAVOR IF YOU'D LOOK THEM OVER AND FILL ME IN ON THE IMPORTANT PARTS.
ES, SIR. HAT WILL BE NO ROBLEM.
ぴた PAUSE
...YUMI-HARA.
I KNOW A GOOD YAKITORI PLACE.
...YOU WANNA GO SOME-TIME?

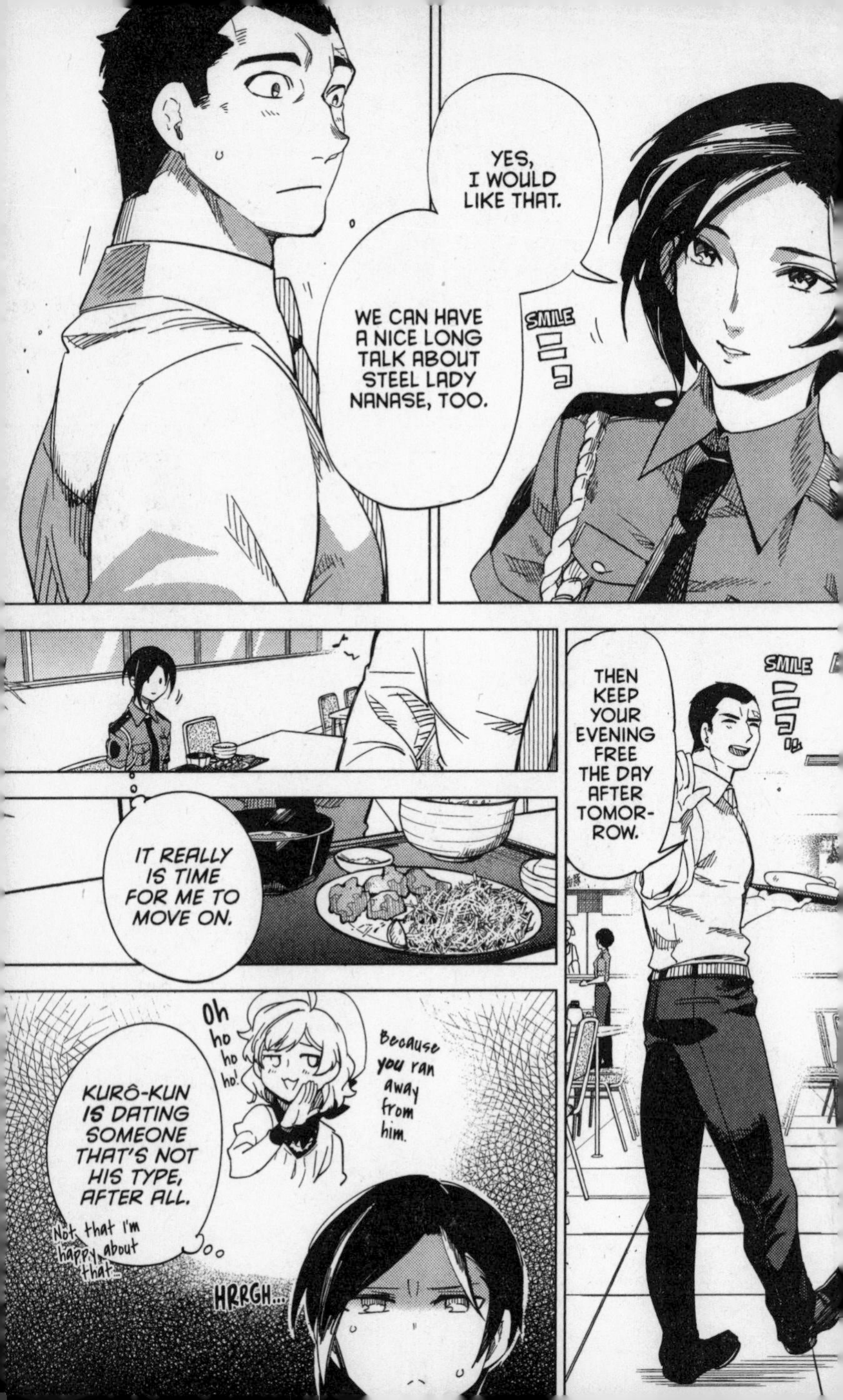
YES, I WOULD LIKE THAT.
SMILE
WE CAN HAVE A NICE LONG TALK ABOUT STEEL LADY NANASE, TOO.
SMILE
THEN KEEP YOUR EVENING FREE THE DAY AFTER TOMOR-ROW.
IT REALLY IS TIME FOR ME TO MOVE ON.
Oh ho ho ho!
Because you ran away from him.
KURÔ-KUN IS DATING SOMEONE THAT'S NOT HIS TYPE, AFTER ALL.
Not that I'm happy about that...
HRRGH...

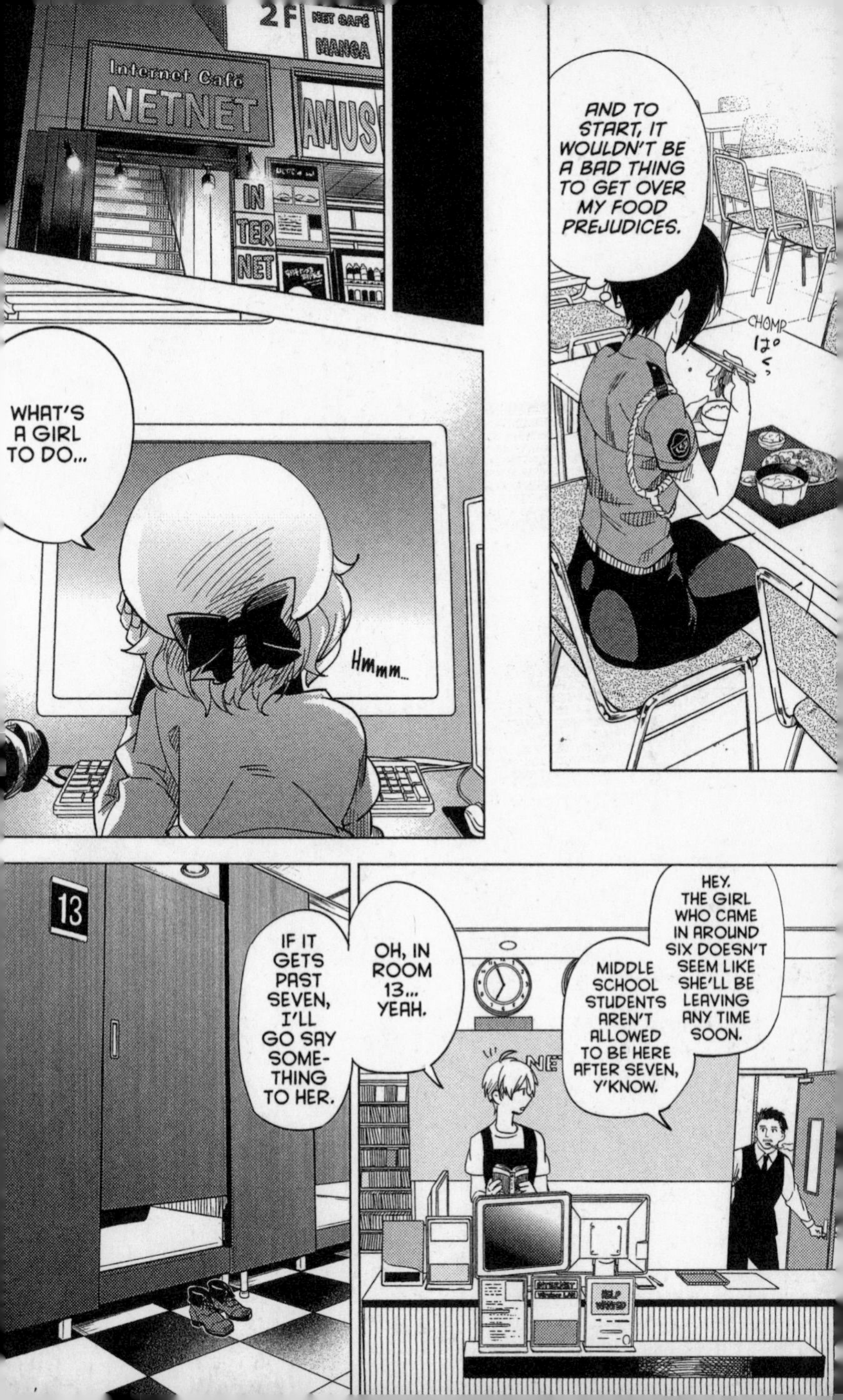
AND TO START, IT WOULDN'T BE A BAD THING TO GET OVER MY FOOD PREJUDICES.
CHOMP
ぱく
2F
NET CAFÉ
MANGA
Internet Café
NETNET
AMUS
IN TER NET
WHAT'S A GIRL TO DO...
Hmmm...
HEY. THE GIRL WHO CAME IN AROUND SIX DOESN'T SEEM LIKE SHE'LL BE LEAVING ANY TIME SOON.
MIDDLE SCHOOL STUDENTS AREN'T ALLOWED TO BE HERE AFTER SEVEN, Y'KNOW.
OH, IN ROOM 13... YEAH.
IF IT GETS PAST SEVEN, I'LL GO SAY SOME-THING TO HER.
13

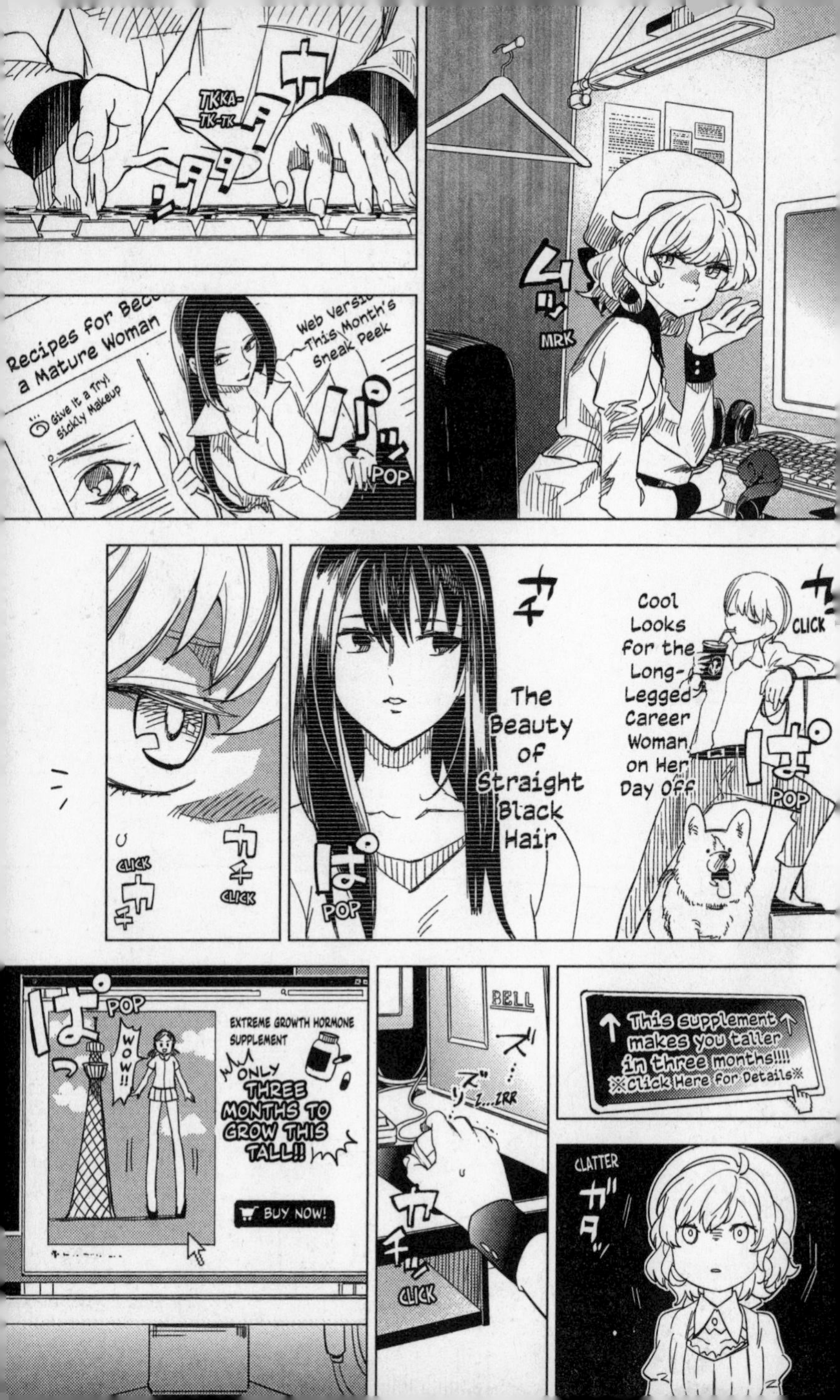
MRK
TKKA-TK-TK
Recipes for Bec
a Mature Woman
Web Versi
This Month's Sneak Peek
Give It a Try! Sickly Makeup
POP
Cool Looks for the Long-Legged Career Woman on Her Day Off
CLICK
POP
The Beauty of Straight Black Hair
POP
CLICK
CLICK
This supplement makes you taller in three months!!!!
※Click Here for Details※
CLATTER
BELL
ZZZ...ZRR
CLICK
POP
WOW!!
EXTREME GROWTH HORMONE SUPPLEMENT
ONLY THREE MONTHS TO GROW THIS TALL!!
BUY NOW!

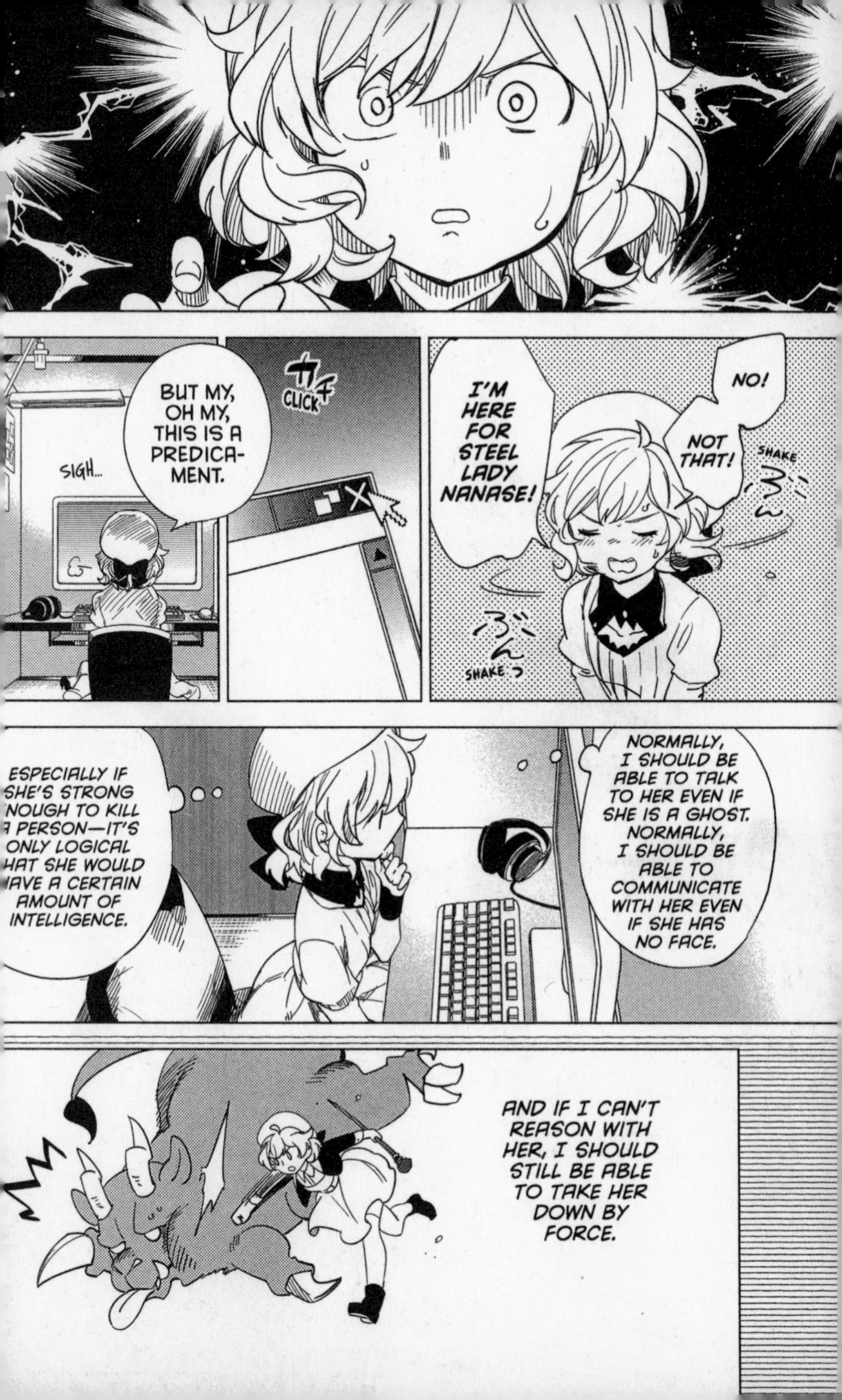
I'M HERE FOR STEEL LADY NANASE!
NO!
NOT THAT!
SHAKE
SHAKE
CLICK
BUT MY, OH MY, THIS IS A PREDICA-MENT.
SIGH...
NORMALLY, I SHOULD BE ABLE TO TALK TO HER EVEN IF SHE IS A GHOST. NORMALLY, I SHOULD BE ABLE TO COMMUNICATE WITH HER EVEN IF SHE HAS NO FACE.
ESPECIALLY IF SHE'S STRONG NOUGH TO KILL A PERSON—IT'S ONLY LOGICAL HAT SHE WOULD AVE A CERTAIN AMOUNT OF INTELLIGENCE.
AND IF I CAN'T REASON WITH HER, I SHOULD STILL BE ABLE TO TAKE HER DOWN BY FORCE.

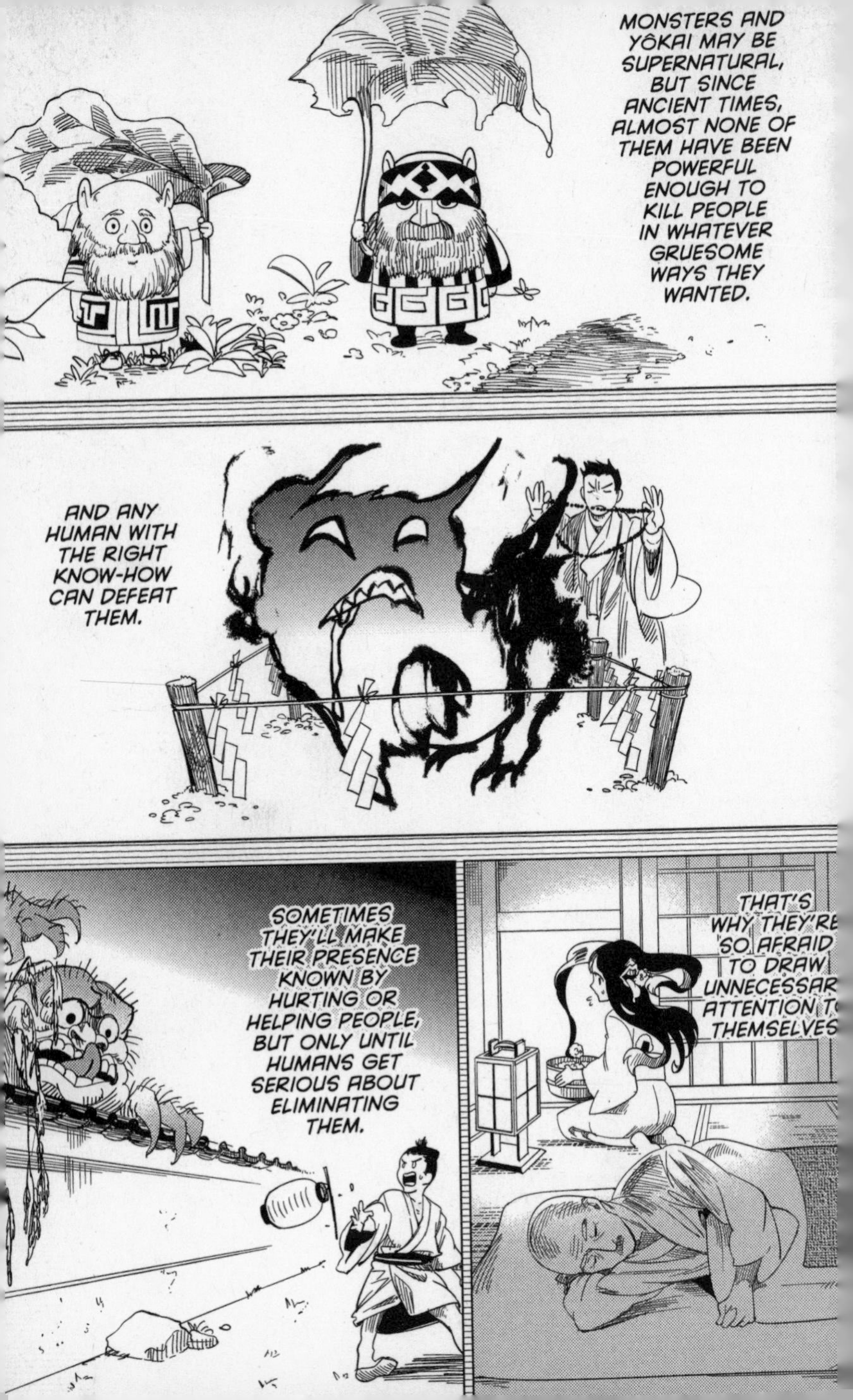
MONSTERS AND YÔKAI MAY BE SUPERNATURAL, BUT SINCE ANCIENT TIMES, ALMOST NONE OF THEM HAVE BEEN POWERFUL ENOUGH TO KILL PEOPLE IN WHATEVER GRUESOME WAYS THEY WANTED.
AND ANY HUMAN WITH THE RIGHT KNOW-HOW CAN DEFEAT THEM.
THAT'S WHY THEY'RE SO AFRAID TO DRAW UNNECESSAR ATTENTION T THEMSELVES
SOMETIMES THEY'LL MAKE THEIR PRESENCE KNOWN BY HURTING OR HELPING PEOPLE, BUT ONLY UNTIL HUMANS GET SERIOUS ABOUT ELIMINATING THEM.

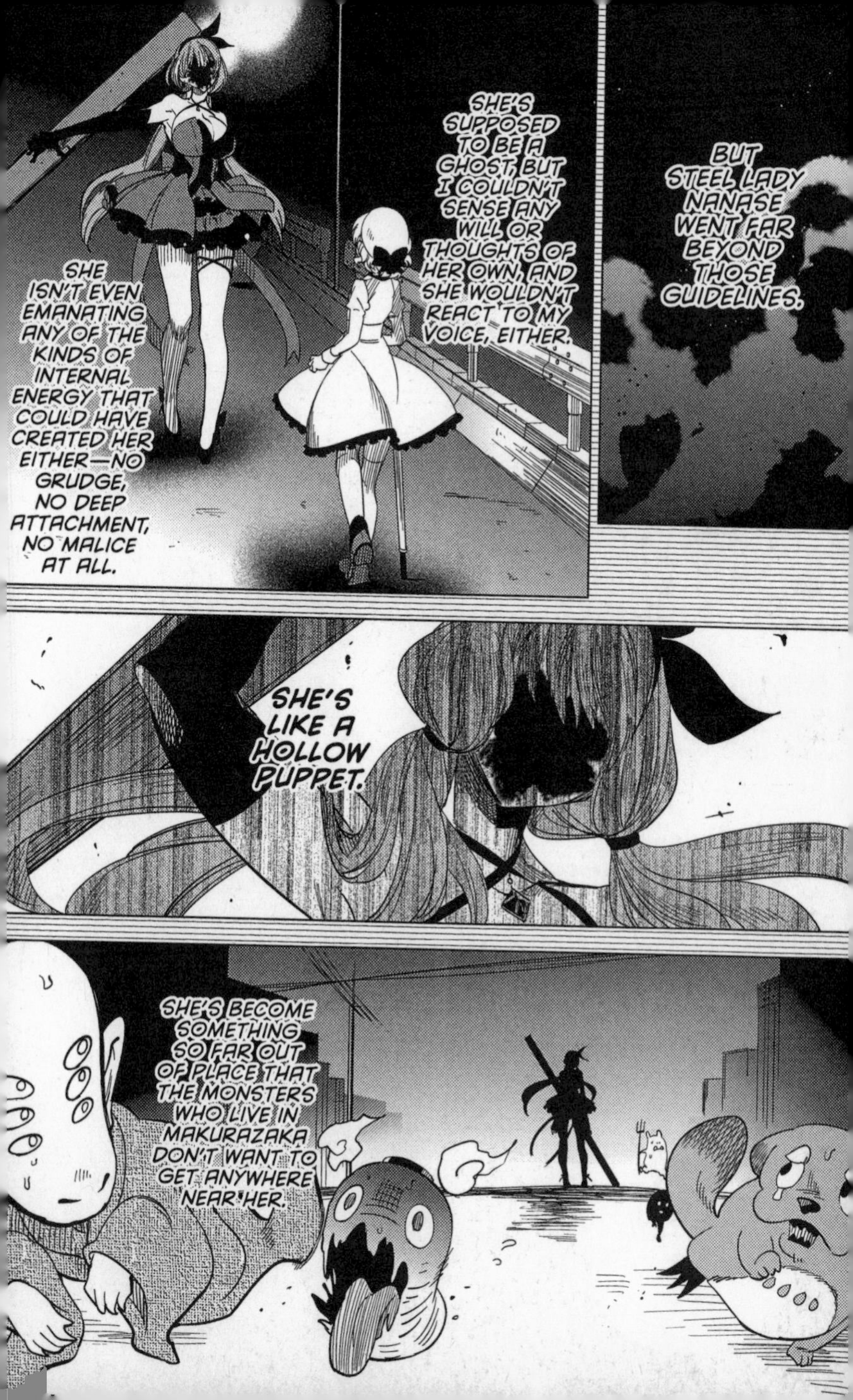
BUT STEEL LADY NANASE WENT FAR BEYOND THOSE GUIDELINES.
SHE'S SUPPOSED TO BE A GHOST, BUT I COULDN'T SENSE ANY WILL OR THOUGHTS OF HER OWN, AND SHE WOULDN'T REACT TO MY VOICE, EITHER.
SHE ISN'T EVEN EMANATING ANY OF THE KINDS OF INTERNAL ENERGY THAT COULD HAVE CREATED HER EITHER—NO GRUDGE, NO DEEP ATTACHMENT, NO MALICE AT ALL.
SHE'S LIKE A HOLLOW PUPPET.
SHE'S BECOME SOMETHING SO FAR OUT OF PLACE THAT THE MONSTERS WHO LIVE IN MAKURAZAKA DON'T WANT TO GET ANYWHERE NEAR HER.

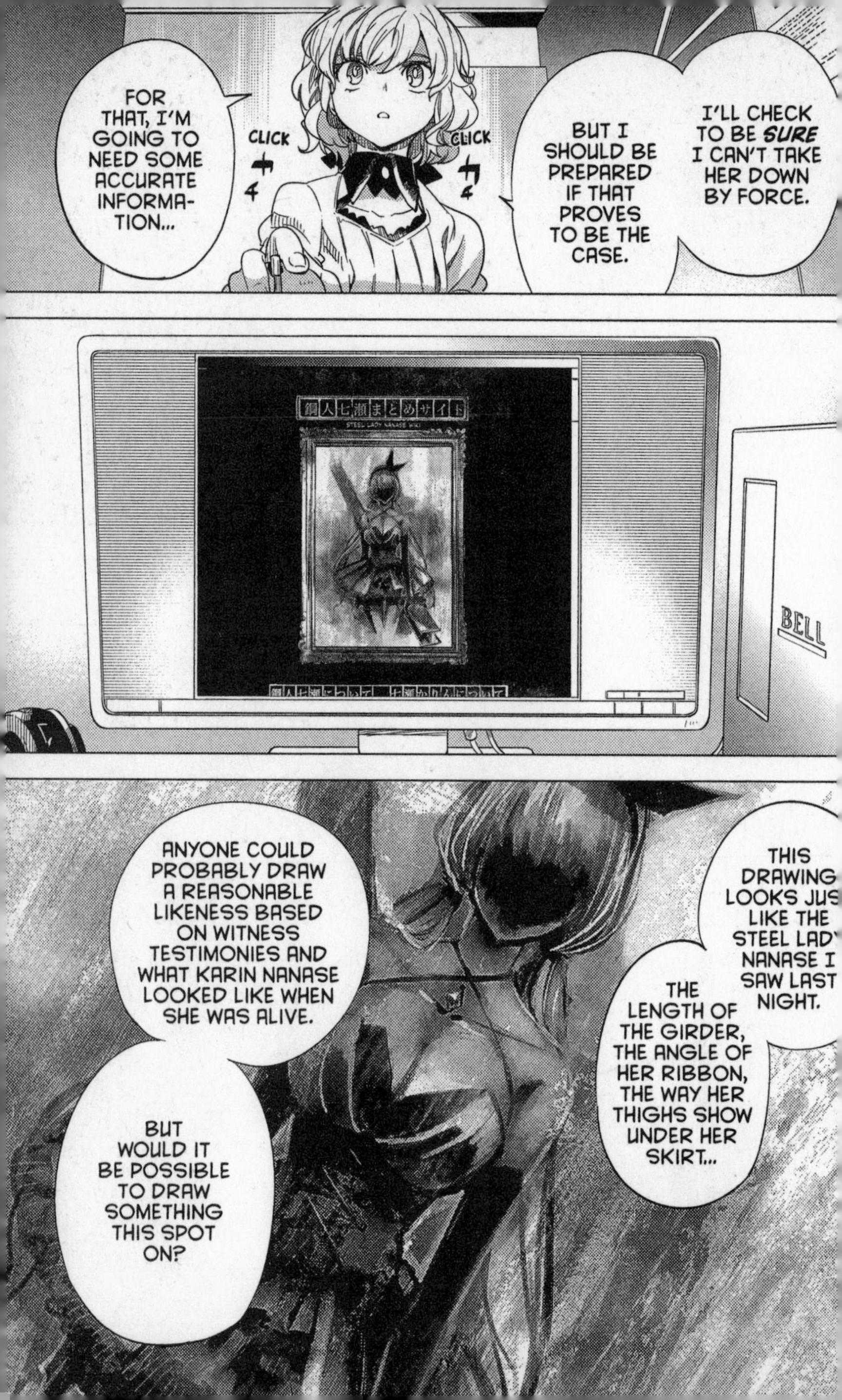
I'LL CHECK TO BE *SURE* I CAN'T TAKE HER DOWN BY FORCE.
BUT I SHOULD BE PREPARED IF THAT PROVES TO BE THE CASE.
CLICK
CLICK
FOR THAT, I'M GOING TO NEED SOME ACCURATE INFORMATION...
鋼人七瀬まとめサイト
STEEL LADY NANASE WIKI
鋼人七瀬について 七瀬かりんについて
BELL
THIS DRAWING LOOKS JUS LIKE THE STEEL LAD NANASE I SAW LAST NIGHT.
THE LENGTH OF THE GIRDER, THE ANGLE OF HER RIBBON, THE WAY HER THIGHS SHOW UNDER HER SKIRT...
ANYONE COULD PROBABLY DRAW A REASONABLE LIKENESS BASED ON WITNESS TESTIMONIES AND WHAT KARIN NANASE LOOKED LIKE WHEN SHE WAS ALIVE.
BUT WOULD IT BE POSSIBLE TO DRAW SOMETHING THIS SPOT ON?

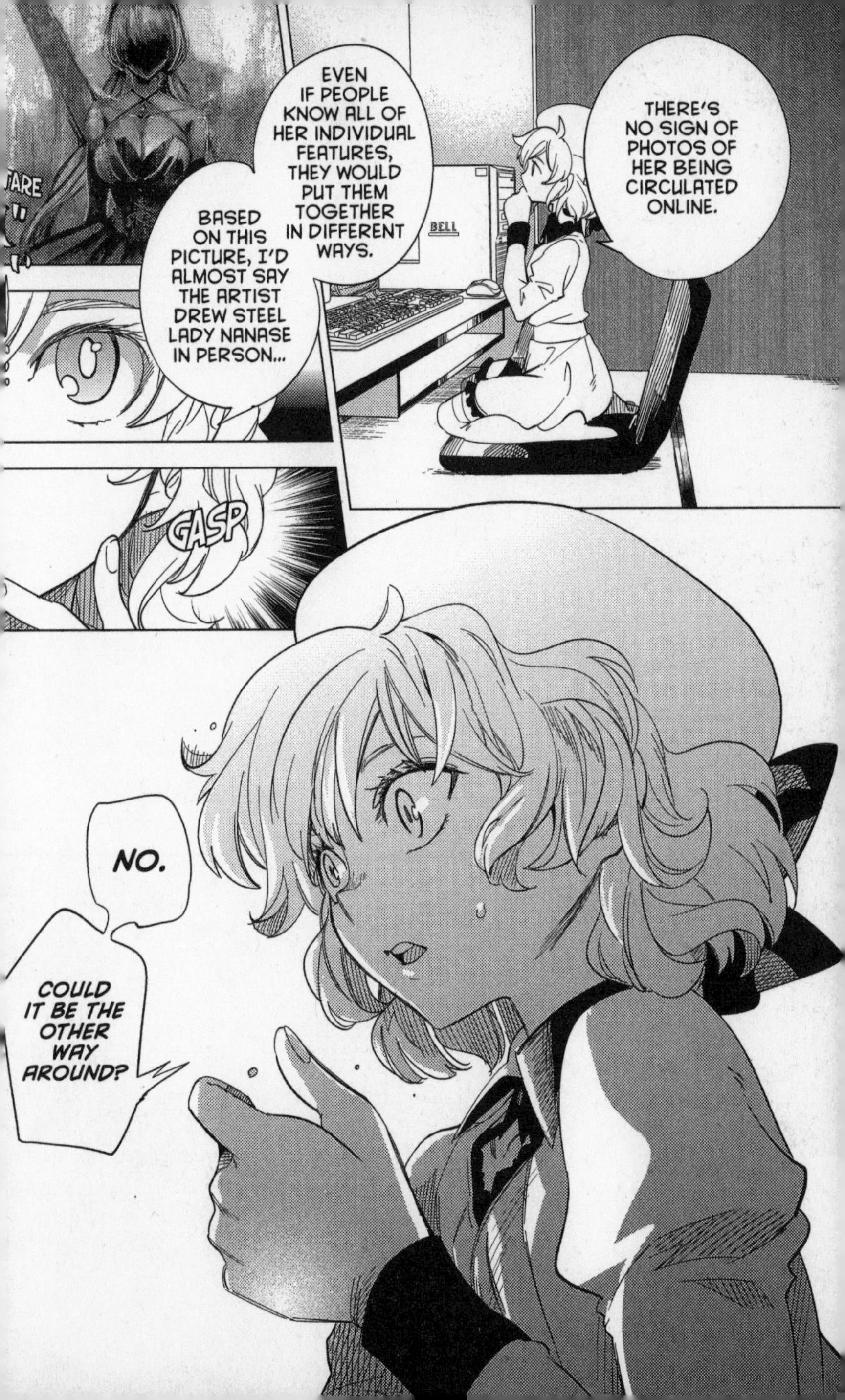
BELL
THERE'S NO SIGN OF PHOTOS OF HER BEING CIRCULATED ONLINE.
EVEN IF PEOPLE KNOW ALL OF HER INDIVIDUAL FEATURES, THEY WOULD PUT THEM TOGETHER IN DIFFERENT WAYS.
BASED ON THIS PICTURE, I'D ALMOST SAY THE ARTIST DREW STEEL LADY NANASE IN PERSON...
GASP
NO.
COULD IT BE THE OTHER WAY AROUND?

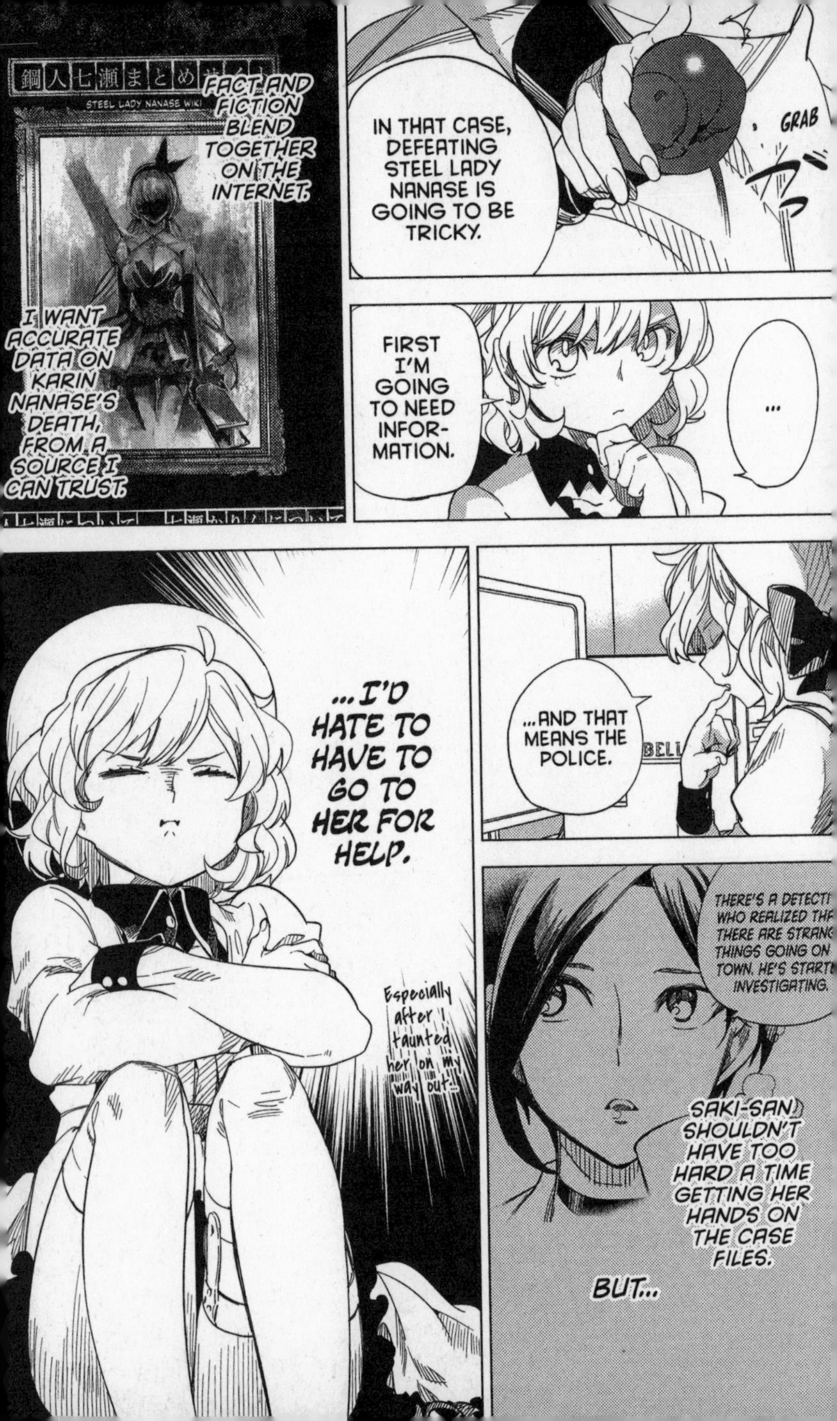
GRAB
IN THAT CASE, DEFEATING STEEL LADY NANASE IS GOING TO BE TRICKY.
...
FIRST I'M GOING TO NEED INFOR-MATION.
鋼人七瀬まとめ
STEEL LADY NANASE WIKI
FACT AND FICTION BLEND TOGETHER ON THE INTERNET.
I WANT ACCURATE DATA ON KARIN NANASE'S DEATH, FROM A SOURCE I CAN TRUST.
...AND THAT MEANS THE POLICE.
THERE'S A DETECTI WHO REALIZED TH THERE ARE STRANG THINGS GOING ON TOWN. HE'S START INVESTIGATING.
SAKI-SAN SHOULDN'T HAVE TOO HARD A TIME GETTING HER HANDS ON THE CASE FILES.
BUT...
...I'D HATE TO HAVE TO GO TO HER FOR HELP.
Especially after I taunted her on my way out...

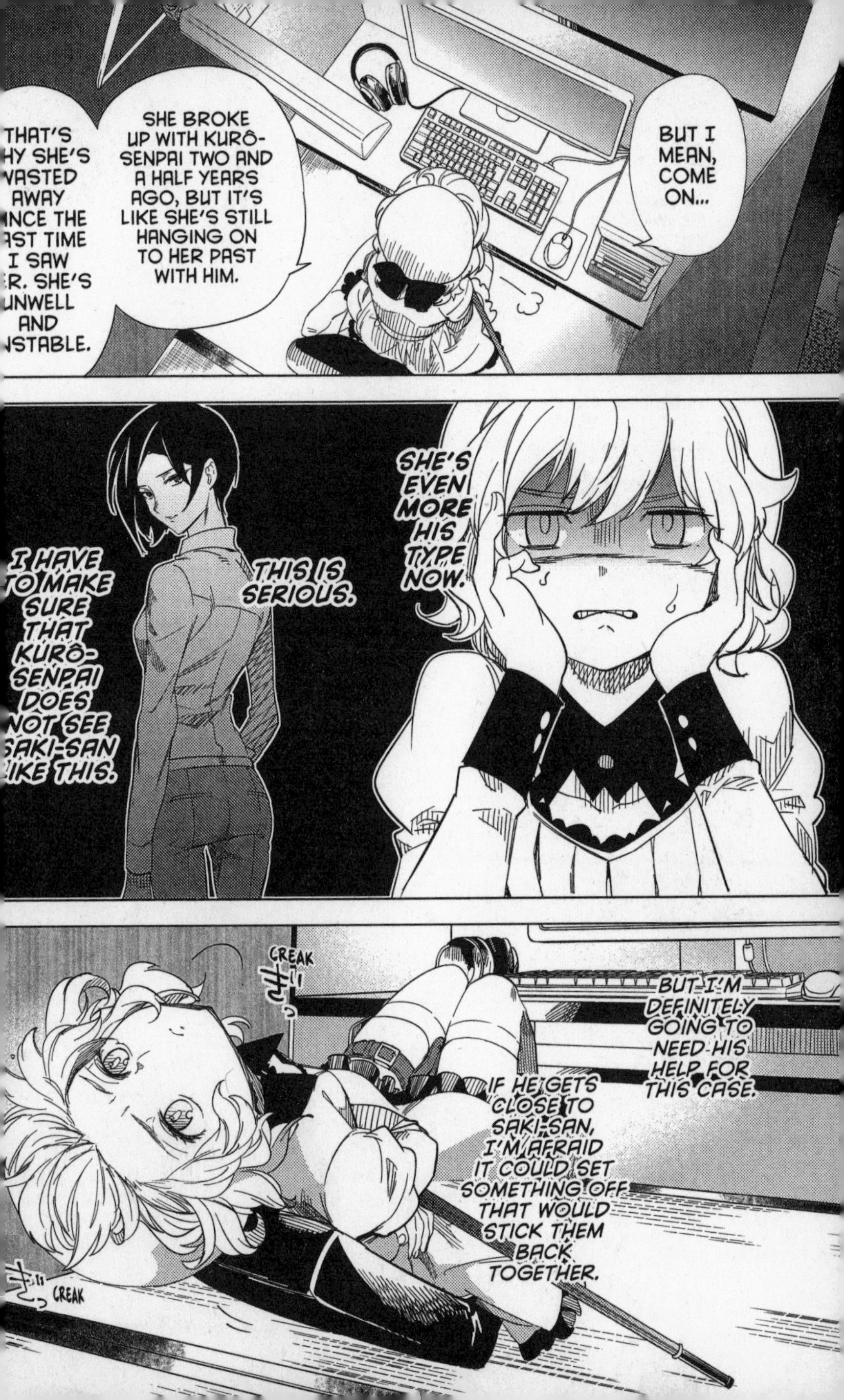
BUT I MEAN, COME ON...
SHE BROKE UP WITH KURÔ-SENPAI TWO AND A HALF YEARS AGO, BUT IT'S LIKE SHE'S STILL HANGING ON TO HER PAST WITH HIM.
THAT'S HY SHE'S VASTED AWAY INCE THE AST TIME I SAW R. SHE'S UNWELL AND NSTABLE.
SHE'S EVEN MORE HIS TYPE NOW.
THIS IS SERIOUS.
I HAVE O MAKE SURE THAT KURÔ-SENPAI DOES NOT SEE AKI-SAN IKE THIS.
CREAK
BUT I'M DEFINITELY GOING TO NEED HIS HELP FOR THIS CASE.
IF HE GETS CLOSE TO SAKI-SAN, I'M AFRAID IT COULD SET SOMETHING OFF THAT WOULD STICK THEM BACK TOGETHER.
CREAK

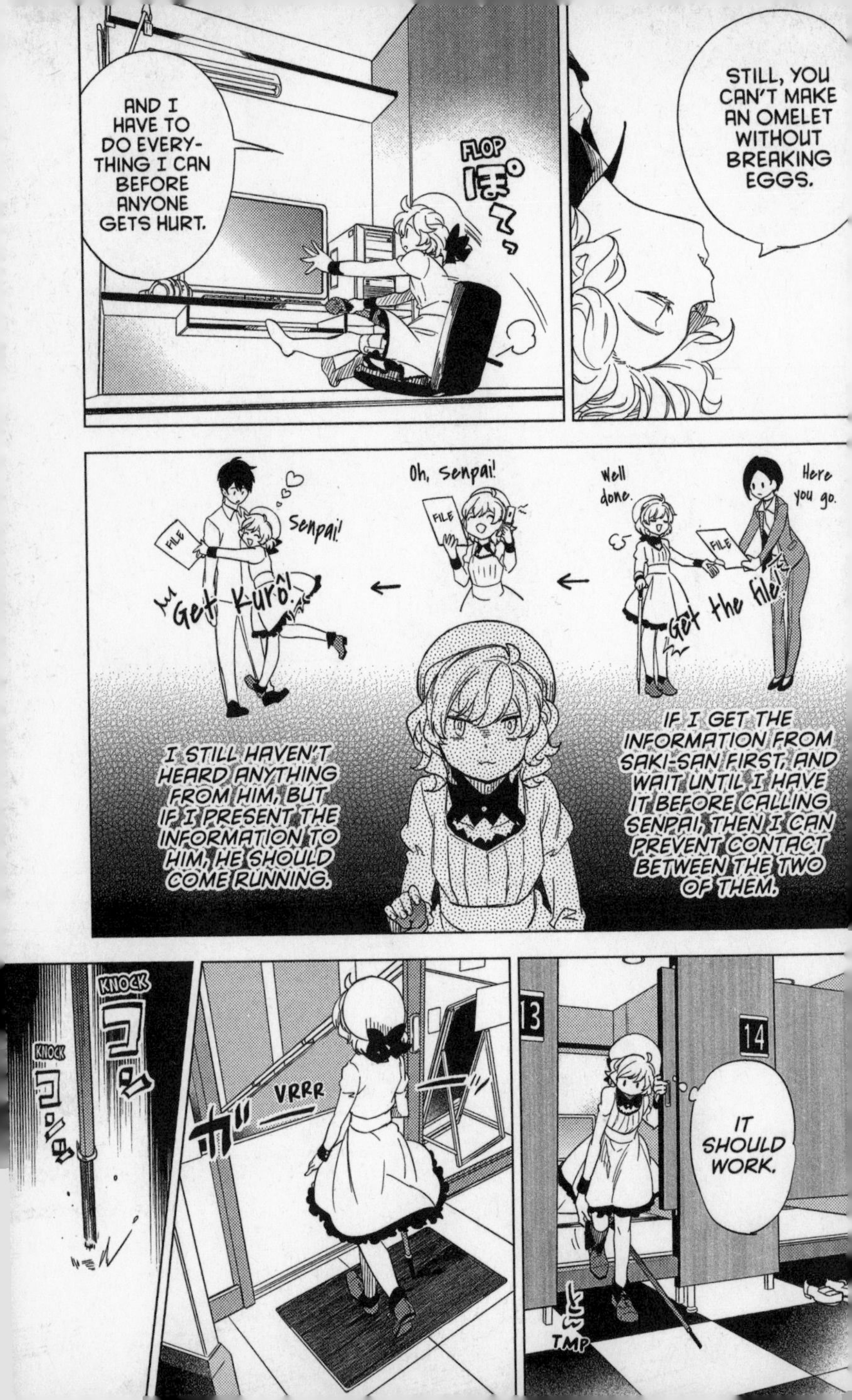
STILL, YOU CAN'T MAKE AN OMELET WITHOUT BREAKING EGGS.
AND I HAVE TO DO EVERY-THING I CAN BEFORE ANYONE GETS HURT.
FLOP
ぽて
Here you go.
Well done.
Get the file!
Oh, Senpai!
Senpai!
Get Kurô!
IF I GET THE INFORMATION FROM SAKI-SAN FIRST, AND WAIT UNTIL I HAVE IT BEFORE CALLING SENPAI, THEN I CAN PREVENT CONTACT BETWEEN THE TWO OF THEM.
I STILL HAVEN'T HEARD ANYTHING FROM HIM, BUT IF I PRESENT THE INFORMATION TO HIM, HE SHOULD COME RUNNING.
14
13
IT SHOULD WORK.
TMP
KNOCK
KNOCK
VRRR

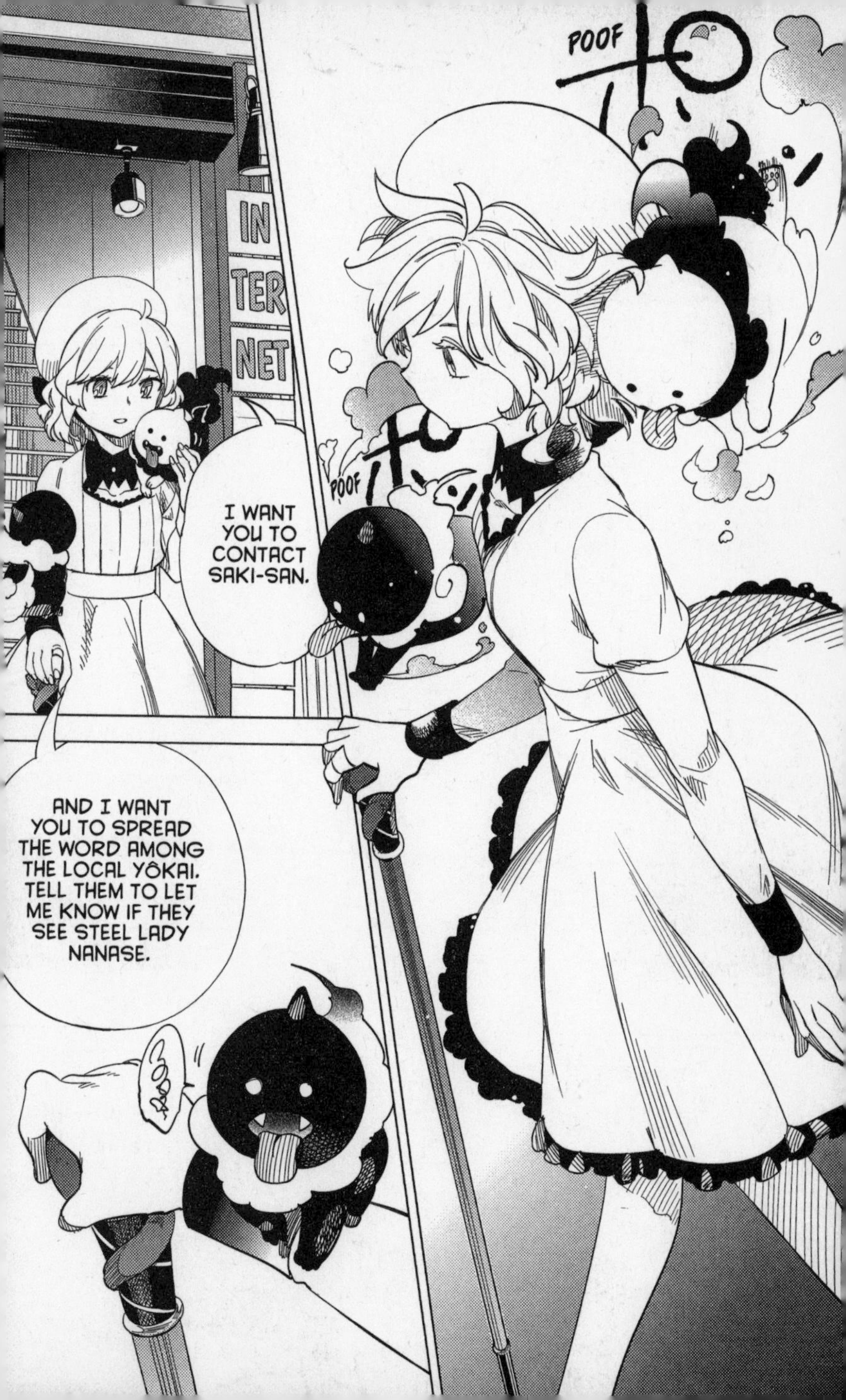
POOF
POOF
IN TER NET
I WANT YOU TO CONTACT SAKI-SAN.
AND I WANT YOU TO SPREAD THE WORD AMONG THE LOCAL YÔKAI. TELL THEM TO LET ME KNOW IF THEY SEE STEEL LADY NANASE.

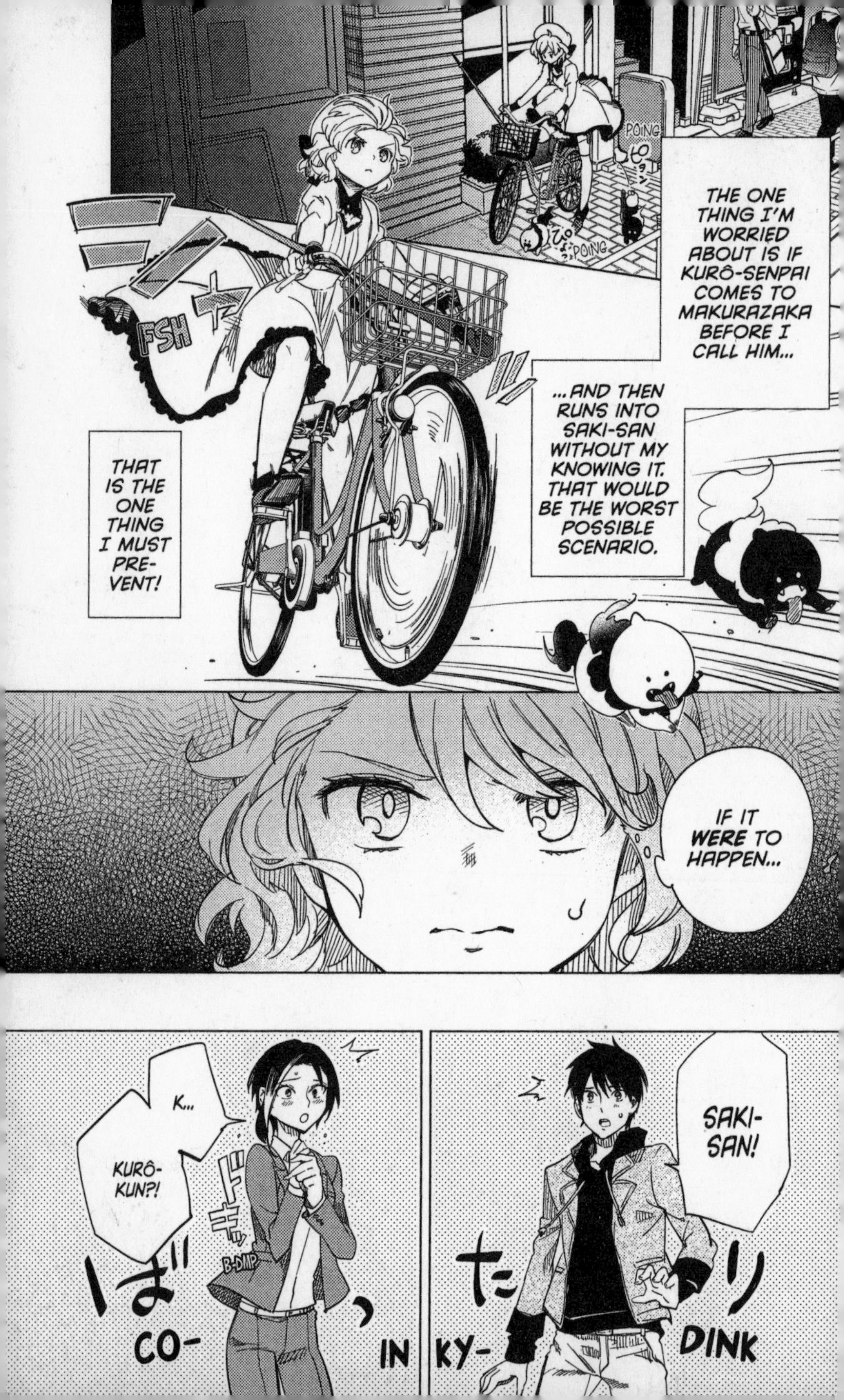
POING
POING
THE ONE THING I'M WORRIED ABOUT IS IF KURÔ-SENPAI COMES TO MAKURAZAKA BEFORE I CALL HIM...
...AND THEN RUNS INTO SAKI-SAN WITHOUT MY KNOWING IT. THAT WOULD BE THE WORST POSSIBLE SCENARIO.
FSH
THAT IS THE ONE THING I MUST PRE-VENT!
IF IT WERE TO HAPPEN...
SAKI-SAN!
DINK
KY-
K...
KURÔ-KUN?!
B-DMP
IN
CO-

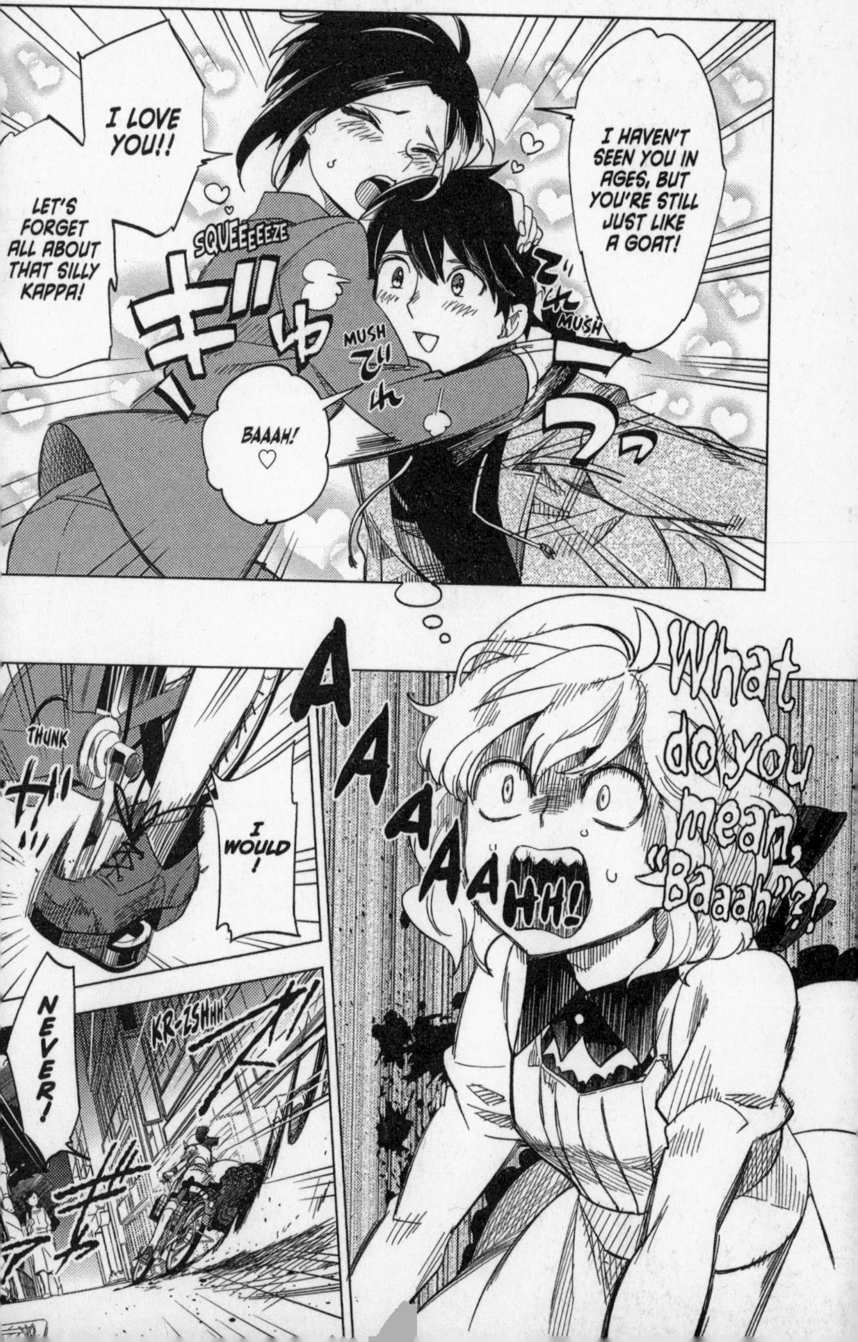
I HAVEN'T SEEN YOU IN AGES, BUT YOU'RE STILL JUST LIKE A GOAT!
MUSH
I LOVE YOU!!
LET'S FORGET ALL ABOUT THAT SILLY KAPPA!
SQUEEEEEZE
MUSH
BAAAH! ♡
What do you mean, "Baaah"?!
AAAAAHH!
THUNK
I WOULD!
NEVER!
KR-ZSHHH

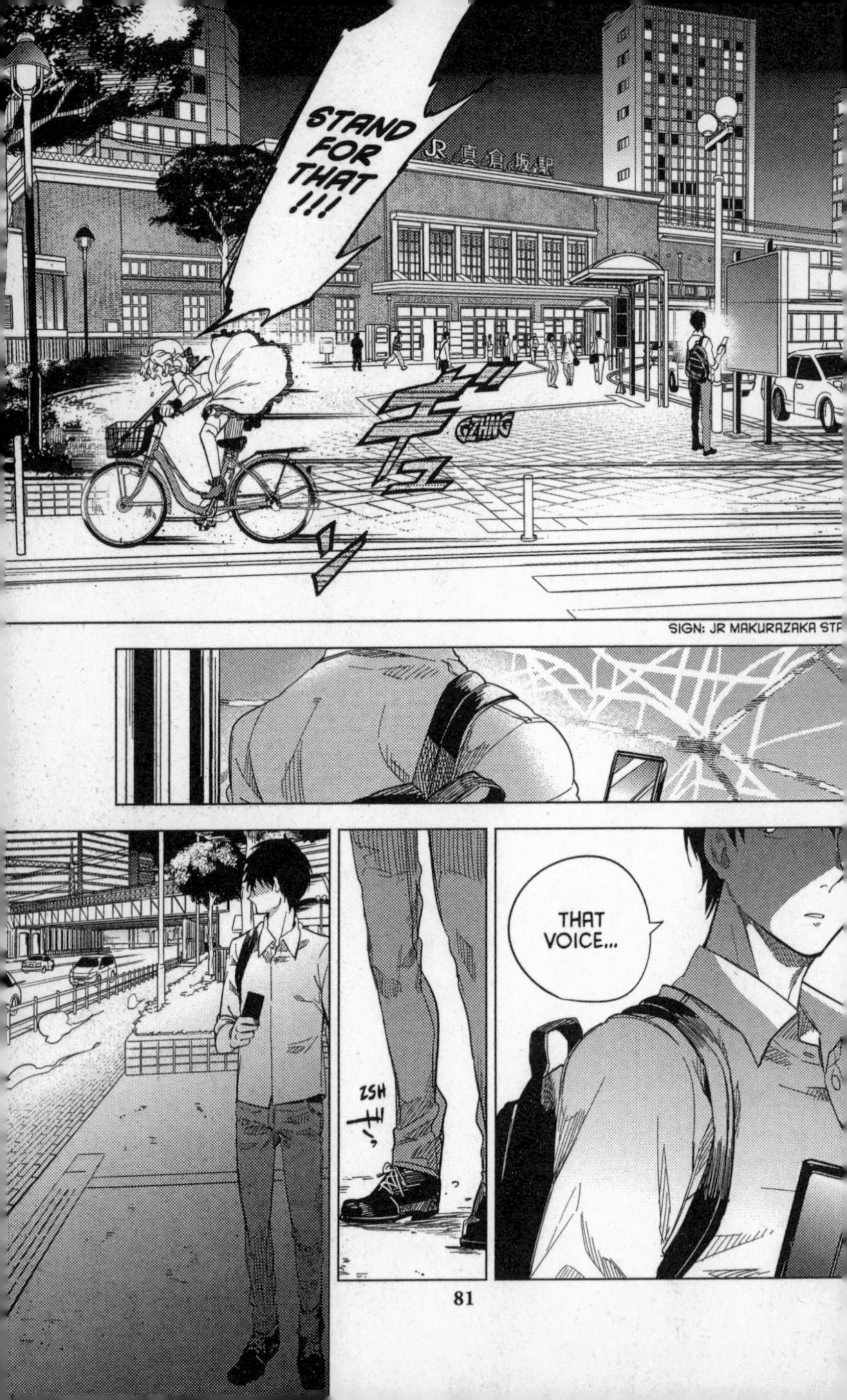
STAND FOR THAT!!!
GZHING
SIGN: JR MAKURAZAKA STA
THAT VOICE...
ZSH

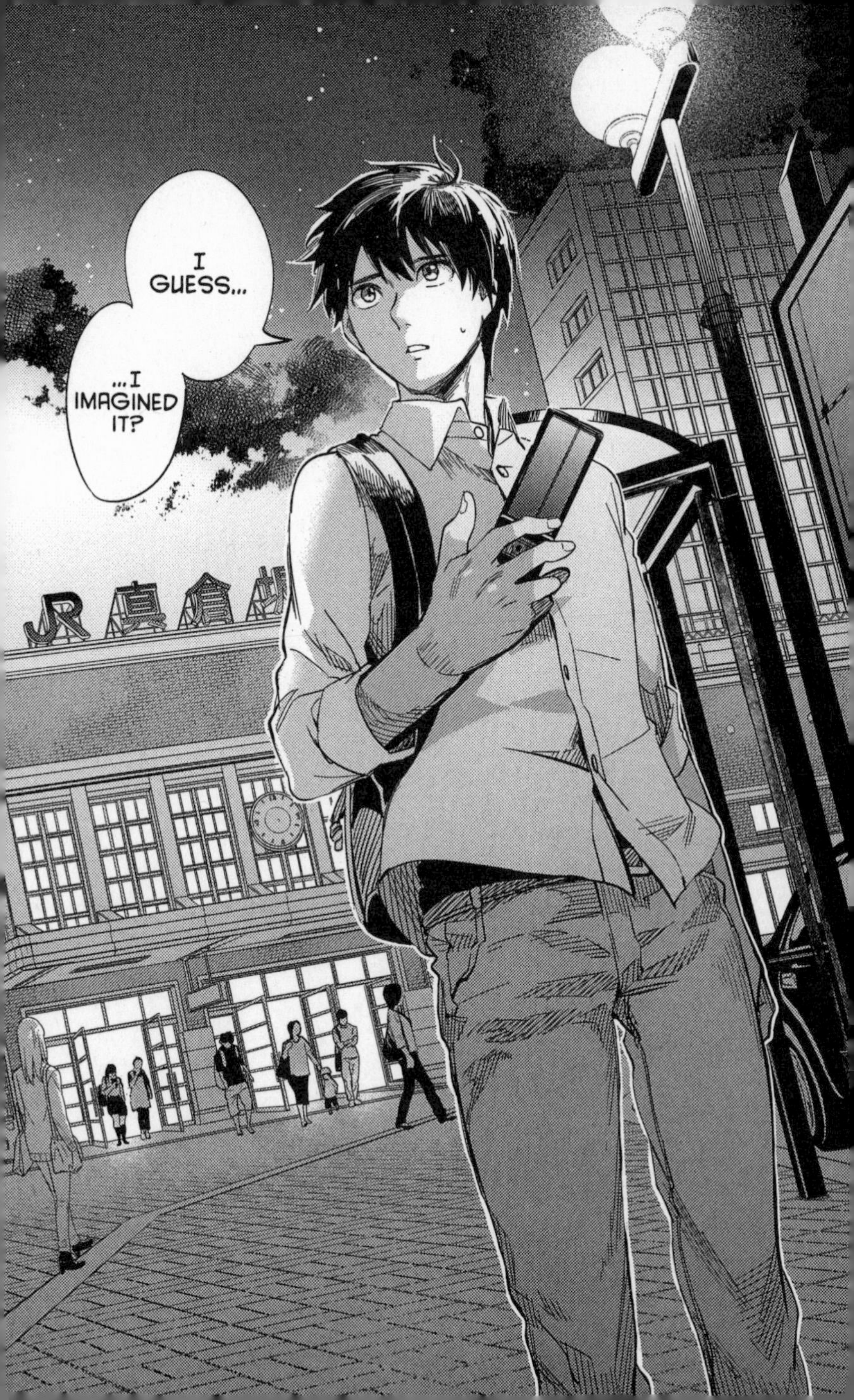
I GUESS...
...I IMAGINED IT?

KORO-POK-GURU

KOTO-POK-GURU

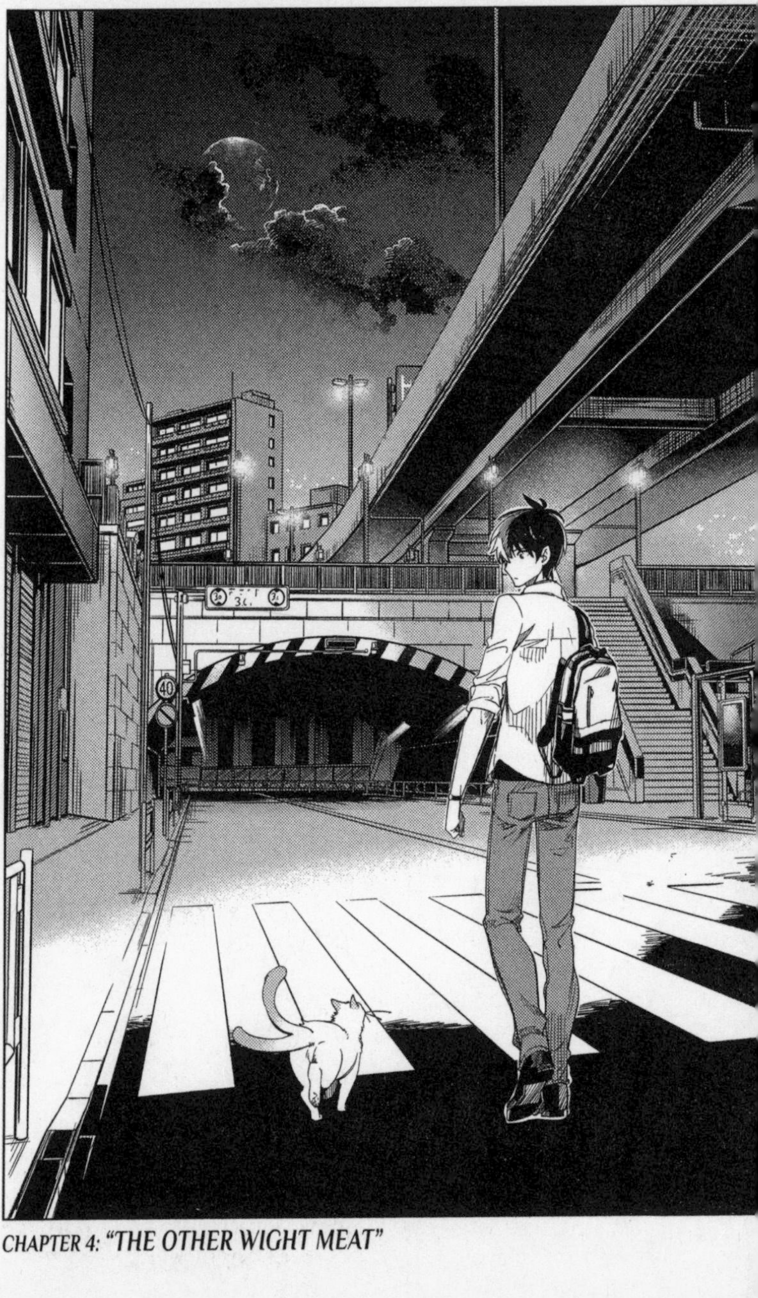
40

CHAPTER 4: "THE OTHER WIGHT MEAT"

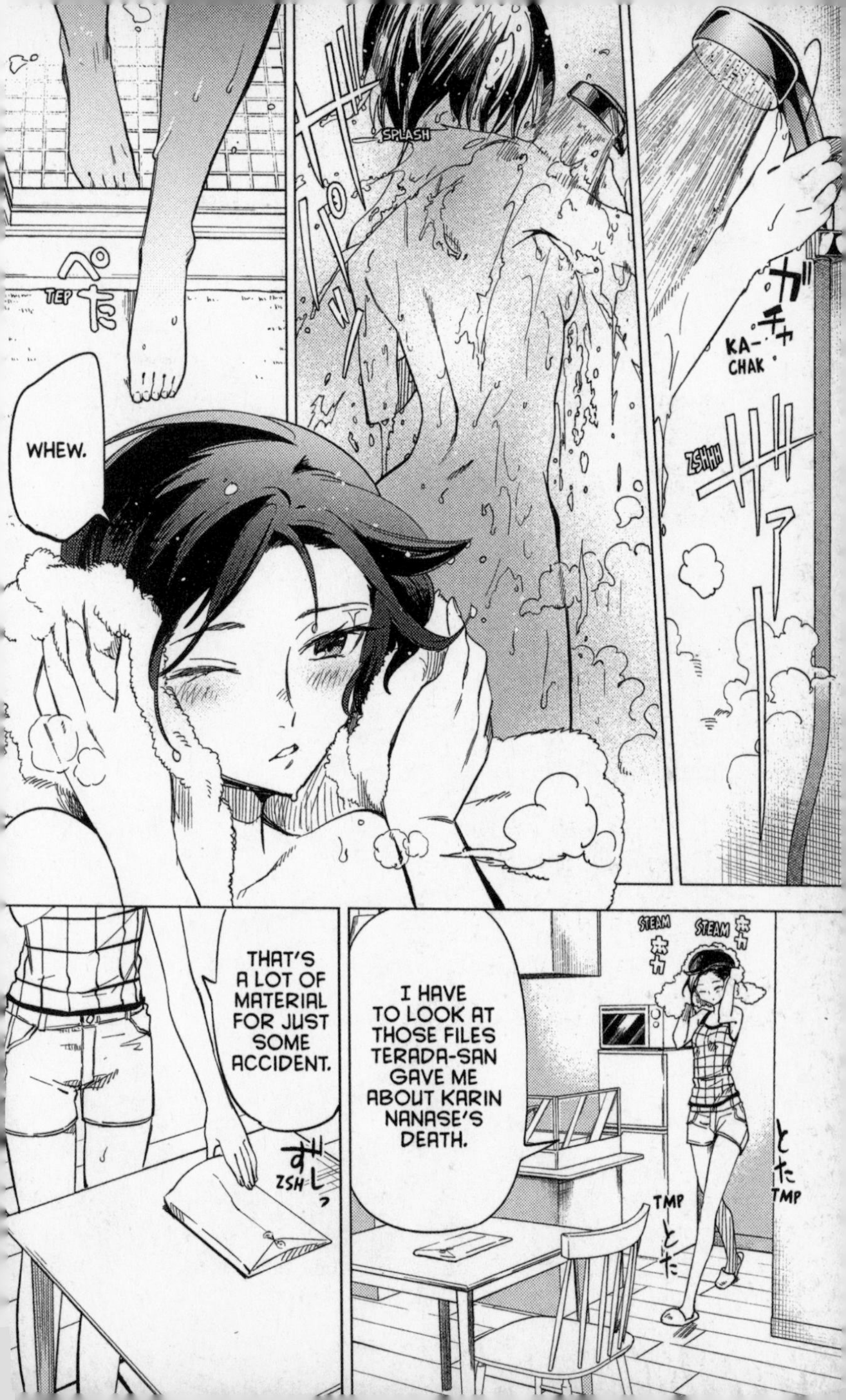
ガチャ
KA-CHAK
ZSHHH
SPLASH
ぺた
TEP
WHEW.
STEAM
STEAM
I HAVE TO LOOK AT THOSE FILES TERADA-SAN GAVE ME ABOUT KARIN NANASE'S DEATH.
とた
TMP
TMP
とた
ZSH
ずしっ
THAT'S A LOT OF MATERIAL FOR JUST SOME ACCIDENT.

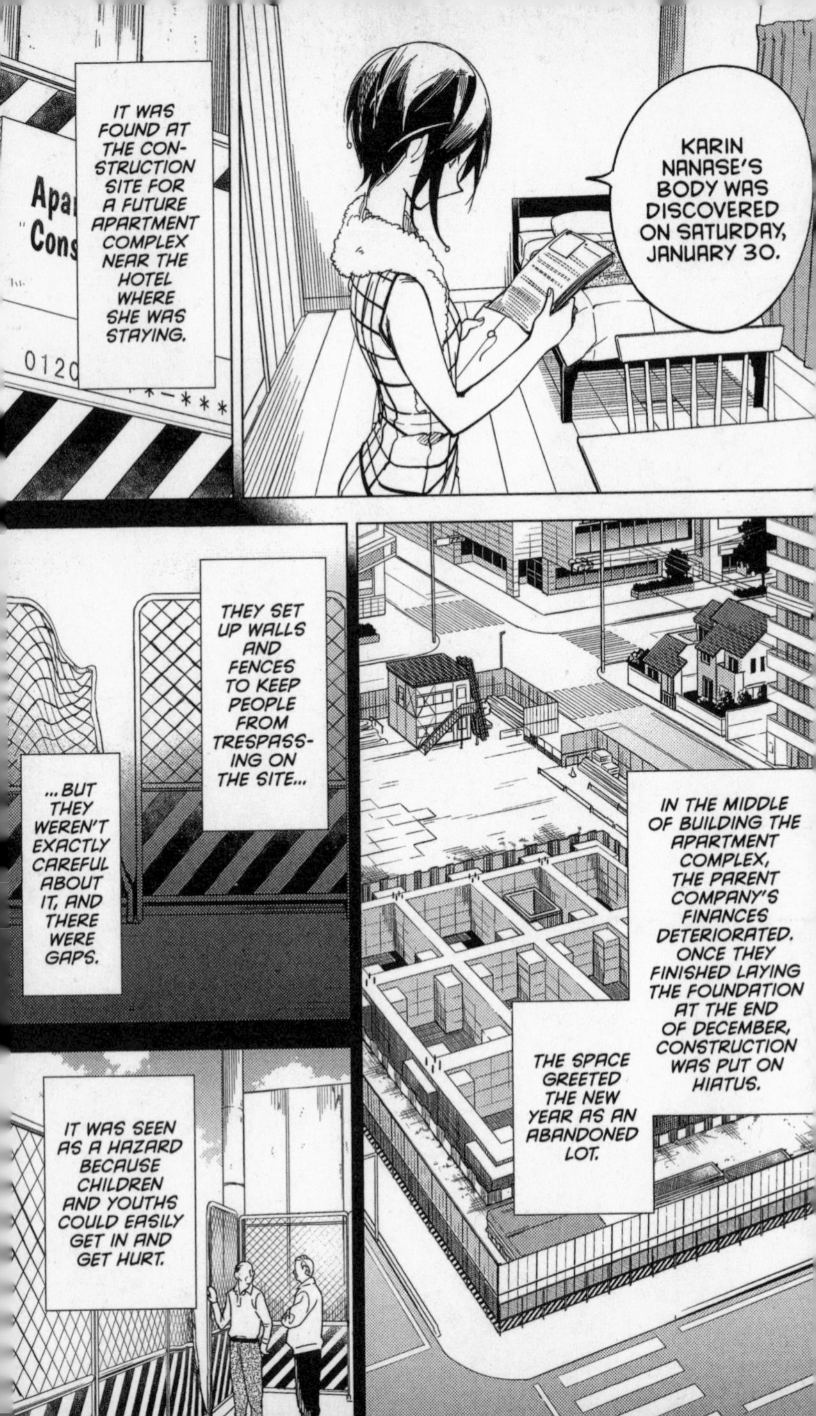
KARIN NANASE'S BODY WAS DISCOVERED ON SATURDAY, JANUARY 30.
IT WAS FOUND AT THE CON-STRUCTION SITE FOR A FUTURE APARTMENT COMPLEX NEAR THE HOTEL WHERE SHE WAS STAYING.
IN THE MIDDLE OF BUILDING THE APARTMENT COMPLEX, THE PARENT COMPANY'S FINANCES DETERIORATED. ONCE THEY FINISHED LAYING THE FOUNDATION AT THE END OF DECEMBER, CONSTRUCTION WAS PUT ON HIATUS.
THE SPACE GREETED THE NEW YEAR AS AN ABANDONED LOT.
THEY SET UP WALLS AND FENCES TO KEEP PEOPLE FROM TRESPASS-ING ON THE SITE...
...BUT THEY WEREN'T EXACTLY CAREFUL ABOUT IT, AND THERE WERE GAPS.
IT WAS SEEN AS A HAZARD BECAUSE CHILDREN AND YOUTHS COULD EASILY GET IN AND GET HURT.

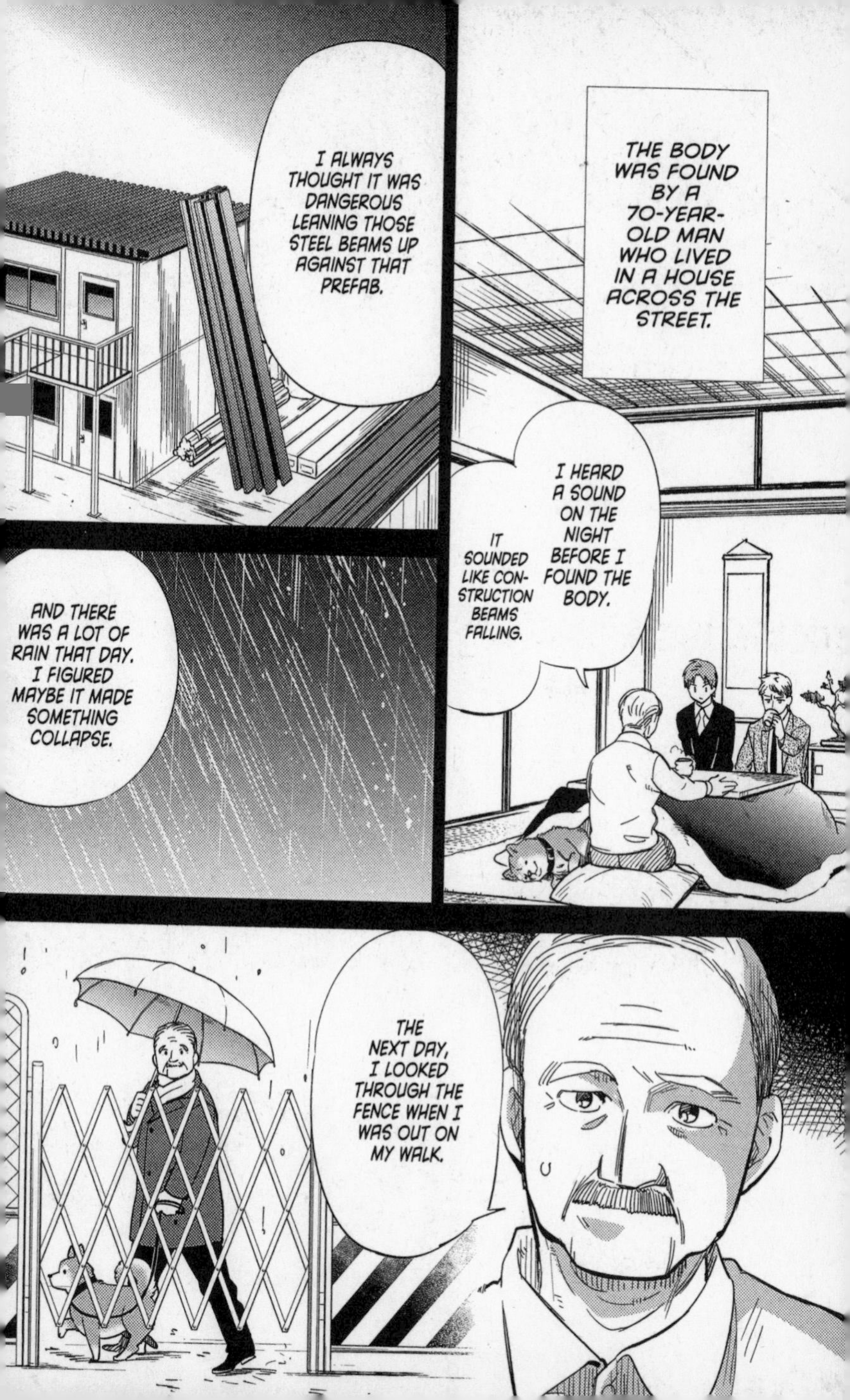
THE BODY WAS FOUND BY A 70-YEAR-OLD MAN WHO LIVED IN A HOUSE ACROSS THE STREET.
I HEARD A SOUND ON THE NIGHT BEFORE I FOUND THE BODY.
IT SOUNDED LIKE CONSTRUCTION BEAMS FALLING.
I ALWAYS THOUGHT IT WAS DANGEROUS LEANING THOSE STEEL BEAMS UP AGAINST THAT PREFAB.
AND THERE WAS A LOT OF RAIN THAT DAY. I FIGURED MAYBE IT MADE SOMETHING COLLAPSE.
THE NEXT DAY, I LOOKED THROUGH THE FENCE WHEN I WAS OUT ON MY WALK.

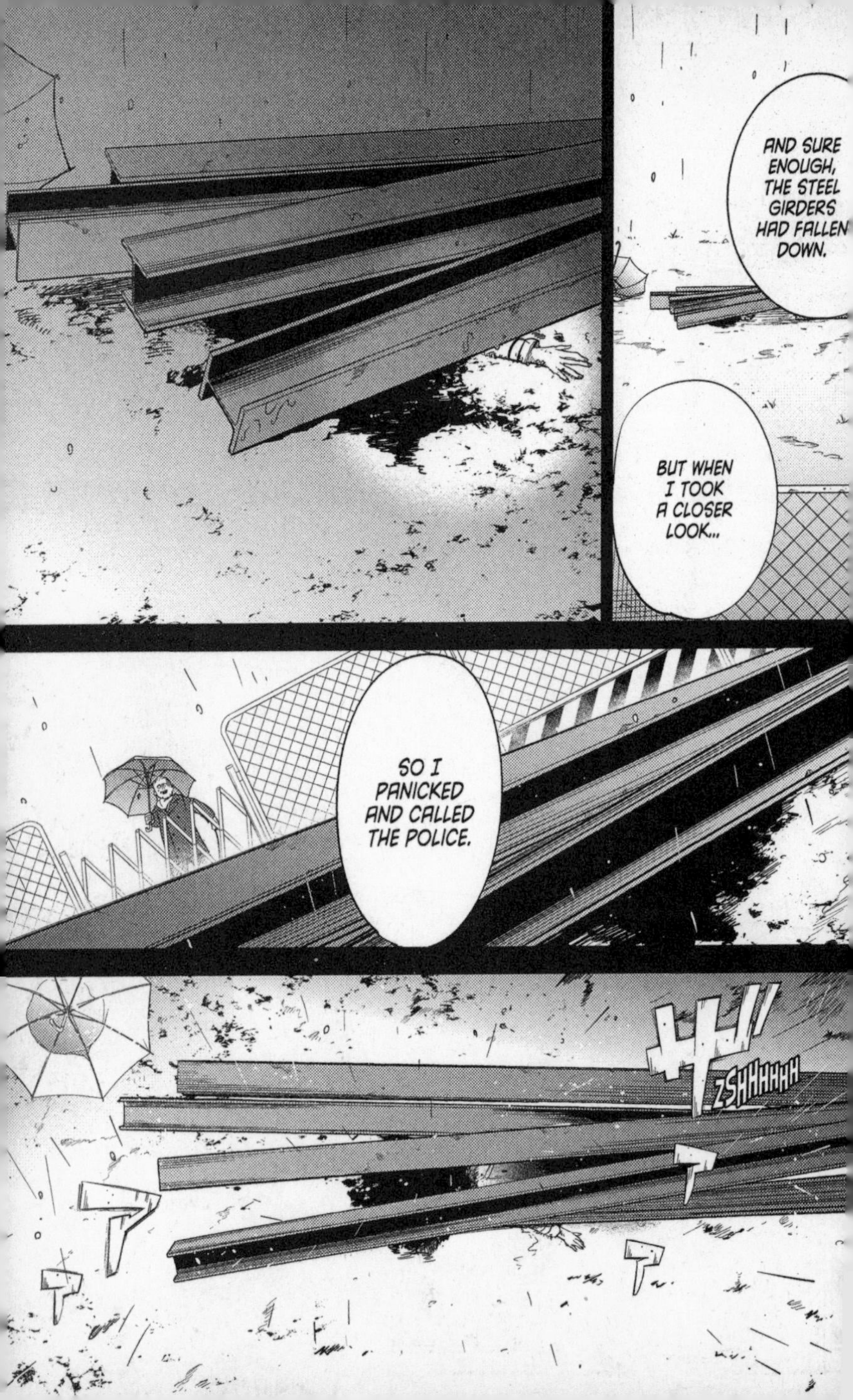
AND SURE ENOUGH, THE STEEL GIRDERS HAD FALLEN DOWN.
BUT WHEN I TOOK A CLOSER LOOK...
SO I PANICKED AND CALLED THE POLICE.
ZSHHHHHH

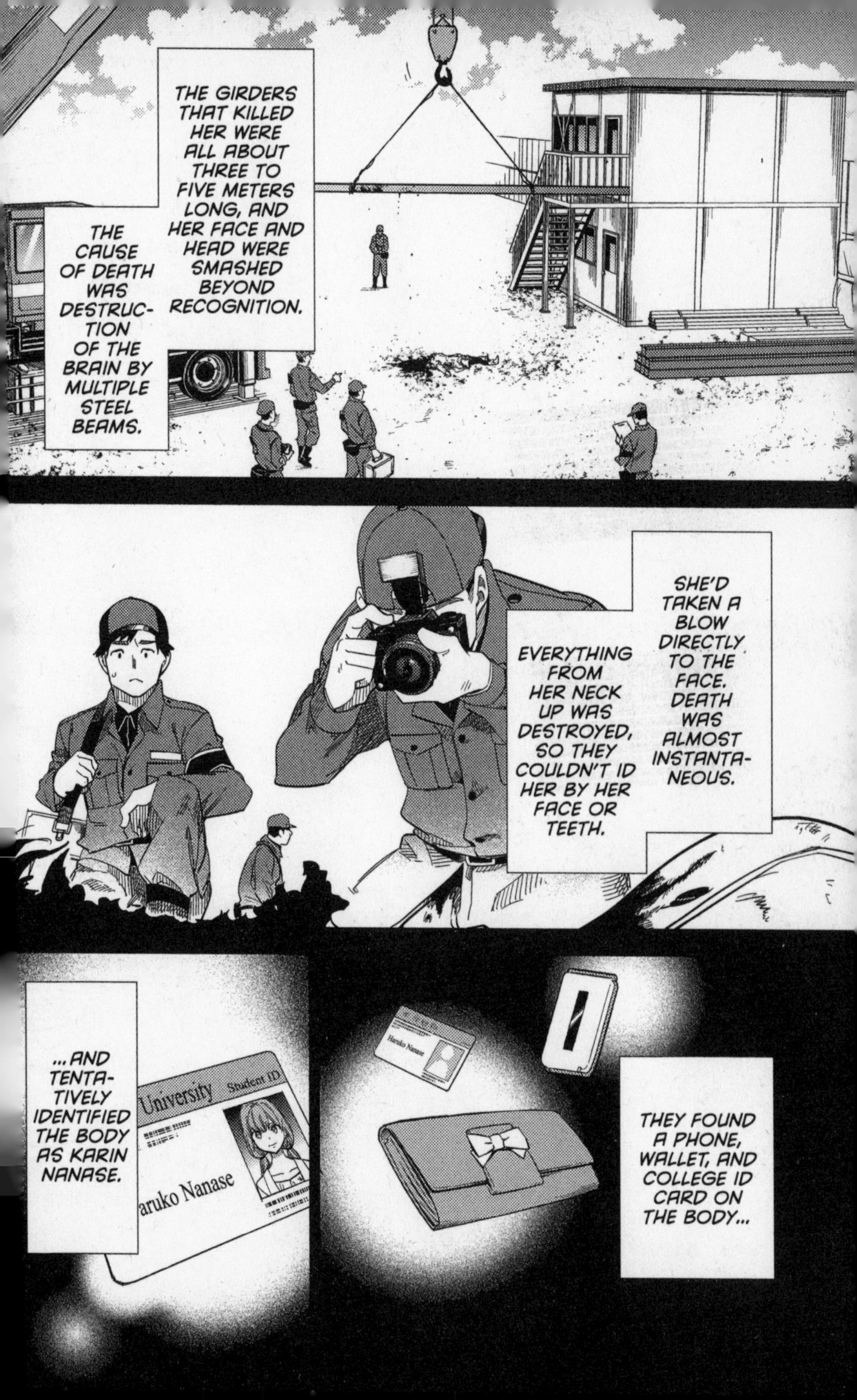
THE GIRDERS THAT KILLED HER WERE ALL ABOUT THREE TO FIVE METERS LONG, AND HER FACE AND HEAD WERE SMASHED BEYOND RECOGNITION.
THE CAUSE OF DEATH WAS DESTRUCTION OF THE BRAIN BY MULTIPLE STEEL BEAMS.
SHE'D TAKEN A BLOW DIRECTLY TO THE FACE. DEATH WAS ALMOST INSTANTANEOUS.
EVERYTHING FROM HER NECK UP WAS DESTROYED, SO THEY COULDN'T ID HER BY HER FACE OR TEETH.
Haruko Nanase
THEY FOUND A PHONE, WALLET, AND COLLEGE ID CARD ON THE BODY...
...AND TENTATIVELY IDENTIFIED THE BODY AS KARIN NANASE.
University
Student ID
aruko Nanase

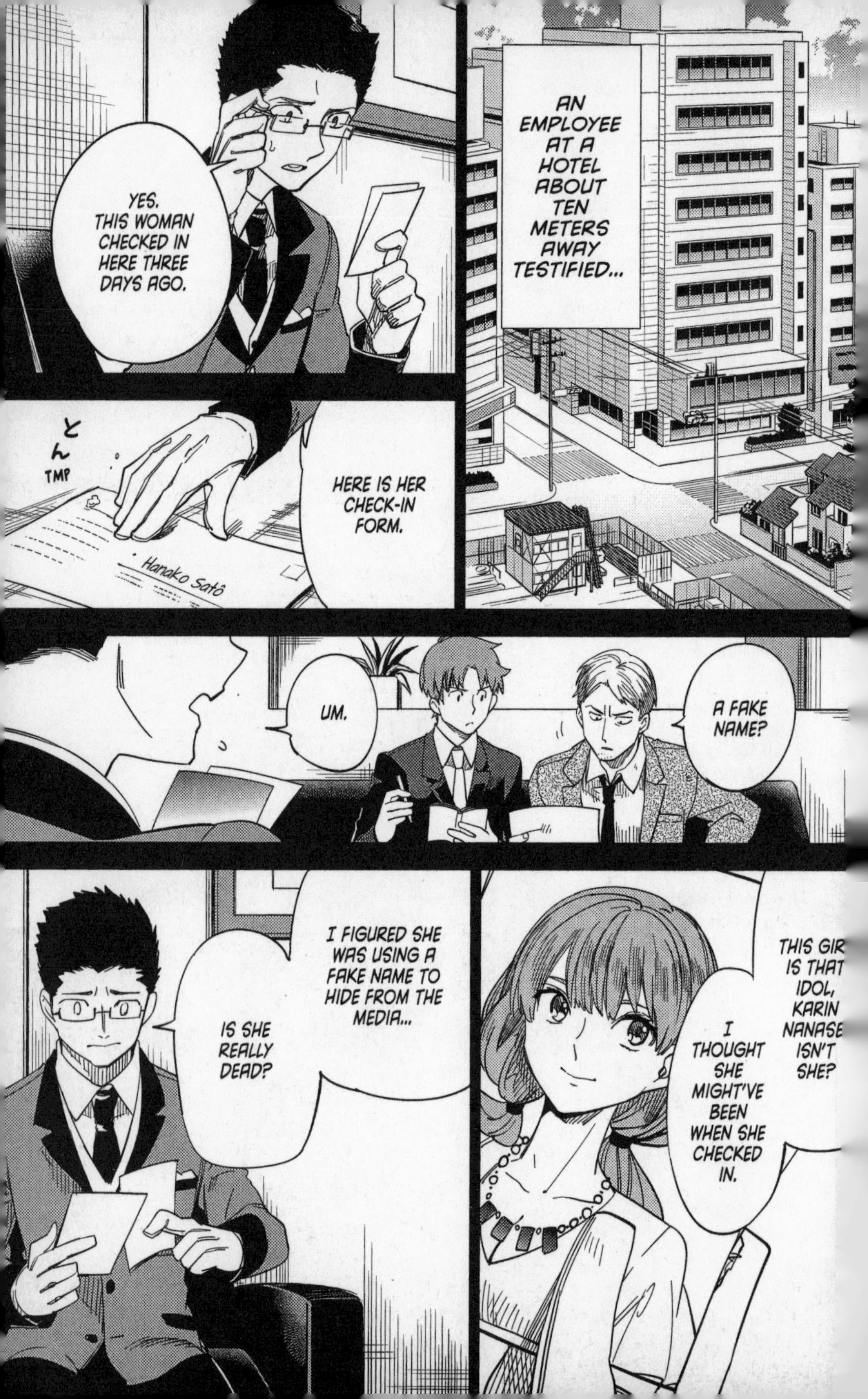
AN EMPLOYEE AT A HOTEL ABOUT TEN METERS AWAY TESTIFIED...
YES. THIS WOMAN CHECKED IN HERE THREE DAYS AGO.
とん TMP
HERE IS HER CHECK-IN FORM.
Hanako Satô
A FAKE NAME?
UM.
THIS GIRL IS THAT IDOL, KARIN NANASE ISN'T SHE?
I THOUGHT SHE MIGHT'VE BEEN WHEN SHE CHECKED IN.
I FIGURED SHE WAS USING A FAKE NAME TO HIDE FROM THE MEDIA...
IS SHE REALLY DEAD?

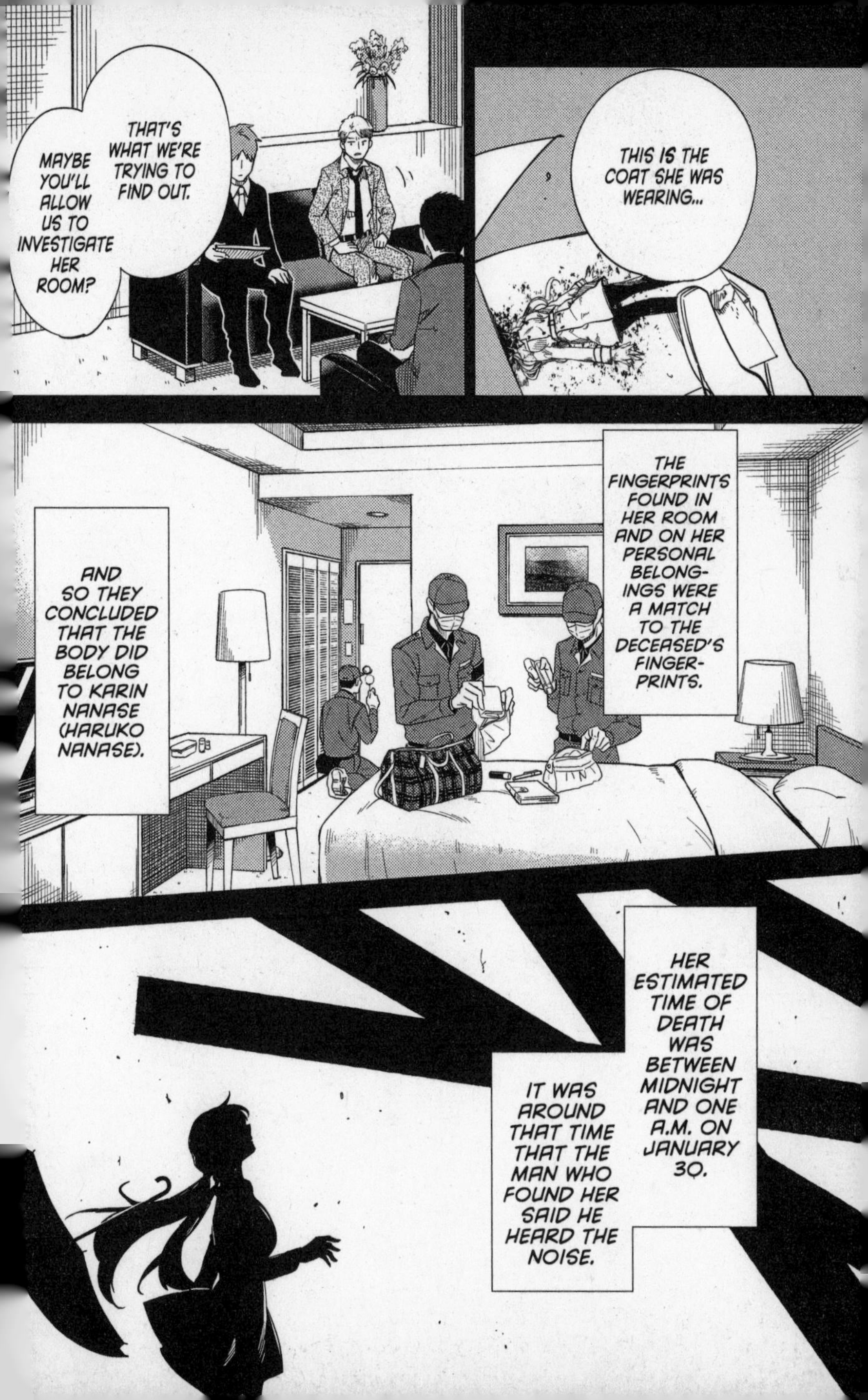
THIS IS THE COAT SHE WAS WEARING...
THAT'S WHAT WE'RE TRYING TO FIND OUT.
MAYBE YOU'LL ALLOW US TO INVESTIGATE HER ROOM?
THE FINGERPRINTS FOUND IN HER ROOM AND ON HER PERSONAL BELONG-INGS WERE A MATCH TO THE DECEASED'S FINGER-PRINTS.
AND SO THEY CONCLUDED THAT THE BODY DID BELONG TO KARIN NANASE (HARUKO NANASE).
HER ESTIMATED TIME OF DEATH WAS BETWEEN MIDNIGHT AND ONE A.M. ON JANUARY 30.
IT WAS AROUND THAT TIME THAT THE MAN WHO FOUND HER SAID HE HEARD THE NOISE.

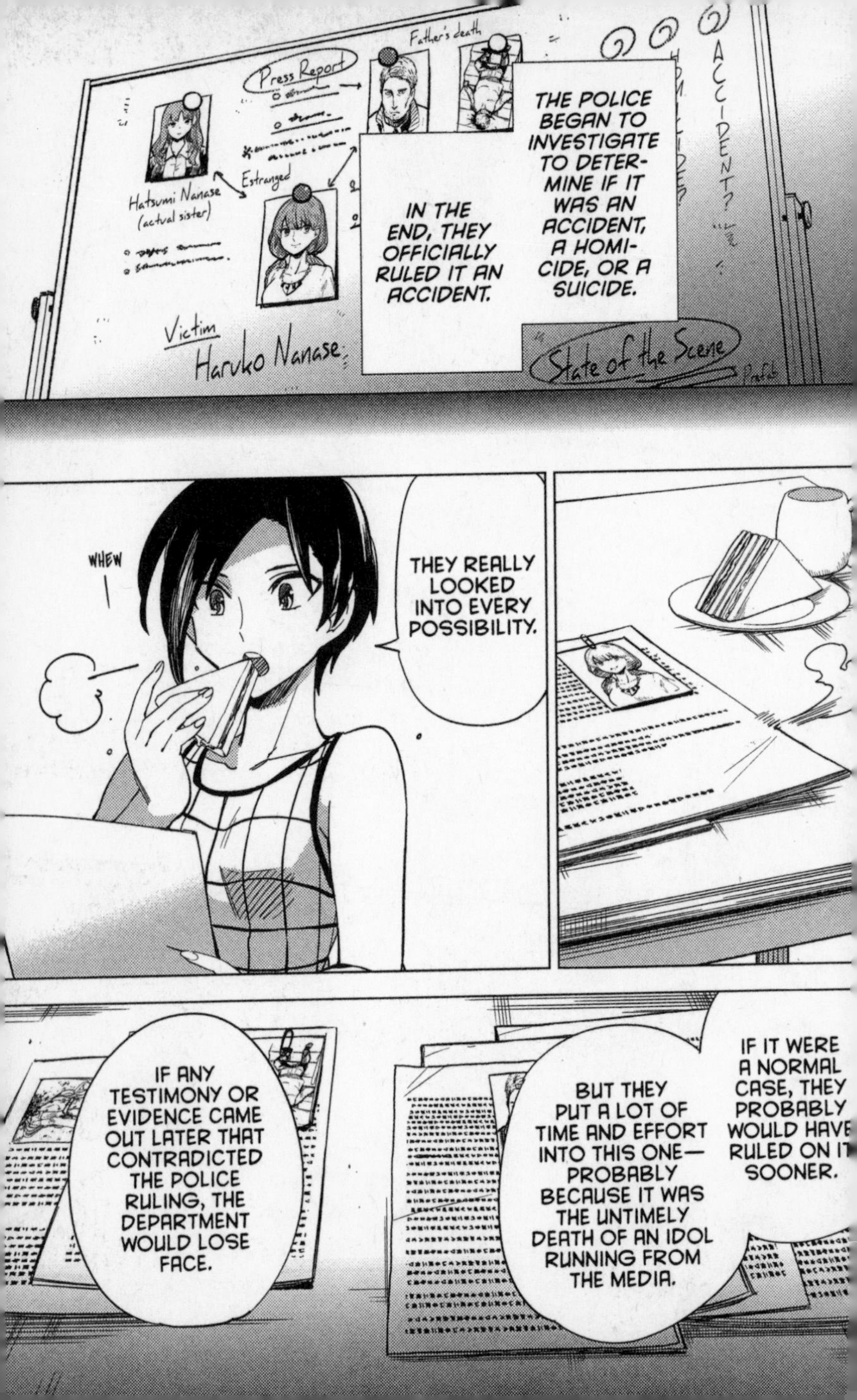
Father's death
Press Report
Hatsumi Nanase (actual sister)
Estranged
Victim
Haruko Nanase
State of the Scene
ACCIDENT?
THE POLICE BEGAN TO INVESTIGATE TO DETERMINE IF IT WAS AN ACCIDENT, A HOMICIDE, OR A SUICIDE.
IN THE END, THEY OFFICIALLY RULED IT AN ACCIDENT.
THEY REALLY LOOKED INTO EVERY POSSIBILITY.
WHEW
IF IT WERE A NORMAL CASE, THEY PROBABLY WOULD HAVE RULED ON IT SOONER.
BUT THEY PUT A LOT OF TIME AND EFFORT INTO THIS ONE—PROBABLY BECAUSE IT WAS THE UNTIMELY DEATH OF AN IDOL RUNNING FROM THE MEDIA.
IF ANY TESTIMONY OR EVIDENCE CAME OUT LATER THAT CONTRADICTED THE POLICE RULING, THE DEPARTMENT WOULD LOSE FACE.

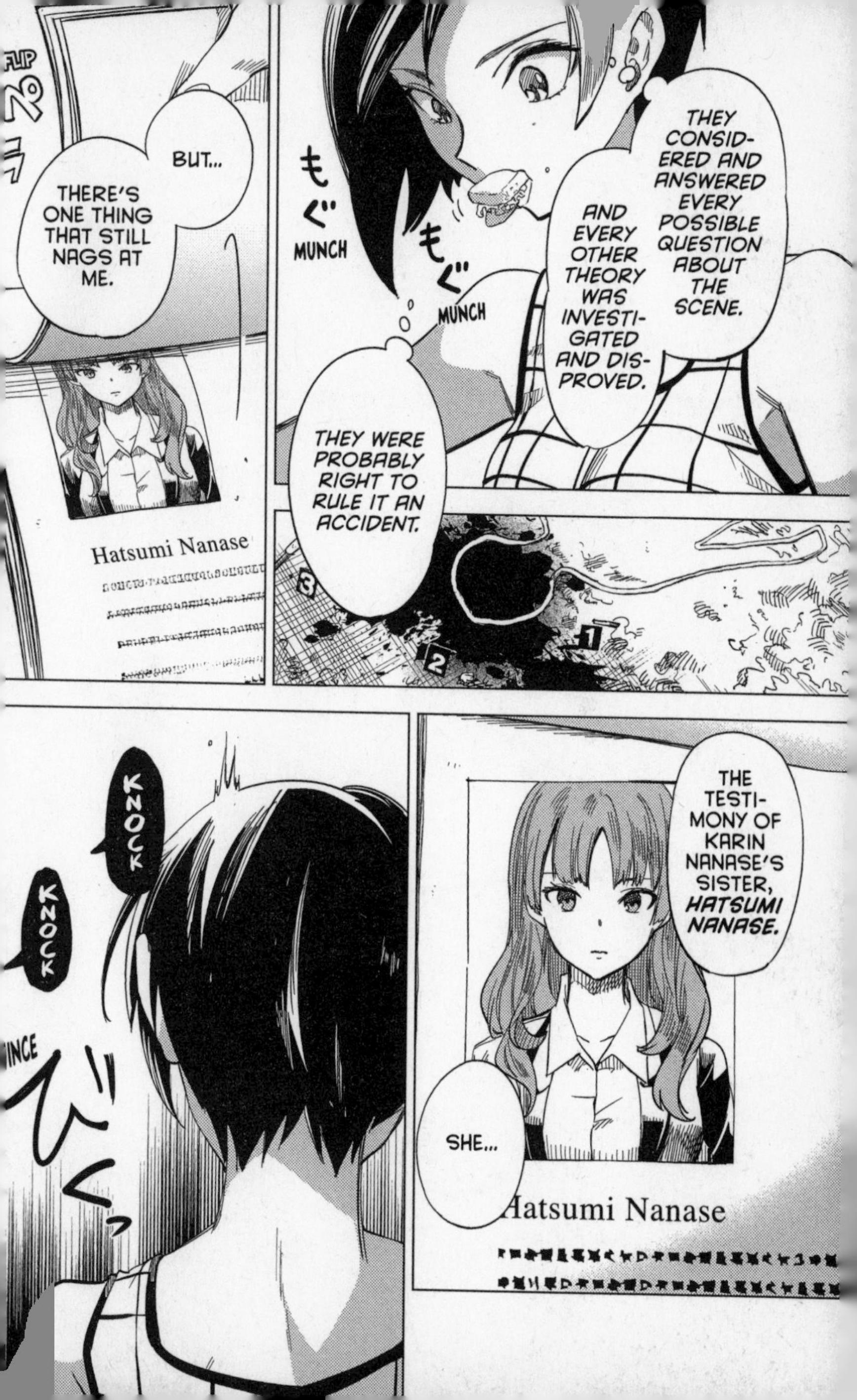
THEY CONSID-ERED AND ANSWERED EVERY POSSIBLE QUESTION ABOUT THE SCENE.
AND EVERY OTHER THEORY WAS INVESTI-GATED AND DIS-PROVED.
もぐ MUNCH
もぐ MUNCH
THEY WERE PROBABLY RIGHT TO RULE IT AN ACCIDENT.
FLIP
BUT...
THERE'S ONE THING THAT STILL NAGS AT ME.
Hatsumi Nanase
THE TESTI-MONY OF KARIN NANASE'S SISTER, HATSUMI NANASE.
SHE...
Hatsumi Nanase
KNOCK
KNOCK

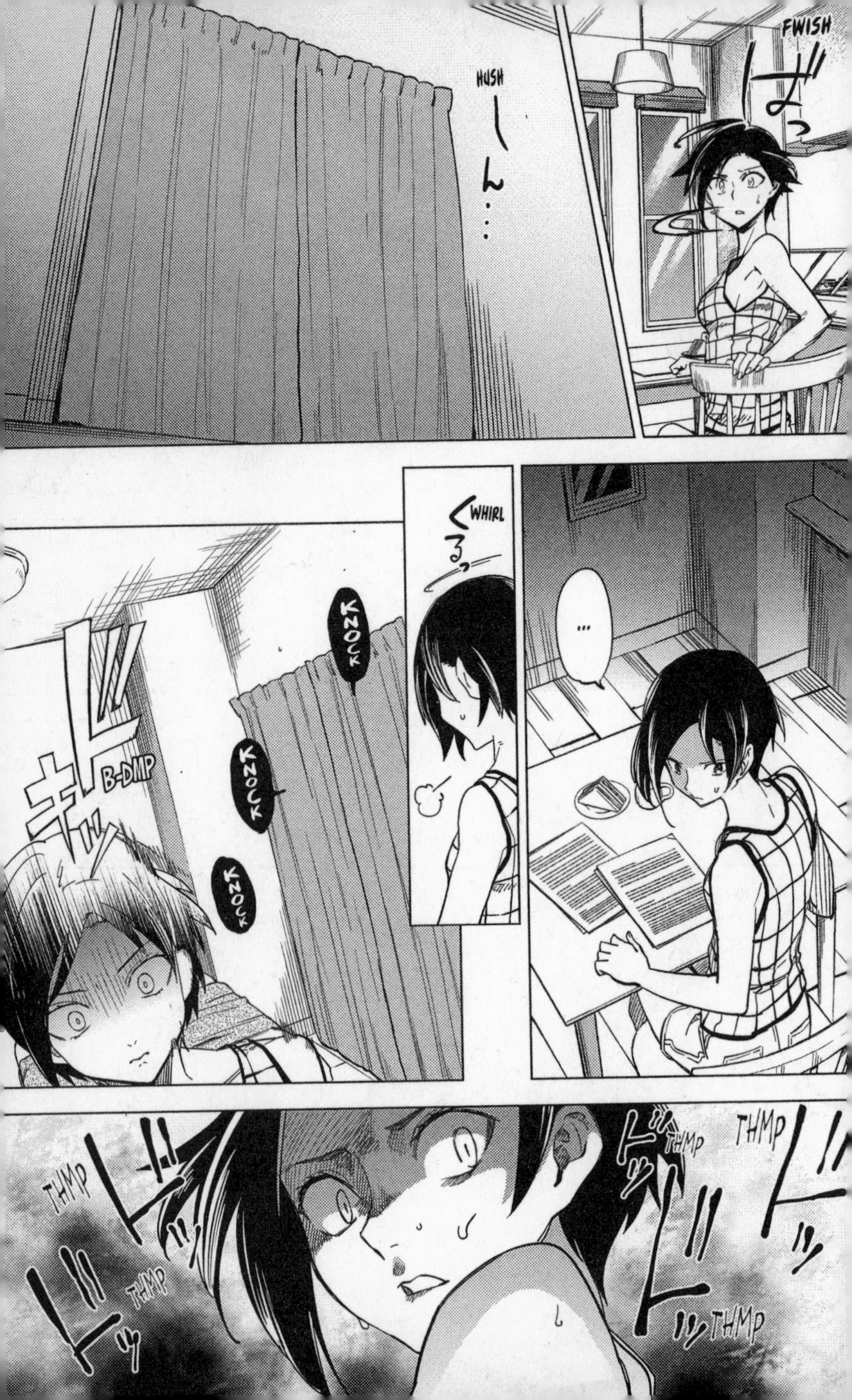
FWISH
ばっ
HUSH
しん…
…
WHIRL
くるっ
KNOCK
KNOCK
KNOCK
B-DMP
ドキッ
THMP
THMP
THMP
THMP
THMP

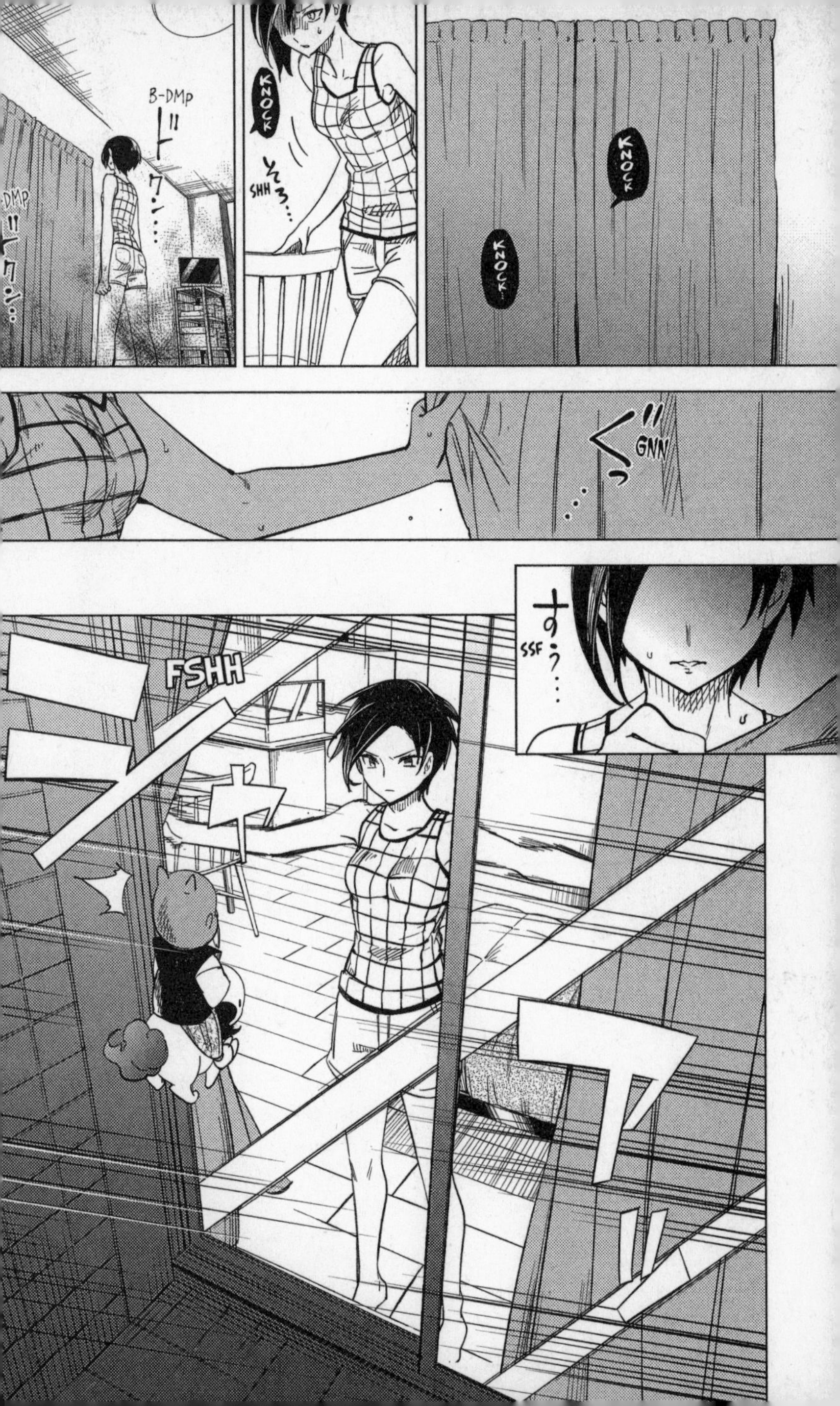

KNOCK
KNOCK...
KNOCK
SHH
そろ…
B-DMP
ドッ
DMP
ドク…
GNN
ぐっ…
SSF
すぅ…
FSHH

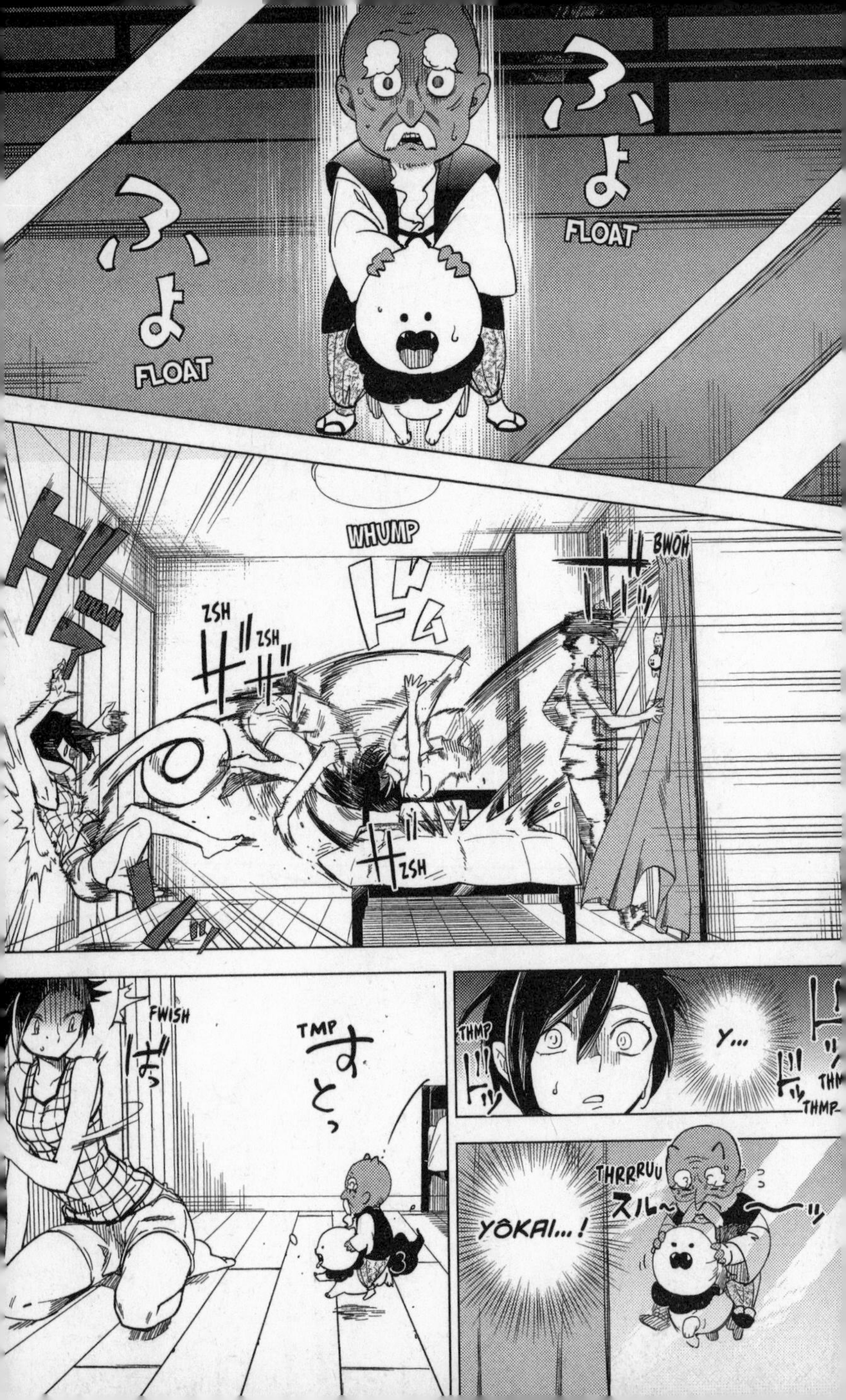

ふよ
FLOAT
ふよ
FLOAT
ザッ
BWOH
ドム
WHUMP
ザッ
ZSH
ザッ
ZSH
ザッ
ZSH
ダン
Y...
ドッ
THMP
ドッ
THMP
THMP
スル～ッ
THRRRUU
YÔKAI...!
ばっ
FWISH
すとっ
TMP

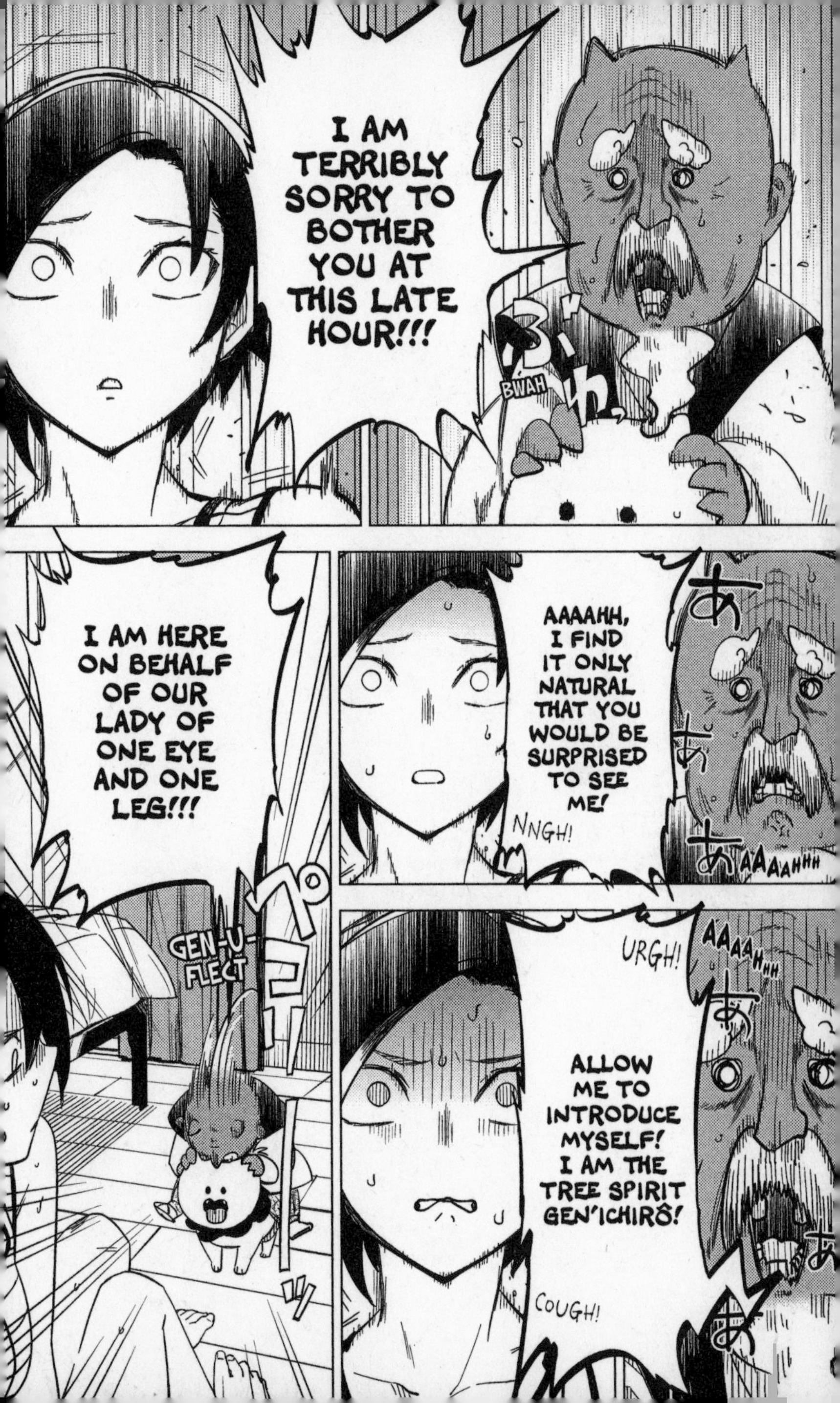
I AM TERRIBLY SORRY TO BOTHER YOU AT THIS LATE HOUR!!!
ぶわっ
BWAH
AAAAHH, I FIND IT ONLY NATURAL THAT YOU WOULD BE SURPRISED TO SEE ME!
NNGH!
あ あ あ AAAAHHH
URGH!
AAAAHHH
ALLOW ME TO INTRODUCE MYSELF! I AM THE TREE SPIRIT GEN'ICHIRÔ!
COUGH!
I AM HERE ON BEHALF OF OUR LADY OF ONE EYE AND ONE LEG!!!
ペコ
GEN-U-FLECT

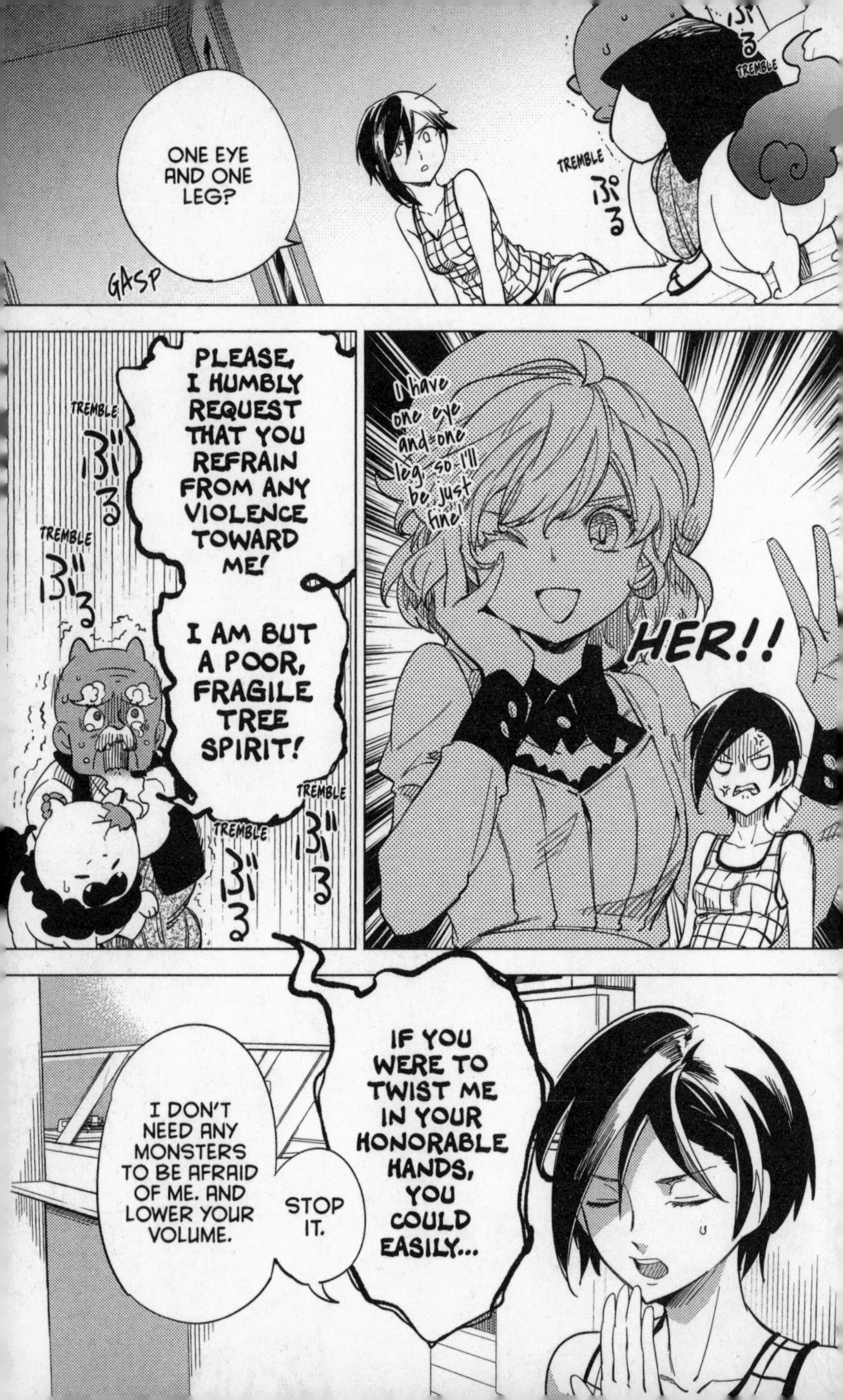

ぷる
TREMBLE
TREMBLE
ぷる
ONE EYE AND ONE LEG?
GASP
I have one eye and one leg, so I'll be just fine!
HER!!
PLEASE, I HUMBLY REQUEST THAT YOU REFRAIN FROM ANY VIOLENCE TOWARD ME!
I AM BUT A POOR, FRAGILE TREE SPIRIT!
TREMBLE
ぶる
TREMBLE
ぶる
TREMBLE
ぶる
TREMBLE
ぶる
IF YOU WERE TO TWIST ME IN YOUR HONORABLE HANDS, YOU COULD EASILY...
STOP IT.
I DON'T NEED ANY MONSTERS TO BE AFRAID OF ME. AND LOWER YOUR VOLUME.

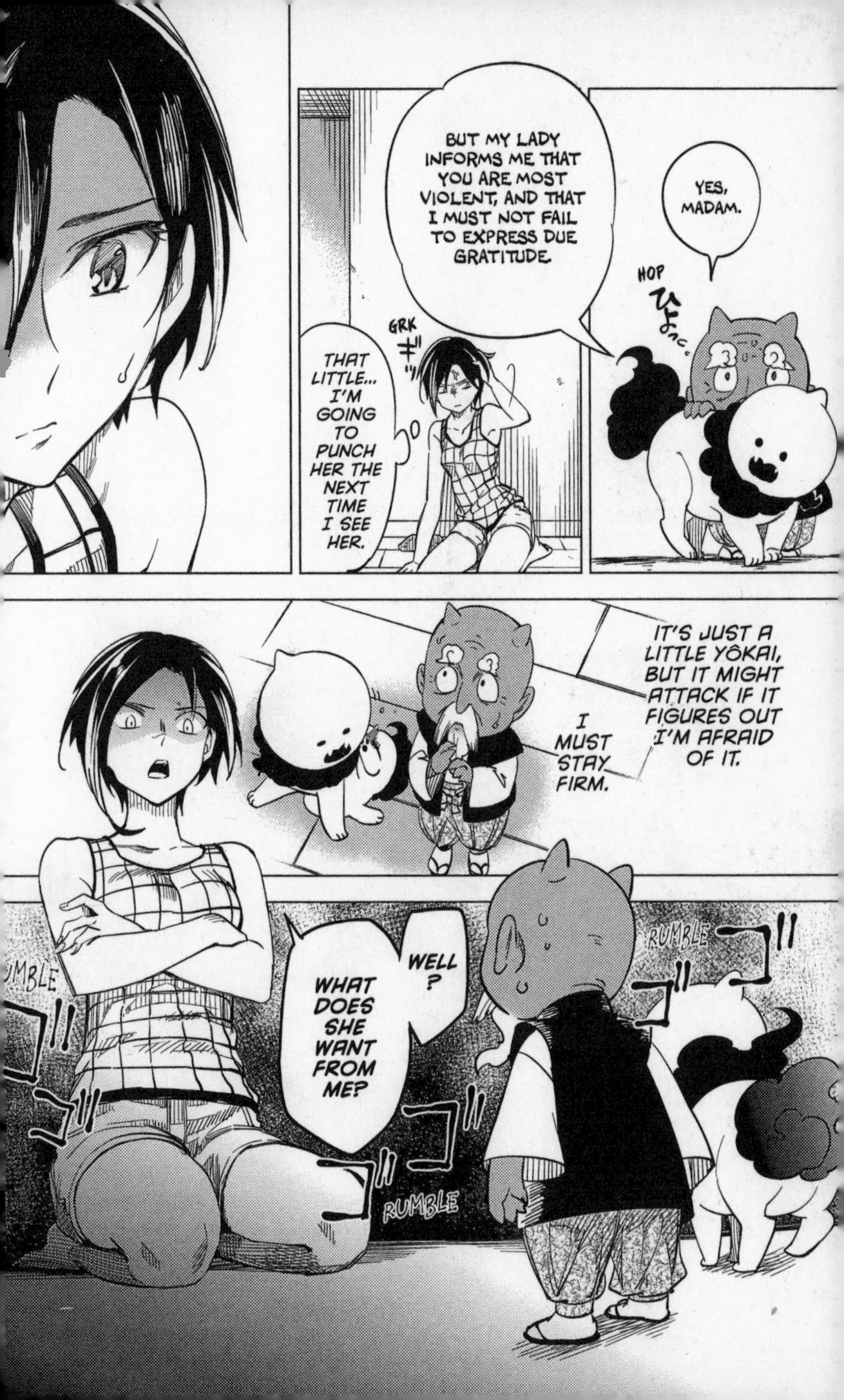
YES, MADAM.
HOP
BUT MY LADY INFORMS ME THAT YOU ARE MOST VIOLENT, AND THAT I MUST NOT FAIL TO EXPRESS DUE GRATITUDE.
GRK
THAT LITTLE... I'M GOING TO PUNCH HER THE NEXT TIME I SEE HER.
IT'S JUST A LITTLE YÔKAI, BUT IT MIGHT ATTACK IF IT FIGURES OUT I'M AFRAID OF IT.
I MUST STAY FIRM.
RUMBLE
WELL?
WHAT DOES SHE WANT FROM ME?
RUMBLE

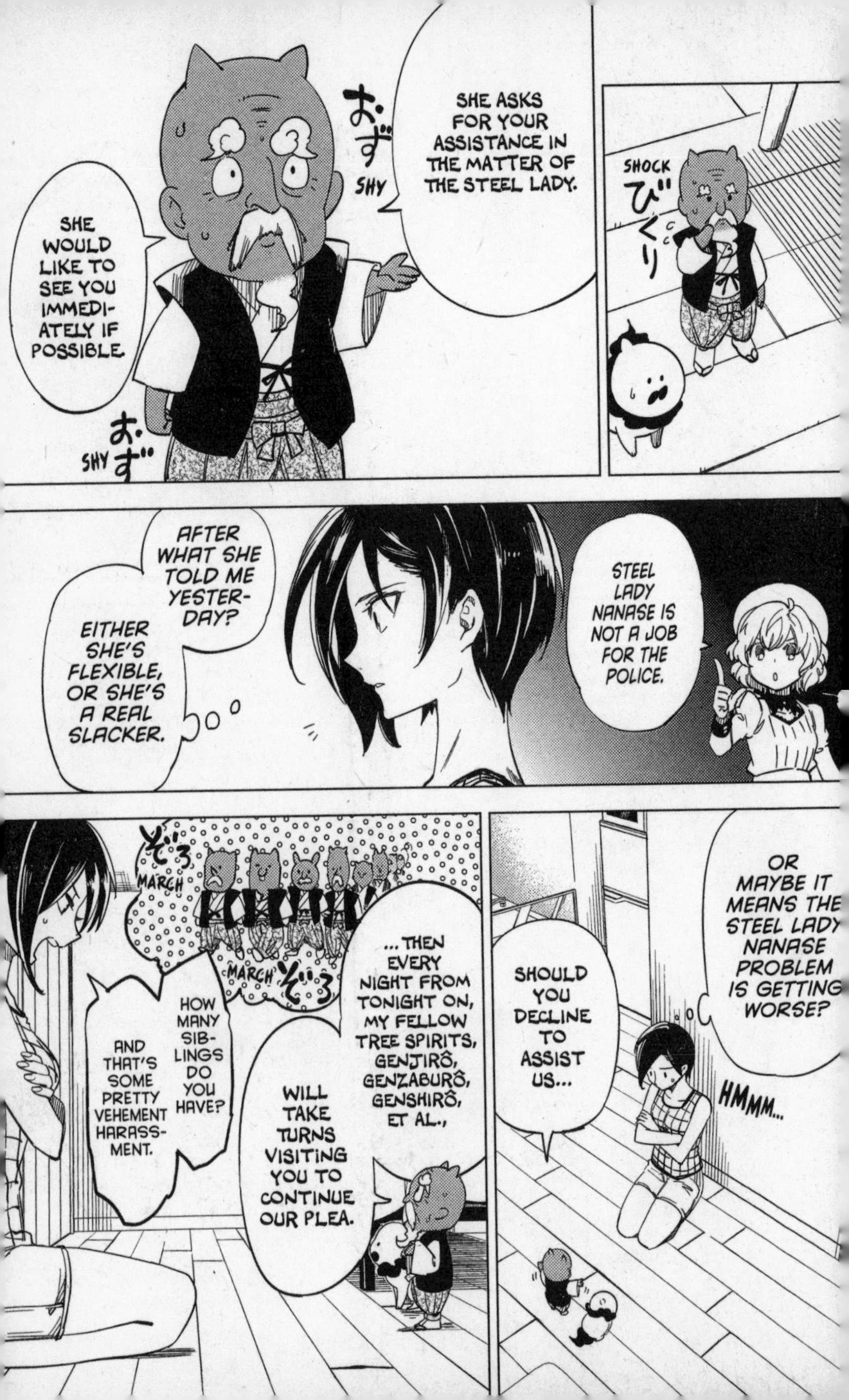

SHOCK
びっくり
SHE ASKS FOR YOUR ASSISTANCE IN THE MATTER OF THE STEEL LADY.
おず
SHY
SHE WOULD LIKE TO SEE YOU IMMEDIATELY IF POSSIBLE.
おず
SHY
STEEL LADY NANASE IS NOT A JOB FOR THE POLICE.
AFTER WHAT SHE TOLD ME YESTERDAY?
EITHER SHE'S FLEXIBLE, OR SHE'S A REAL SLACKER.
OR MAYBE IT MEANS THE STEEL LADY NANASE PROBLEM IS GETTING WORSE?
HMMM...
SHOULD YOU DECLINE TO ASSIST US...
...THEN EVERY NIGHT FROM TONIGHT ON, MY FELLOW TREE SPIRITS, GENJIRÔ, GENZABURÔ, GENSHIRÔ, ET AL.,
WILL TAKE TURNS VISITING YOU TO CONTINUE OUR PLEA.
ぞろ
MARCH
ぞろ
MARCH
HOW MANY SIBLINGS DO YOU HAVE?
AND THAT'S SOME PRETTY VEHEMENT HARASSMENT.

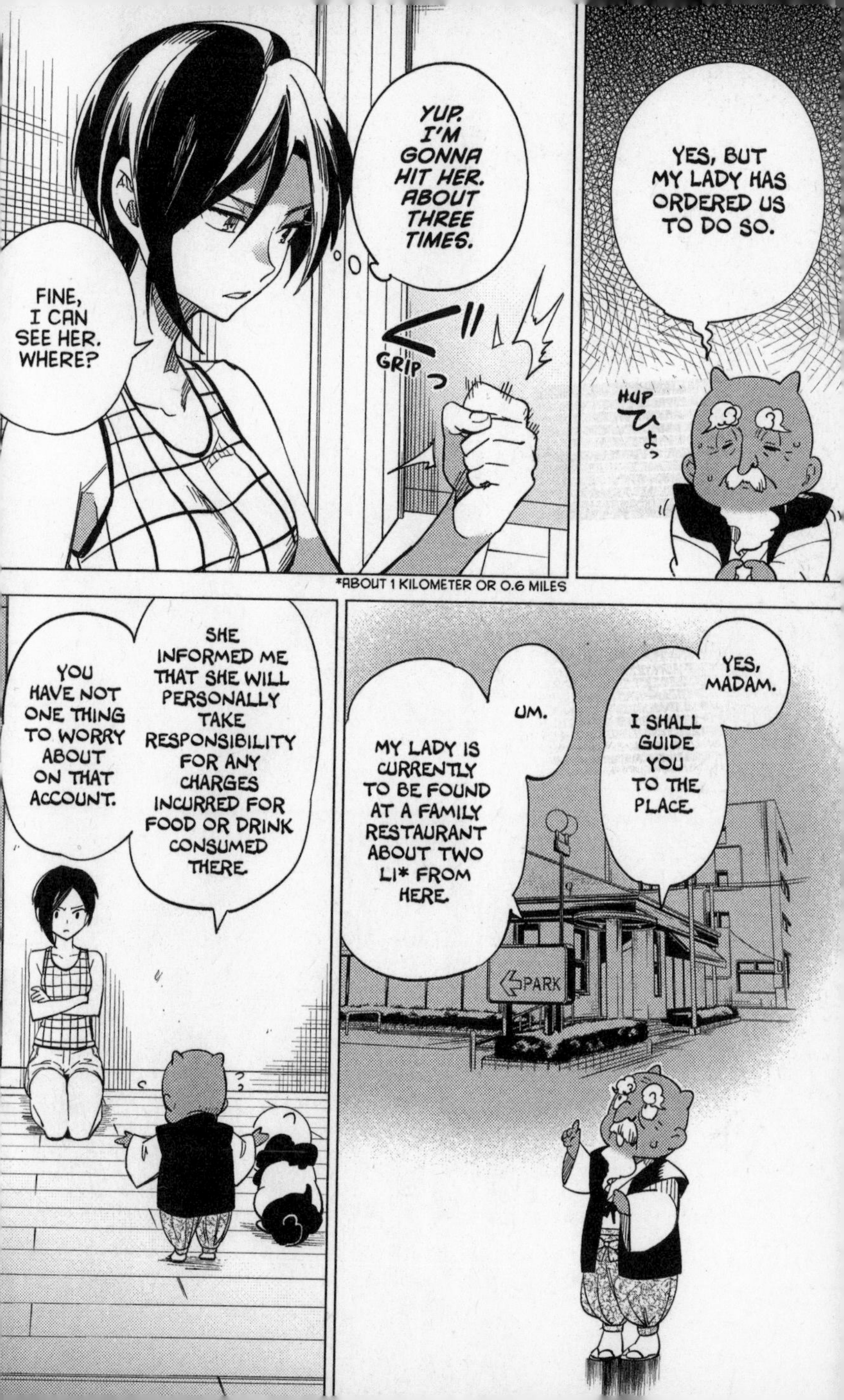
YES, BUT MY LADY HAS ORDERED US TO DO SO.
HUP
ひょっ
YUP. I'M GONNA HIT HER. ABOUT THREE TIMES.
GRIP
FINE, I CAN SEE HER. WHERE?
YES, MADAM.
I SHALL GUIDE YOU TO THE PLACE.
UM.
MY LADY IS CURRENTLY TO BE FOUND AT A FAMILY RESTAURANT ABOUT TWO LI* FROM HERE.
PARK
SHE INFORMED ME THAT SHE WILL PERSONALLY TAKE RESPONSIBILITY FOR ANY CHARGES INCURRED FOR FOOD OR DRINK CONSUMED THERE.
YOU HAVE NOT ONE THING TO WORRY ABOUT ON THAT ACCOUNT.

*ABOUT 1 KILOMETER OR 0.6 MILES

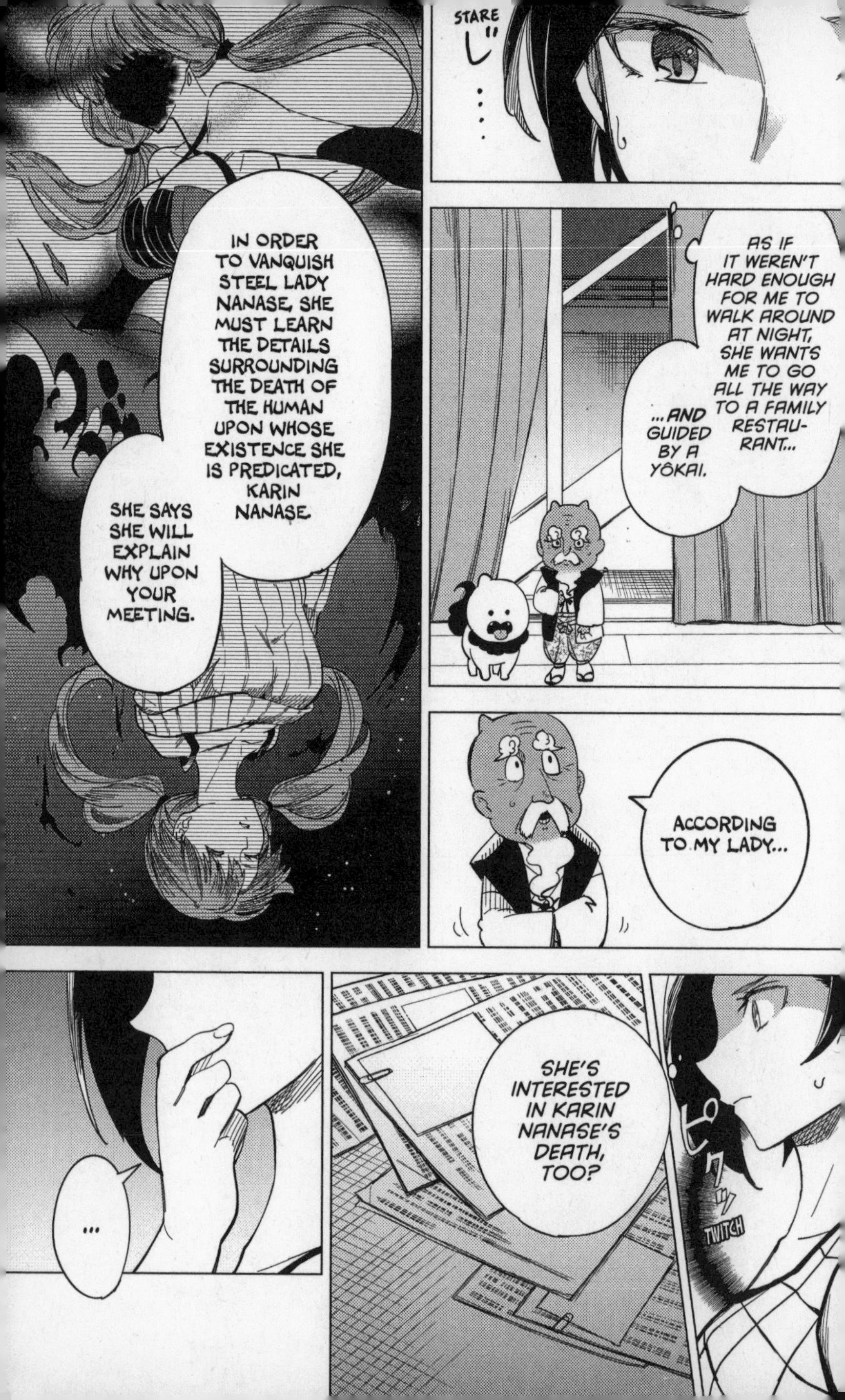
STARE
....
AS IF IT WEREN'T HARD ENOUGH FOR ME TO WALK AROUND AT NIGHT, SHE WANTS ME TO GO ALL THE WAY TO A FAMILY RESTAU-RANT...
...AND GUIDED BY A YÔKAI.
ACCORDING TO MY LADY...
IN ORDER TO VANQUISH STEEL LADY NANASE, SHE MUST LEARN THE DETAILS SURROUNDING THE DEATH OF THE HUMAN UPON WHOSE EXISTENCE SHE IS PREDICATED, KARIN NANASE.
SHE SAYS SHE WILL EXPLAIN WHY UPON YOUR MEETING.
TWITCH
SHE'S INTERESTED IN KARIN NANASE'S DEATH, TOO?
...

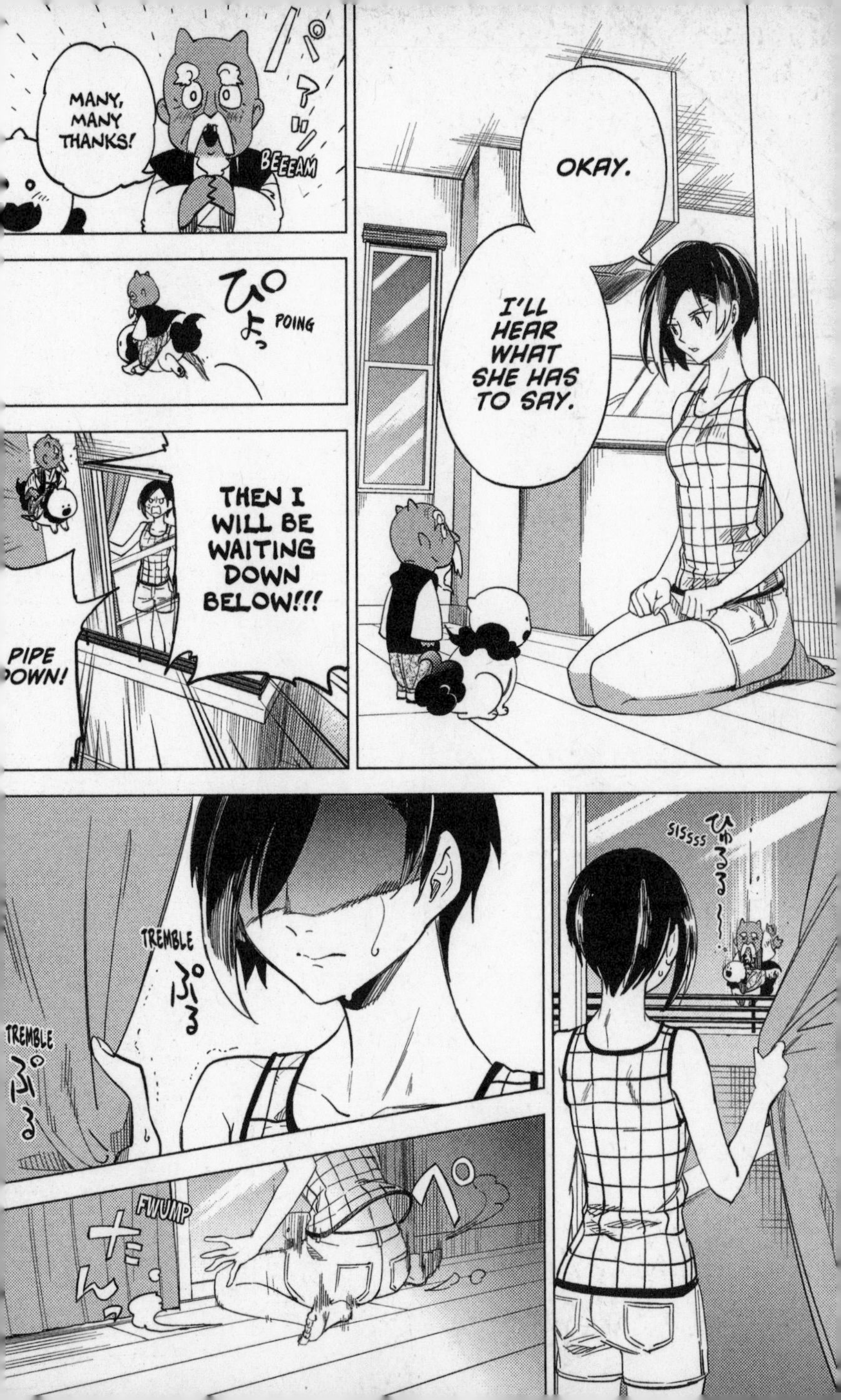
OKAY.
I'LL HEAR WHAT SHE HAS TO SAY.
MANY, MANY THANKS!
BEEEAM
ぴょっ
POING
THEN I WILL BE WAITING DOWN BELOW!!!
PIPE DOWN!
ひゅるる~
SISSSS
TREMBLE
ぷる
TREMBLE
ぷる
ぺ
FWUMP
たんっ

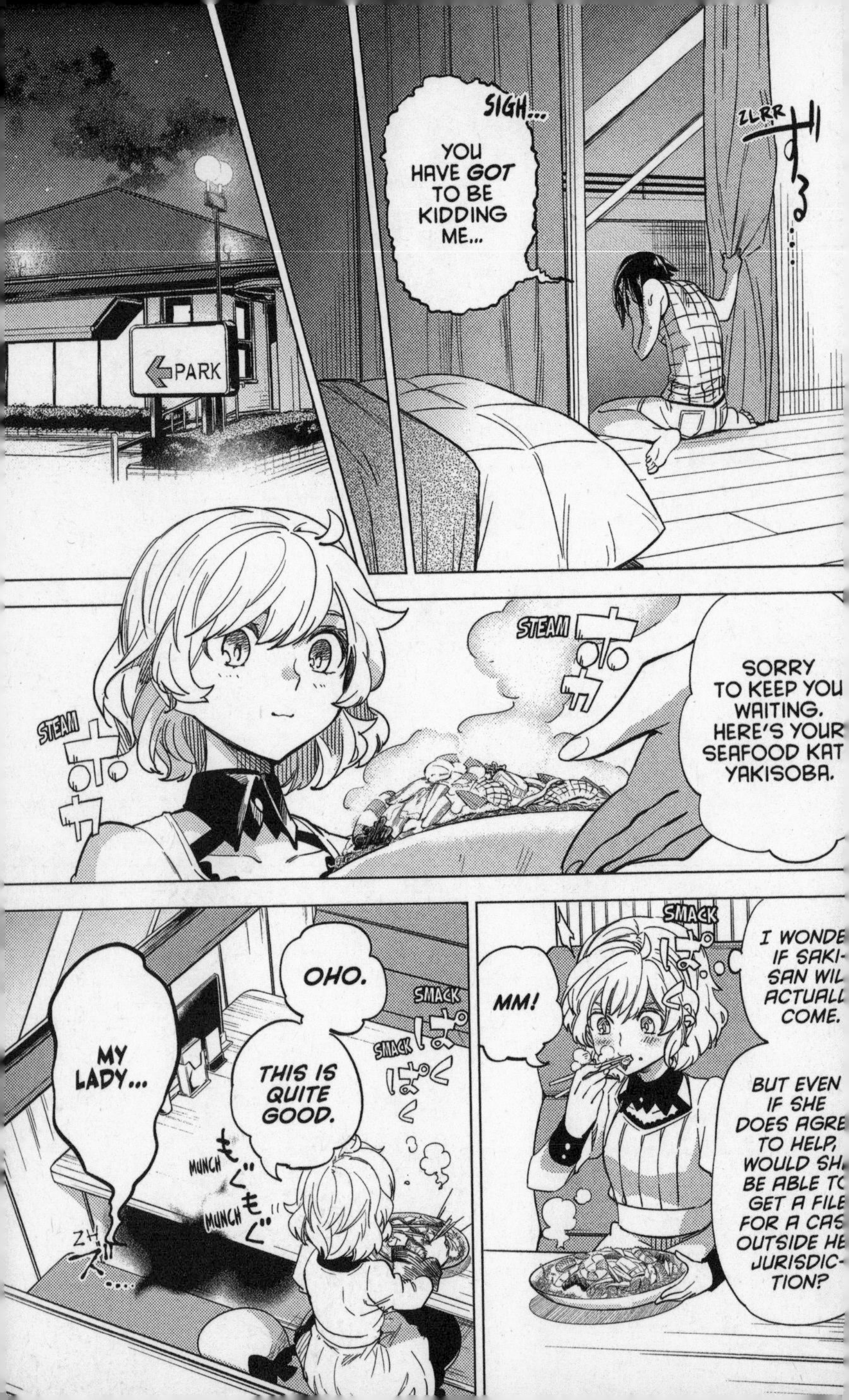
SIGH...
YOU HAVE GOT TO BE KIDDING ME...
ZLRR
PARK
SORRY TO KEEP YOU WAITING. HERE'S YOUR SEAFOOD KAT YAKISOBA.
STEAM
STEAM
I WONDE IF SAKI-SAN WIL ACTUALL COME.
BUT EVEN IF SHE DOES AGRE TO HELP, WOULD SH BE ABLE TO GET A FILE FOR A CAS OUTSIDE HE JURISDIC-TION?
SMACK
MM!
OHO.
SMACK
SMACK
THIS IS QUITE GOOD.
MUNCH
MUNCH
MY LADY...
ZH

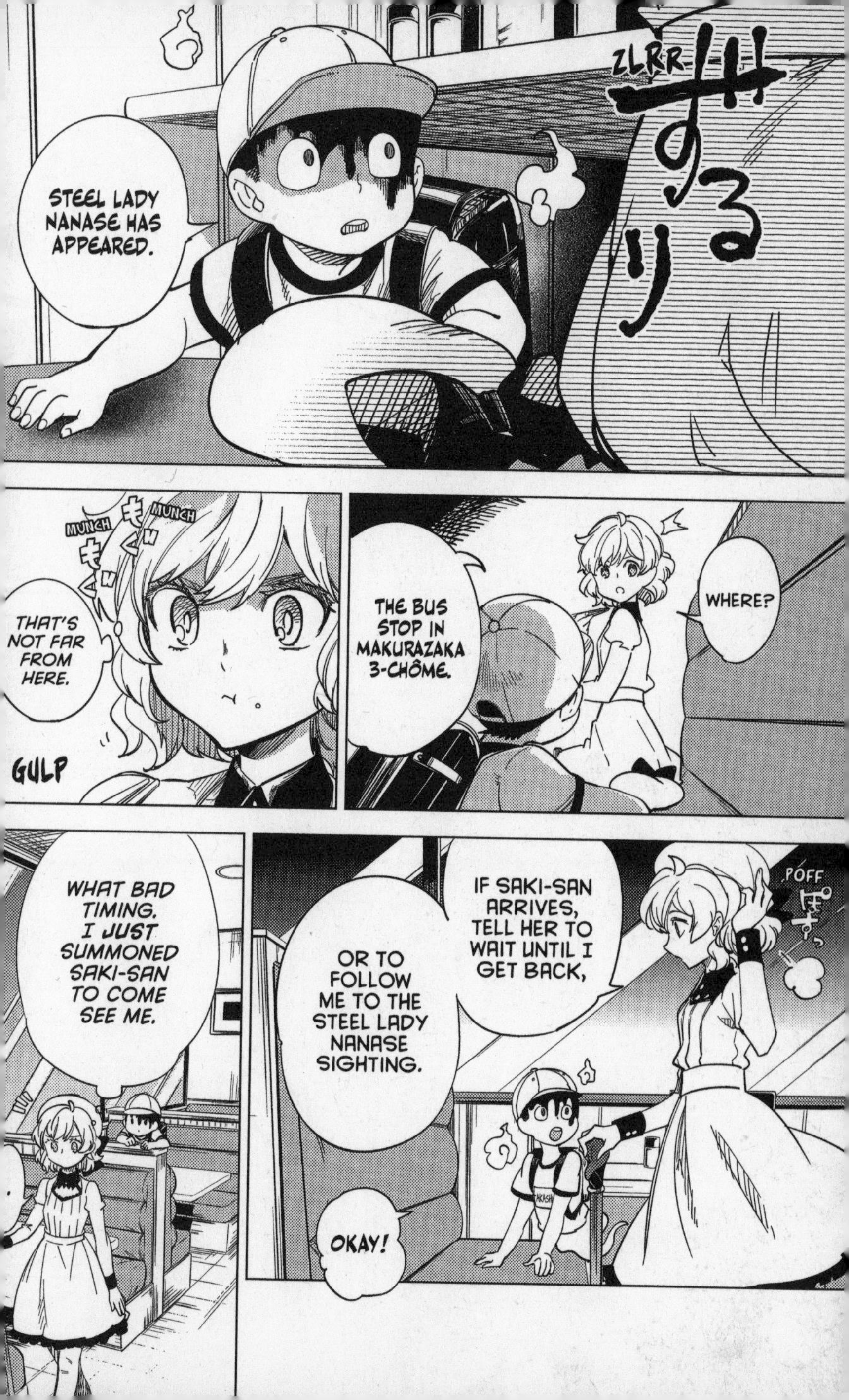
ZLRR
するり
STEEL LADY NANASE HAS APPEARED.
WHERE?
THE BUS STOP IN MAKURAZAKA 3-CHÔME.
MUNCH
MUNCH
THAT'S NOT FAR FROM HERE.
GULP
POFF
ぽすっ
IF SAKI-SAN ARRIVES, TELL HER TO WAIT UNTIL I GET BACK,
OR TO FOLLOW ME TO THE STEEL LADY NANASE SIGHTING.
OKAY!
WHAT BAD TIMING. I JUST SUMMONED SAKI-SAN TO COME SEE ME.

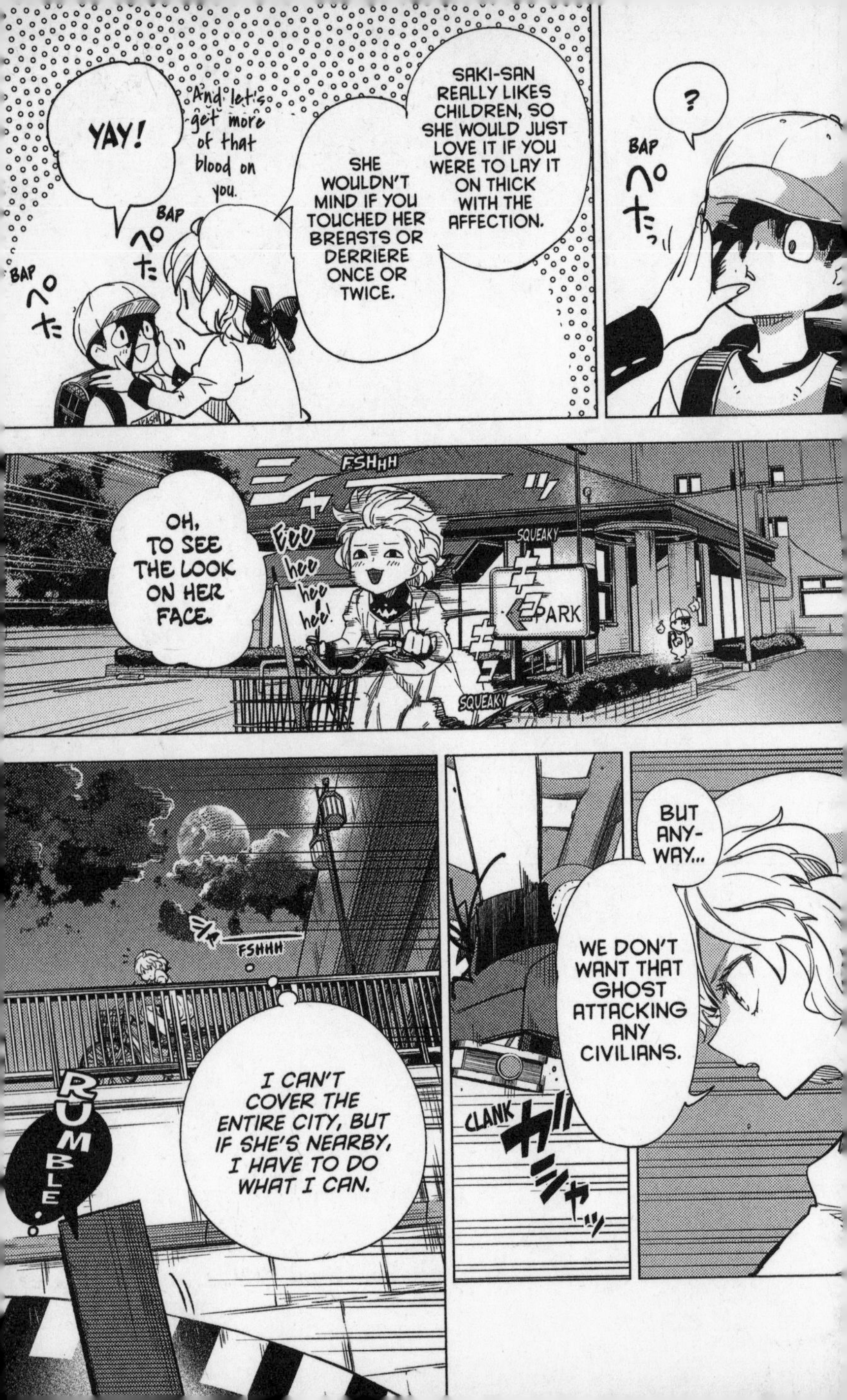
?
BAP
SAKI-SAN REALLY LIKES CHILDREN, SO SHE WOULD JUST LOVE IT IF YOU WERE TO LAY IT ON THICK WITH THE AFFECTION.
SHE WOULDN'T MIND IF YOU TOUCHED HER BREASTS OR DERRIERE ONCE OR TWICE.
And let's get more of that blood on you.
YAY!
BAP
BAP
FSHHH
OH, TO SEE THE LOOK ON HER FACE.
Hee hee hee hee!
SQUEAKY
PARK
SQUEAKY
BUT ANY-WAY...
WE DON'T WANT THAT GHOST ATTACKING ANY CIVILIANS.
CLANK
FSHHH
I CAN'T COVER THE ENTIRE CITY, BUT IF SHE'S NEARBY, I HAVE TO DO WHAT I CAN.
RUMBLE

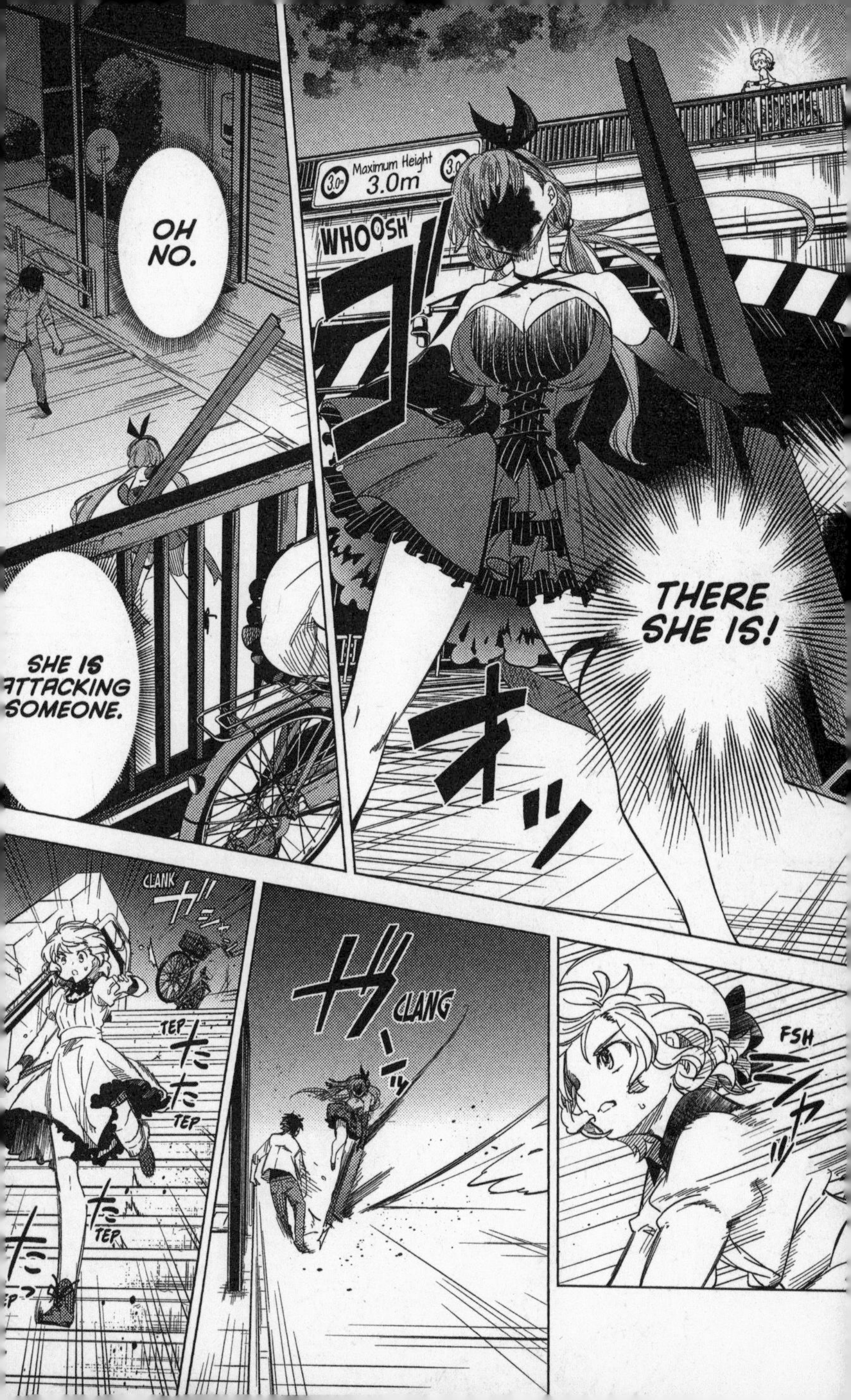
Maximum Height 3.0m
WHOOSH
THERE SHE IS!
OH NO.
SHE IS ATTACKING SOMEONE.
FSH
CLANG
CLANK
TEP
TEP
TEP

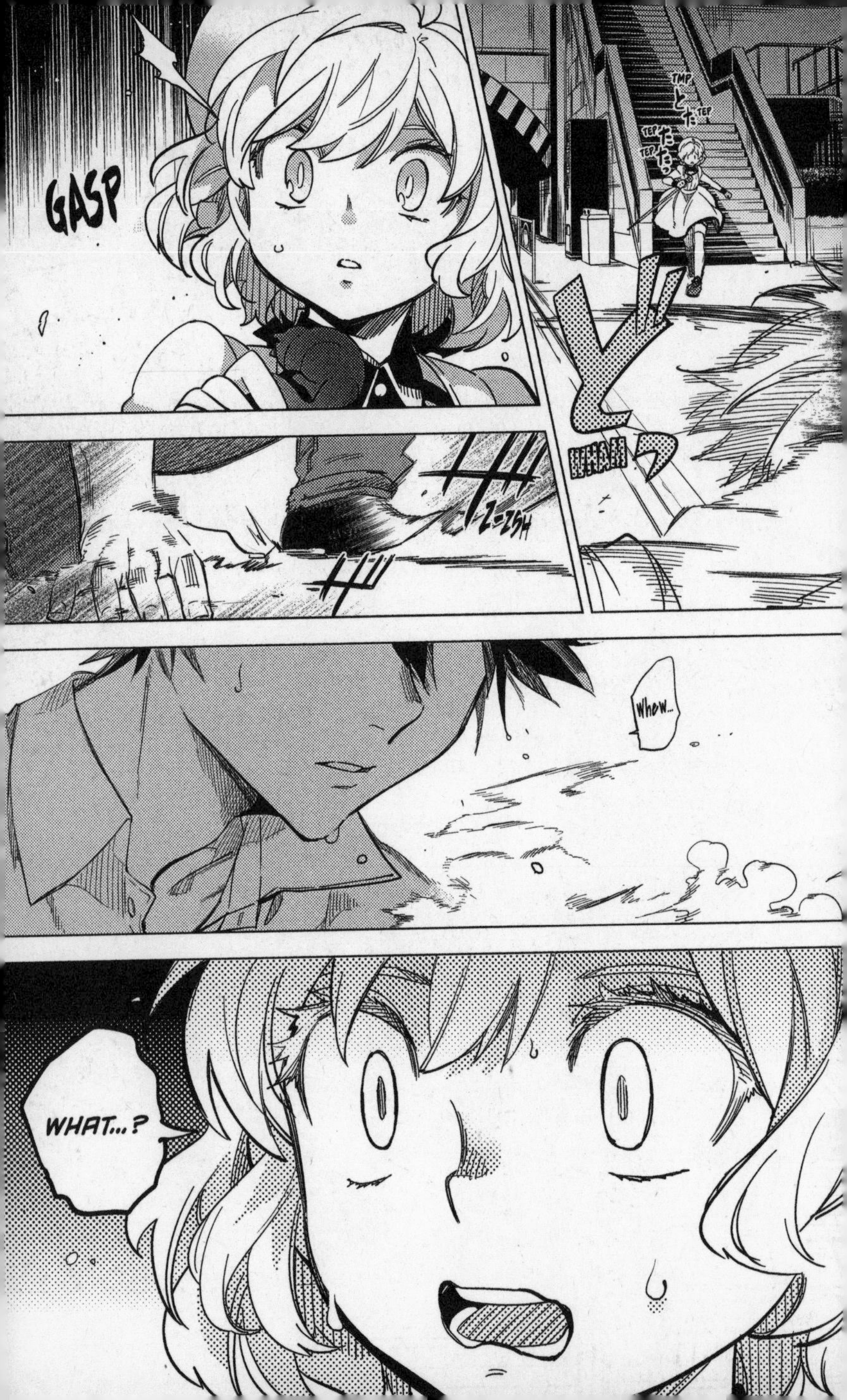
TMP
とた
TEP
TEP
たたっ
TEP
どっ
WHAM
GASP
Z-ZSH
Whew...
WHAT...?

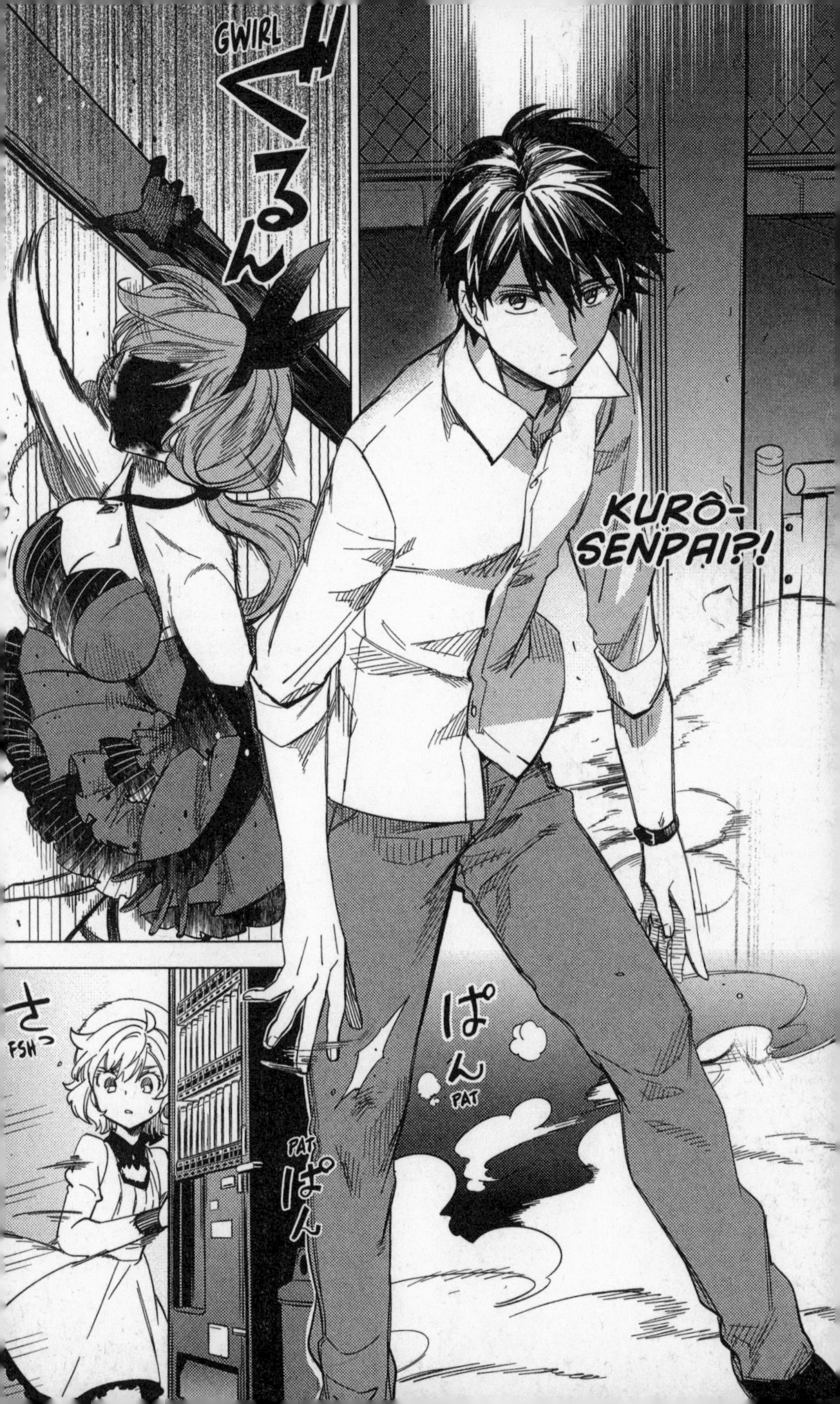
KURÔ-SENPAI?!
ぱん
PAT
PAT
ぱん
くるん
GWIRL
さっ
FSH

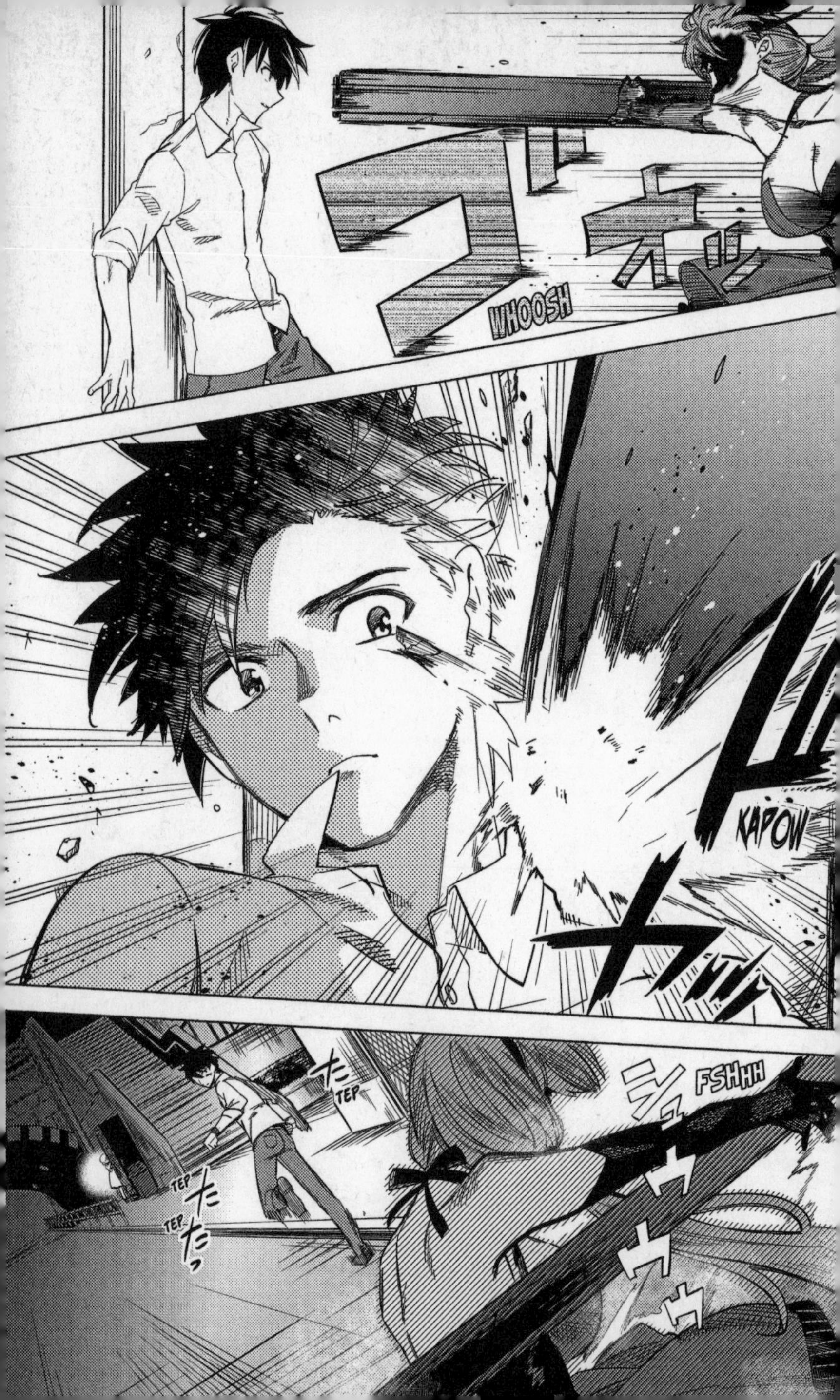
WHOOSH
KAPOW
FSHHH
た
TEP
TEP
た
TEP
たっ

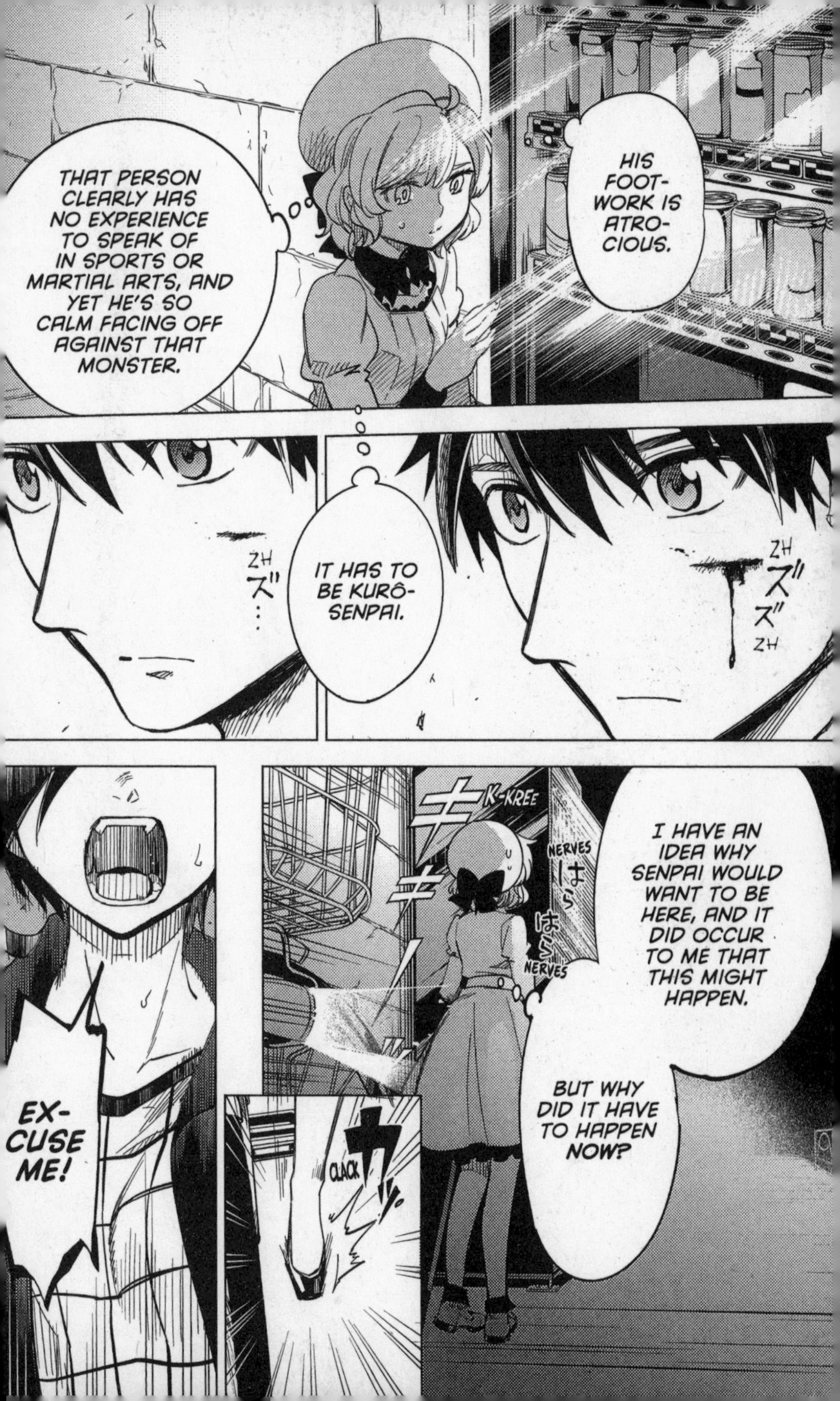

HIS FOOT-WORK IS ATRO-CIOUS.
THAT PERSON CLEARLY HAS NO EXPERIENCE TO SPEAK OF IN SPORTS OR MARTIAL ARTS, AND YET HE'S SO CALM FACING OFF AGAINST THAT MONSTER.
ZH ズズ ZH
IT HAS TO BE KURÔ-SENPAI.
ZH ズ…
K-KREE キキ
NERVES はら はら NERVES
I HAVE AN IDEA WHY SENPAI WOULD WANT TO BE HERE, AND IT DID OCCUR TO ME THAT THIS MIGHT HAPPEN.
BUT WHY DID IT HAVE TO HAPPEN NOW?
CLACK
EX-CUSE ME!

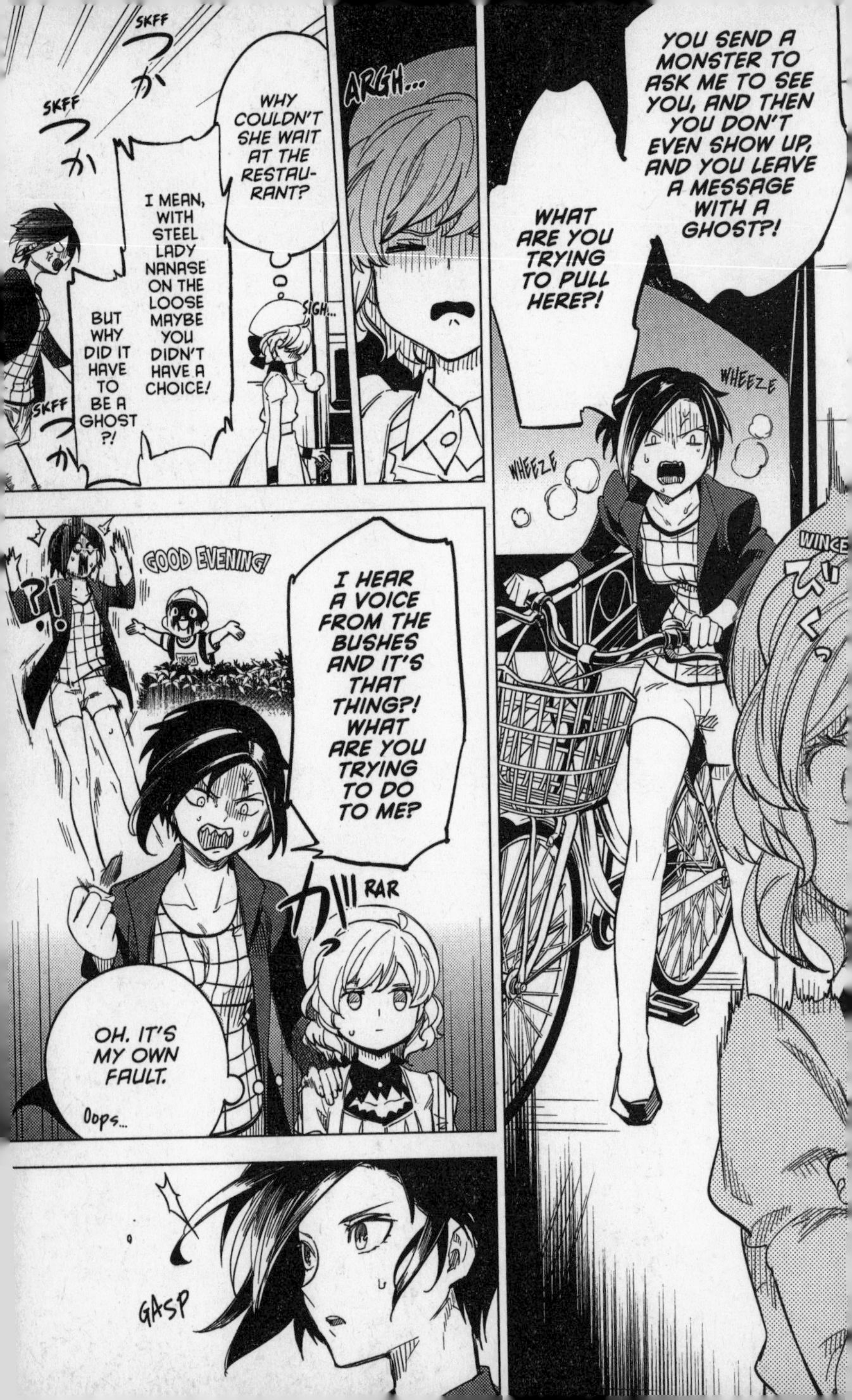
YOU SEND A MONSTER TO ASK ME TO SEE YOU, AND THEN YOU DON'T EVEN SHOW UP, AND YOU LEAVE A MESSAGE WITH A GHOST?!
WHAT ARE YOU TRYING TO PULL HERE?!
WHEEZE
WHEEZE
WINCE
ARGH...
WHY COULDN'T SHE WAIT AT THE RESTAU-RANT?
SIGH...
SKFF
つか
SKFF
つか
I MEAN, WITH STEEL LADY NANASE ON THE LOOSE MAYBE YOU DIDN'T HAVE A CHOICE!
BUT WHY DID IT HAVE TO BE A GHOST ?!
SKFF
つか
I HEAR A VOICE FROM THE BUSHES AND IT'S THAT THING?! WHAT ARE YOU TRYING TO DO TO ME?
GOOD EVENING!
?!
RAR
OH. IT'S MY OWN FAULT.
Oops...
GASP

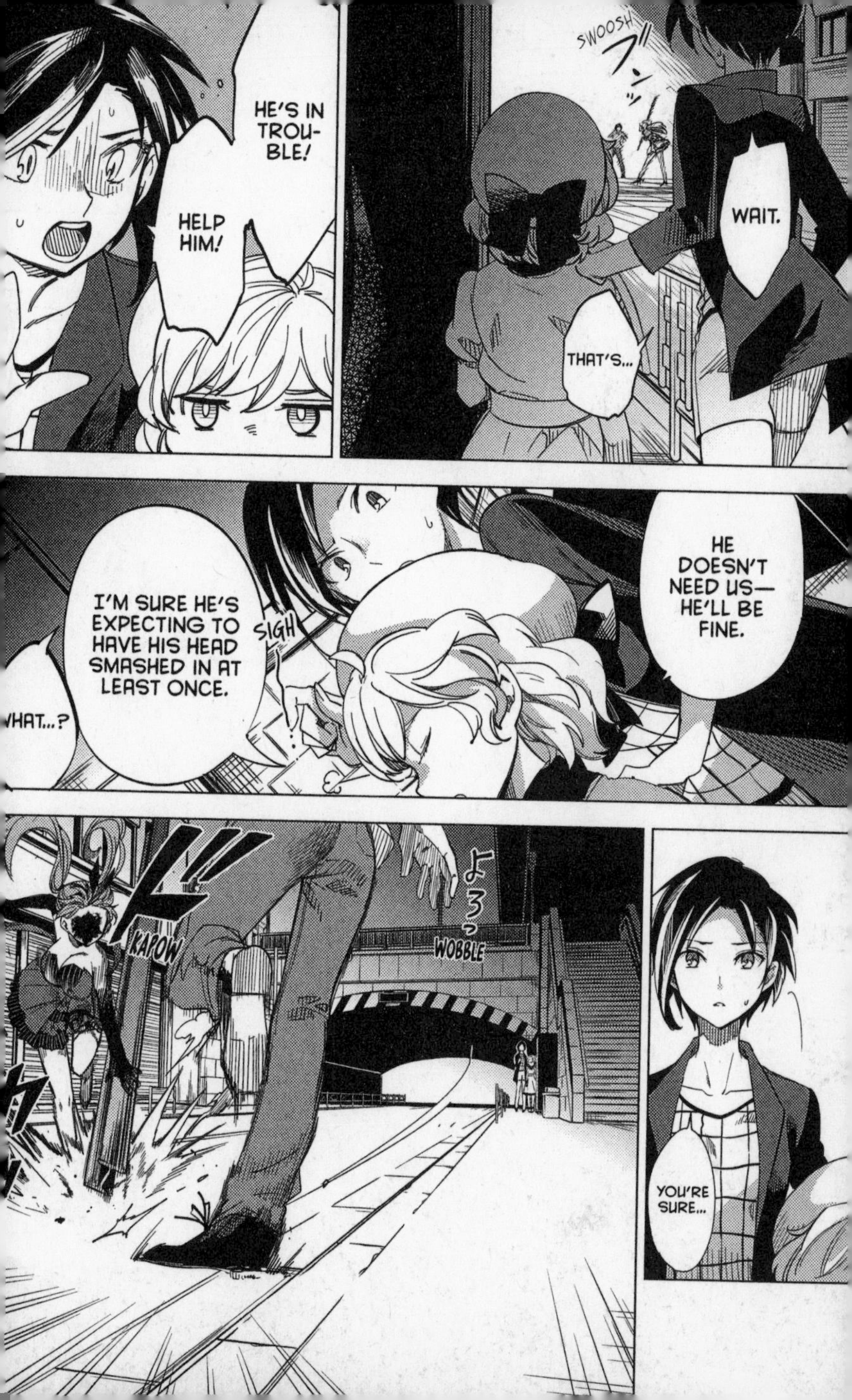
SWOOSH
WAIT.
THAT'S...
HE'S IN TROUBLE!
HELP HIM!
HE DOESN'T NEED US—HE'LL BE FINE.
SIGH
I'M SURE HE'S EXPECTING TO HAVE HIS HEAD SMASHED IN AT LEAST ONCE.
WHAT...?
YOU'RE SURE...
よろっ
WOBBLE
KAPOW

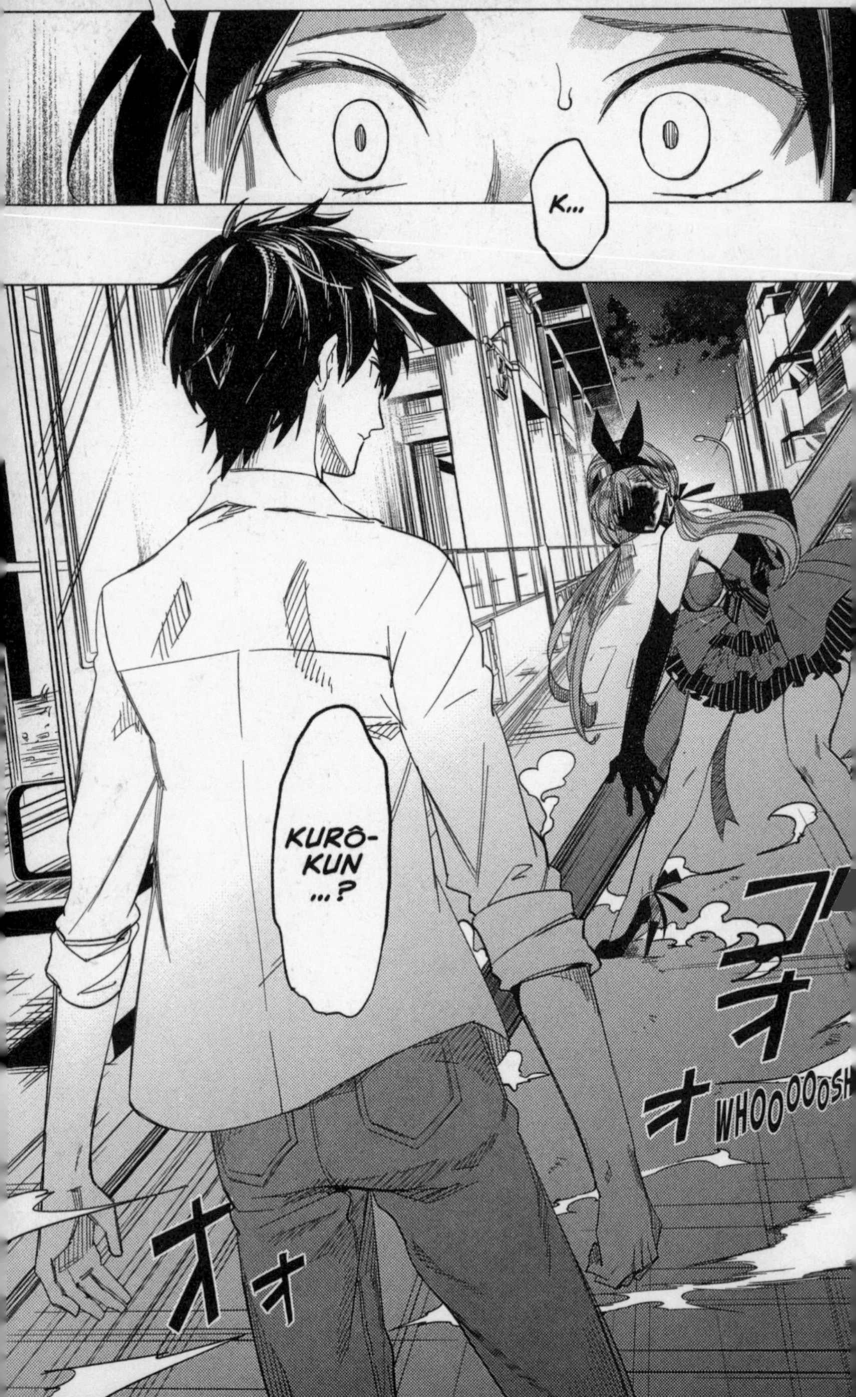
K...
KURÔ-KUN ...?
WHOOOOOSH
オオ

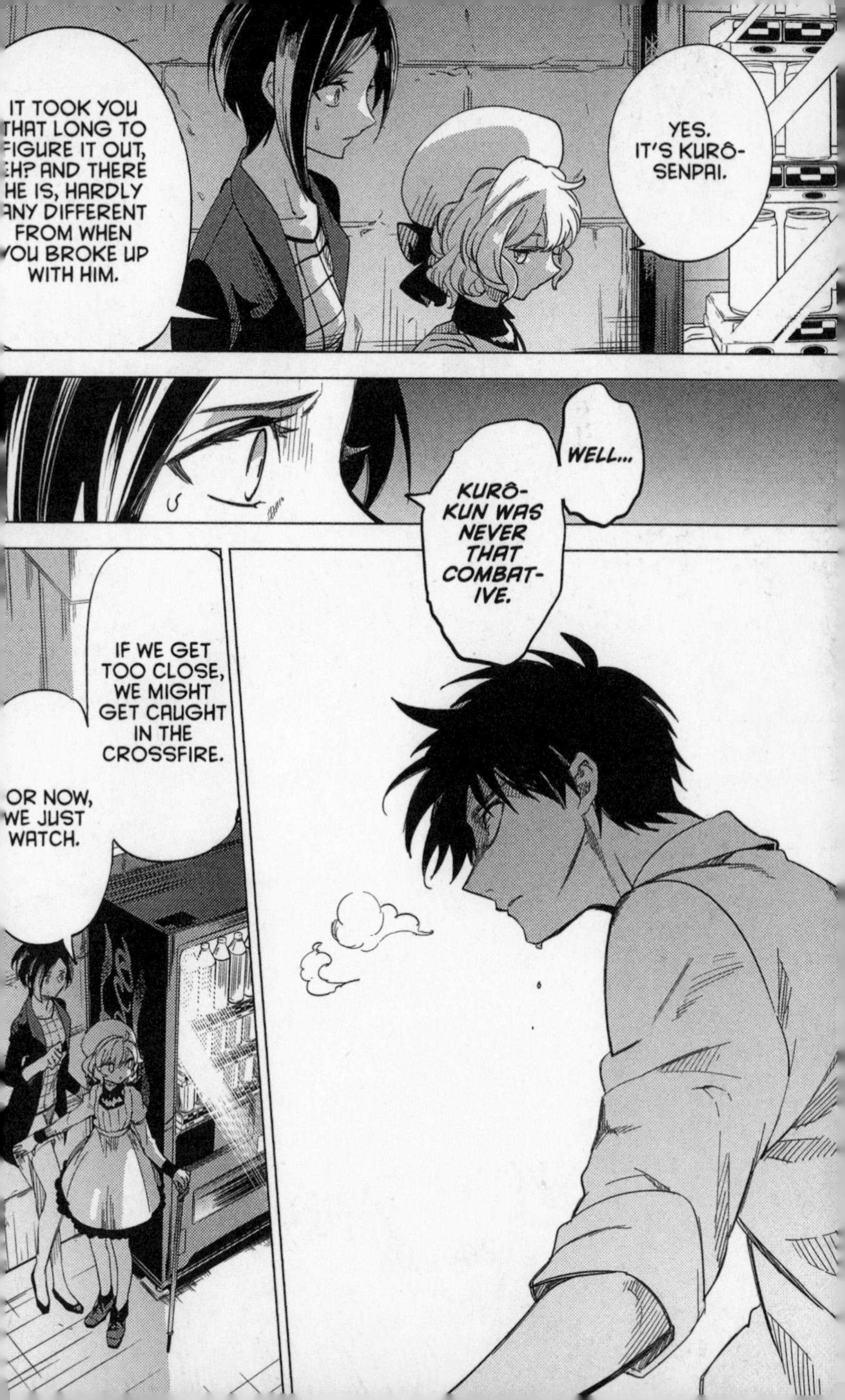
YES. IT'S KURÔ-SENPAI.
IT TOOK YOU THAT LONG TO FIGURE IT OUT, EH? AND THERE HE IS, HARDLY ANY DIFFERENT FROM WHEN YOU BROKE UP WITH HIM.
WELL...
KURÔ-KUN WAS NEVER THAT COMBAT-IVE.
IF WE GET TOO CLOSE, WE MIGHT GET CAUGHT IN THE CROSSFIRE.
FOR NOW, WE JUST WATCH.

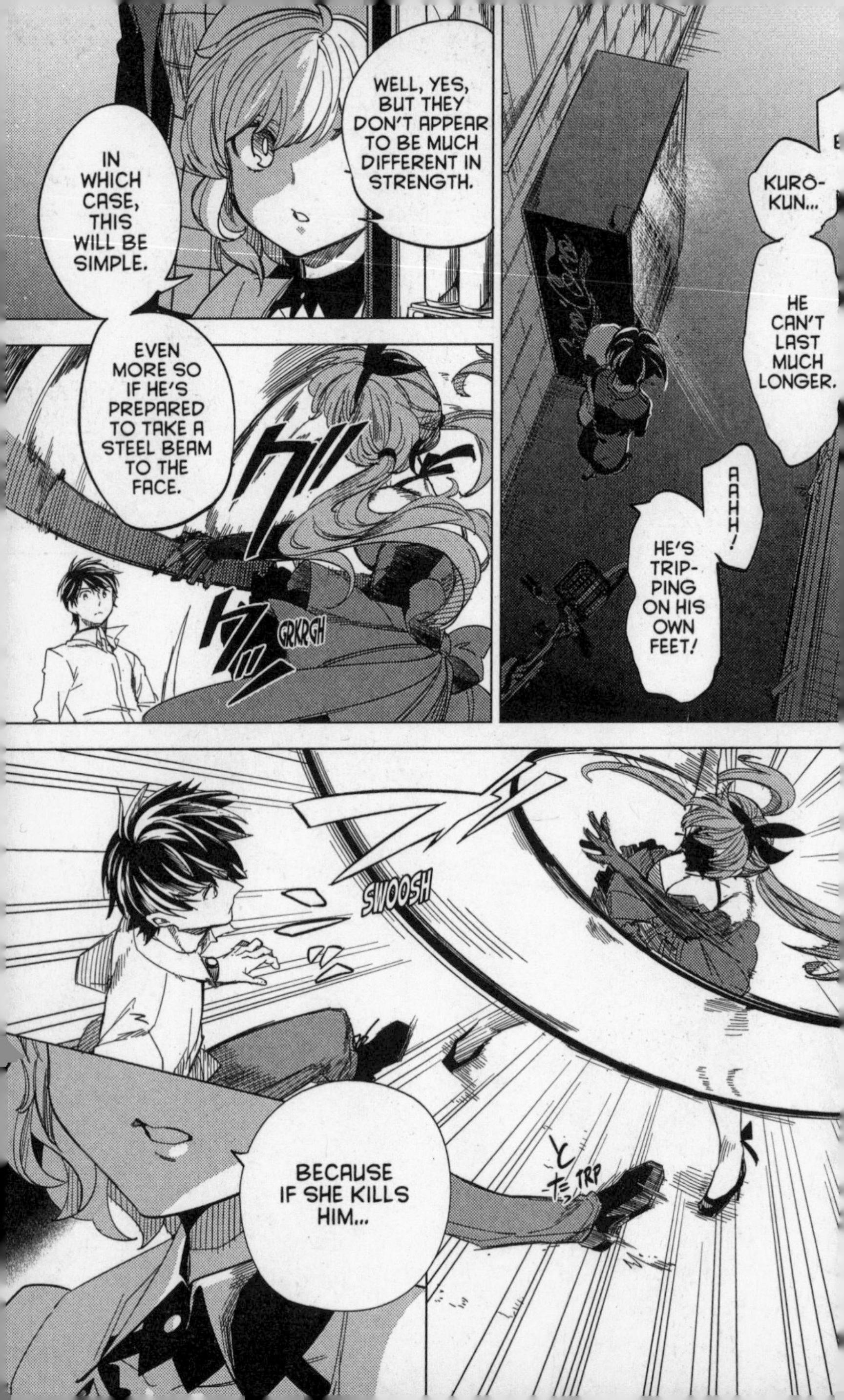
KURÔ-KUN...
HE CAN'T LAST MUCH LONGER.
AAHH!
HE'S TRIP-PING ON HIS OWN FEET!
WELL, YES, BUT THEY DON'T APPEAR TO BE MUCH DIFFERENT IN STRENGTH.
IN WHICH CASE, THIS WILL BE SIMPLE.
EVEN MORE SO IF HE'S PREPARED TO TAKE A STEEL BEAM TO THE FACE.
GRKRGH
SWOOSH
TRP
BECAUSE IF SHE KILLS HIM...

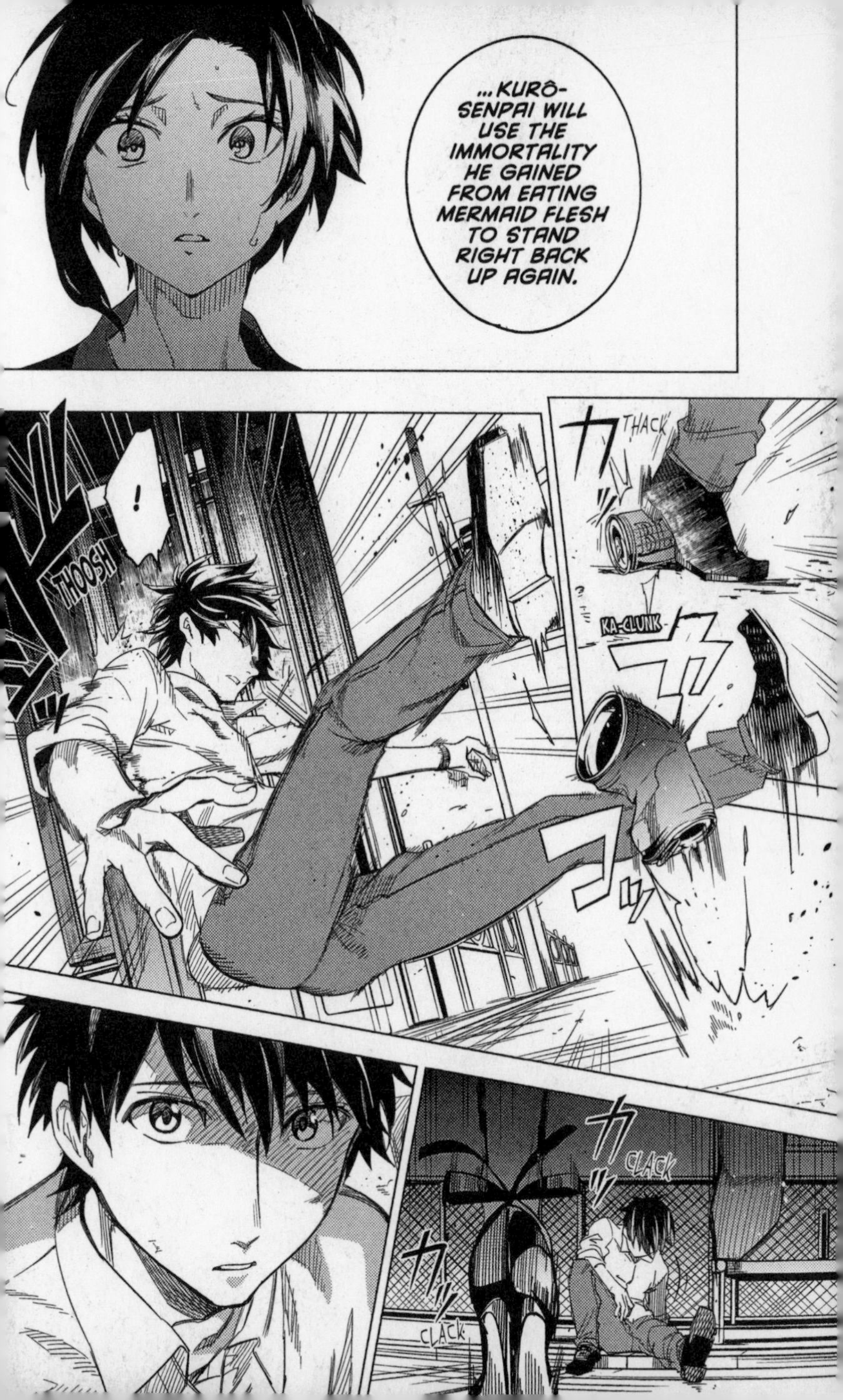
...KURÔ-SENPAI WILL USE THE IMMORTALITY HE GAINED FROM EATING MERMAID FLESH TO STAND RIGHT BACK UP AGAIN.
THACK
KA-CLUNK
!
THOOSH
CLACK
CLACK

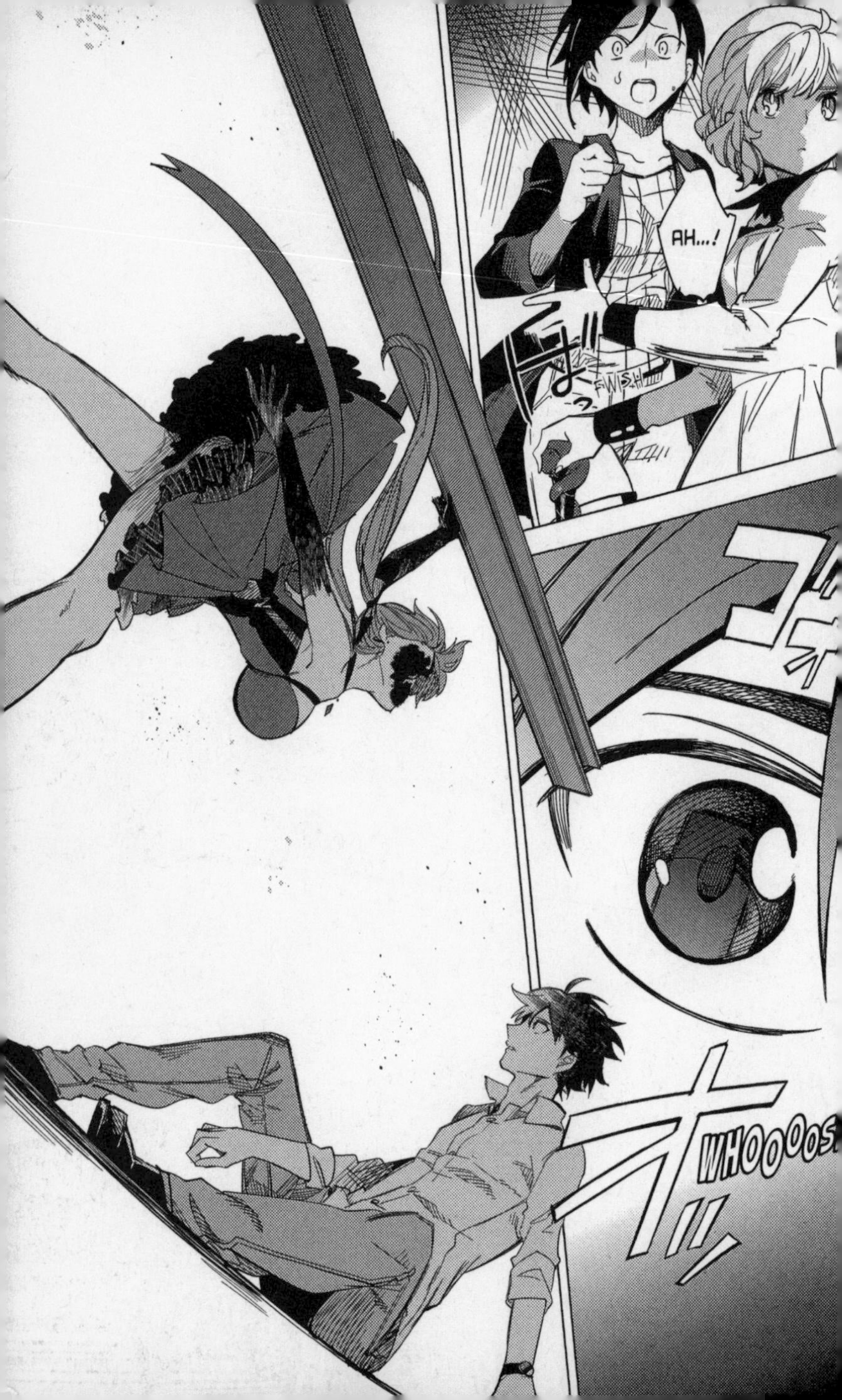
AH...!
FWISH
WHOOOOS

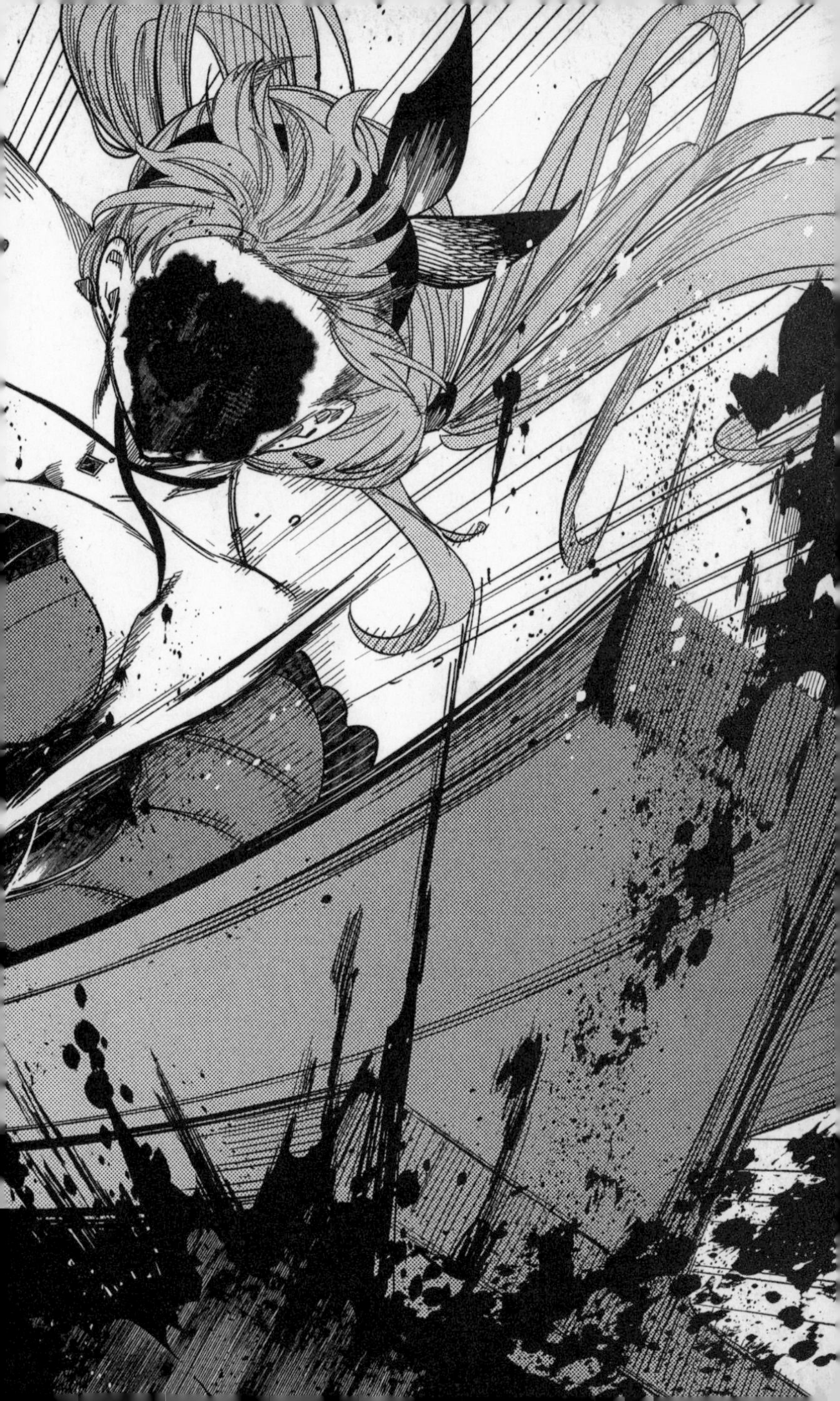

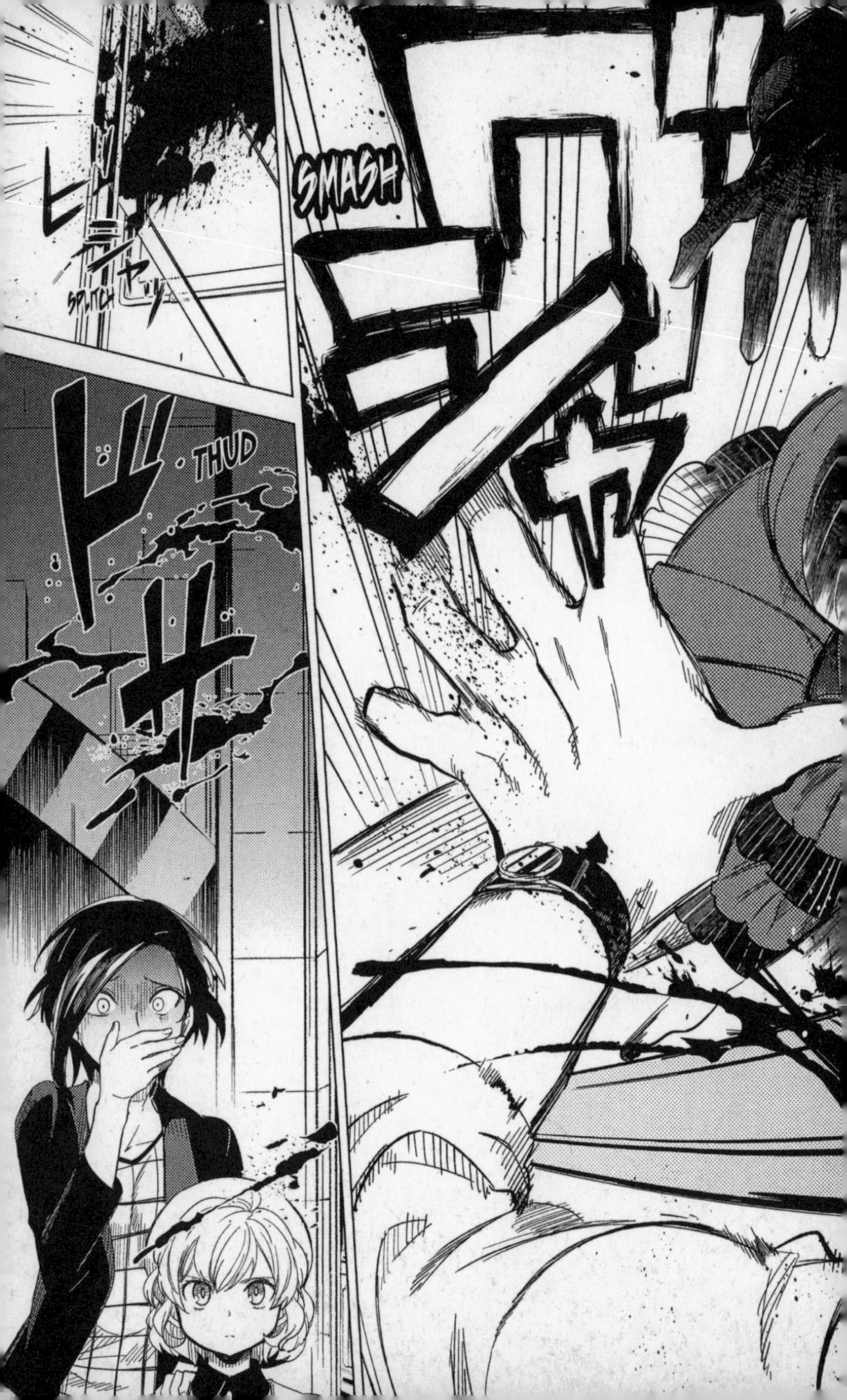
SMASH
SPLTCH
THUD

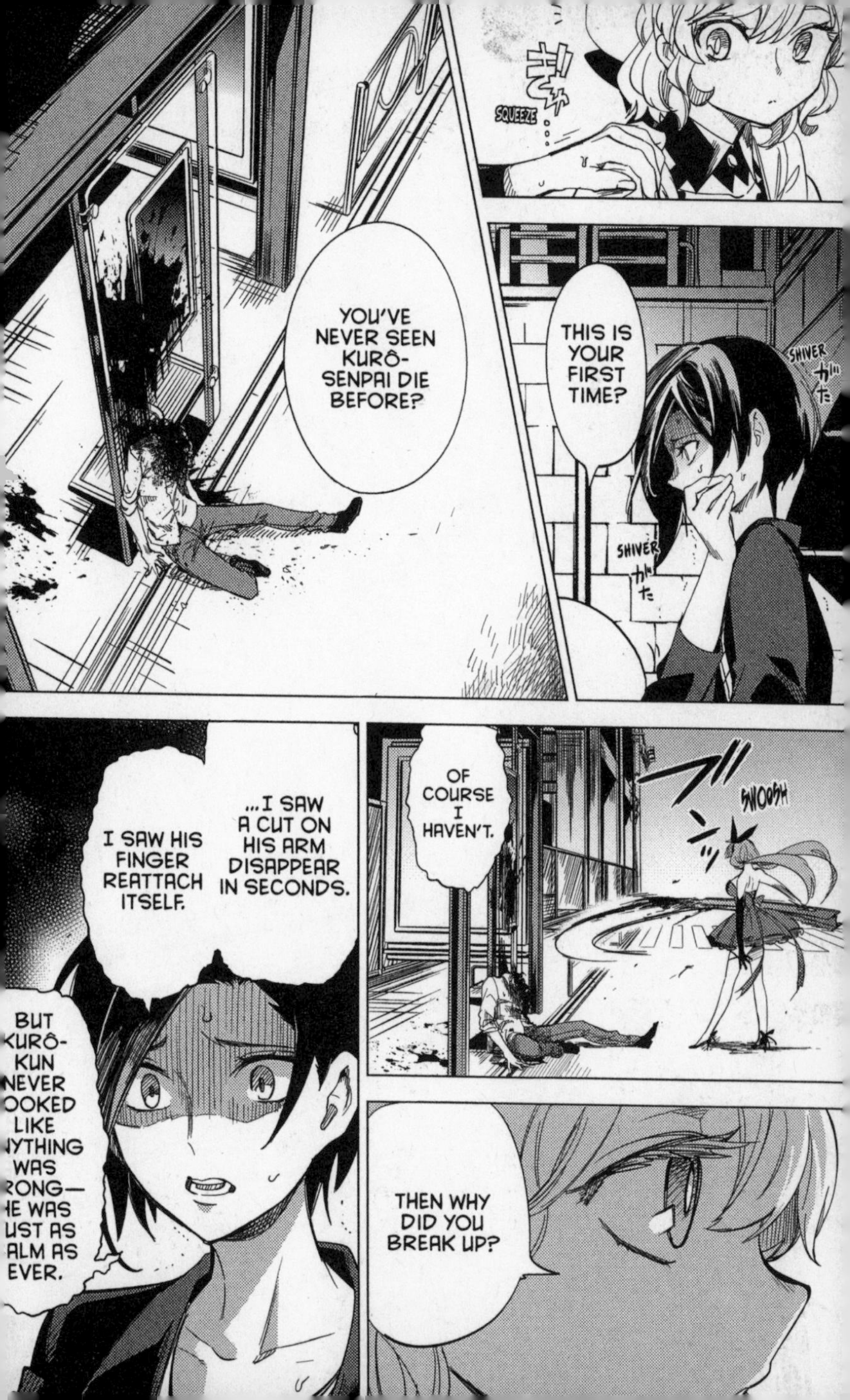
SQUEEZE
THIS IS YOUR FIRST TIME?
SHIVER
SHIVER
YOU'VE NEVER SEEN KURÔ-SENPAI DIE BEFORE?
OF COURSE I HAVEN'T.
SWOOSH
THEN WHY DID YOU BREAK UP?
...I SAW A CUT ON HIS ARM DISAPPEAR IN SECONDS.
I SAW HIS FINGER REATTACH ITSELF.
BUT URÔ-KUN NEVER OOKED LIKE NYTHING WAS RONG— E WAS UST AS ALM AS EVER.

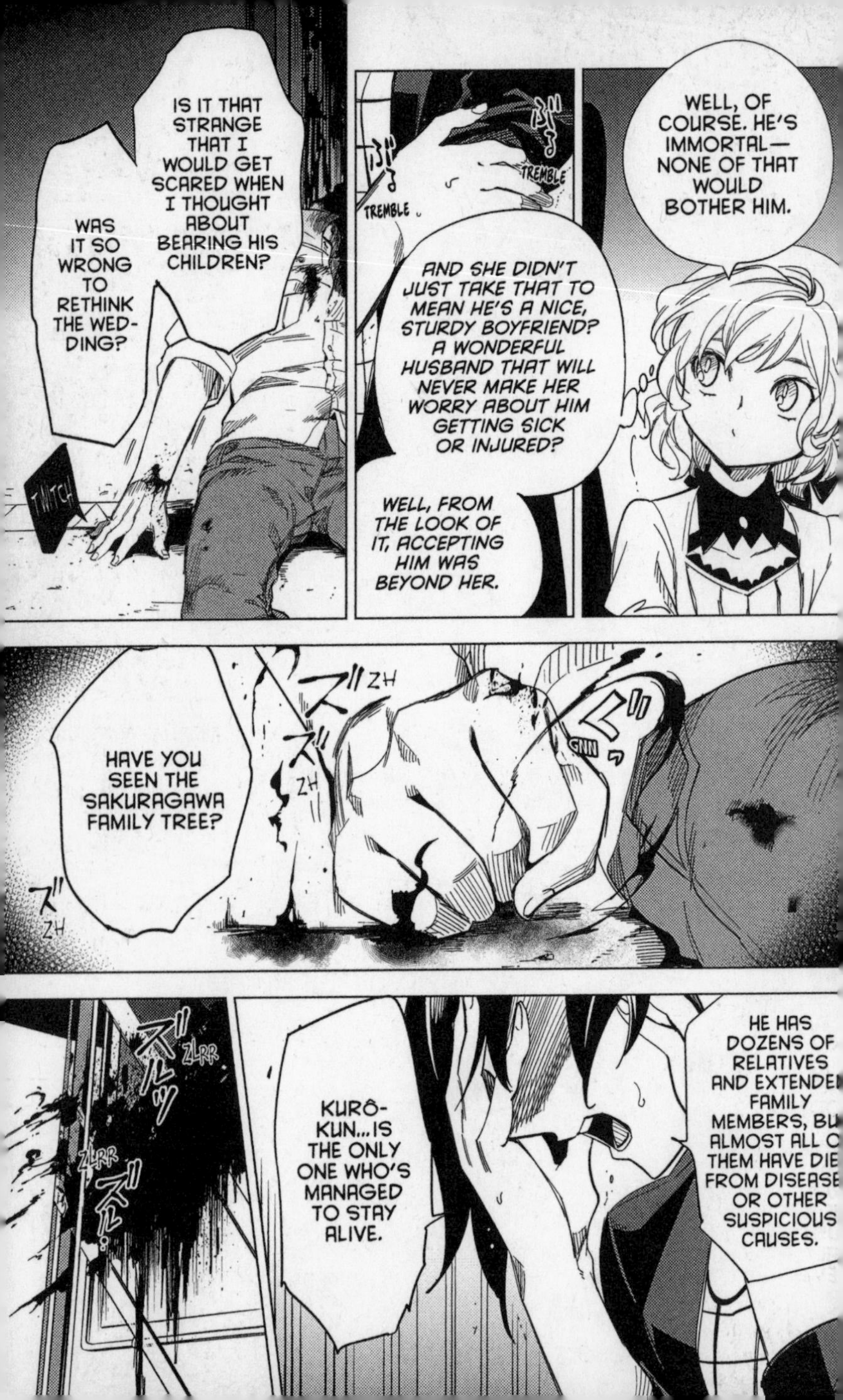
WELL, OF COURSE. HE'S IMMORTAL— NONE OF THAT WOULD BOTHER HIM.
TREMBLE
TREMBLE
AND SHE DIDN'T JUST TAKE THAT TO MEAN HE'S A NICE, STURDY BOYFRIEND? A WONDERFUL HUSBAND THAT WILL NEVER MAKE HER WORRY ABOUT HIM GETTING SICK OR INJURED?
WELL, FROM THE LOOK OF IT, ACCEPTING HIM WAS BEYOND HER.
IS IT THAT STRANGE THAT I WOULD GET SCARED WHEN I THOUGHT ABOUT BEARING HIS CHILDREN?
WAS IT SO WRONG TO RETHINK THE WED-DING?
TWITCH
GNN
ZH
ZH
HAVE YOU SEEN THE SAKURAGAWA FAMILY TREE?
ZH
HE HAS DOZENS OF RELATIVES AND EXTENDE FAMILY MEMBERS, BU ALMOST ALL C THEM HAVE DIE FROM DISEASE OR OTHER SUSPICIOUS CAUSES.
KURÔ-KUN...IS THE ONLY ONE WHO'S MANAGED TO STAY ALIVE.
ZLRR
ZLRR

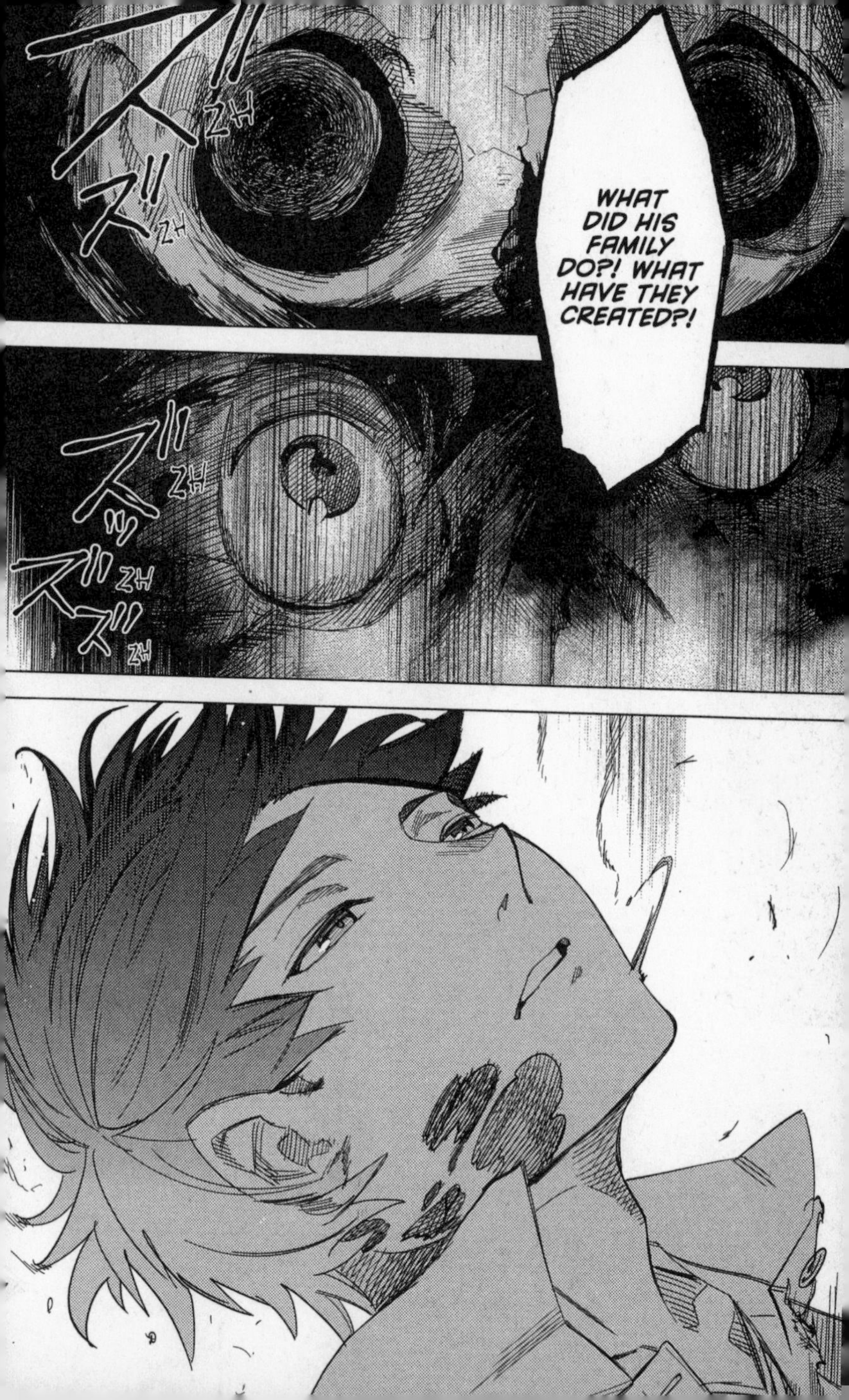
WHAT DID HIS FAMILY DO?! WHAT HAVE THEY CREATED?!
ZH
ZH
ZH
ZH
ZH

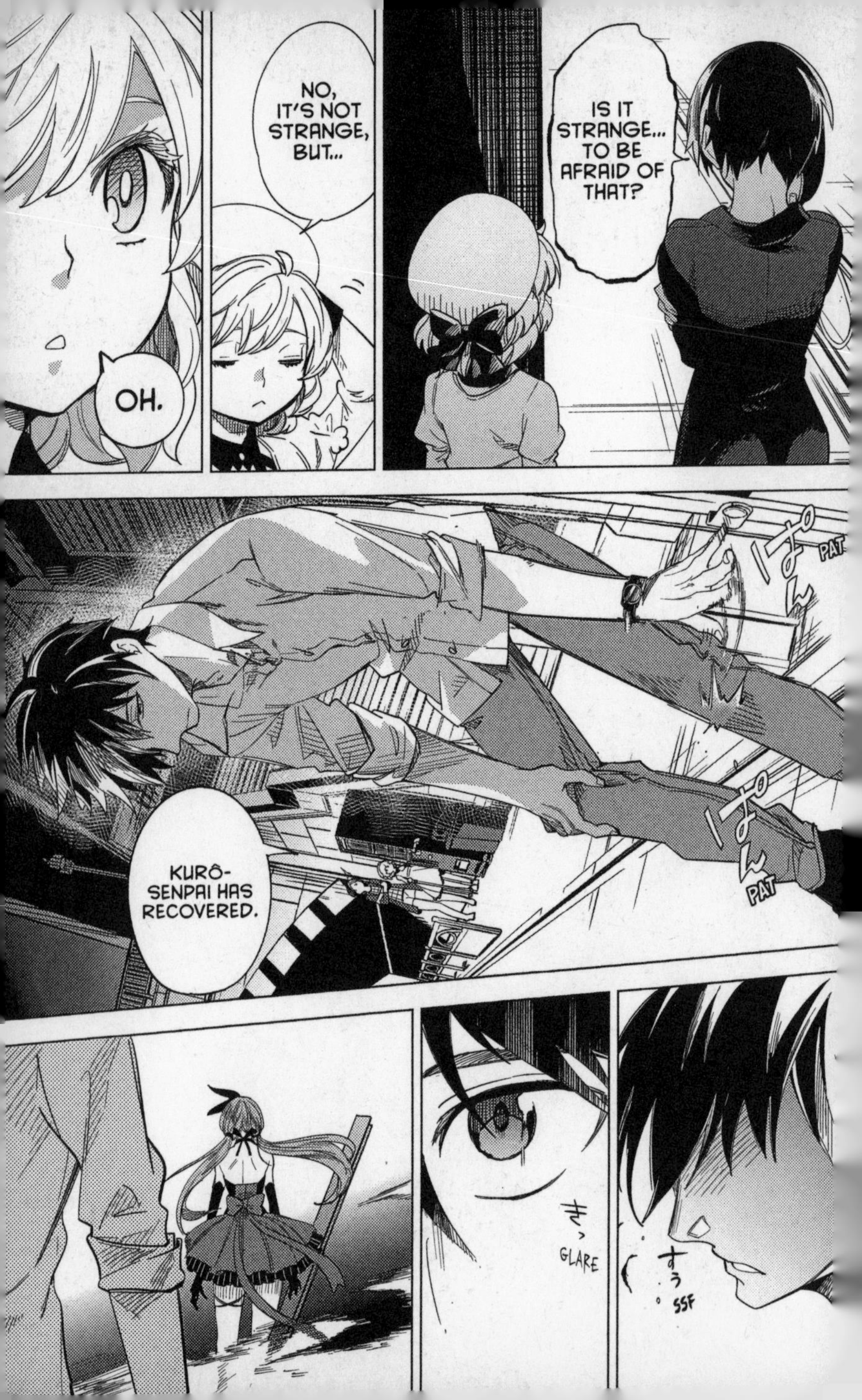
IS IT STRANGE... TO BE AFRAID OF THAT?
NO, IT'S NOT STRANGE, BUT...
OH.
ぱん
PAT
ぱん
PAT
KURÔ-SENPAI HAS RECOVERED.
すぅ
SSF
きっ
GLARE

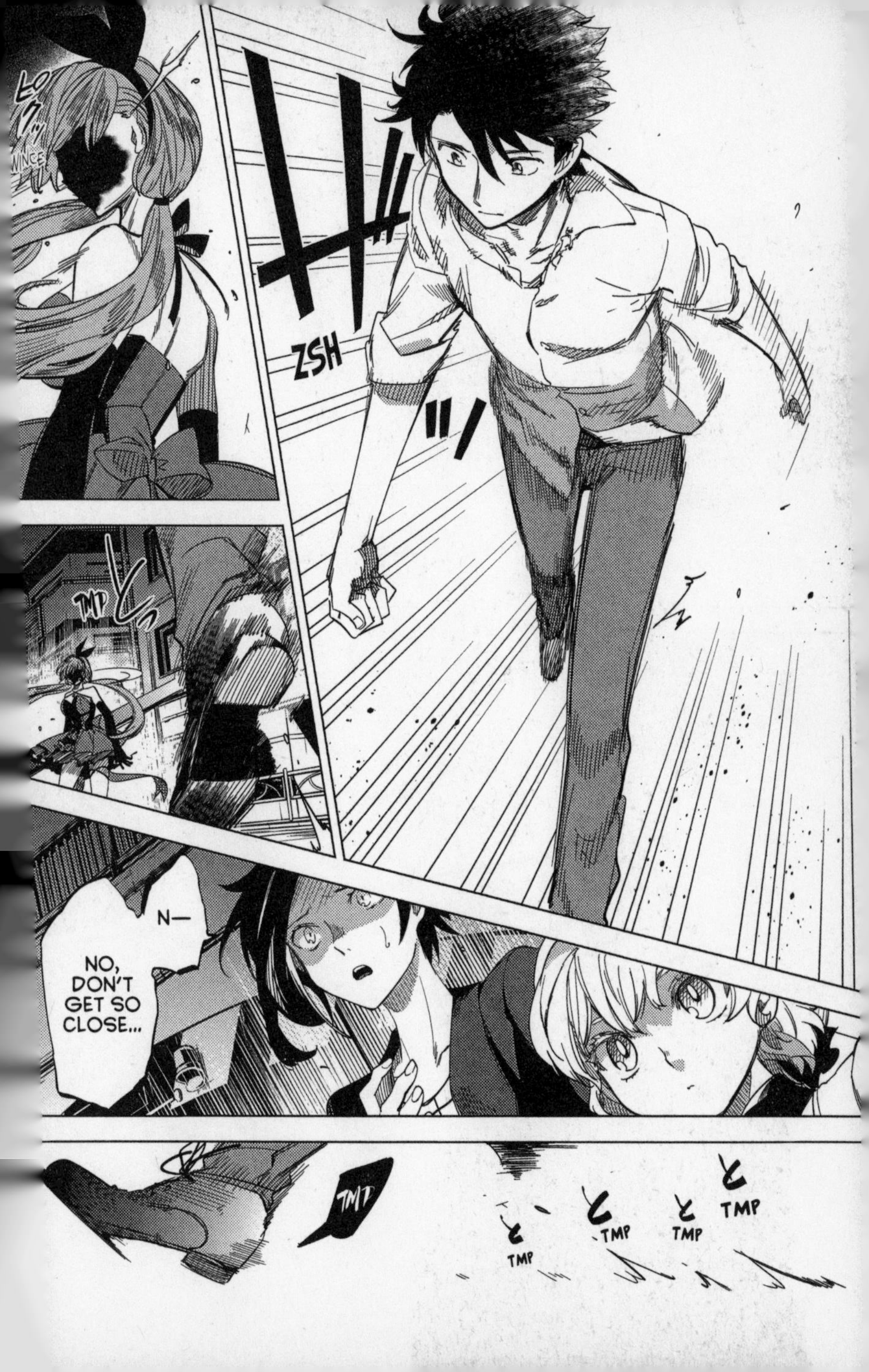
ZSH
ピクッ
WINCE
TMP
N—
NO, DON'T GET SO CLOSE...
と
TMP
と
TMP
と
TMP
と
TMP
TMP

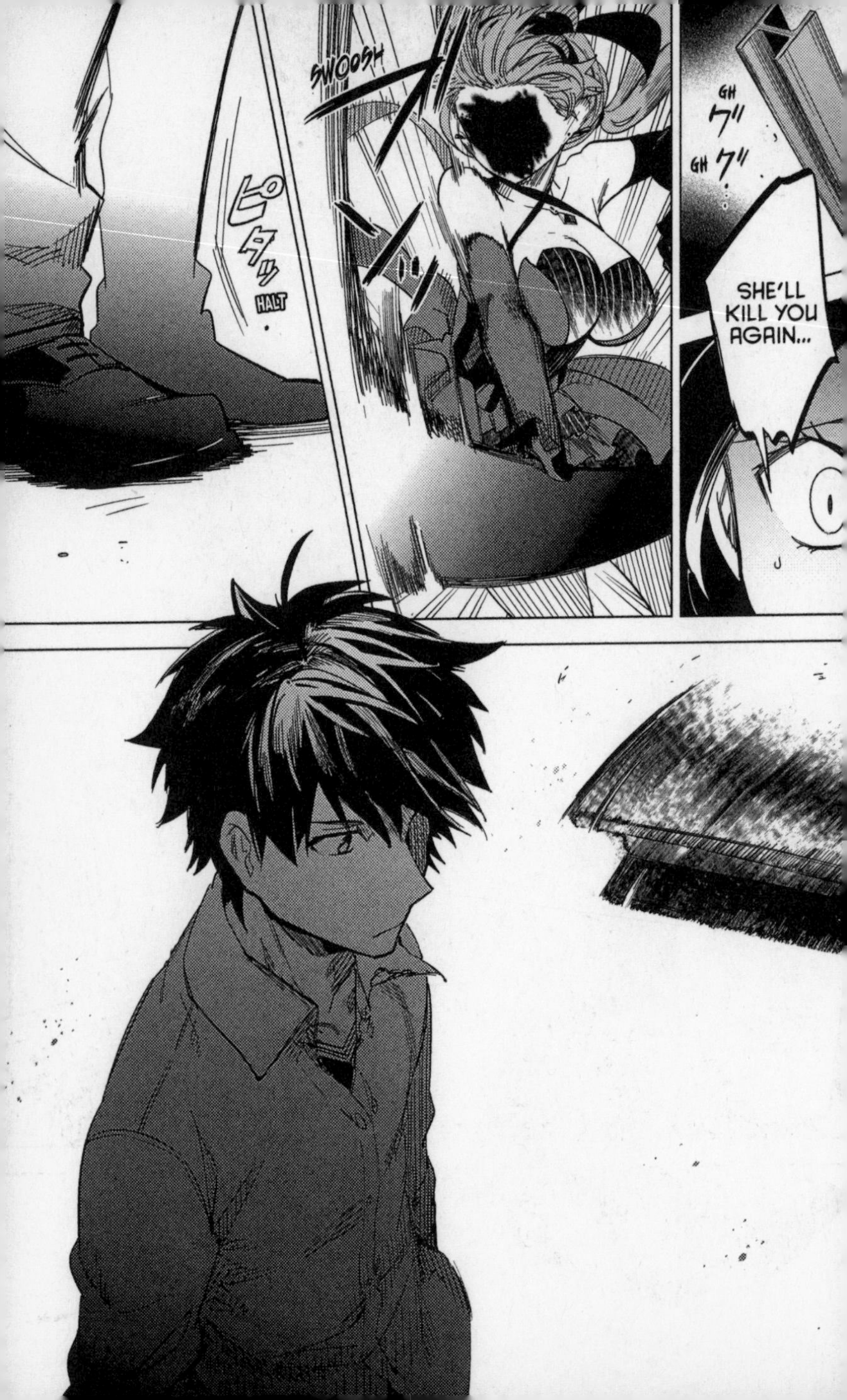
GH グ
GH グ
SHE'LL KILL YOU AGAIN...
SWOOSH
ピタッ
HALT

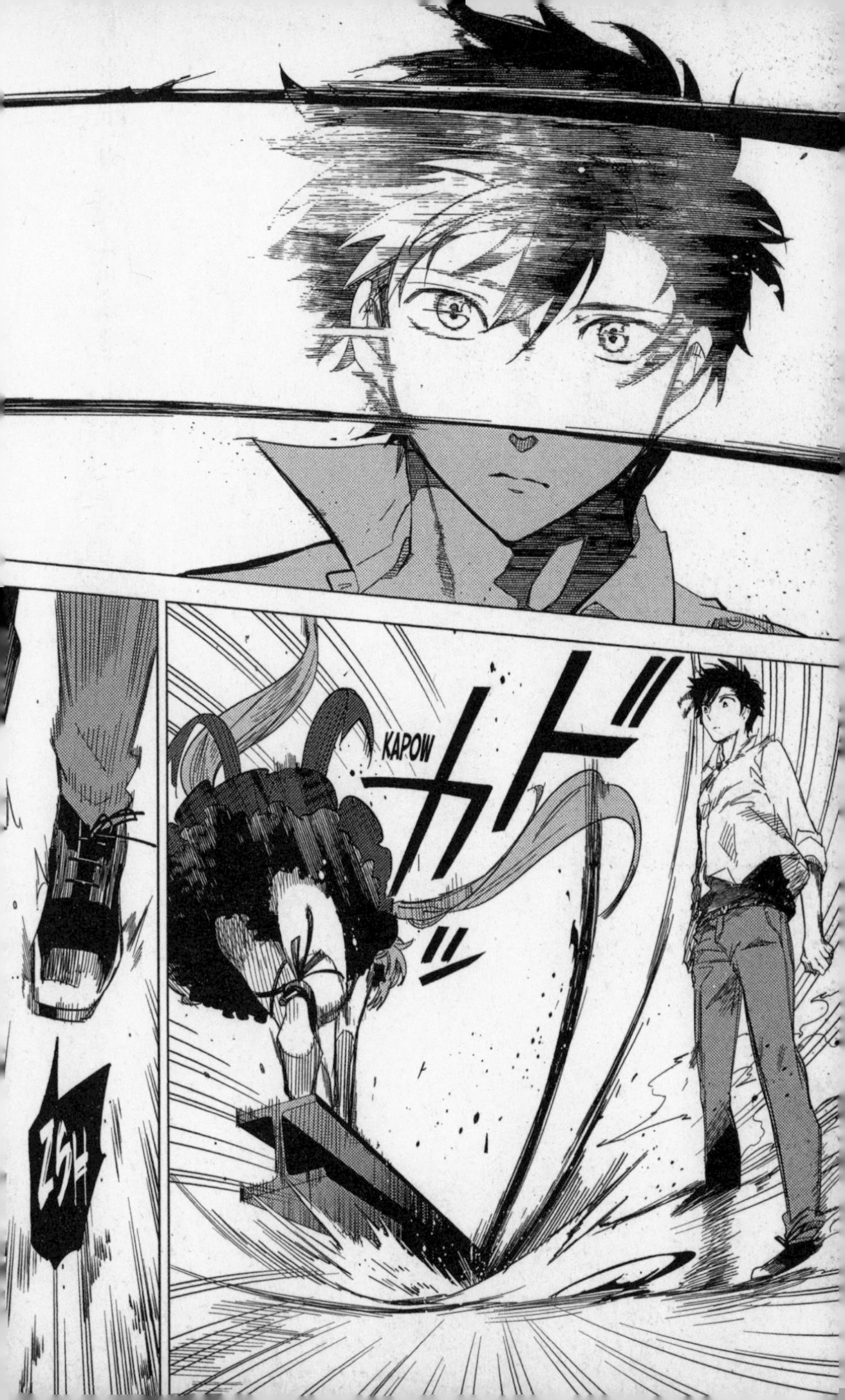
KAPOW
ZSH

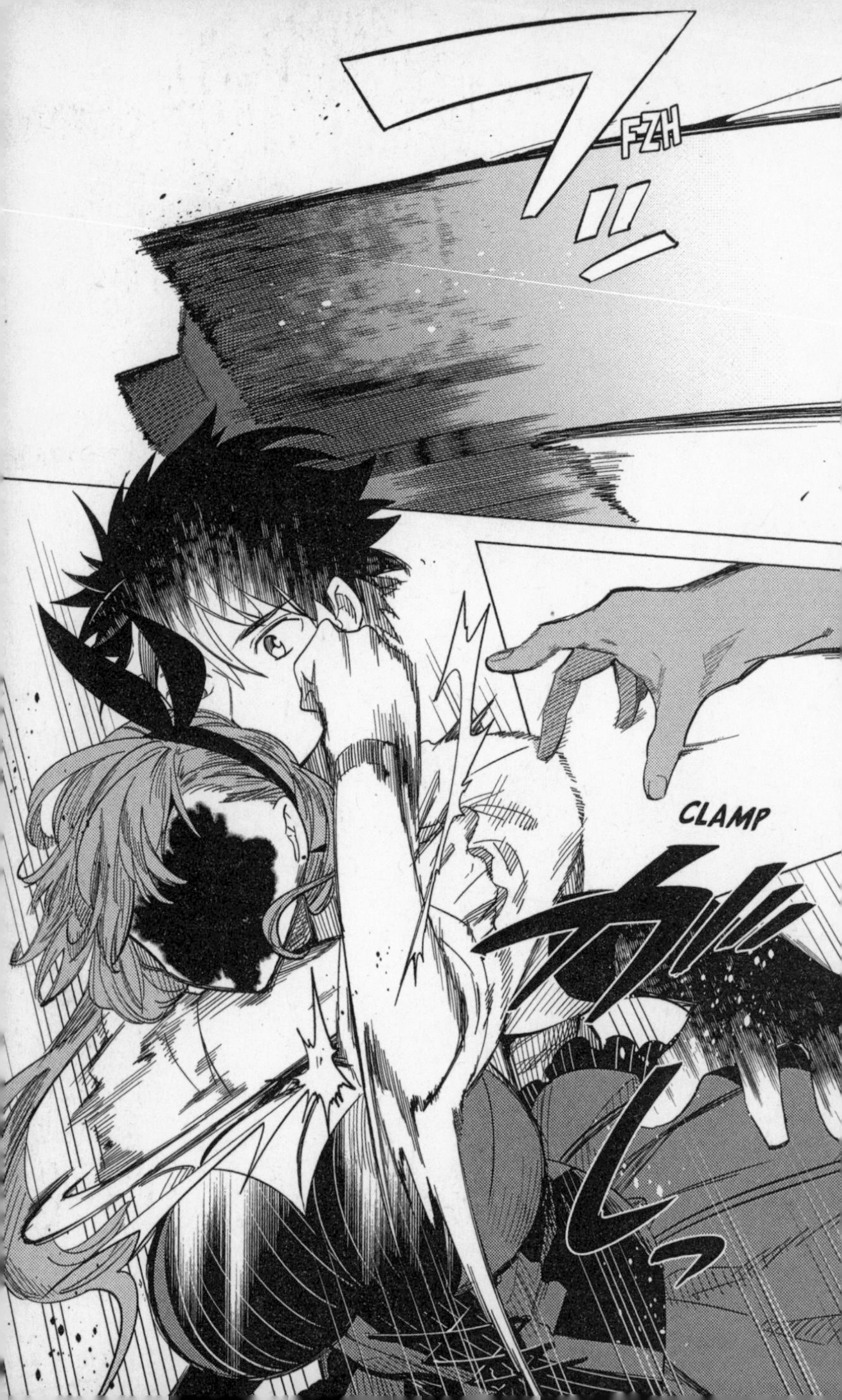
FZH
CLAMP

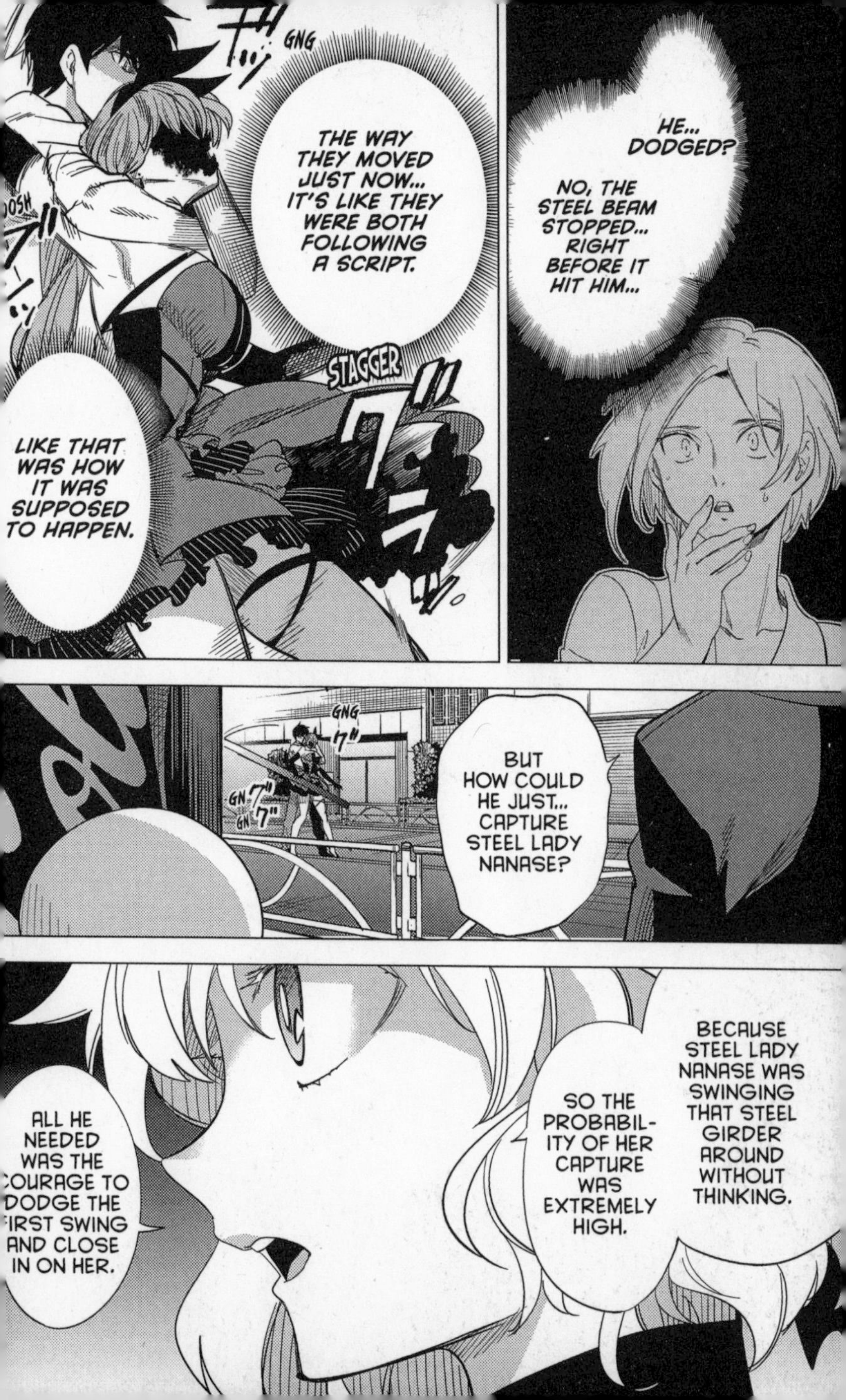

HE... DODGED?
NO, THE STEEL BEAM STOPPED... RIGHT BEFORE IT HIT HIM...
GNG
THE WAY THEY MOVED JUST NOW... IT'S LIKE THEY WERE BOTH FOLLOWING A SCRIPT.
STAGGER
LIKE THAT WAS HOW IT WAS SUPPOSED TO HAPPEN.
GNG
GN
GN
BUT HOW COULD HE JUST... CAPTURE STEEL LADY NANASE?
BECAUSE STEEL LADY NANASE WAS SWINGING THAT STEEL GIRDER AROUND WITHOUT THINKING.
SO THE PROBABIL-ITY OF HER CAPTURE WAS EXTREMELY HIGH.
ALL HE NEEDED WAS THE COURAGE TO DODGE THE FIRST SWING AND CLOSE IN ON HER.

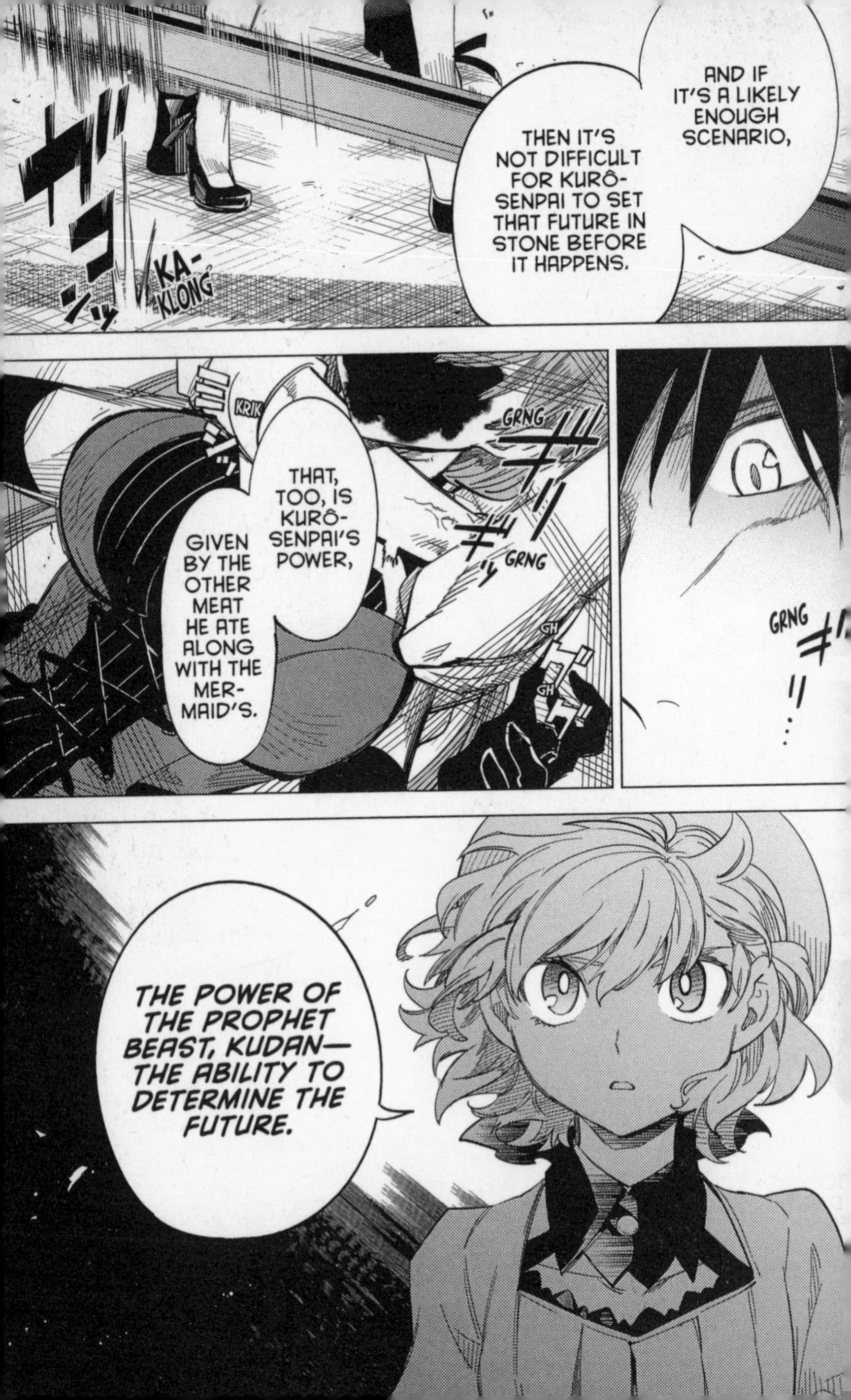
AND IF IT'S A LIKELY ENOUGH SCENARIO,
THEN IT'S NOT DIFFICULT FOR KURÔ-SENPAI TO SET THAT FUTURE IN STONE BEFORE IT HAPPENS.
KA-KLONG
GRNG
GRNG
GRNG
KRIK
THAT, TOO, IS KURÔ-SENPAI'S POWER,
GIVEN BY THE OTHER MEAT HE ATE ALONG WITH THE MER-MAID'S.
GH
GH
THE POWER OF THE PROPHET BEAST, KUDAN—THE ABILITY TO DETERMINE THE FUTURE.

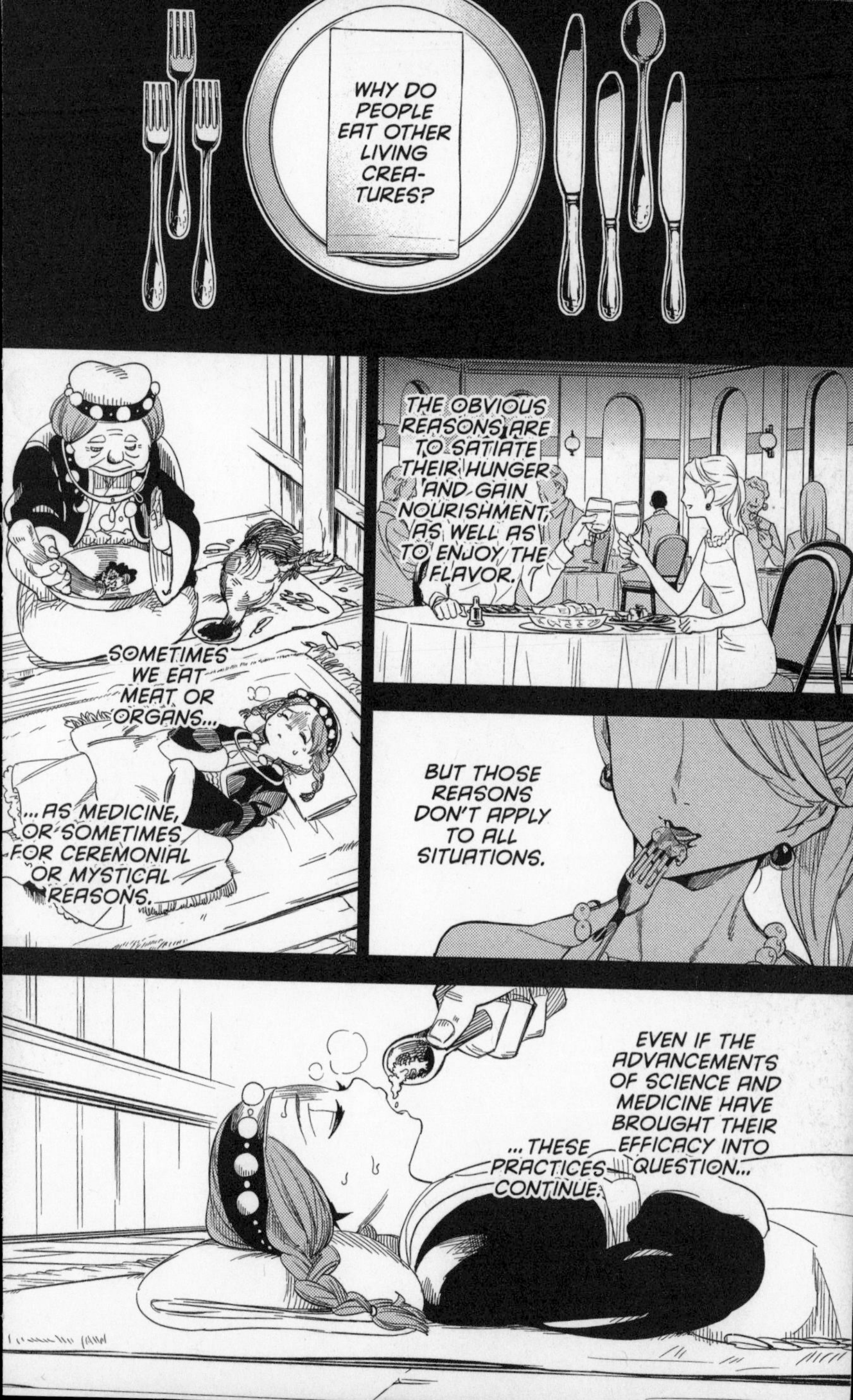
WHY DO PEOPLE EAT OTHER LIVING CREA-TURES?
THE OBVIOUS REASONS ARE TO SATIATE THEIR HUNGER AND GAIN NOURISHMENT, AS WELL AS TO ENJOY THE FLAVOR.
BUT THOSE REASONS DON'T APPLY TO ALL SITUATIONS.
SOMETIMES WE EAT MEAT OR ORGANS...
...AS MEDICINE, OR SOMETIMES FOR CEREMONIAL OR MYSTICAL REASONS.
EVEN IF THE ADVANCEMENTS OF SCIENCE AND MEDICINE HAVE BROUGHT THEIR EFFICACY INTO QUESTION...
...THESE PRACTICES CONTINUE.

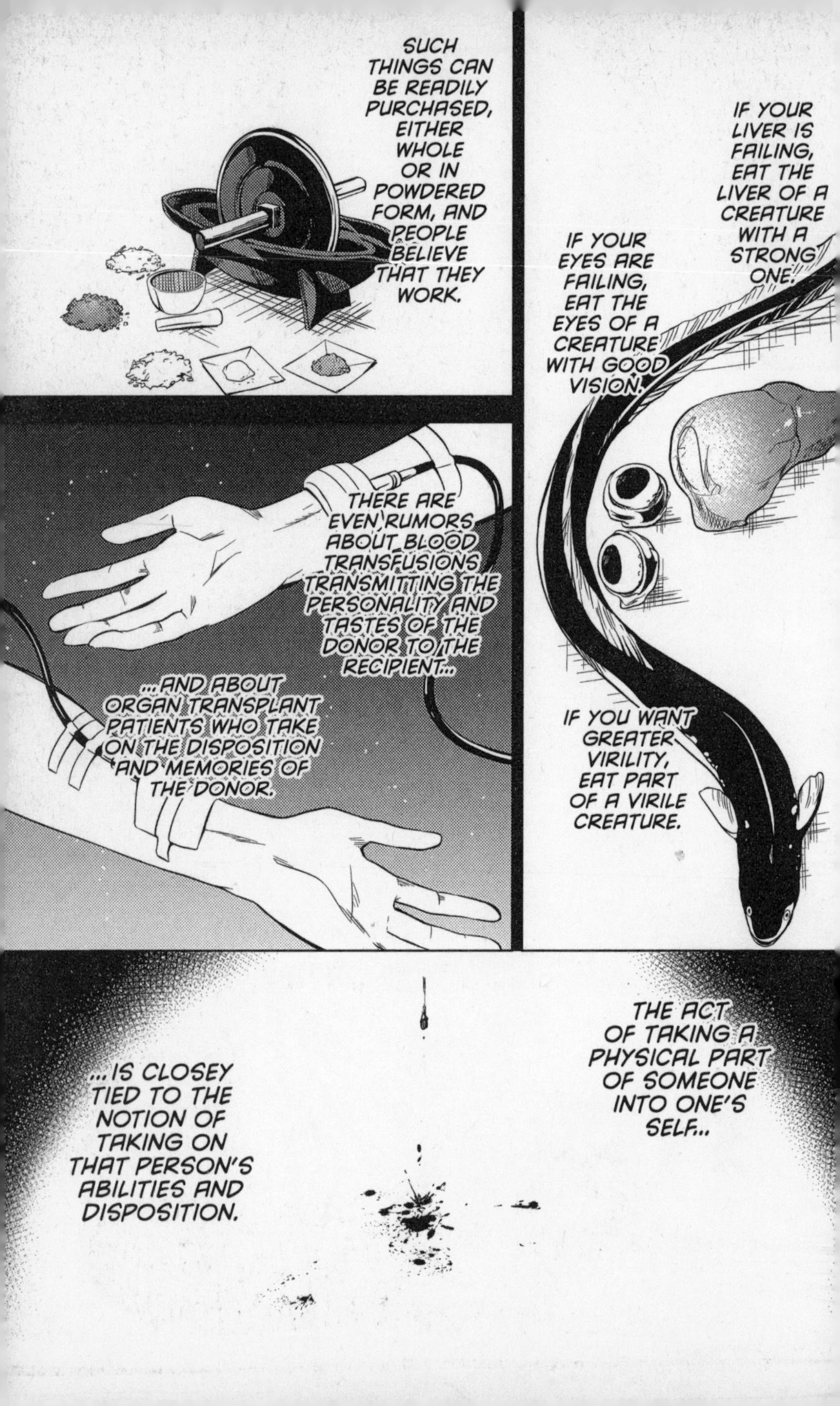
IF YOUR LIVER IS FAILING, EAT THE LIVER OF A CREATURE WITH A STRONG ONE.
IF YOUR EYES ARE FAILING, EAT THE EYES OF A CREATURE WITH GOOD VISION.
IF YOU WANT GREATER VIRILITY, EAT PART OF A VIRILE CREATURE.
SUCH THINGS CAN BE READILY PURCHASED, EITHER WHOLE OR IN POWDERED FORM, AND PEOPLE BELIEVE THAT THEY WORK.
THERE ARE EVEN RUMORS ABOUT BLOOD TRANSFUSIONS TRANSMITTING THE PERSONALITY AND TASTES OF THE DONOR TO THE RECIPIENT...
...AND ABOUT ORGAN TRANSPLANT PATIENTS WHO TAKE ON THE DISPOSITION AND MEMORIES OF THE DONOR.
THE ACT OF TAKING A PHYSICAL PART OF SOMEONE INTO ONE'S SELF...
...IS CLOSEY TIED TO THE NOTION OF TAKING ON THAT PERSON'S ABILITIES AND DISPOSITION.

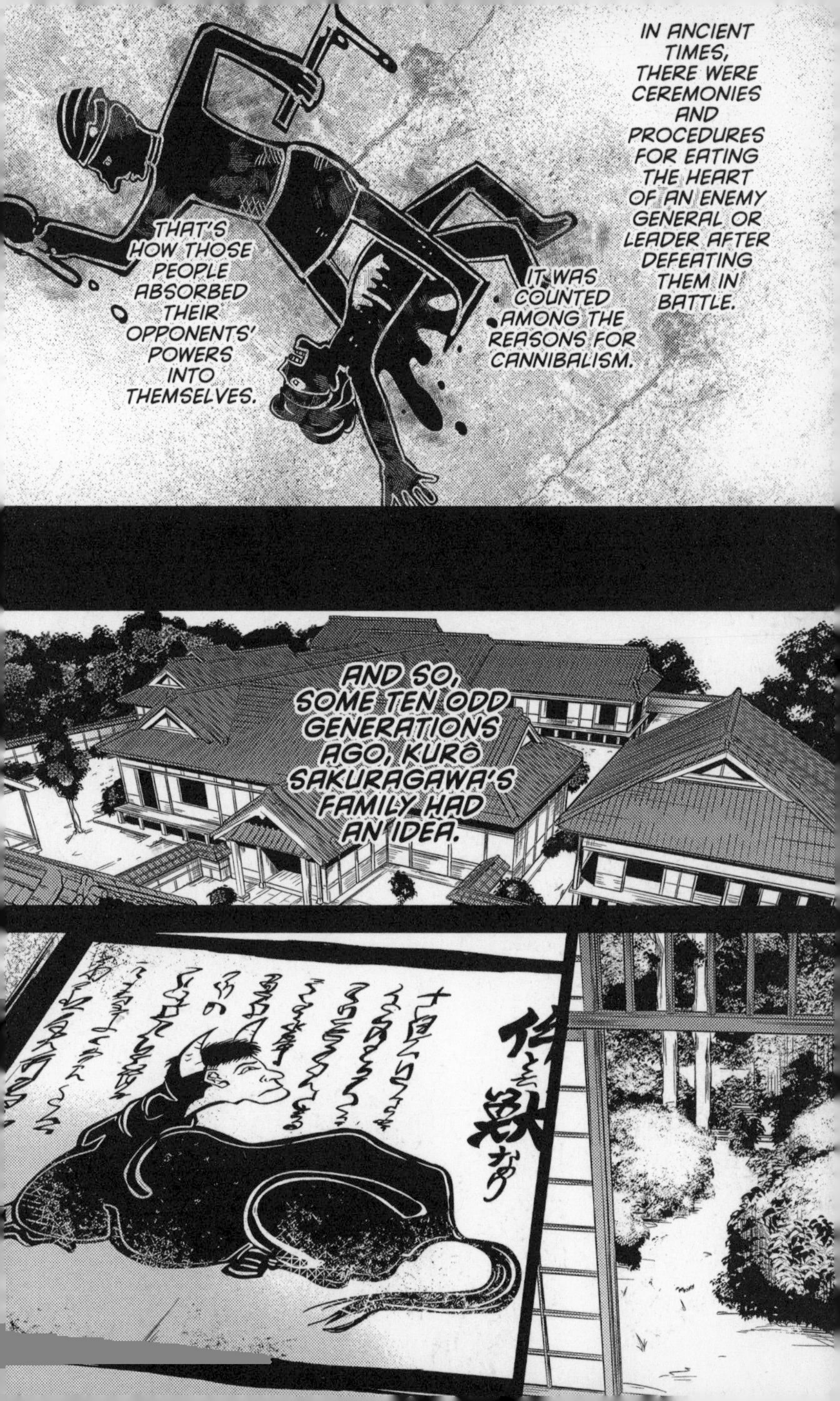
IN ANCIENT TIMES, THERE WERE CEREMONIES AND PROCEDURES FOR EATING THE HEART OF AN ENEMY GENERAL OR LEADER AFTER DEFEATING THEM IN BATTLE.
IT WAS COUNTED AMONG THE REASONS FOR CANNIBALISM.
THAT'S HOW THOSE PEOPLE ABSORBED THEIR OPPONENTS' POWERS INTO THEMSELVES.
AND SO, SOME TEN ODD GENERATIONS AGO, KURÔ SAKURAGAWA'S FAMILY HAD AN IDEA.

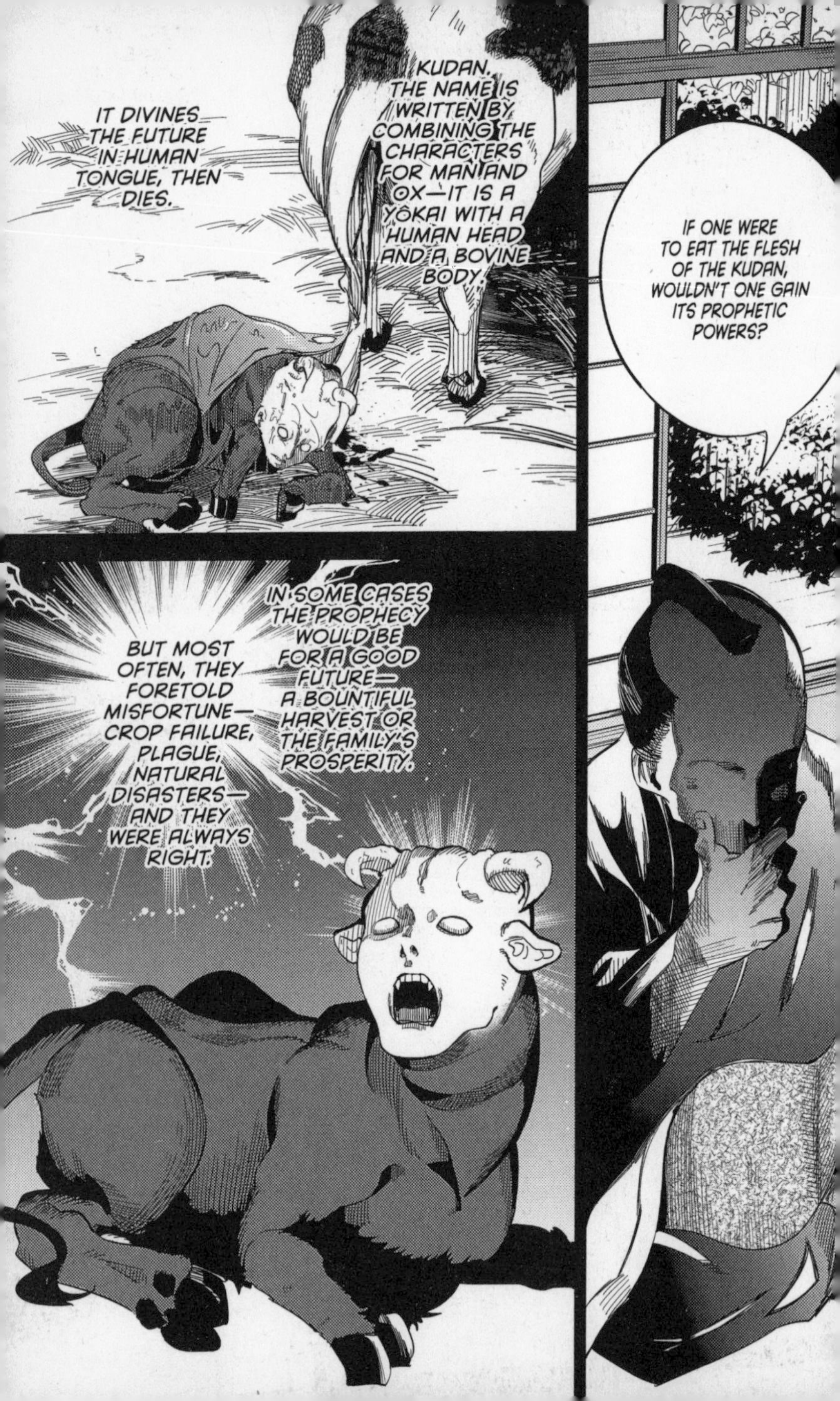
IF ONE WERE TO EAT THE FLESH OF THE KUDAN, WOULDN'T ONE GAIN ITS PROPHETIC POWERS?
KUDAN. THE NAME IS WRITTEN BY COMBINING THE CHARACTERS FOR MAN AND OX—IT IS A YŌKAI WITH A HUMAN HEAD AND A BOVINE BODY.
IT DIVINES THE FUTURE IN HUMAN TONGUE, THEN DIES.
IN SOME CASES THE PROPHECY WOULD BE FOR A GOOD FUTURE—A BOUNTIFUL HARVEST OR THE FAMILY'S PROSPERITY.
BUT MOST OFTEN, THEY FORETOLD MISFORTUNE—CROP FAILURE, PLAGUE, NATURAL DISASTERS—AND THEY WERE ALWAYS RIGHT.

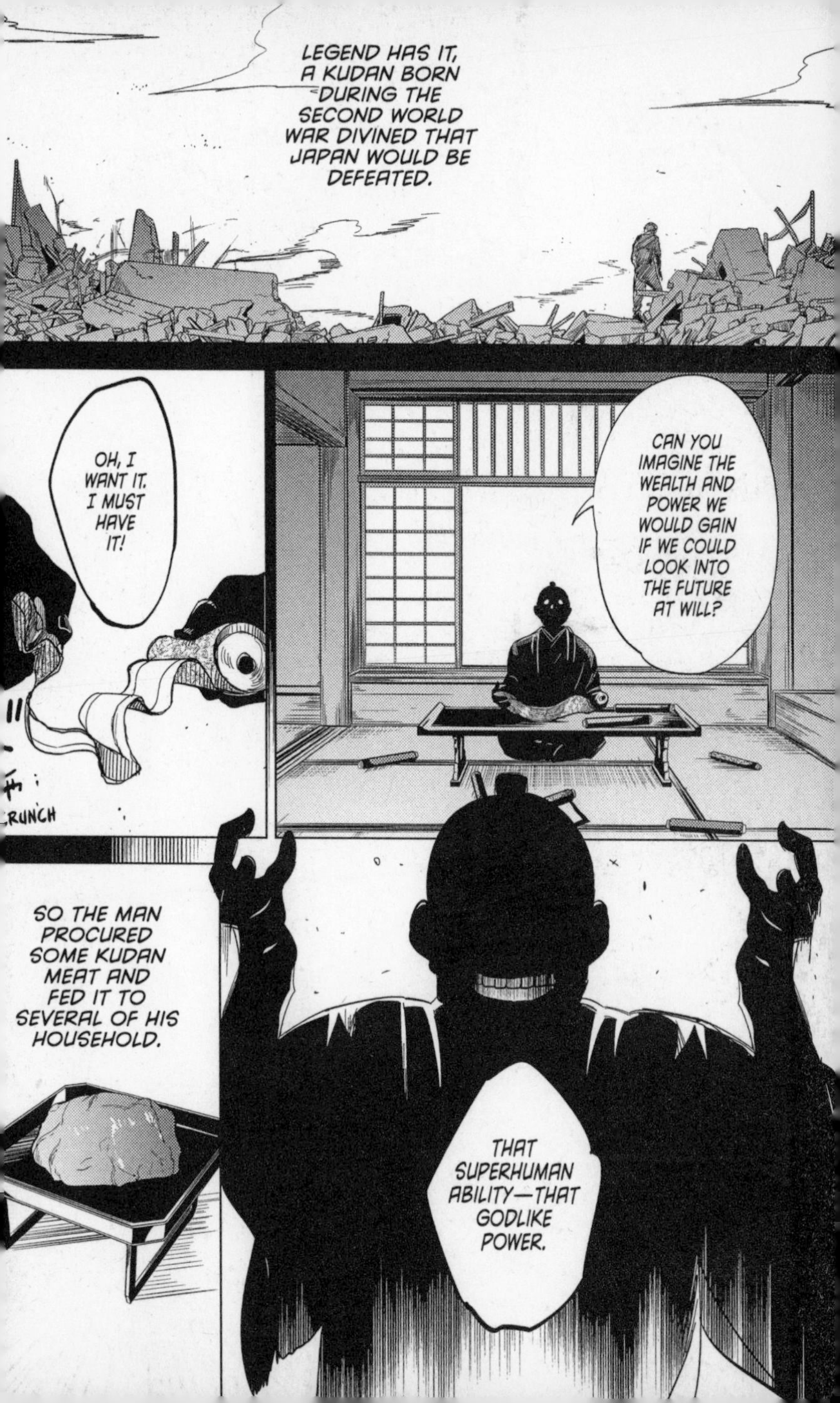
LEGEND HAS IT, A KUDAN BORN DURING THE SECOND WORLD WAR DIVINED THAT JAPAN WOULD BE DEFEATED.
CAN YOU IMAGINE THE WEALTH AND POWER WE WOULD GAIN IF WE COULD LOOK INTO THE FUTURE AT WILL?
OH, I WANT IT. I MUST HAVE IT!
CRUNCH
THAT SUPERHUMAN ABILITY—THAT GODLIKE POWER.
SO THE MAN PROCURED SOME KUDAN MEAT AND FED IT TO SEVERAL OF HIS HOUSEHOLD.

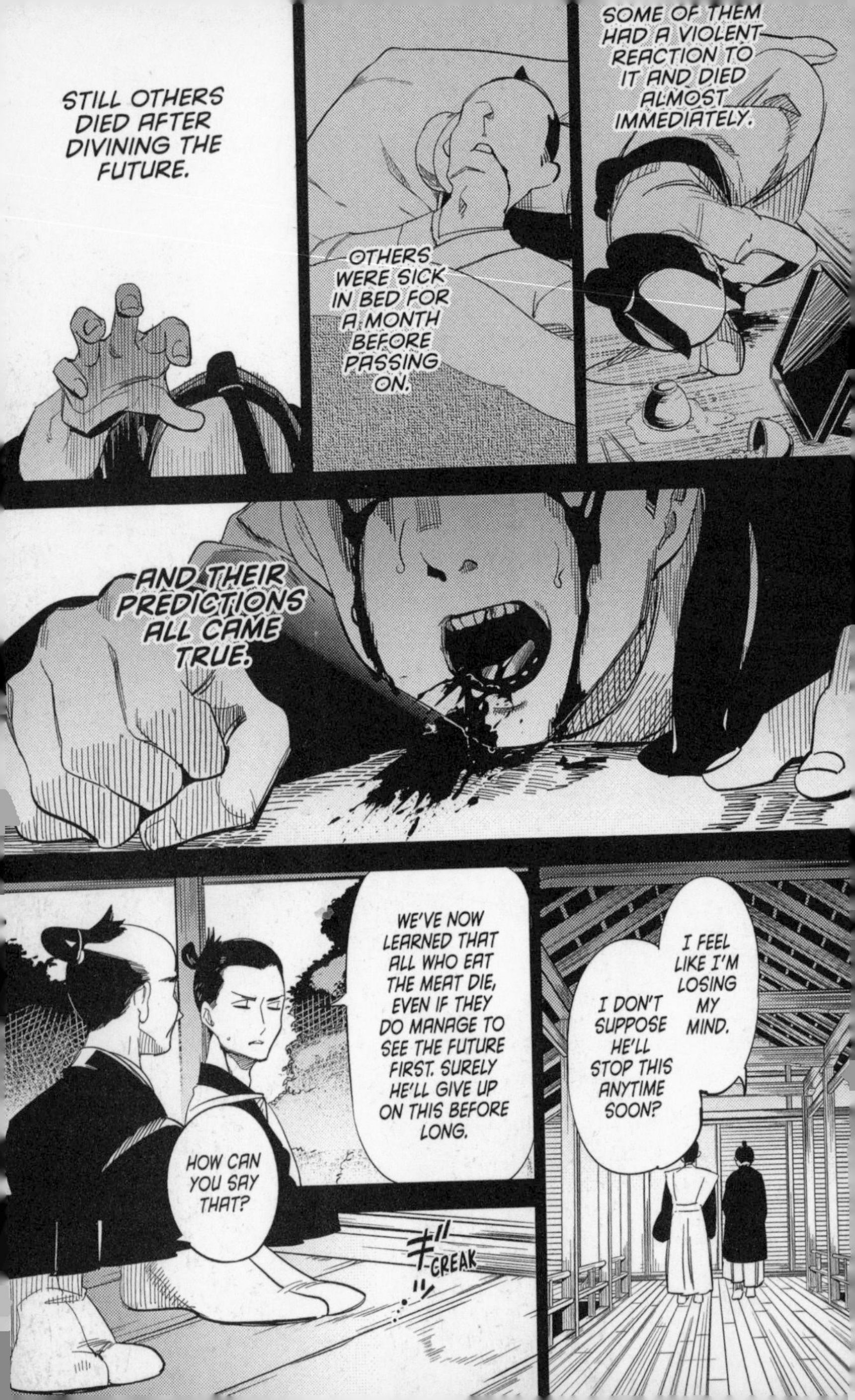
SOME OF THEM HAD A VIOLENT REACTION TO IT AND DIED ALMOST IMMEDIATELY.
OTHERS WERE SICK IN BED FOR A MONTH BEFORE PASSING ON.
STILL OTHERS DIED AFTER DIVINING THE FUTURE.
AND THEIR PREDICTIONS ALL CAME TRUE.
I FEEL LIKE I'M LOSING MY MIND.
I DON'T SUPPOSE HE'LL STOP THIS ANYTIME SOON?
WE'VE NOW LEARNED THAT ALL WHO EAT THE MEAT DIE, EVEN IF THEY DO MANAGE TO SEE THE FUTURE FIRST. SURELY HE'LL GIVE UP ON THIS BEFORE LONG.
HOW CAN YOU SAY THAT?
CREAK

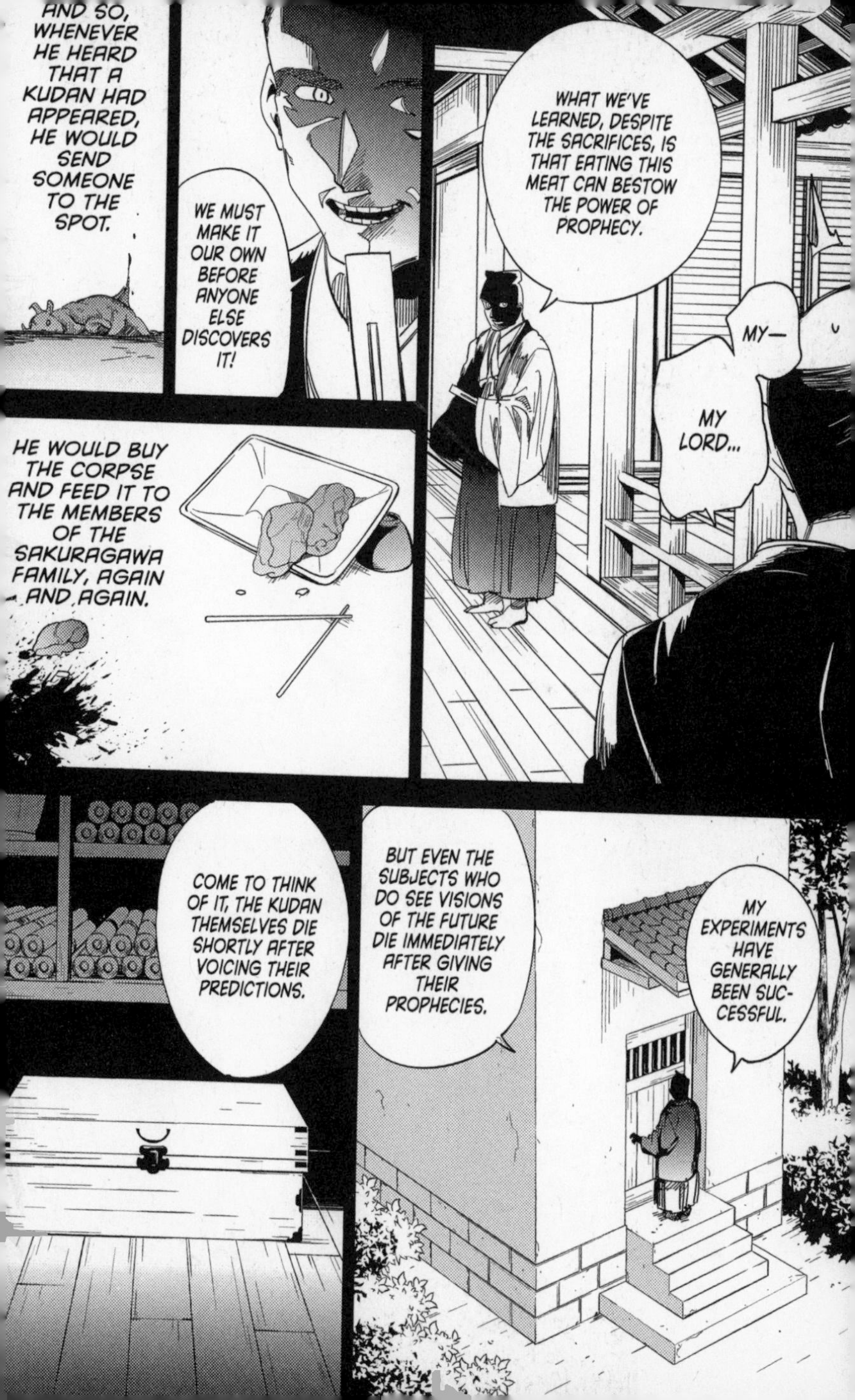
WHAT WE'VE LEARNED, DESPITE THE SACRIFICES, IS THAT EATING THIS MEAT CAN BESTOW THE POWER OF PROPHECY.
MY—
MY LORD...
WE MUST MAKE IT OUR OWN BEFORE ANYONE ELSE DISCOVERS IT!
AND SO, WHENEVER HE HEARD THAT A KUDAN HAD APPEARED, HE WOULD SEND SOMEONE TO THE SPOT.
HE WOULD BUY THE CORPSE AND FEED IT TO THE MEMBERS OF THE SAKURAGAWA FAMILY, AGAIN AND AGAIN.
MY EXPERIMENTS HAVE GENERALLY BEEN SUC-CESSFUL.
BUT EVEN THE SUBJECTS WHO DO SEE VISIONS OF THE FUTURE DIE IMMEDIATELY AFTER GIVING THEIR PROPHECIES.
COME TO THINK OF IT, THE KUDAN THEMSELVES DIE SHORTLY AFTER VOICING THEIR PREDICTIONS.

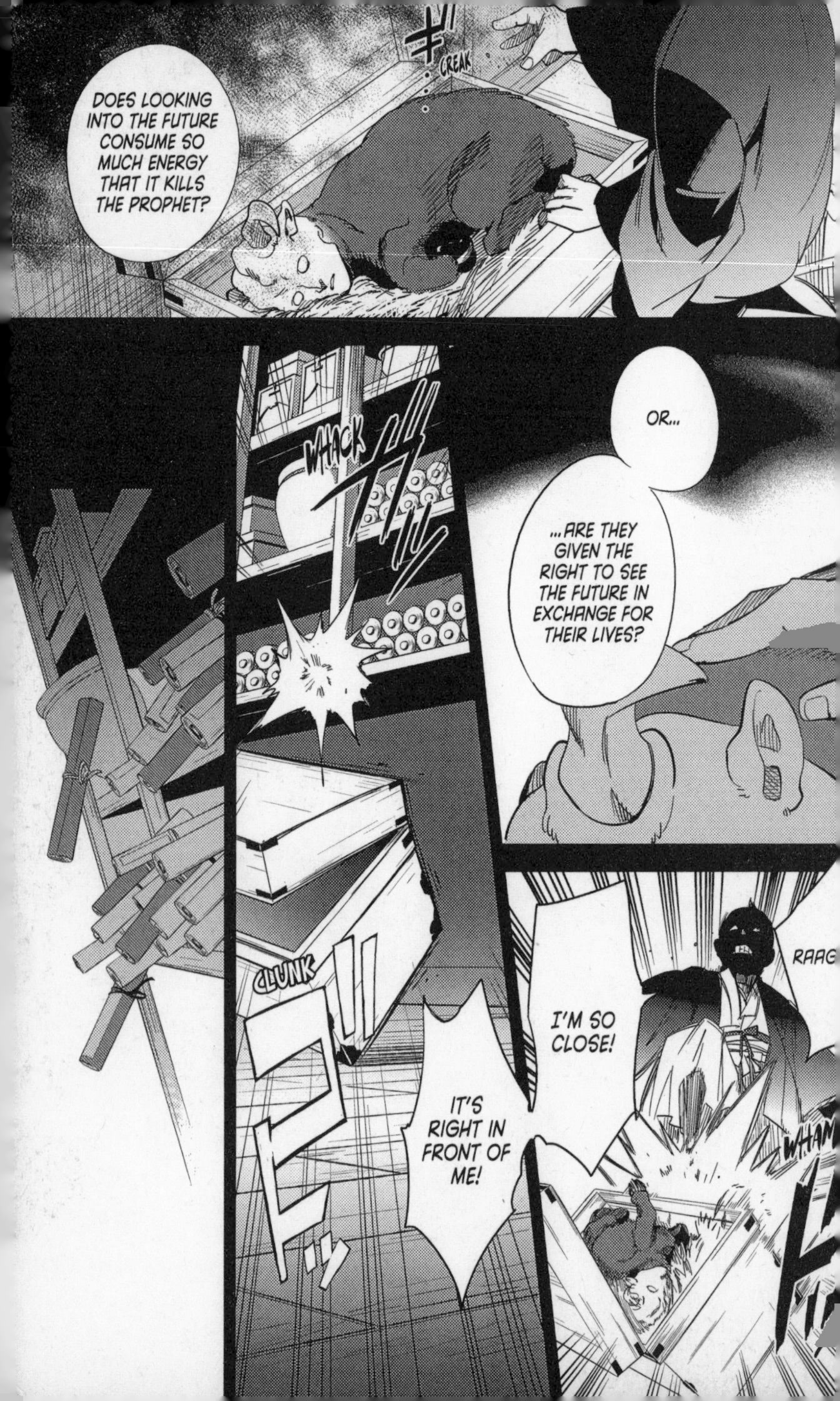
CREAK
DOES LOOKING INTO THE FUTURE CONSUME SO MUCH ENERGY THAT IT KILLS THE PROPHET?
OR...
...ARE THEY GIVEN THE RIGHT TO SEE THE FUTURE IN EXCHANGE FOR THEIR LIVES?
RAAG
I'M SO CLOSE!
IT'S RIGHT IN FRONT OF ME!
WHAM
WHACK
CLUNK

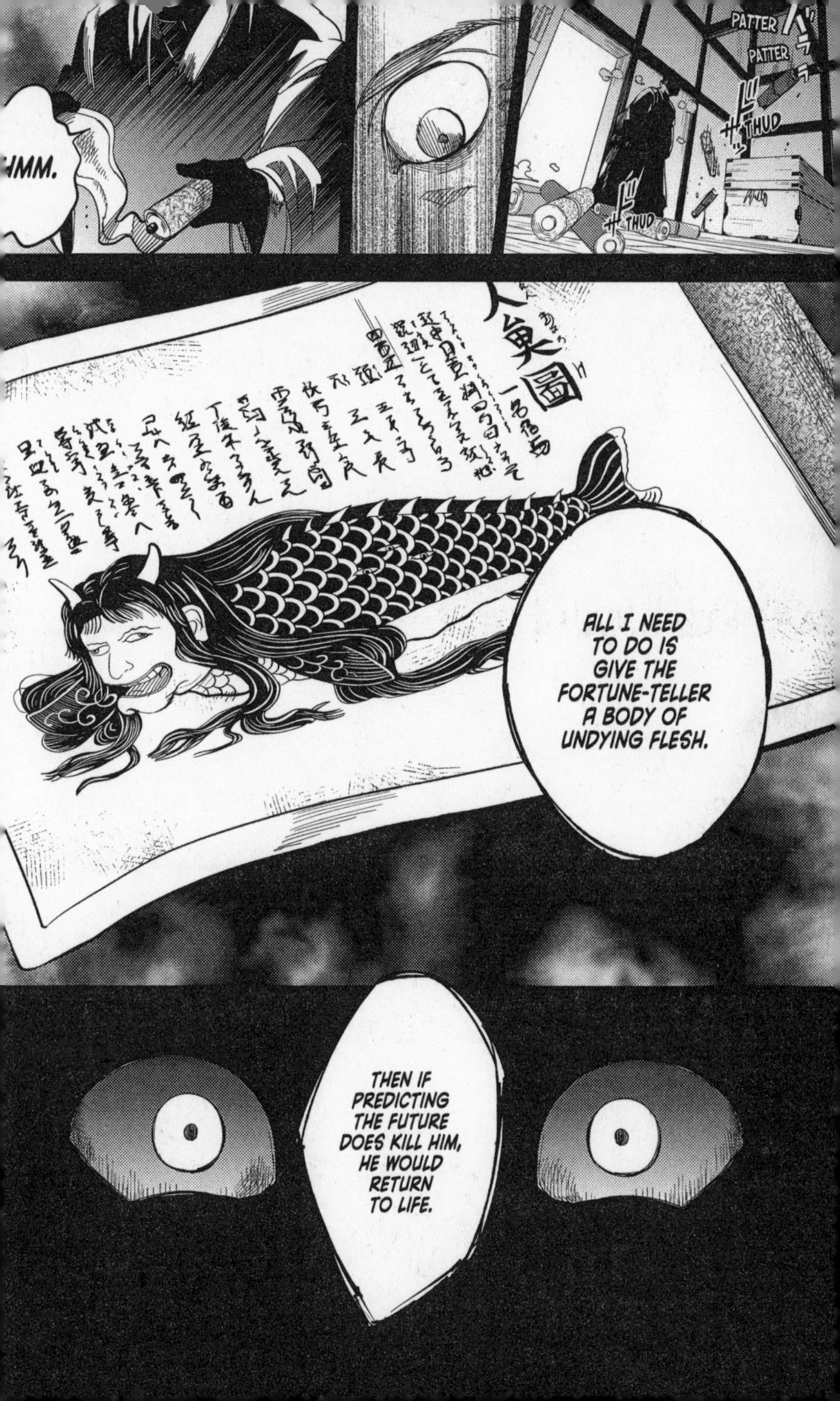
PATTER
PATTER
THUD
THUD
HMM.
ALL I NEED TO DO IS GIVE THE FORTUNE-TELLER A BODY OF UNDYING FLESH.
THEN IF PREDICTING THE FUTURE DOES KILL HIM, HE WOULD RETURN TO LIFE.

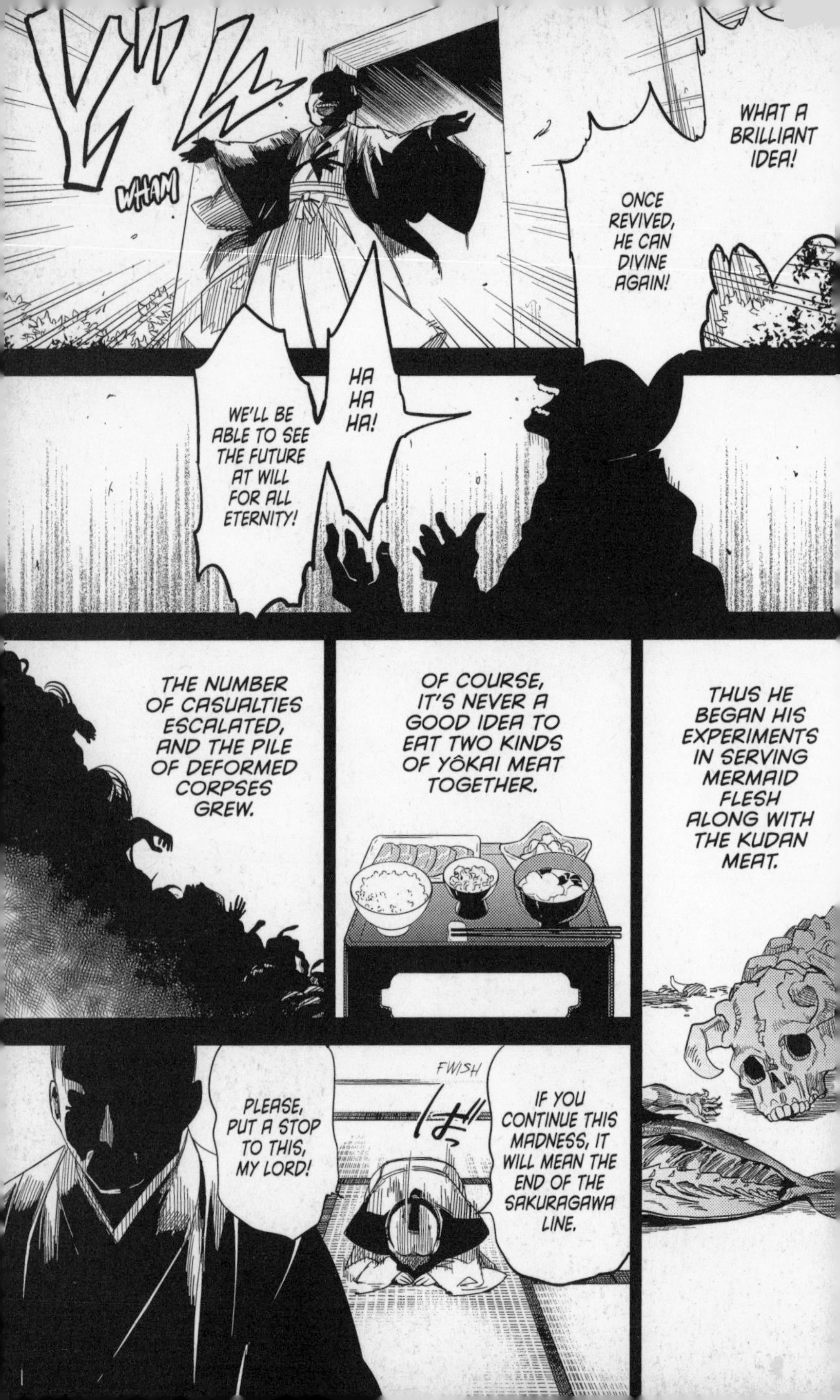
WHAT A BRILLIANT IDEA!
ONCE REVIVED, HE CAN DIVINE AGAIN!
WHAM
HA HA HA!
WE'LL BE ABLE TO SEE THE FUTURE AT WILL FOR ALL ETERNITY!
THUS HE BEGAN HIS EXPERIMENTS IN SERVING MERMAID FLESH ALONG WITH THE KUDAN MEAT.
OF COURSE, IT'S NEVER A GOOD IDEA TO EAT TWO KINDS OF YÔKAI MEAT TOGETHER.
THE NUMBER OF CASUALTIES ESCALATED, AND THE PILE OF DEFORMED CORPSES GREW.
FWISH
IF YOU CONTINUE THIS MADNESS, IT WILL MEAN THE END OF THE SAKURAGAWA LINE.
PLEASE, PUT A STOP TO THIS, MY LORD!

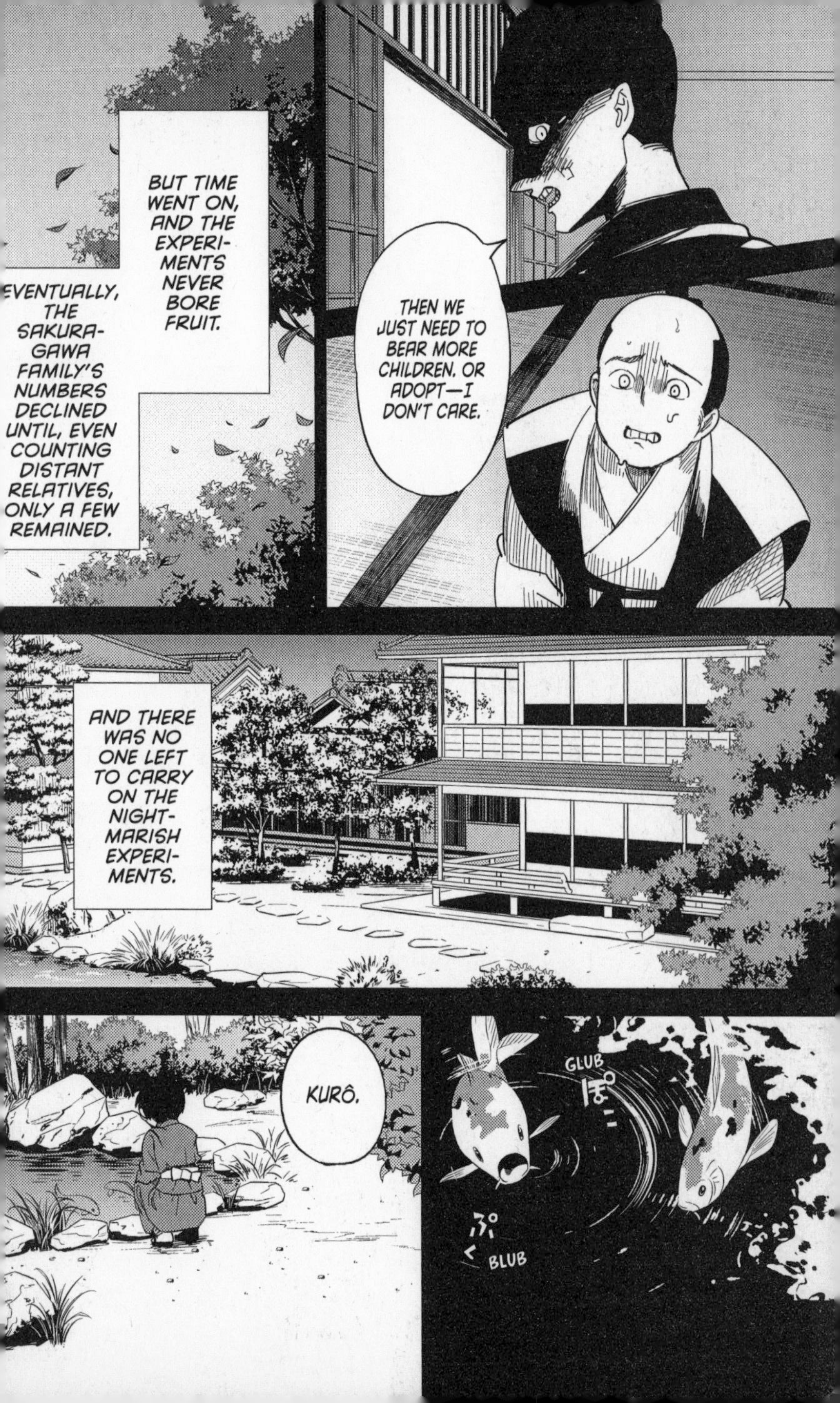

THEN WE JUST NEED TO BEAR MORE CHILDREN. OR ADOPT—I DON'T CARE.
BUT TIME WENT ON, AND THE EXPERIMENTS NEVER BORE FRUIT.
EVENTUALLY, THE SAKURAGAWA FAMILY'S NUMBERS DECLINED UNTIL, EVEN COUNTING DISTANT RELATIVES, ONLY A FEW REMAINED.
AND THERE WAS NO ONE LEFT TO CARRY ON THE NIGHTMARISH EXPERIMENTS.
GLUB
ぽ
ぷ
BLUB
KURÔ.

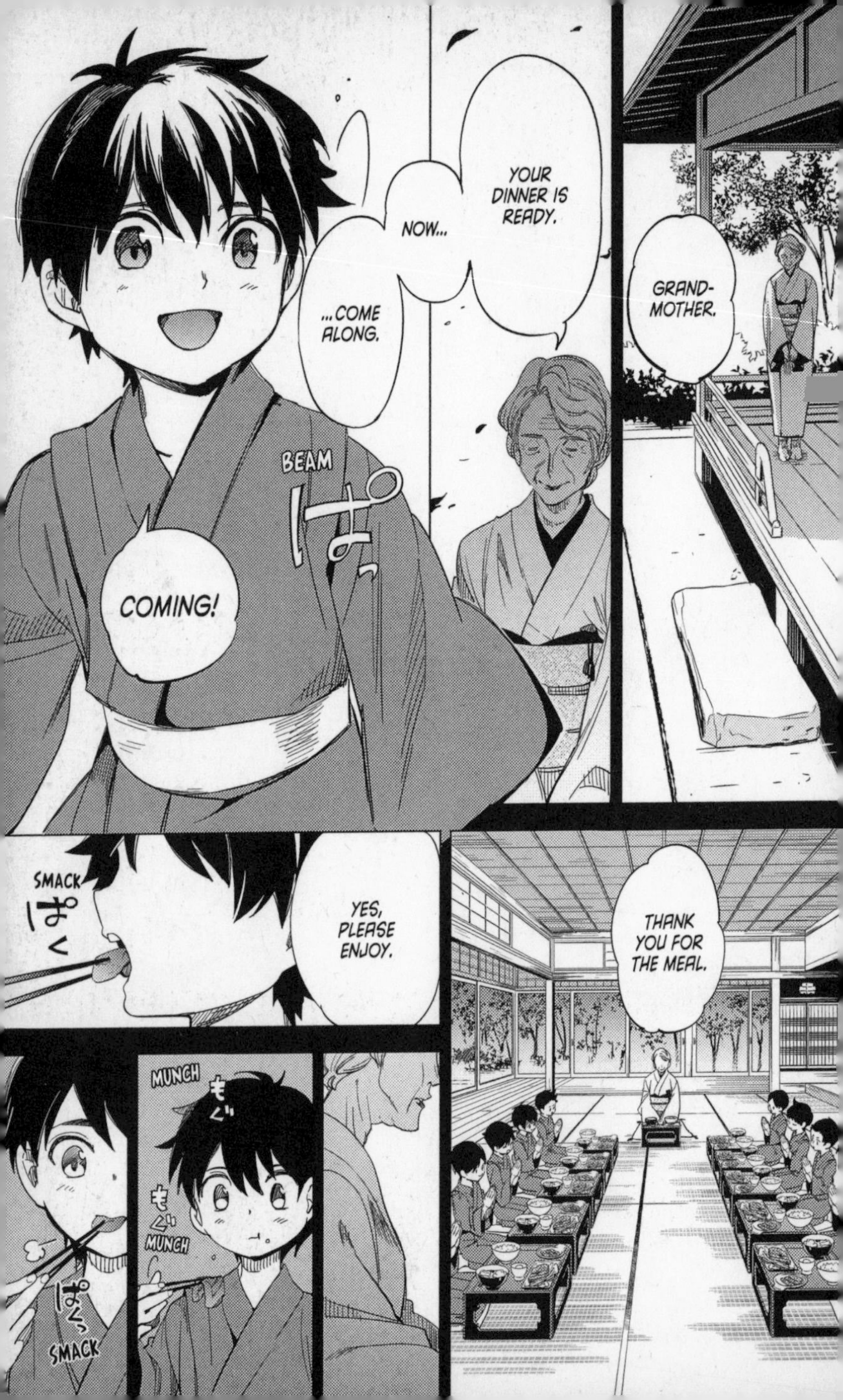
GRAND-MOTHER.
YOUR DINNER IS READY.
NOW...
...COME ALONG.
BEAM
ぱっ
COMING!
THANK YOU FOR THE MEAL.
YES, PLEASE ENJOY.
SMACK
ぱく
MUNCH
もぐ
もぐ
MUNCH
ぱくっ
SMACK

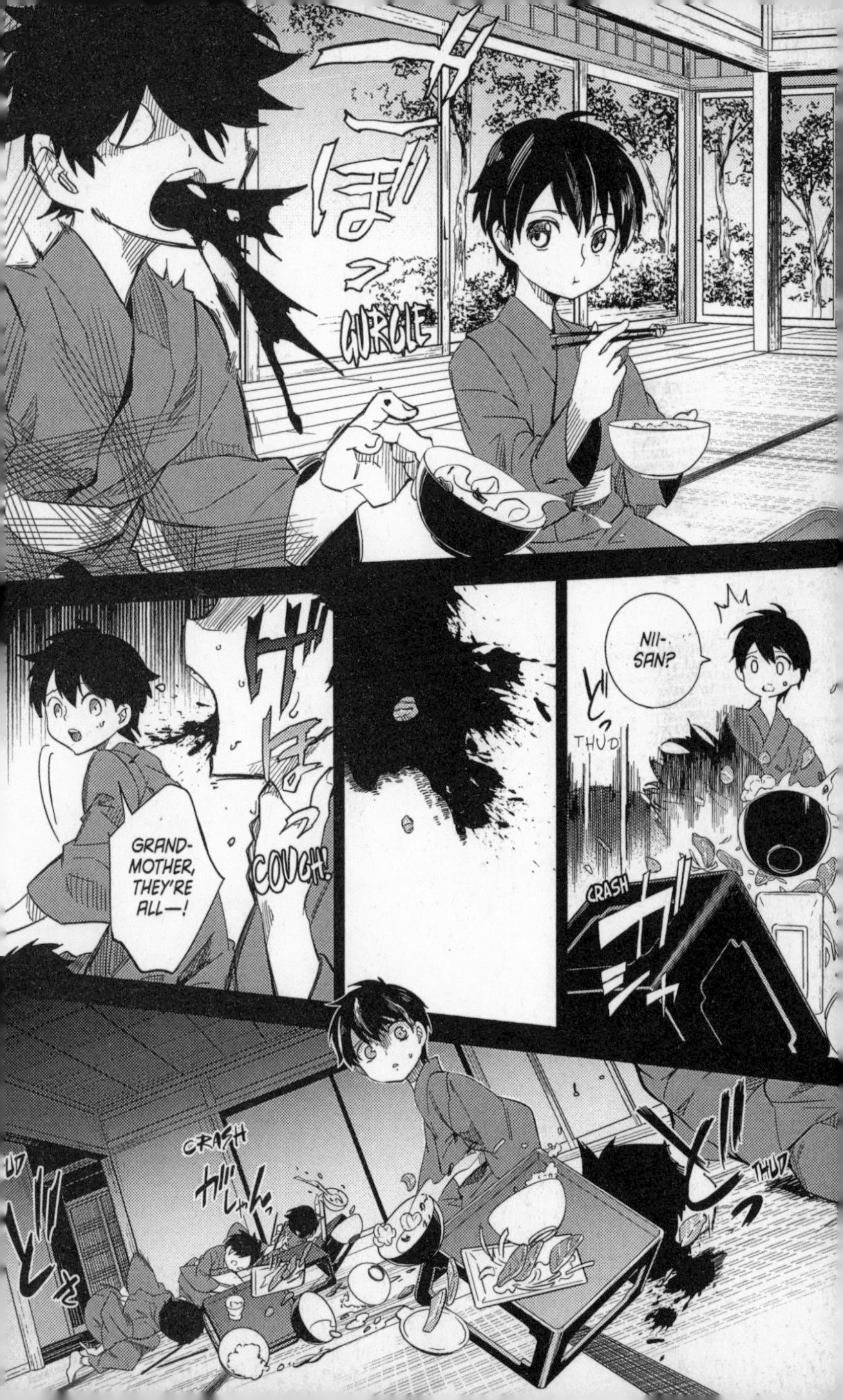

ごぼっ
GURGLE
NII-SAN?
どっ
THUD
CRASH
ガシャ
げほっ
COUGH!
GRANDMOTHER, THEY'RE ALL—!
どっ
THUD
CRASH
がしゃん
どさ

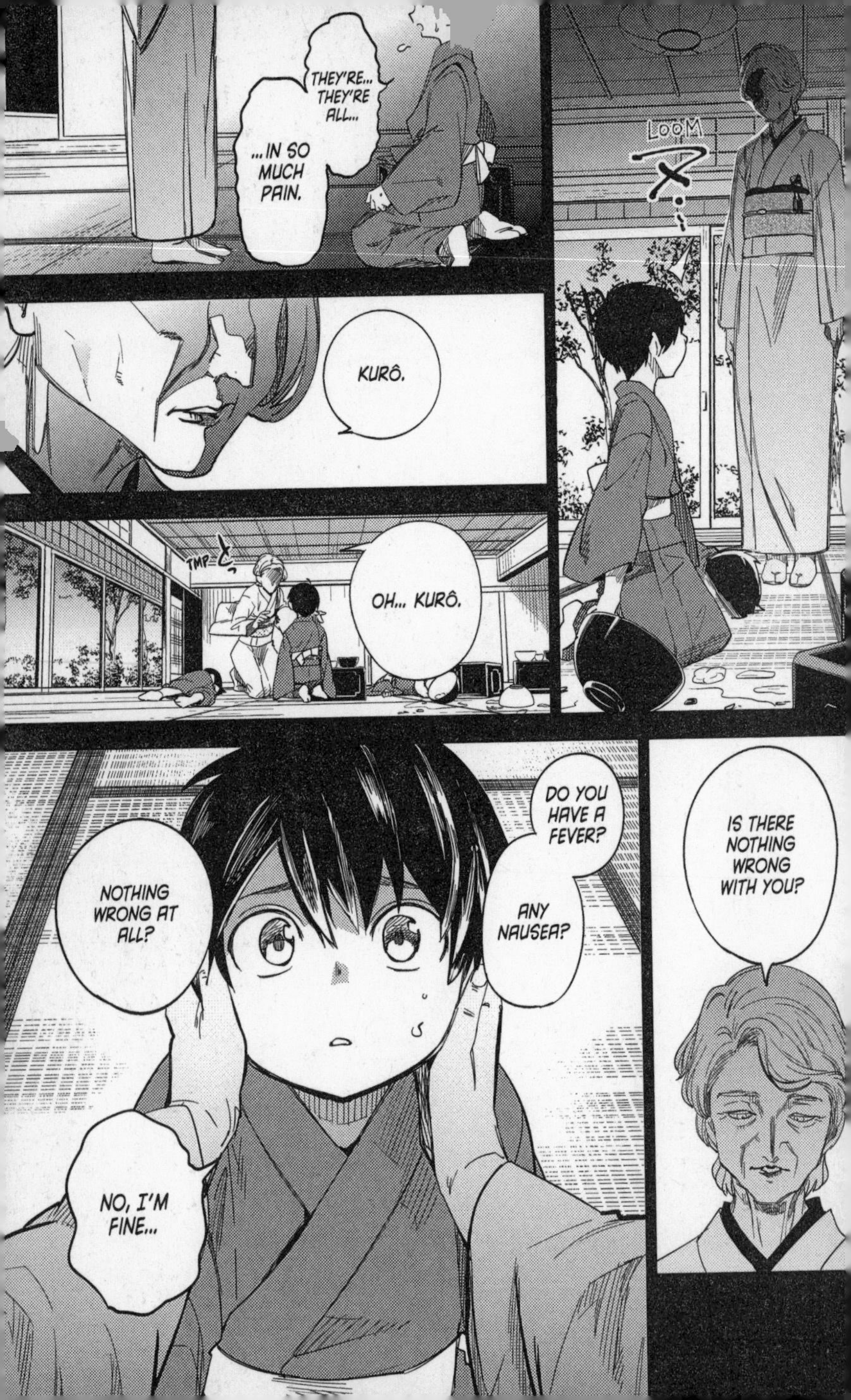
LOOM
THEY'RE... THEY'RE ALL...
...IN SO MUCH PAIN.
KURÔ.
TMP
OH... KURÔ.
IS THERE NOTHING WRONG WITH YOU?
DO YOU HAVE A FEVER?
ANY NAUSEA?
NOTHING WRONG AT ALL?
NO, I'M FINE...

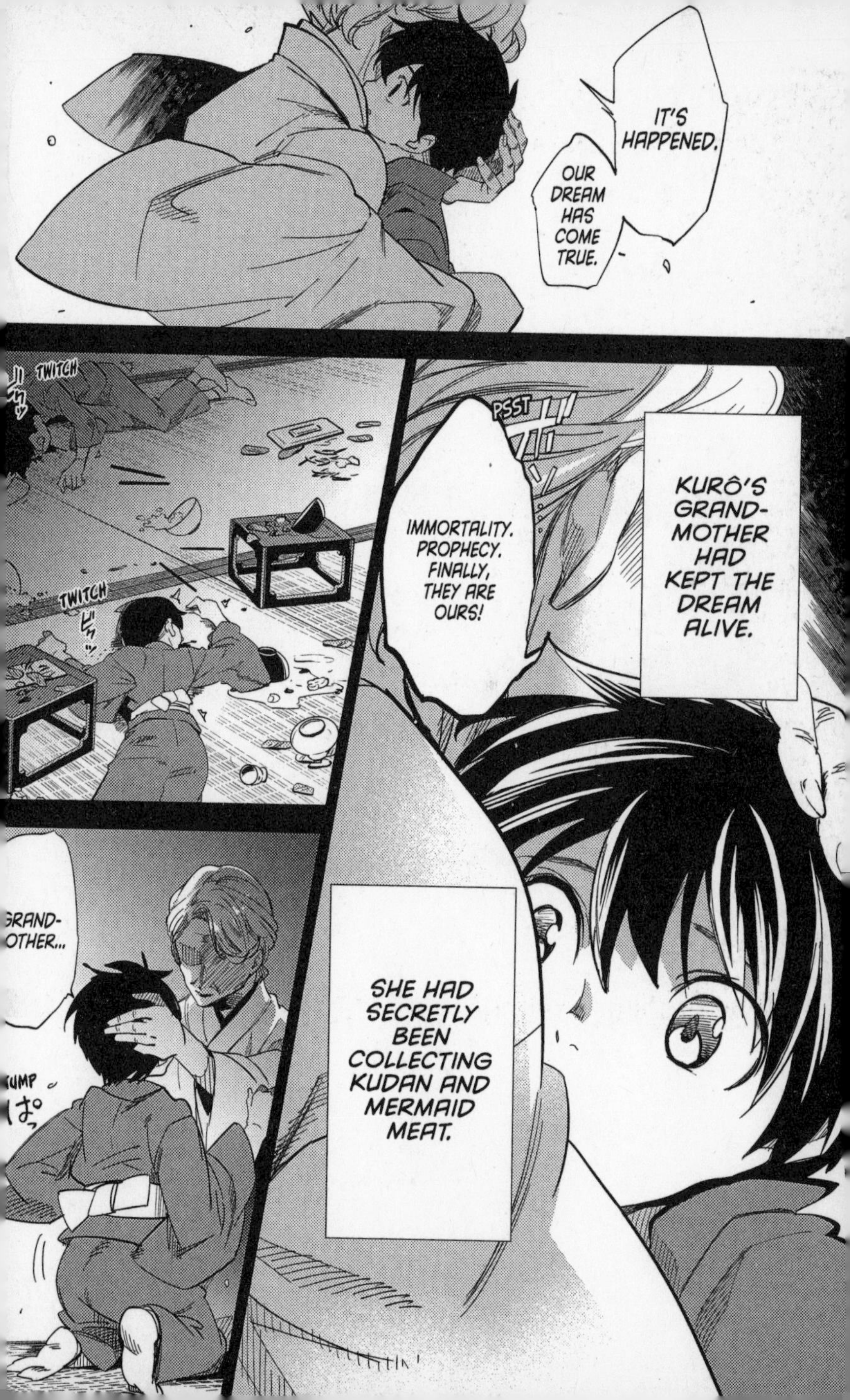
IT'S HAPPENED.
OUR DREAM HAS COME TRUE.
PSST
KURÔ'S GRANDMOTHER HAD KEPT THE DREAM ALIVE.
IMMORTALITY. PROPHECY. FINALLY, THEY ARE OURS!
SHE HAD SECRETLY BEEN COLLECTING KUDAN AND MERMAID MEAT.
TWITCH
TWITCH
GRAND- OTHER...
UMP

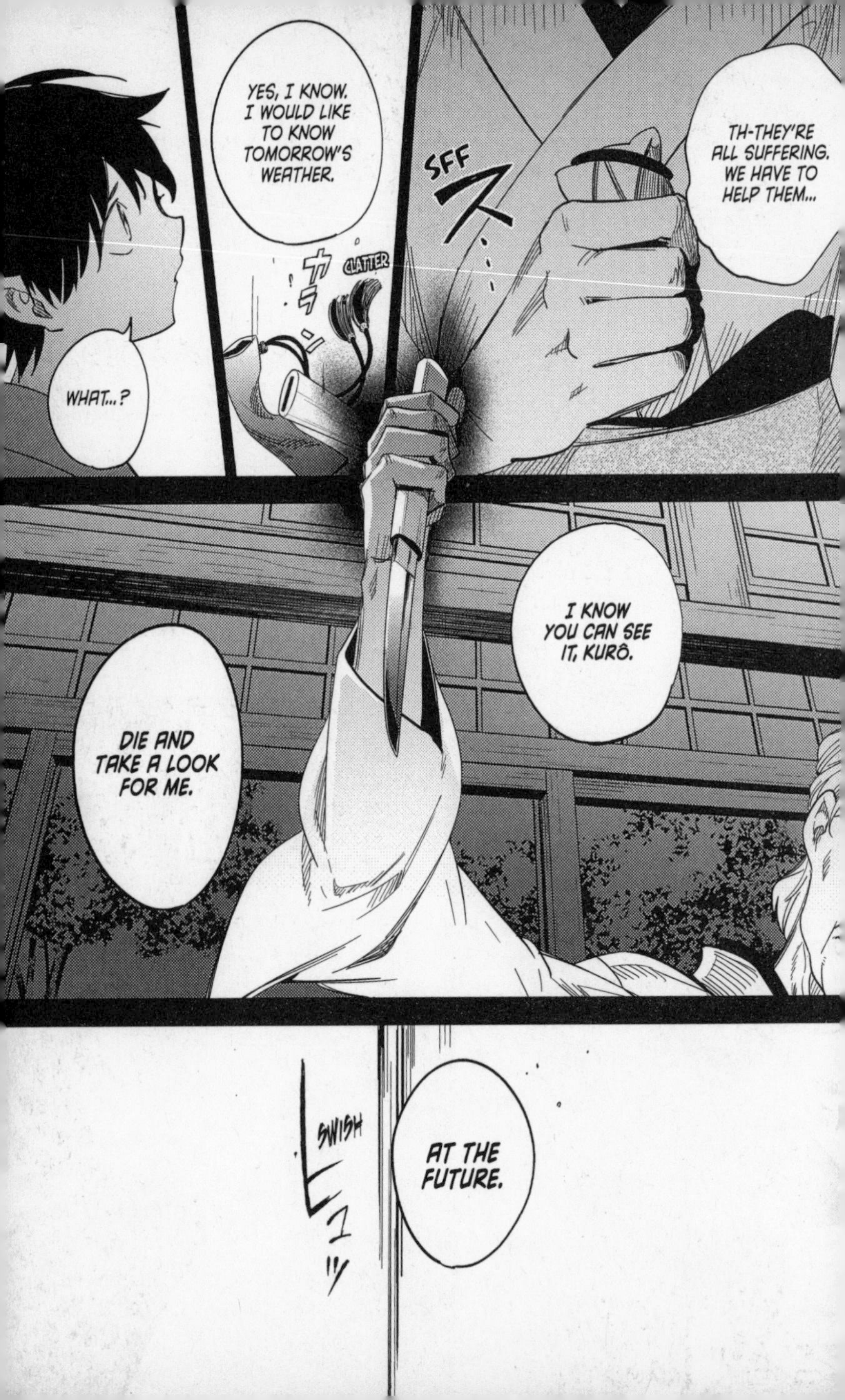
TH-THEY'RE ALL SUFFERING. WE HAVE TO HELP THEM...
SFF
YES, I KNOW. I WOULD LIKE TO KNOW TOMORROW'S WEATHER.
CLATTER
WHAT...?
I KNOW YOU CAN SEE IT, KURÔ.
DIE AND TAKE A LOOK FOR ME.
AT THE FUTURE.
SWISH

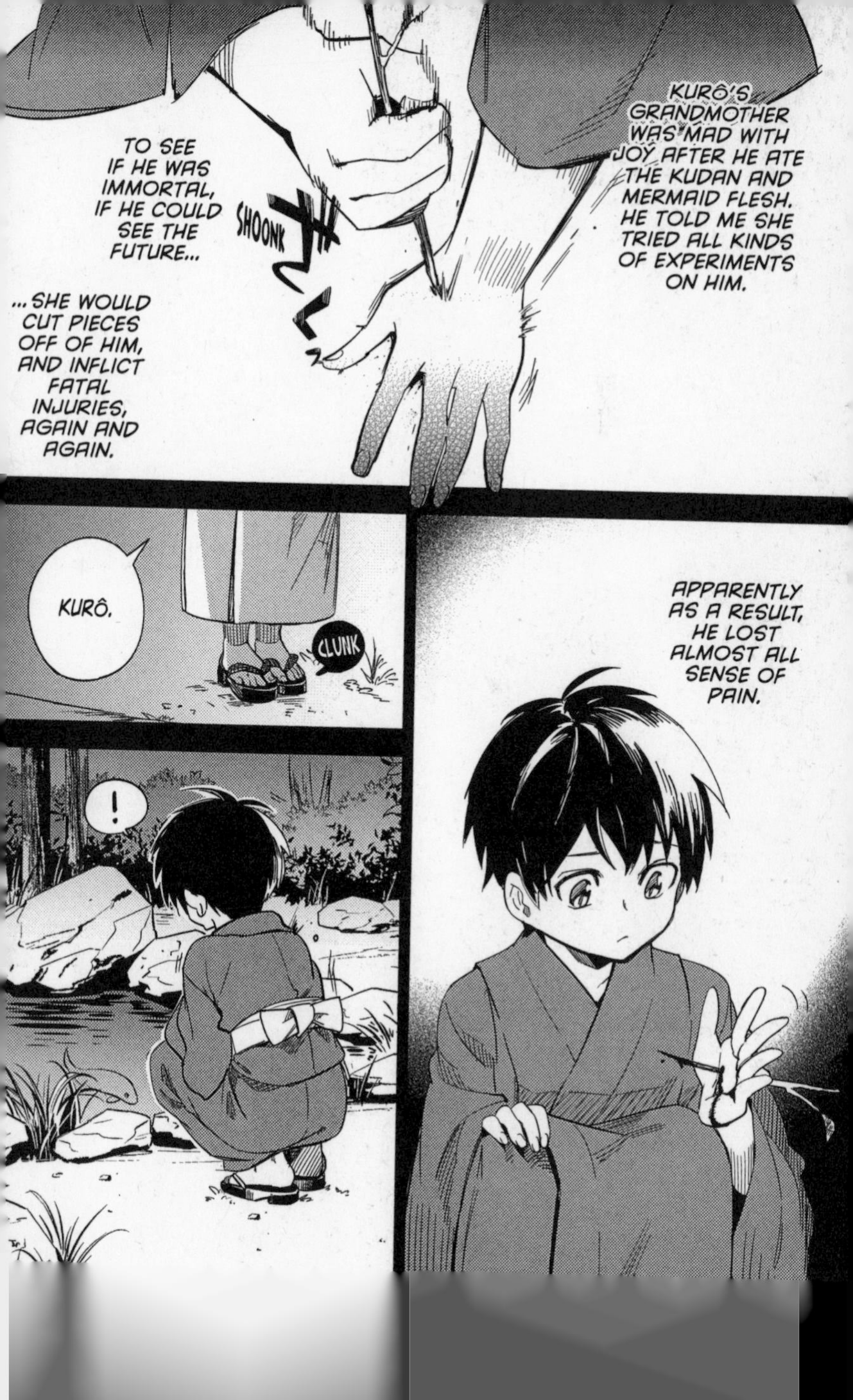
KURÔ'S GRANDMOTHER WAS MAD WITH JOY AFTER HE ATE THE KUDAN AND MERMAID FLESH. HE TOLD ME SHE TRIED ALL KINDS OF EXPERIMENTS ON HIM.
TO SEE IF HE WAS IMMORTAL, IF HE COULD SEE THE FUTURE...
SHOONK
...SHE WOULD CUT PIECES OFF OF HIM, AND INFLICT FATAL INJURIES, AGAIN AND AGAIN.
APPARENTLY AS A RESULT, HE LOST ALMOST ALL SENSE OF PAIN.
KURÔ.
CLUNK
!

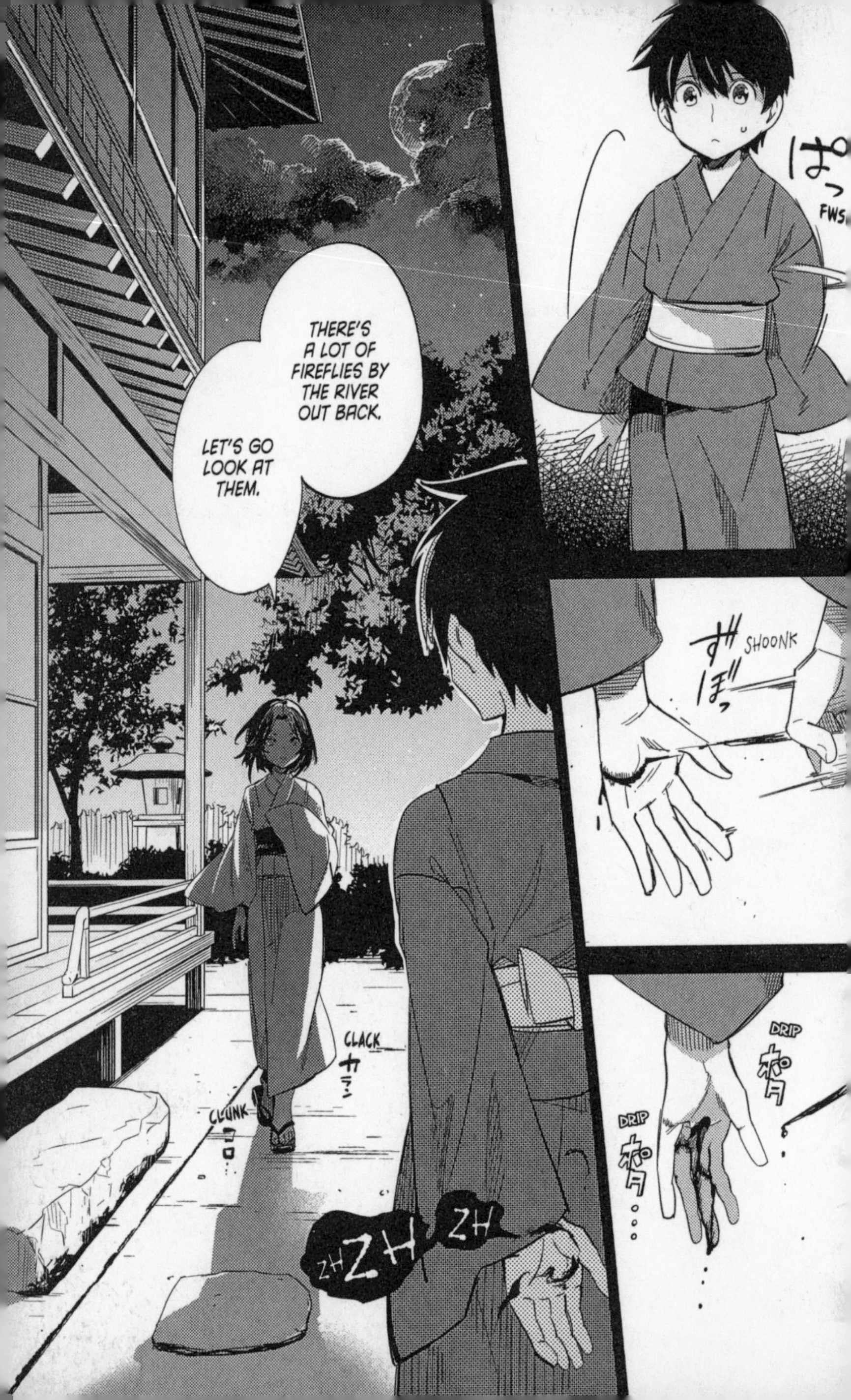
ぱっ
FWS
ずぼっ
SHOONK
DRIP
ぽた
DRIP
ぽた…
THERE'S A LOT OF FIREFLIES BY THE RIVER OUT BACK.
LET'S GO LOOK AT THEM.
CLACK
カラン
CLUNK
コロ…

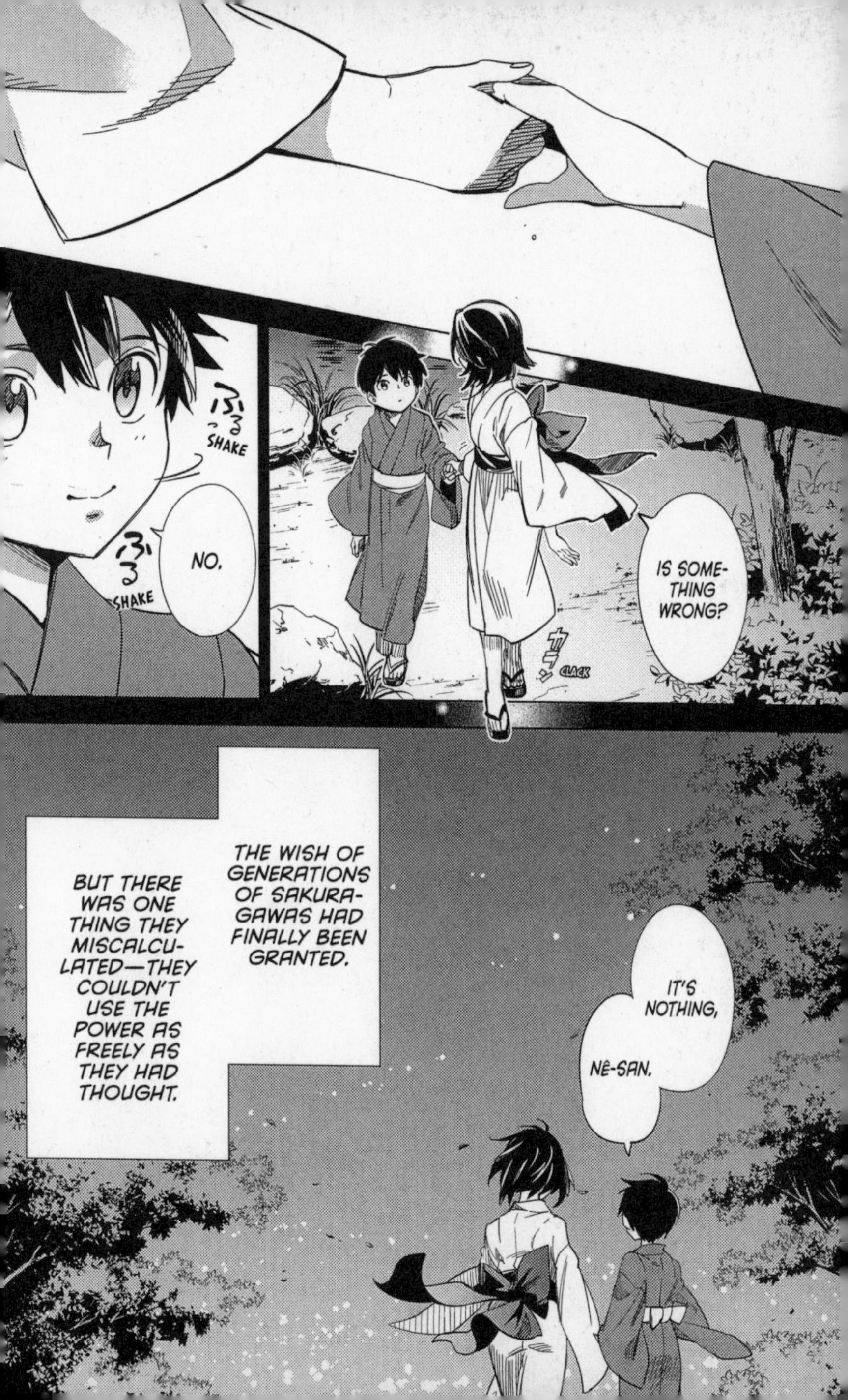
IS SOME-THING WRONG?
CLACK
SHAKE
SHAKE
NO.
THE WISH OF GENERATIONS OF SAKURA-GAWAS HAD FINALLY BEEN GRANTED.
BUT THERE WAS ONE THING THEY MISCALCU-LATED—THEY COULDN'T USE THE POWER AS FREELY AS THEY HAD THOUGHT.
IT'S NOTHING,
NÊ-SAN.

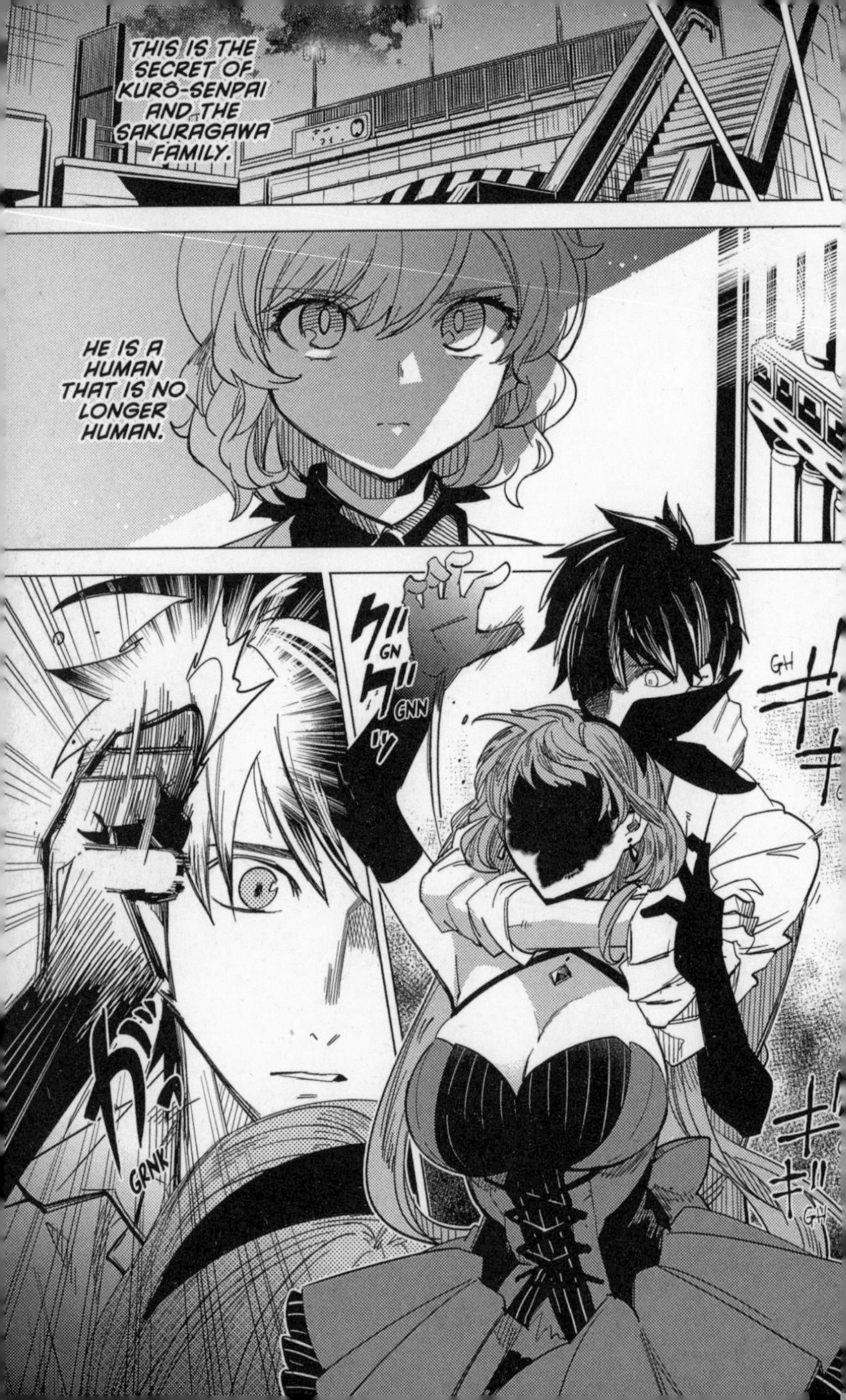
THIS IS THE SECRET OF KURÔ-SENPAI AND THE SAKURAGAWA FAMILY.
HE IS A HUMAN THAT IS NO LONGER HUMAN.
GH
GN
GNN
GRNK
GH

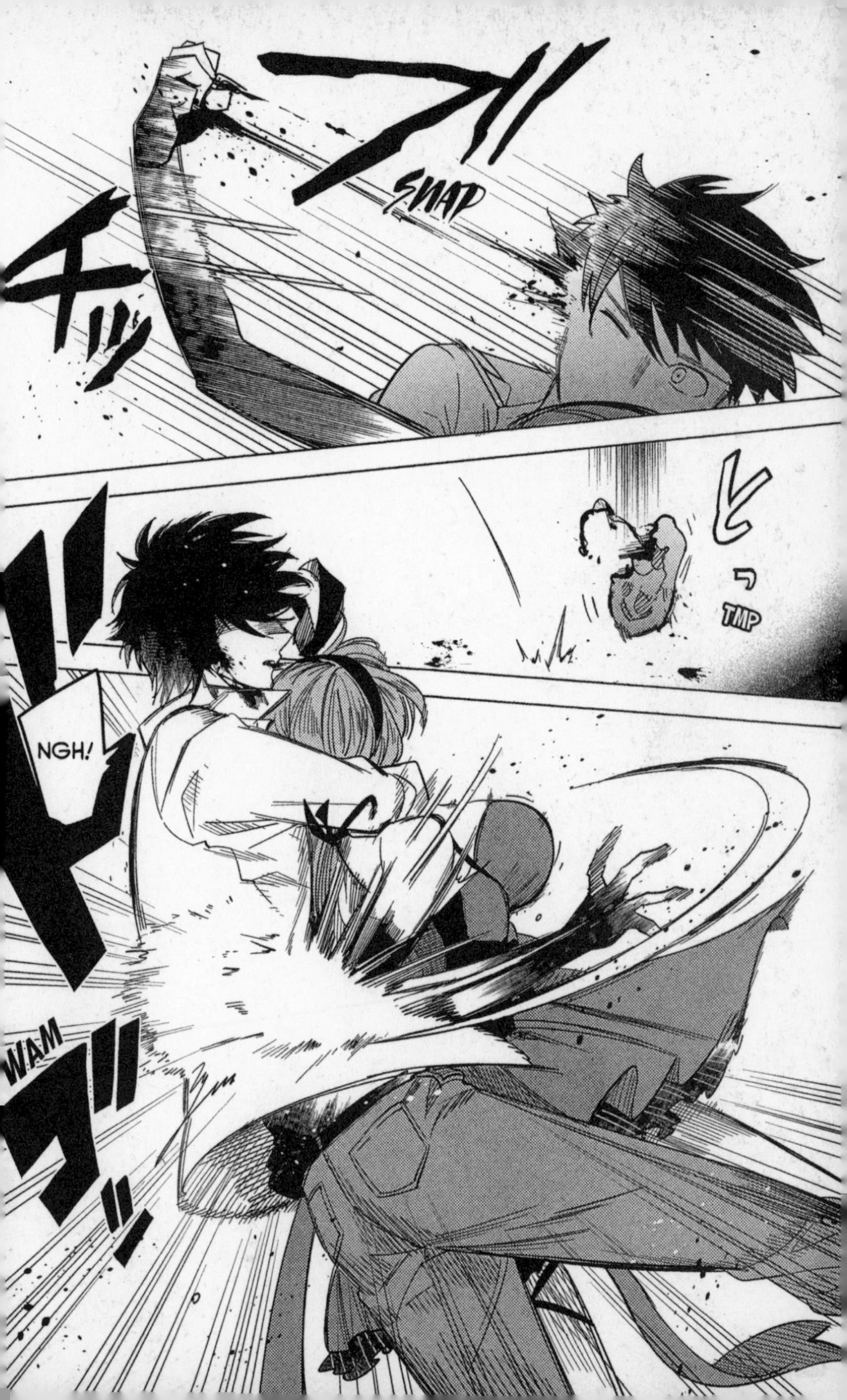
SNAP
TMP
NGH!
WAM

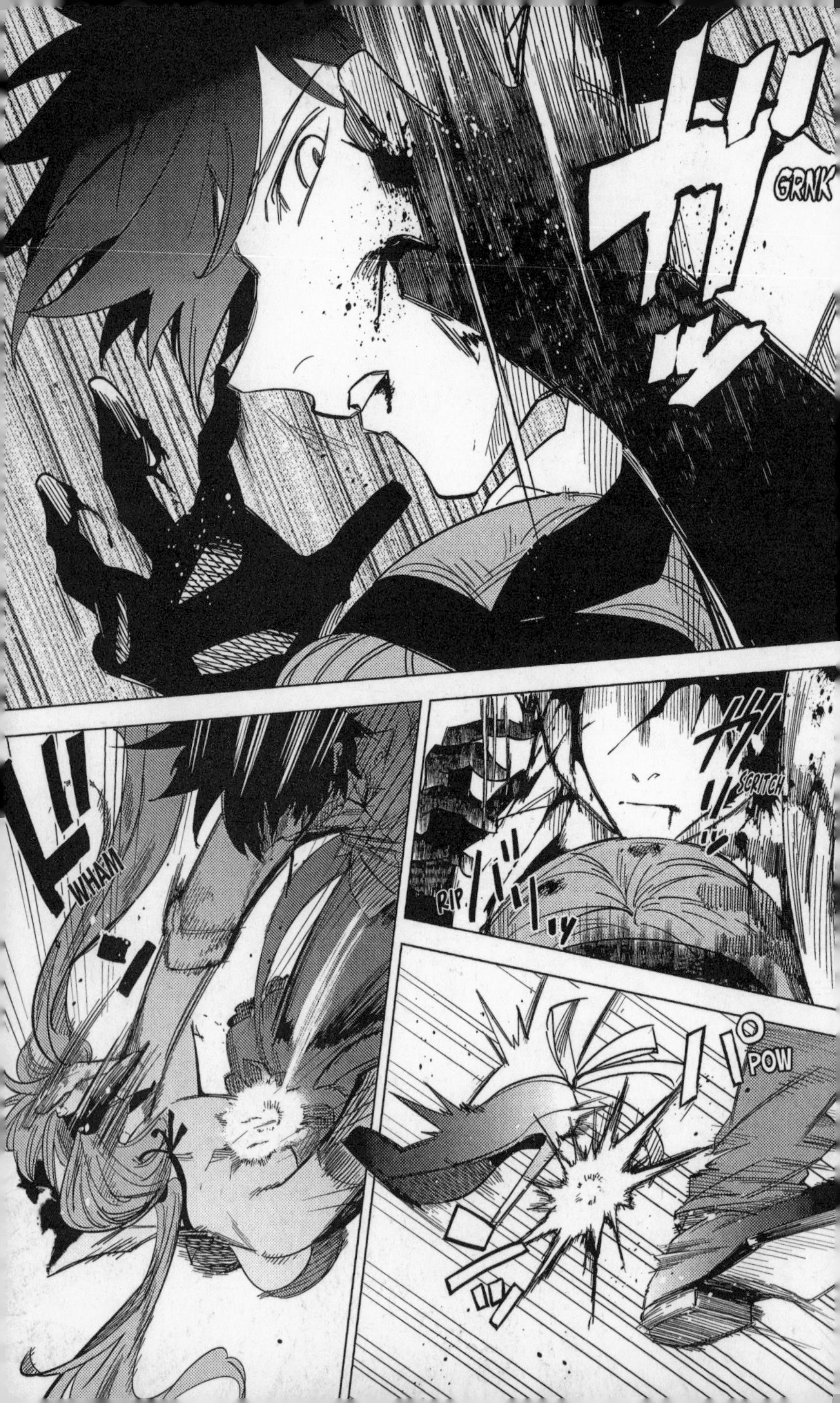
GRNK
SCRITCH
RIP
WHAM
POW

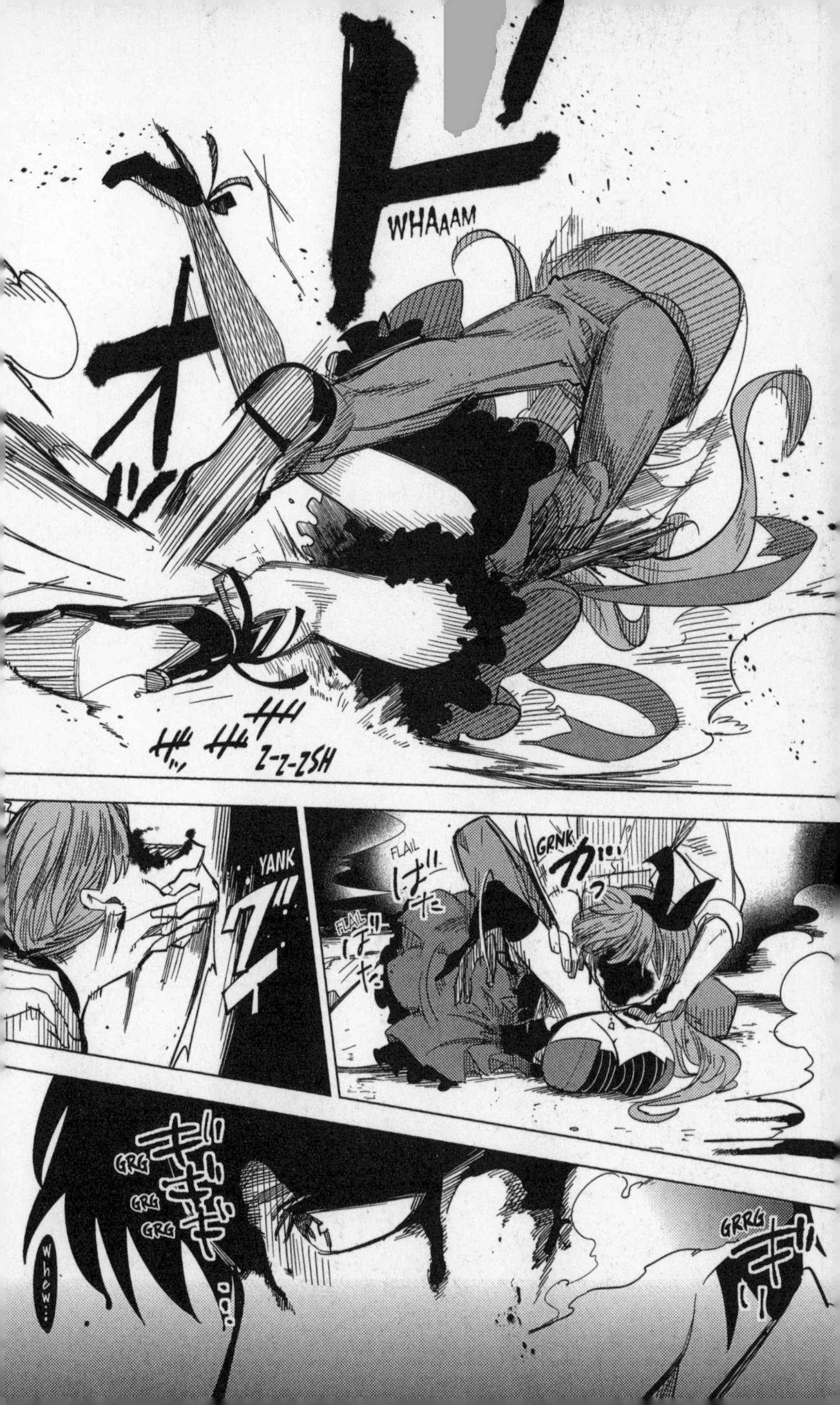
WHAAAM
Z-Z-ZSH
GRNK
FLAIL
FLAIL
YANK
GRRG
GRG
GRG
GRG
Whew...

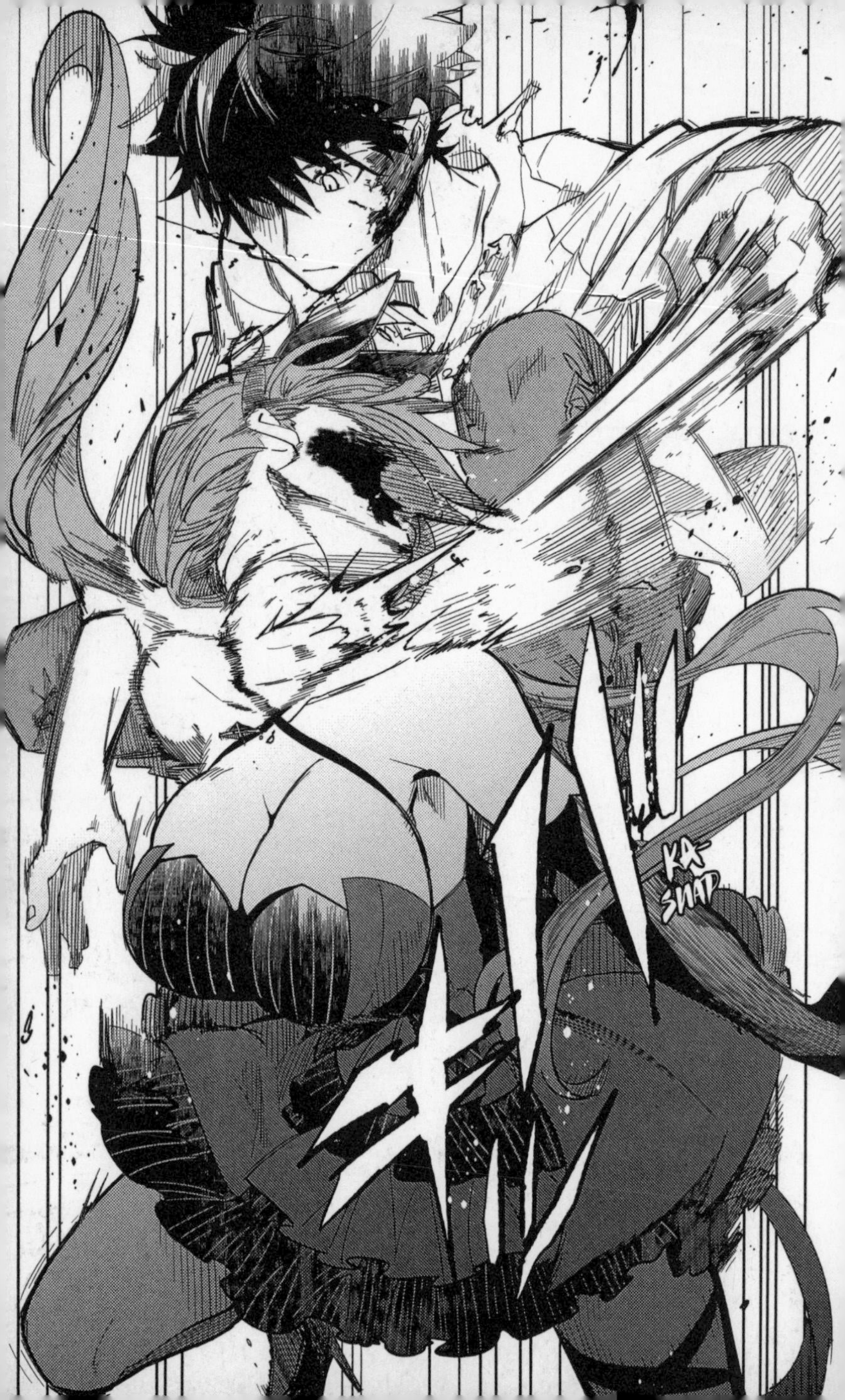
KA-SNAP

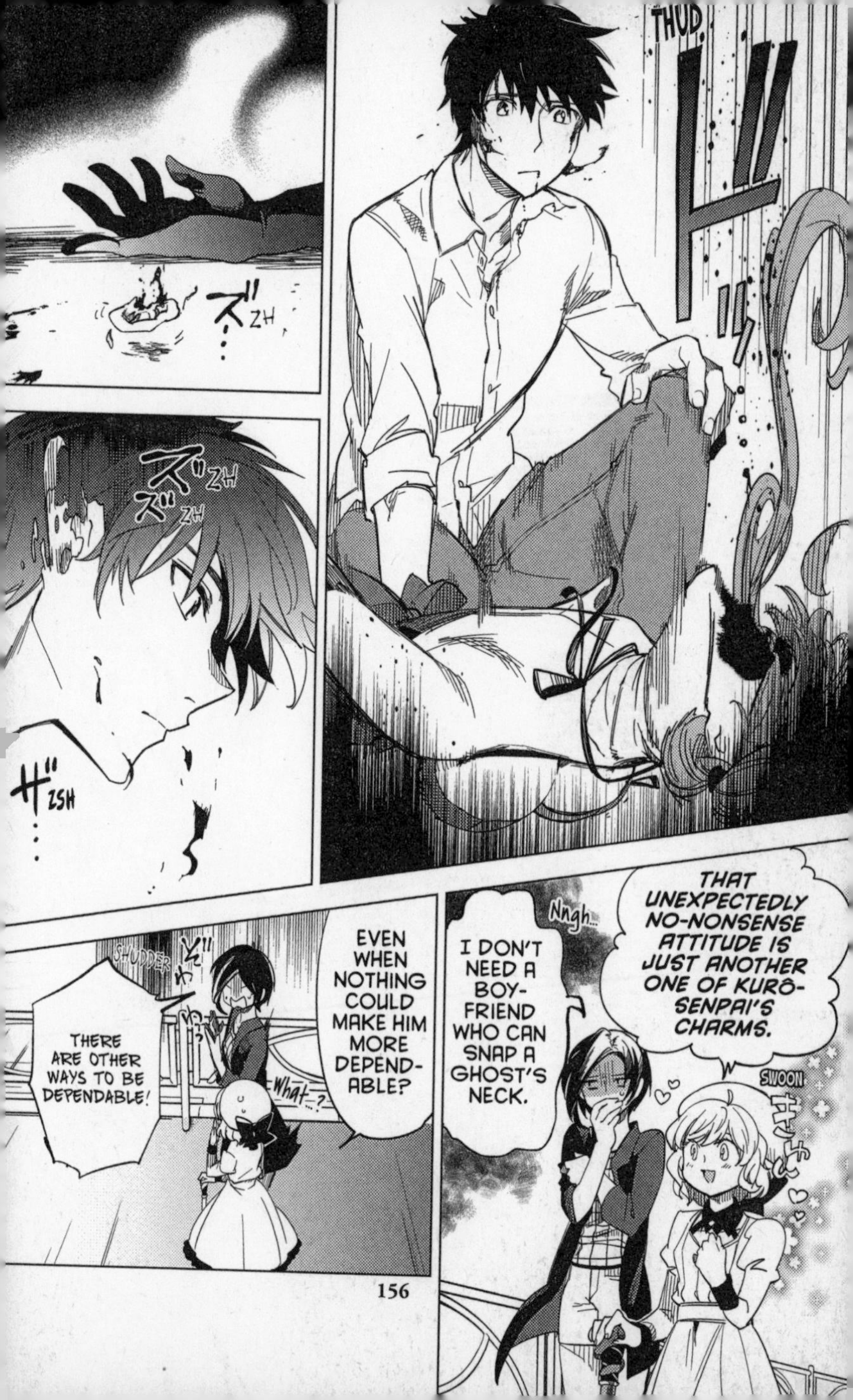
THUD
ZH
ZH
ZH
ZSH
THAT UNEXPECTEDLY NO-NONSENSE ATTITUDE IS JUST ANOTHER ONE OF KURÔ-SENPAI'S CHARMS.
Nngh...
I DON'T NEED A BOY-FRIEND WHO CAN SNAP A GHOST'S NECK.
SWOON
EVEN WHEN NOTHING COULD MAKE HIM MORE DEPEND-ABLE?
SHUDDER
What...?
THERE ARE OTHER WAYS TO BE DEPENDABLE!

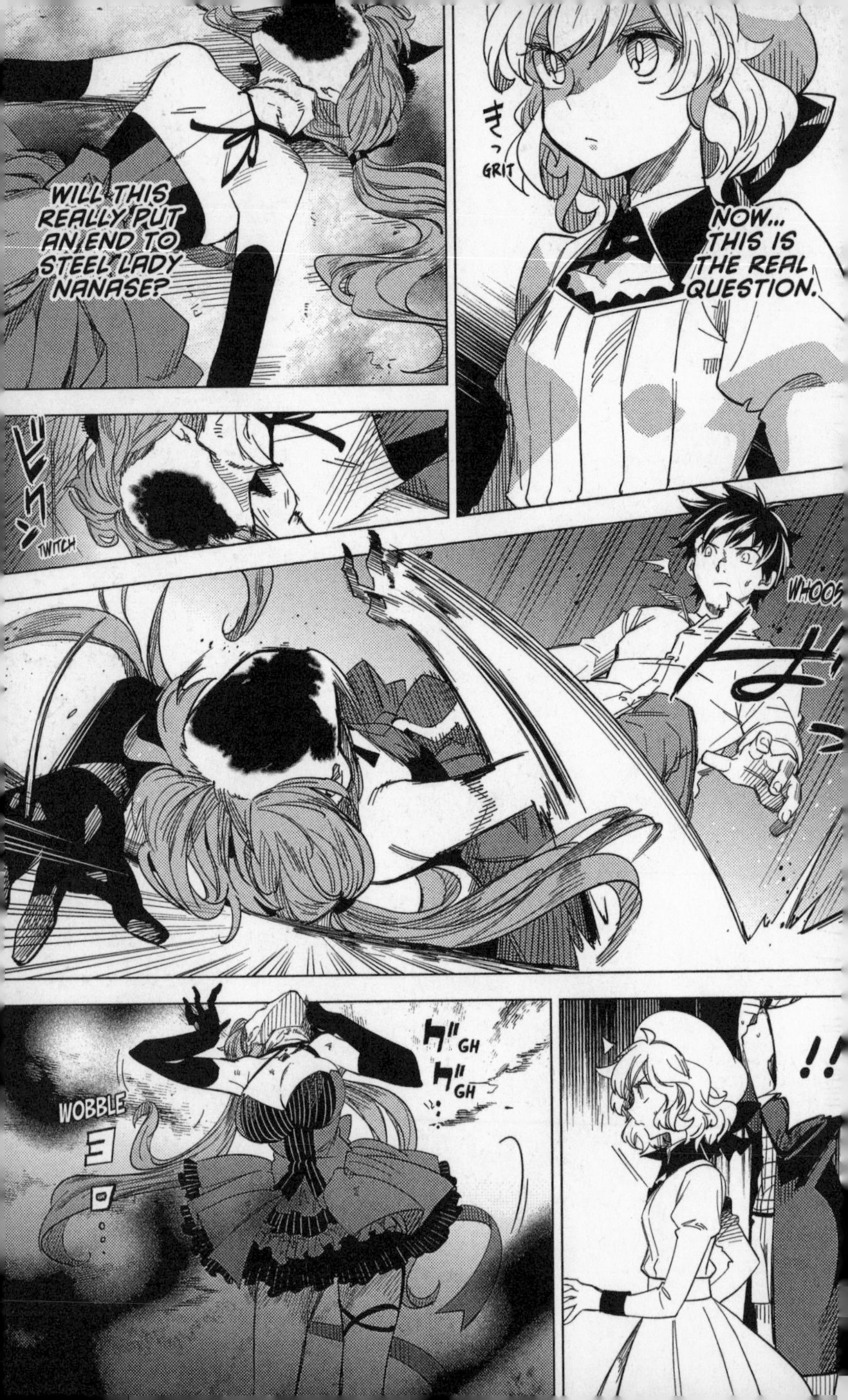
きっ
GRIT
NOW... THIS IS THE REAL QUESTION.
WILL THIS REALLY PUT AN END TO STEEL LADY NANASE?
ビクン
TWITCH
WHOOS
!!
グ GH
グ GH
WOBBLE
ヨロ

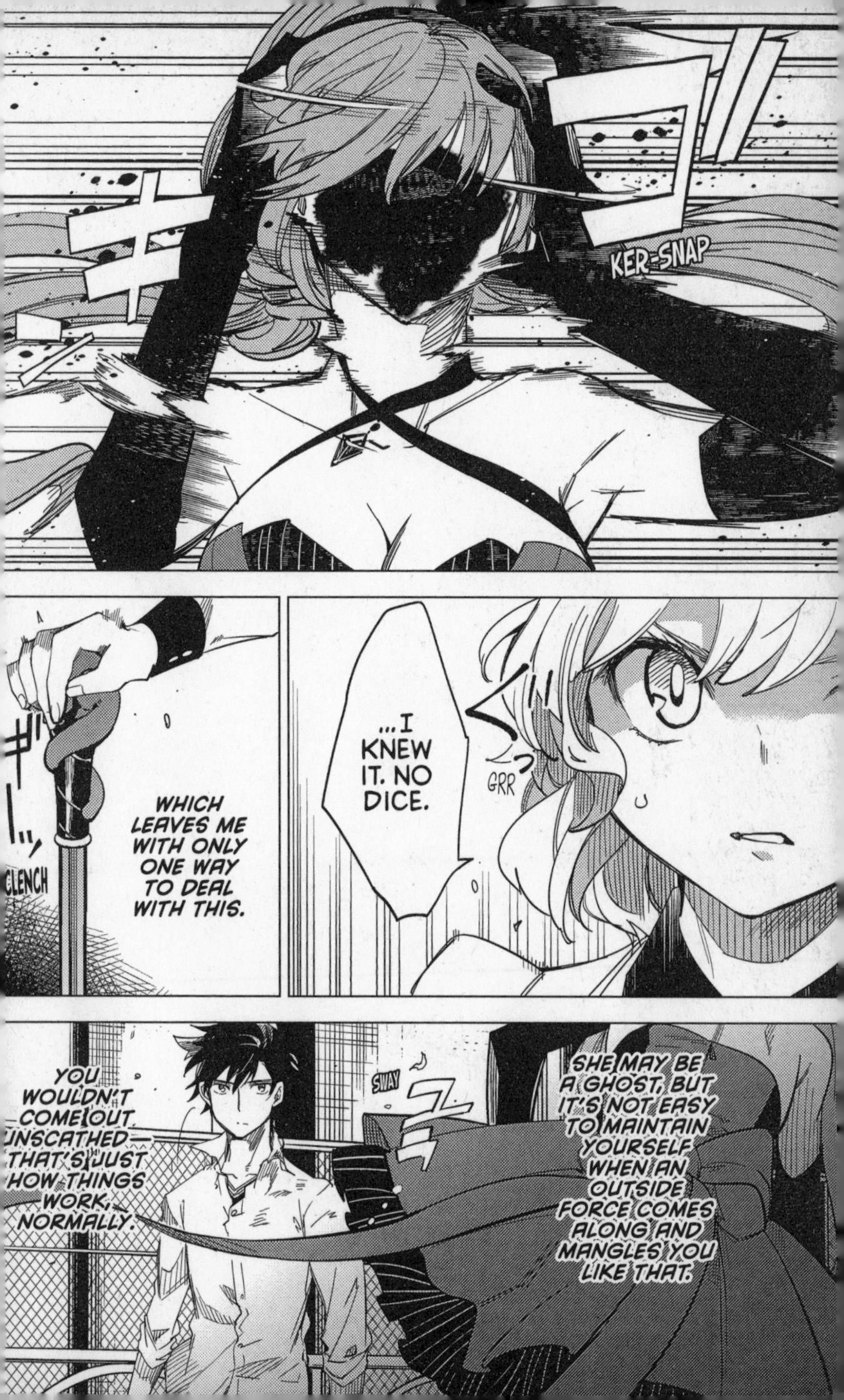
KER-SNAP
...I KNEW IT. NO DICE.
GRR
WHICH LEAVES ME WITH ONLY ONE WAY TO DEAL WITH THIS.
CLENCH
SHE MAY BE A GHOST, BUT IT'S NOT EASY TO MAINTAIN YOURSELF WHEN AN OUTSIDE FORCE COMES ALONG AND MANGLES YOU LIKE THAT.
SWAY
YOU WOULDN'T COME OUT UNSCATHED— THAT'S JUST HOW THINGS WORK, NORMALLY.

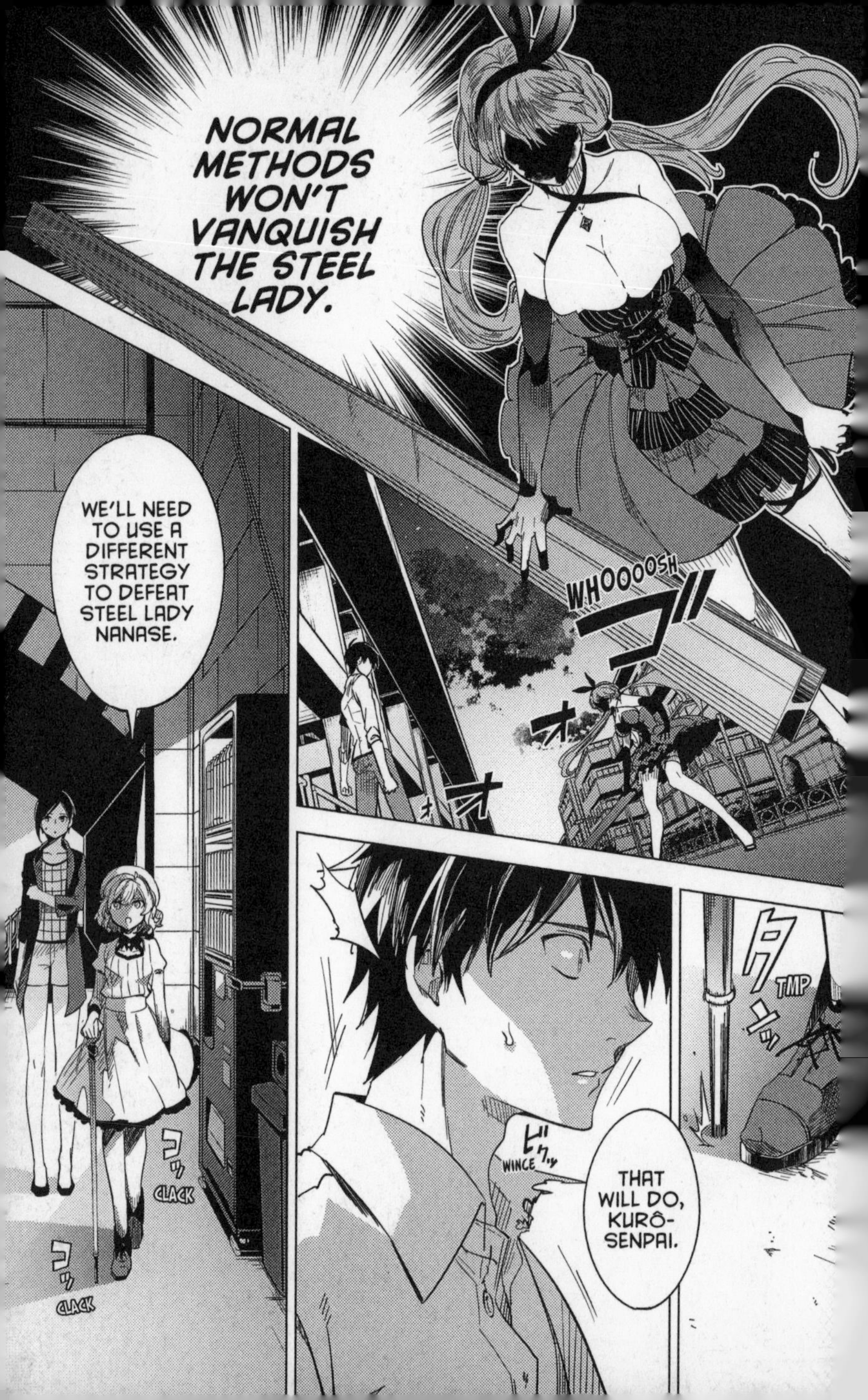
NORMAL METHODS WON'T VANQUISH THE STEEL LADY.
WHOOOOSH
TMP
WINCE
THAT WILL DO, KURÔ-SENPAI.
WE'LL NEED TO USE A DIFFERENT STRATEGY TO DEFEAT STEEL LADY NANASE.
CLACK
CLACK

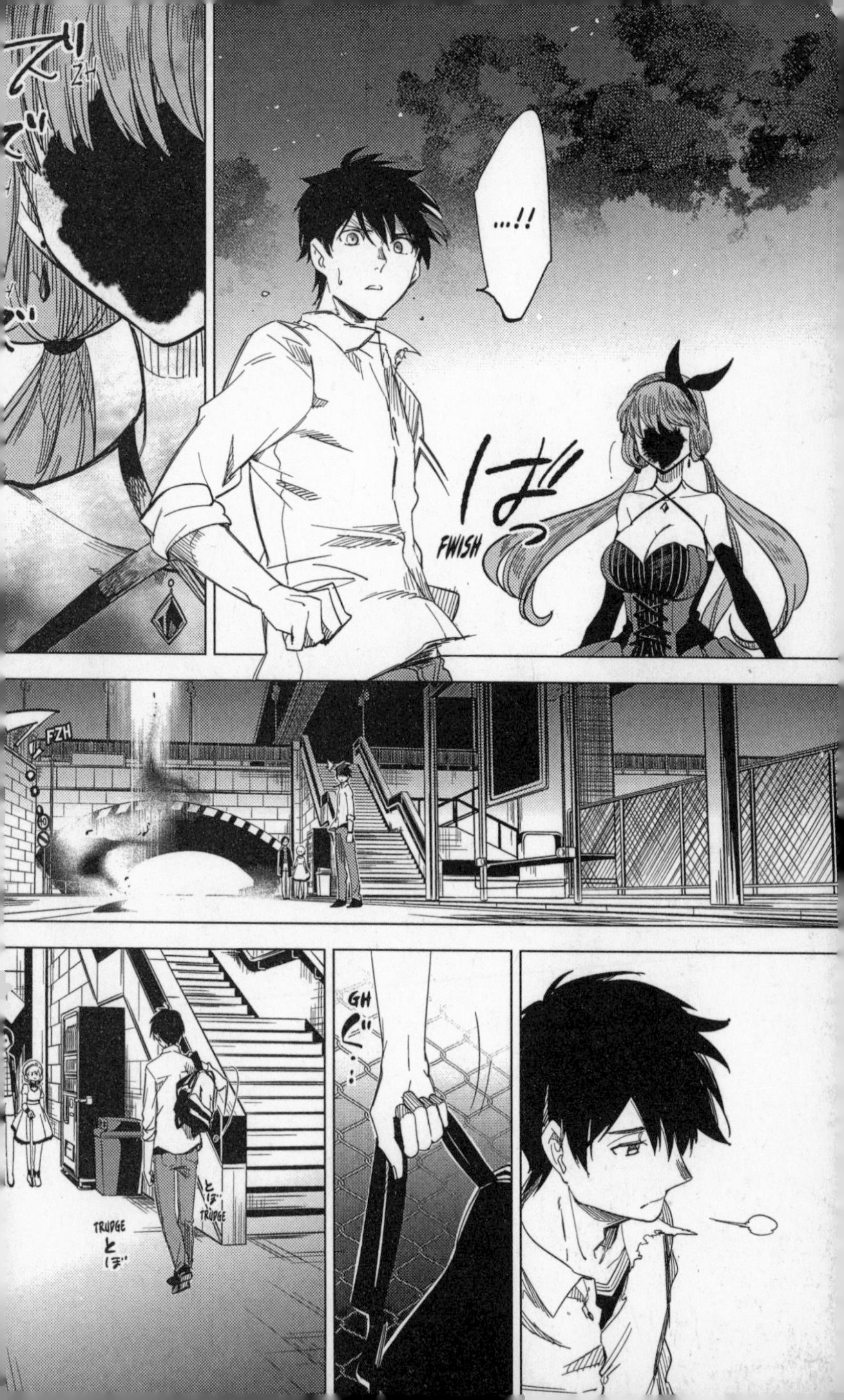
...!!
ばっ
FWISH
ZH
FZH
GH
ぐ...
TRUDGE
とぼ
TRUDGE
とぼ

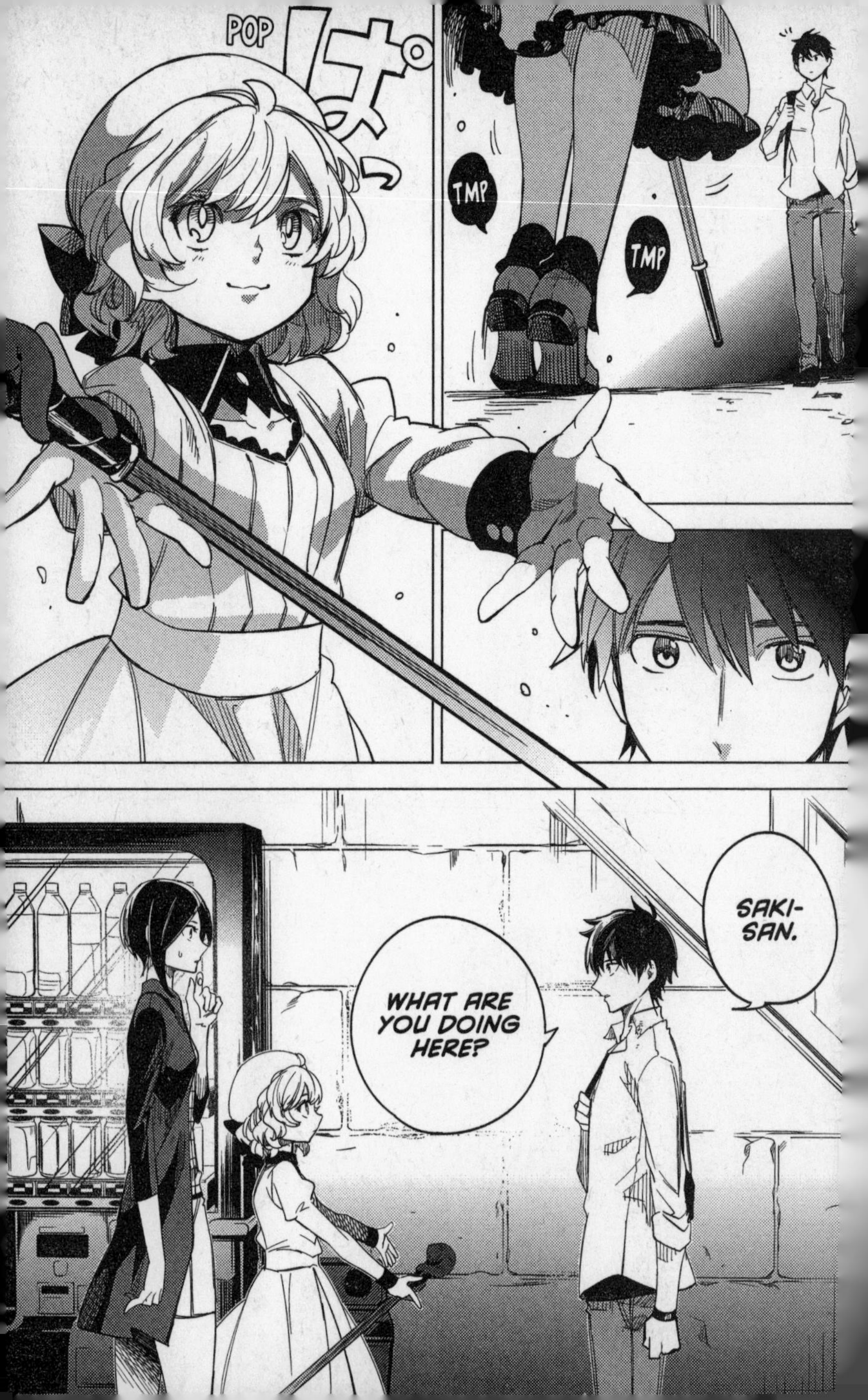
TMP
TMP
POP
ぱっ
SAKI-SAN.
WHAT ARE YOU DOING HERE?

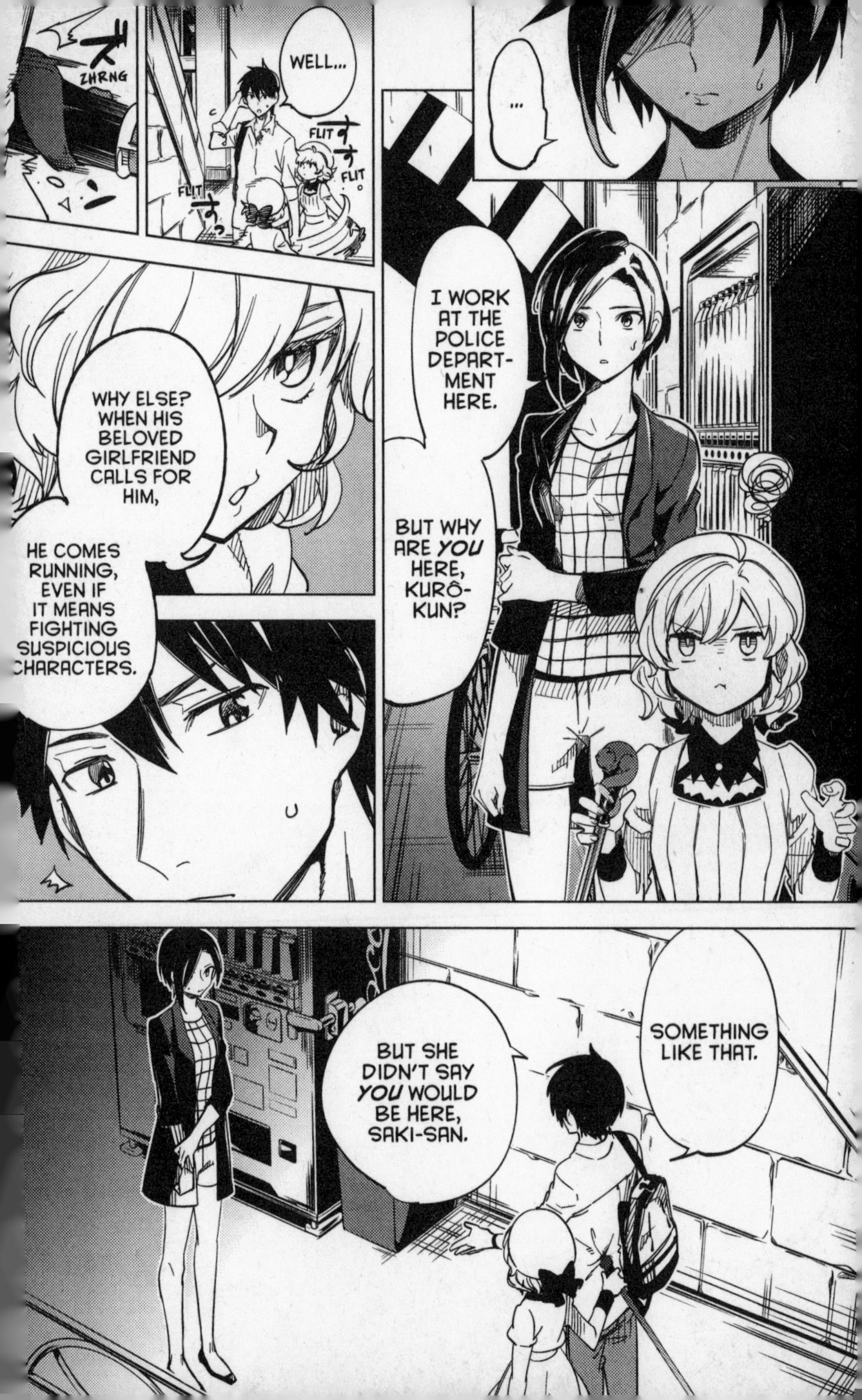
...
I WORK AT THE POLICE DEPARTMENT HERE.
BUT WHY ARE *YOU* HERE, KURÔ-KUN?
WELL...
FLIT
FLIT
FLIT
ZHRNG
WHY ELSE? WHEN HIS BELOVED GIRLFRIEND CALLS FOR HIM,
HE COMES RUNNING, EVEN IF IT MEANS FIGHTING SUSPICIOUS CHARACTERS.
SOMETHING LIKE THAT.
BUT SHE DIDN'T SAY *YOU* WOULD BE HERE, SAKI-SAN.

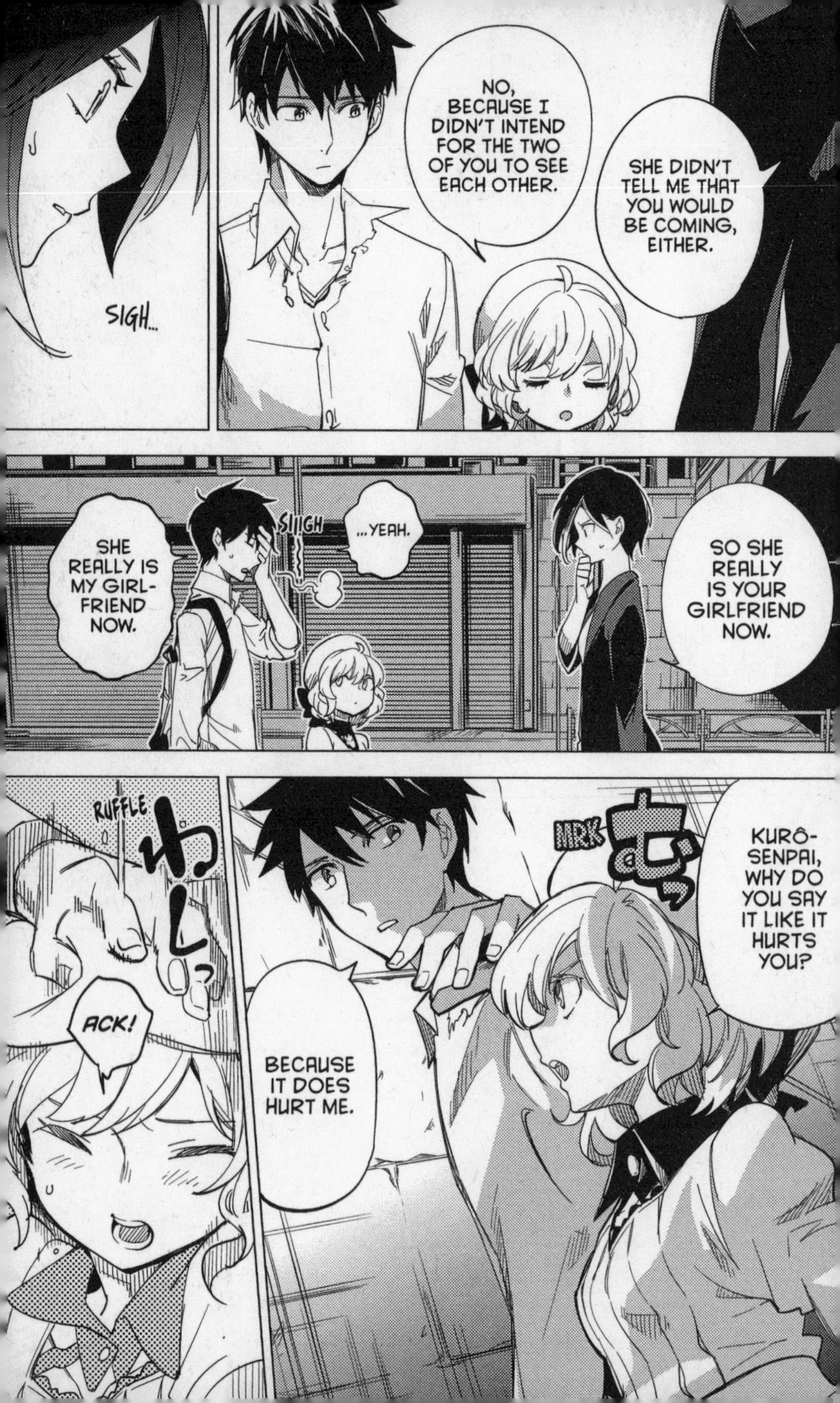

NO, BECAUSE I DIDN'T INTEND FOR THE TWO OF YOU TO SEE EACH OTHER.
SHE DIDN'T TELL ME THAT YOU WOULD BE COMING, EITHER.
SIGH...
SO SHE REALLY IS YOUR GIRLFRIEND NOW.
...YEAH.
SIIIGH
SHE REALLY IS MY GIRL-FRIEND NOW.
KURÔ-SENPAI, WHY DO YOU SAY IT LIKE IT HURTS YOU?
NRK
むっ
BECAUSE IT DOES HURT ME.
RUFFLE
わしっ
ACK!

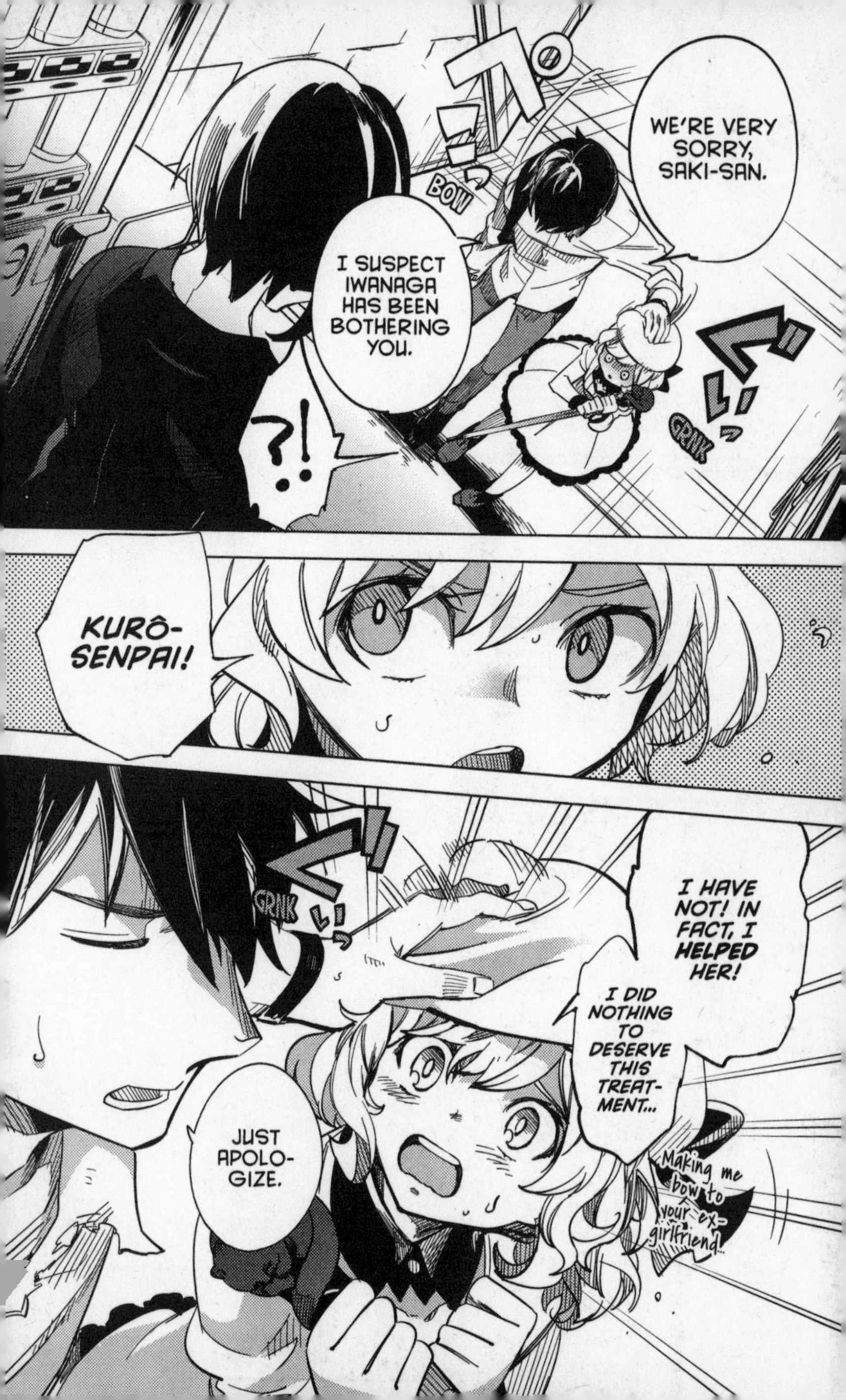
WE'RE VERY SORRY, SAKI-SAN.
BOW
I SUSPECT IWANAGA HAS BEEN BOTHERING YOU.
GRNK
?!
KURÔ-SENPAI!
I HAVE NOT! IN FACT, I HELPED HER!
I DID NOTHING TO DESERVE THIS TREAT-MENT...
Making me bow to your ex-girlfriend...
GRNK
JUST APOLO-GIZE.

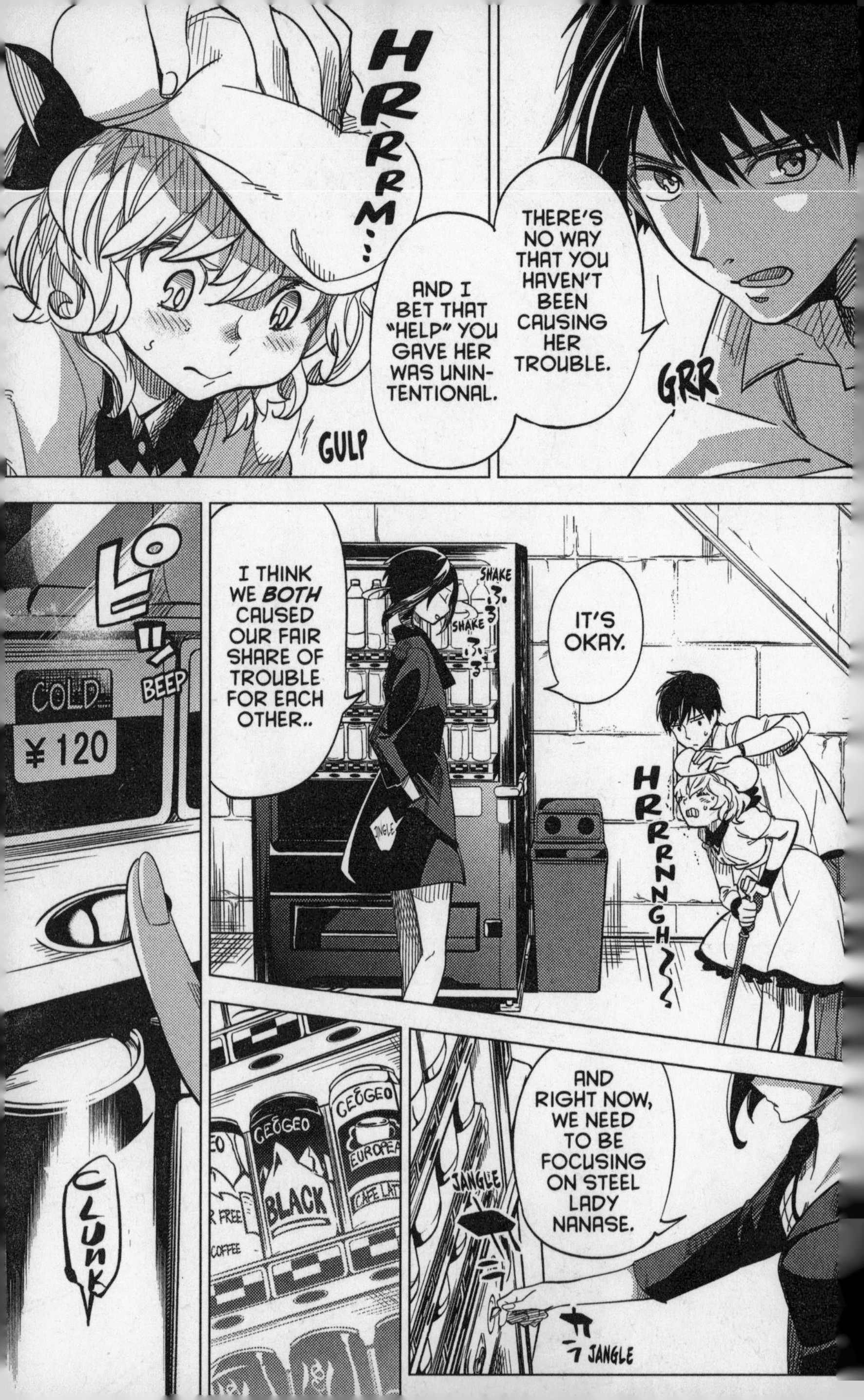

THERE'S NO WAY THAT YOU HAVEN'T BEEN CAUSING HER TROUBLE.
GRR
HRRRM...
AND I BET THAT "HELP" YOU GAVE HER WAS UNINTENTIONAL.
GULP
IT'S OKAY.
SHAKE ふる
SHAKE ふる
I THINK WE *BOTH* CAUSED OUR FAIR SHARE OF TROUBLE FOR EACH OTHER..
HRRRNNGH
JANGLE
ピッ
BEEP
COLD
¥120
AND RIGHT NOW, WE NEED TO BE FOCUSING ON STEEL LADY NANASE.
JANGLE
JANGLE
GEOGEO
BLACK
GEOGEO
EUROPEA
CAFE LAT
COFFEE
CLUNK

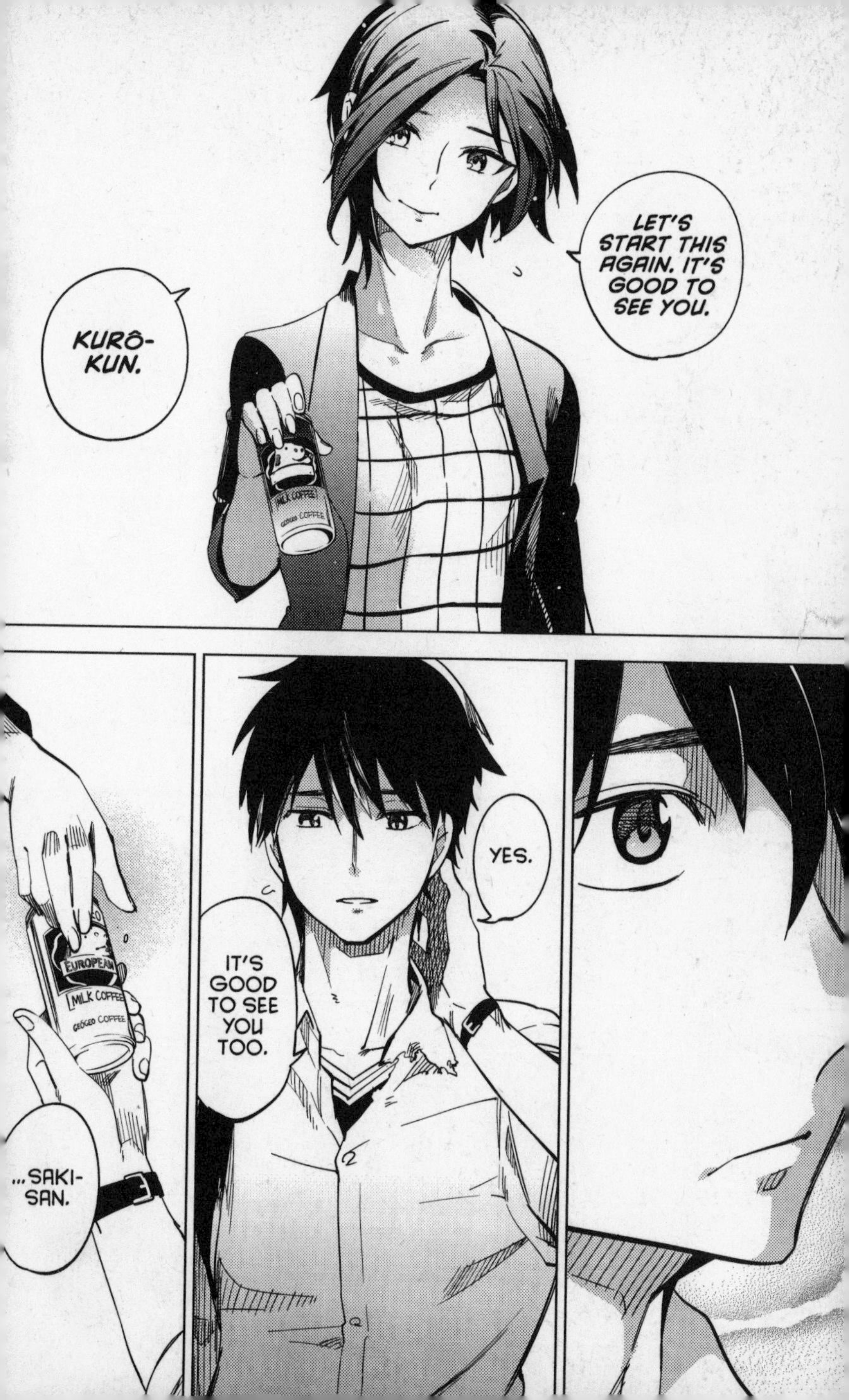
LET'S START THIS AGAIN. IT'S GOOD TO SEE YOU.
KURÔ-KUN.
MILK COFFEE
YES.
IT'S GOOD TO SEE YOU TOO.
EUROPEAN
MILK COFFEE
...SAKI-SAN.

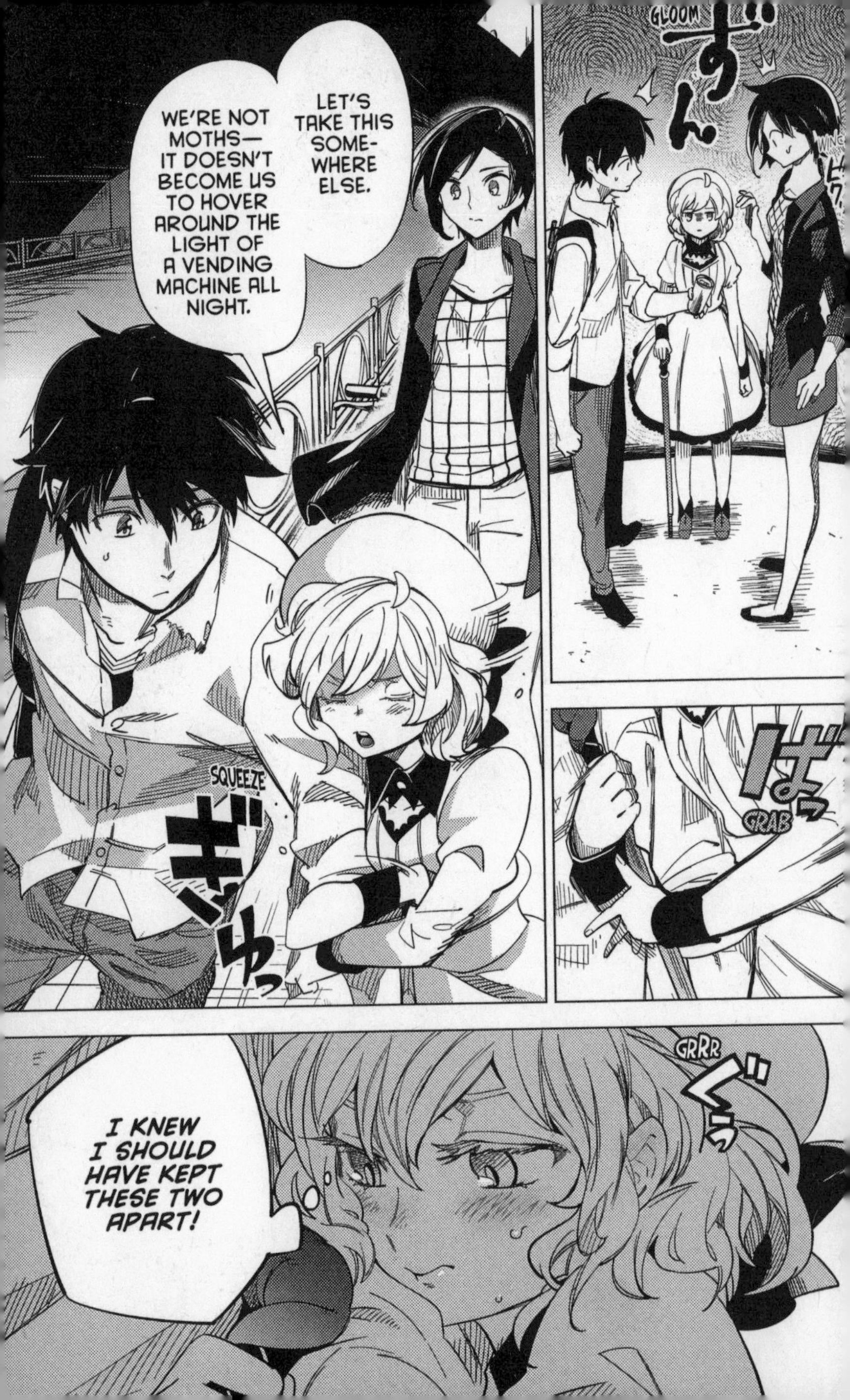
GLOOM
GRAB
LET'S TAKE THIS SOMEWHERE ELSE.
WE'RE NOT MOTHS—IT DOESN'T BECOME US TO HOVER AROUND THE LIGHT OF A VENDING MACHINE ALL NIGHT.
SQUEEZE
GRRR
I KNEW I SHOULD HAVE KEPT THESE TWO APART!

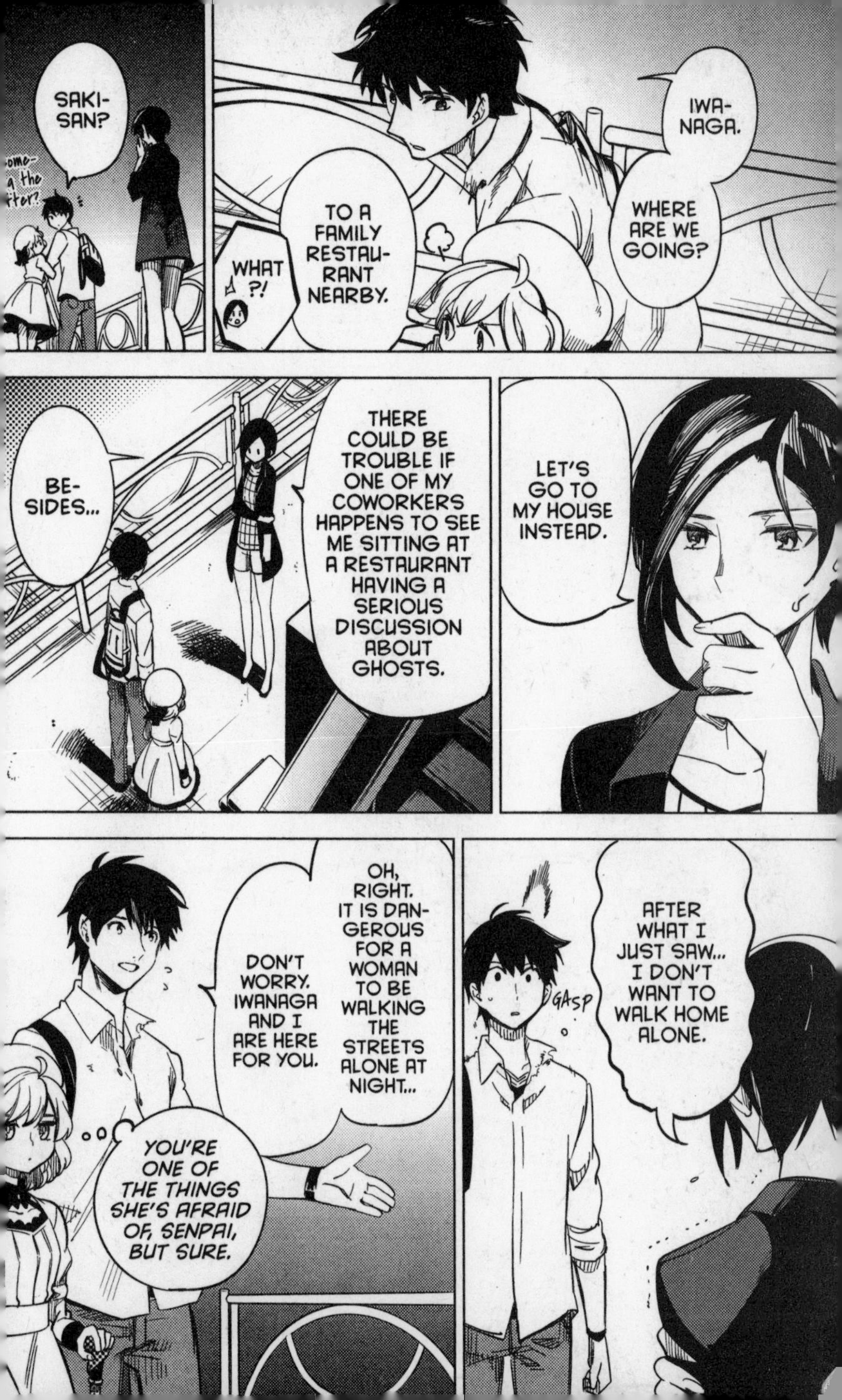
IWA-NAGA.
WHERE ARE WE GOING?
TO A FAMILY RESTAU-RANT NEARBY.
WHAT ?!
SAKI-SAN?
LET'S GO TO MY HOUSE INSTEAD.
THERE COULD BE TROUBLE IF ONE OF MY COWORKERS HAPPENS TO SEE ME SITTING AT A RESTAURANT HAVING A SERIOUS DISCUSSION ABOUT GHOSTS.
BE-SIDES...
AFTER WHAT I JUST SAW... I DON'T WANT TO WALK HOME ALONE.
GASP
OH, RIGHT. IT IS DAN-GEROUS FOR A WOMAN TO BE WALKING THE STREETS ALONE AT NIGHT...
DON'T WORRY. IWANAGA AND I ARE HERE FOR YOU.
YOU'RE ONE OF THE THINGS SHE'S AFRAID OF, SENPAI, BUT SURE.

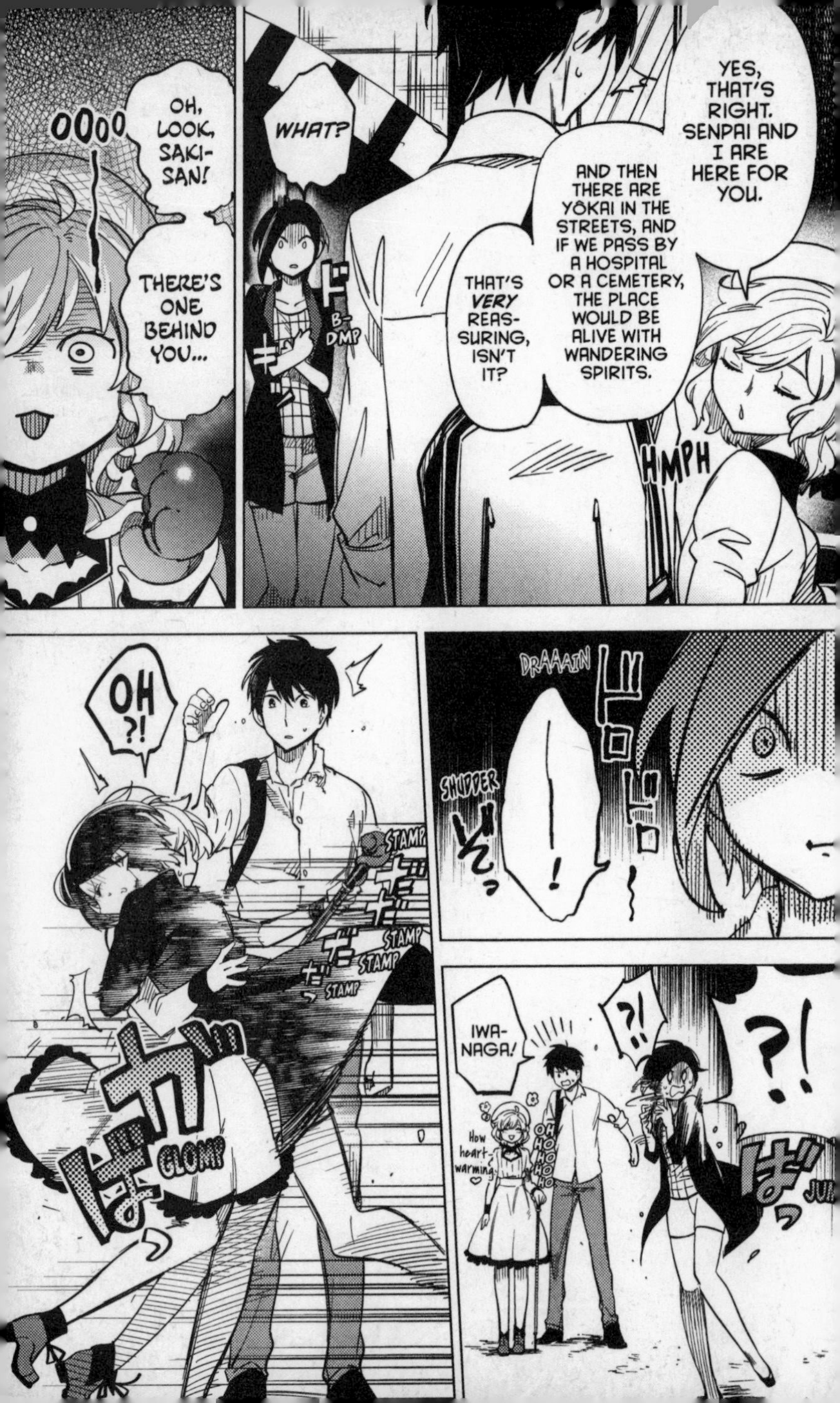
YES, THAT'S RIGHT. SENPAI AND I ARE HERE FOR YOU.
AND THEN THERE ARE YÔKAI IN THE STREETS, AND IF WE PASS BY A HOSPITAL OR A CEMETERY, THE PLACE WOULD BE ALIVE WITH WANDERING SPIRITS.
THAT'S *VERY* REASSURING, ISN'T IT?
HMPH
WHAT?
B-DMP
OOOO
OH, LOOK, SAKI-SAN!
THERE'S ONE BEHIND YOU...
DRAAAIN
SHUDDER
?!
JU
?!
IWA-NAGA!
OHOHOHOHO
How heart-warming ♡
OH ?!
STAMP
STAMP
STAMP
STAMP
GLOMP

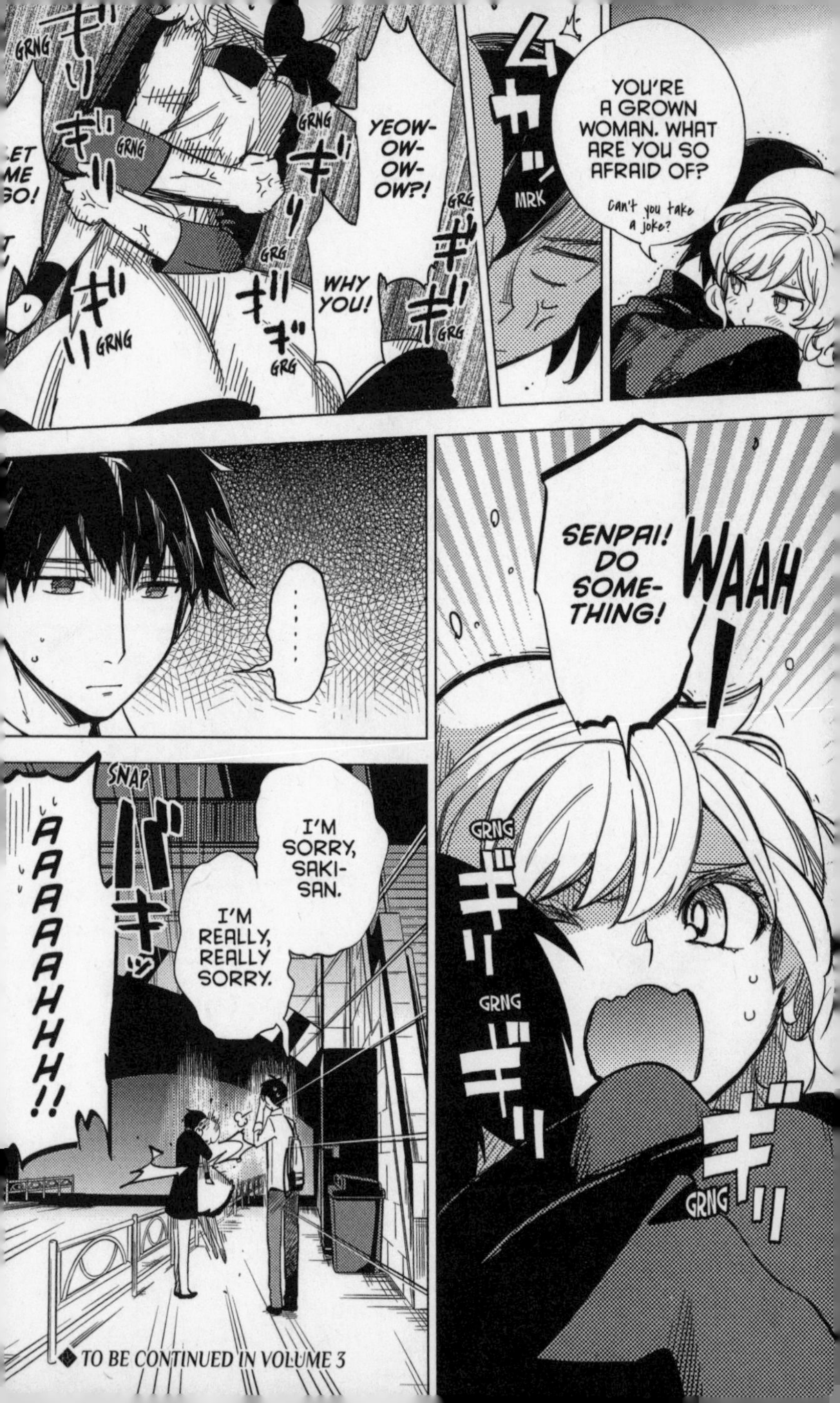

YOU'RE A GROWN WOMAN. WHAT ARE YOU SO AFRAID OF?
Can't you take a joke?
MRK
GRG
YEOW-OW-OW-OW?!
WHY YOU!
GRNG
ET ME GO!
GRNG
SENPAI! DO SOMETHING!
WAAH!
GRNG
GRNG
GRNG
......
SNAP
AAAAAAAHHHH!!
I'M SORRY, SAKI-SAN.
I'M REALLY, REALLY SORRY.
TO BE CONTINUED IN VOLUME 3

IN/SPECTRE

Something Like a Comment from the Author

I am Kyo Shirodaira, the original author who, as with volume one, didn't really have any hand in the story's manga version. This is volume two.

I think the highlights of this volume are the scenes from Karin Nanase's drama, *"Youth! The Girl Who Breathes Fire!"* that showed up in chapter three.

They're important scenes that are necessary to give the readers a clear impression of what the idol Karin Nanase was like in life, but only the title of the show and the name of the song were mentioned in the original novel. The book didn't have any other details, let alone an entire scene. And when the story became a manga, I didn't give the artist any background details or anything, so the scenes were a complete manga original.

When I was writing the novel, I had to come up with a title for Karin Nanase's TV series, so I pulled out the "Funny Words that I May Use for Something Someday" notebook that I keep habitually to help with my writing, and picked something fitting—I didn't bother to think about any sort of content for the show at all.

It started with one of my notes, "*Kaenhôshaki* (Flamethrower) Girl," and because I felt like it sounded a little cool and stylish, I turned it into the more Japanese-sounding "*Hifuki Musume* (the Girl Who Breathes Fire)." Then I thought about what word I could attach to it to make it even funnier, and the word "*seishun* (youth, adolescence)" came into my mind. I remember thinking it felt too heavy all on its own, so I added an exclamation point to bring out its "pop" essence. That's where I ran

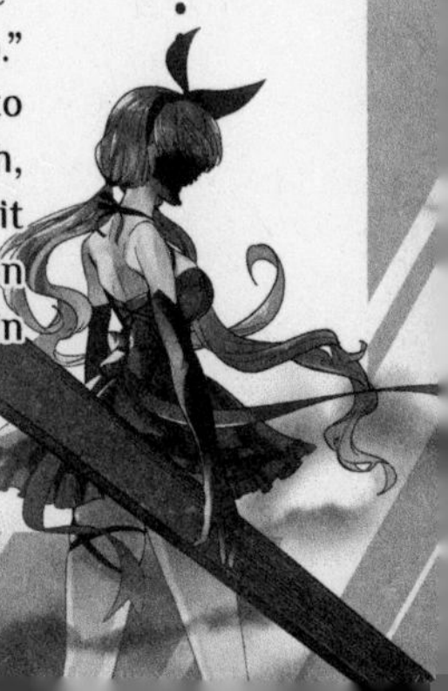

completely out of energy, so the whole endeavor ended with nothing but a title.

And yet, here in the manga, it has a story and characters that fit the title, and there's even some action! I was in total awe, like the shoemaker who woke up to find all the shoes that were made while he slept. Fairy tale events do happen in real life. There's hope for the real world after all.

On the other hand, Chashiba Katase-sensei had to create a comic of this fictional drama with that title and no other clues whatsoever, and may have been grumbling and snarling, "If this is reality, then it's a cruel and unreasonable world that I live in." Um, I'm really sorry.

Nevertheless, this title, *"Youth! The Girl Who Breathes Fire!,"* is something that I was very particular about when I put it in my book. For instance, for the entire rest of the book, I managed to maintain my personal aesthetic of using no exclamation points, but in this case, I thought, "It won't feel right if I take the exclamation point out, and there's no better title than this one," so in the end, I did not remove the exclamation points or change the title. So believe it or not, I didn't settle on this title just because I needed something and it didn't really matter. But it is a pretty insignificant thing to be particular about.

As for the manga itself, it continues to be a self-proclaimed mystery manga that is not very mystery-like, but I think it may just be possible that all the groundwork has been laid for it to start being a mystery series.

With that in mind, I hope you'll read the next volume.

Kyo Shirodaira

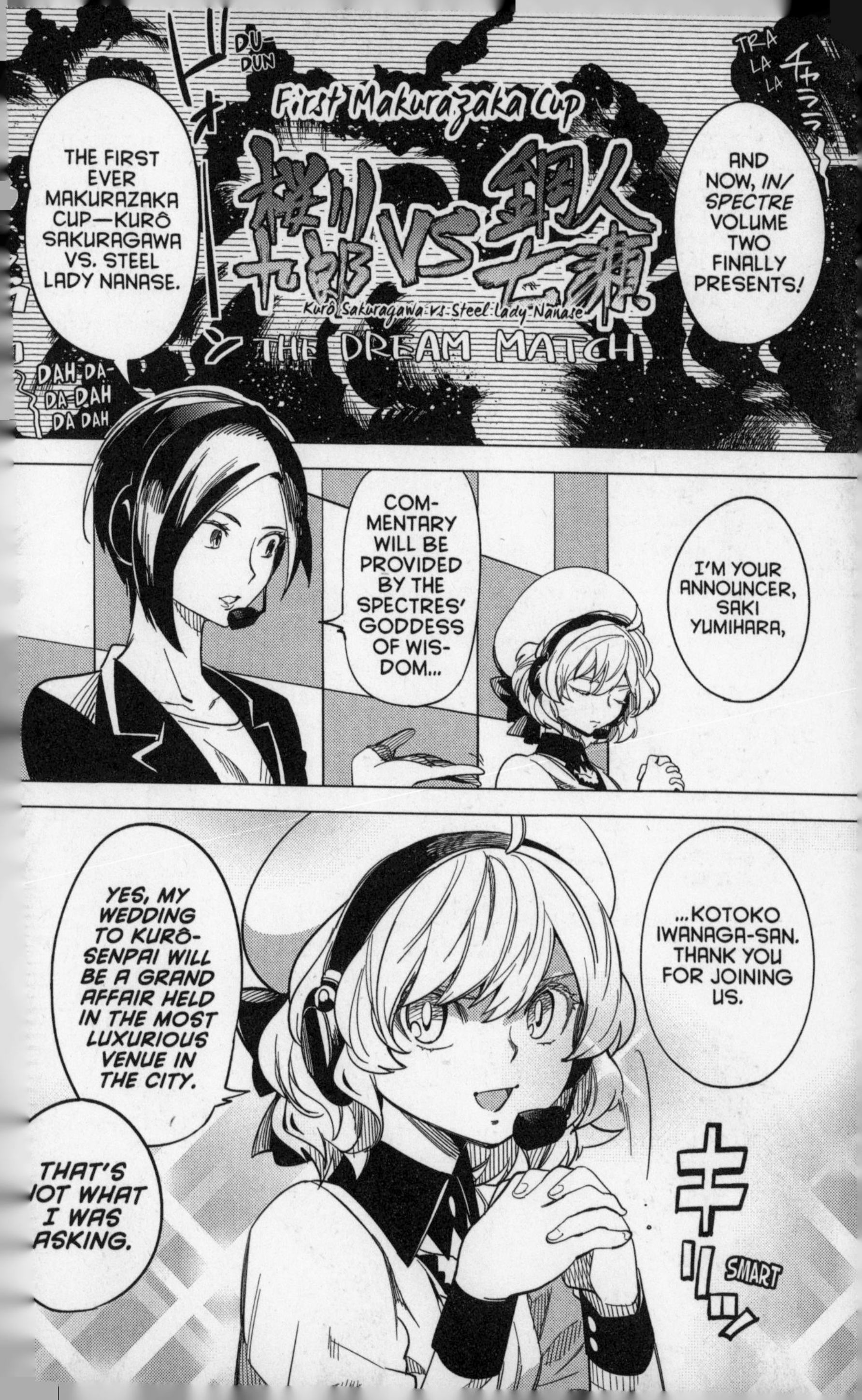
TRA LA LA
AND NOW, IN/SPECTRE VOLUME TWO FINALLY PRESENTS!
First Makurazaka Cup
Kurô Sakuragawa vs Steel Lady Nanase
THE DREAM MATCH
DU-DUN
THE FIRST EVER MAKURAZAKA CUP—KURÔ SAKURAGAWA VS. STEEL LADY NANASE.
DAH DA-DA-DAH DA DAH
I'M YOUR ANNOUNCER, SAKI YUMIHARA,
COMMENTARY WILL BE PROVIDED BY THE SPECTRES' GODDESS OF WISDOM...
...KOTOKO IWANAGA-SAN. THANK YOU FOR JOINING US.
SMART
YES, MY WEDDING TO KURÔ-SENPAI WILL BE A GRAND AFFAIR HELD IN THE MOST LUXURIOUS VENUE IN THE CITY.
THAT'S OT WHAT I WAS ASKING.

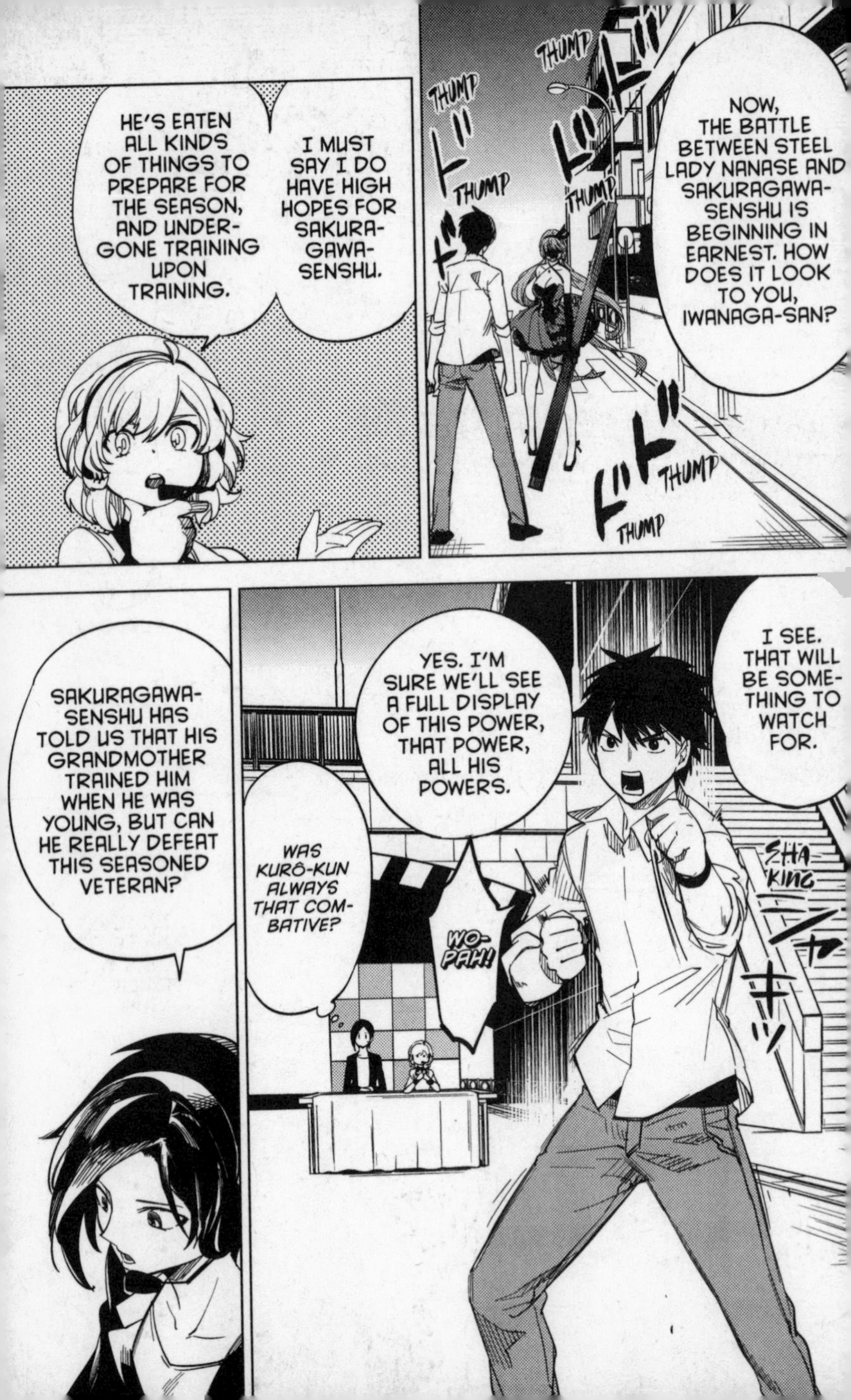
NOW, THE BATTLE BETWEEN STEEL LADY NANASE AND SAKURAGAWA-SENSHU IS BEGINNING IN EARNEST. HOW DOES IT LOOK TO YOU, IWANAGA-SAN?
THUMP
THUMP
THUMP
THUMP
THUMP
THUMP
I MUST SAY I DO HAVE HIGH HOPES FOR SAKURAGAWA-SENSHU.
HE'S EATEN ALL KINDS OF THINGS TO PREPARE FOR THE SEASON, AND UNDERGONE TRAINING UPON TRAINING.
I SEE. THAT WILL BE SOMETHING TO WATCH FOR.
YES. I'M SURE WE'LL SEE A FULL DISPLAY OF THIS POWER, THAT POWER, ALL HIS POWERS.
SHAKING
WO-PAH!
WAS KURÔ-KUN ALWAYS THAT COMBATIVE?
SAKURAGAWA-SENSHU HAS TOLD US THAT HIS GRANDMOTHER TRAINED HIM WHEN HE WAS YOUNG, BUT CAN HE REALLY DEFEAT THIS SEASONED VETERAN?

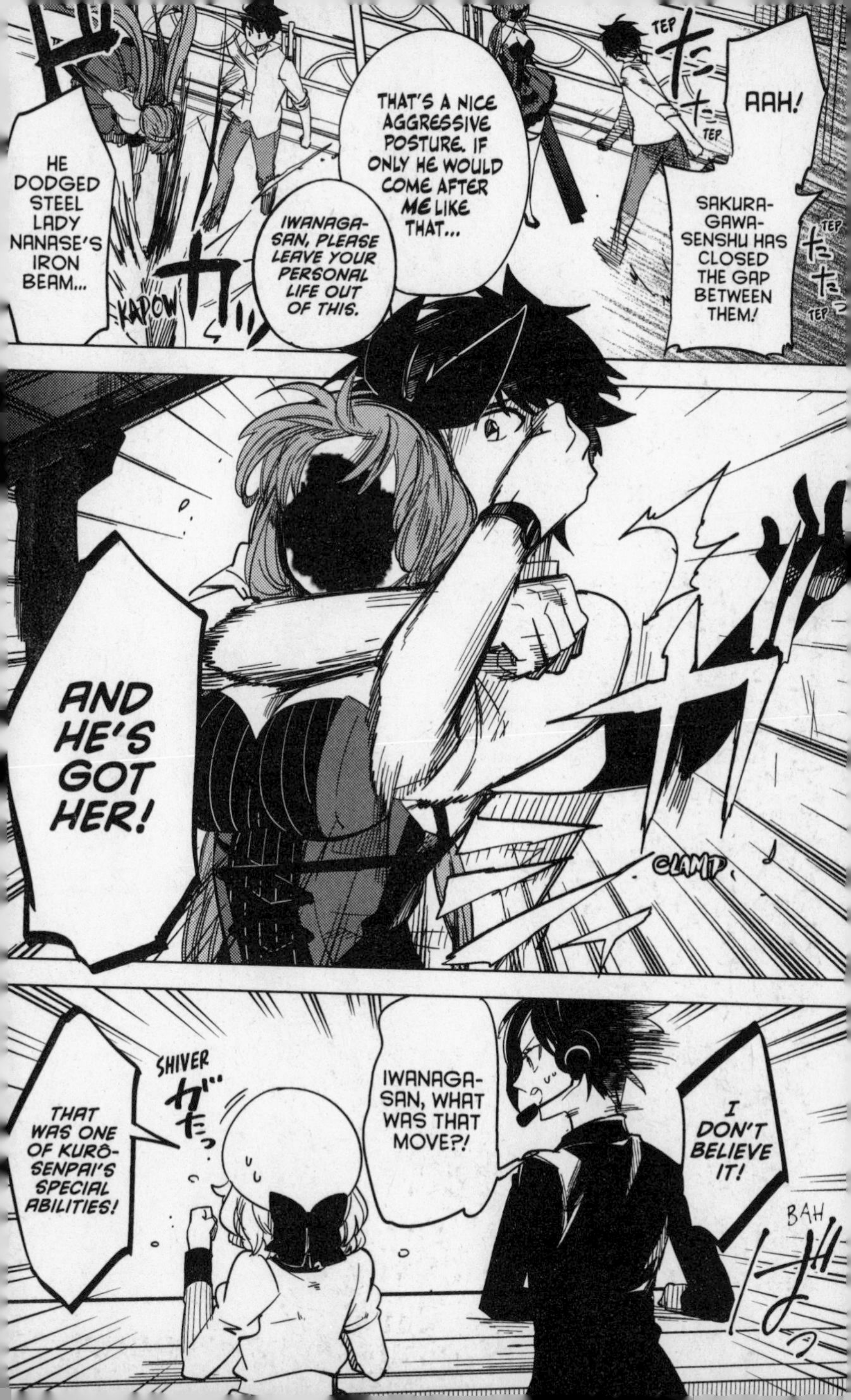
TEP
AAH!
TEP
SAKURA-GAWA-SENSHU HAS CLOSED THE GAP BETWEEN THEM!
TEP
TEP
THAT'S A NICE AGGRESSIVE POSTURE. IF ONLY HE WOULD COME AFTER ME LIKE THAT...
IWANAGA-SAN, PLEASE LEAVE YOUR PERSONAL LIFE OUT OF THIS.
HE DODGED STEEL LADY NANASE'S IRON BEAM...
KADOW
AND HE'S GOT HER!
CLAMP
I DON'T BELIEVE IT!
BAH
IWANAGA-SAN, WHAT WAS THAT MOVE?!
SHIVER
THAT WAS ONE OF KURÔ-SENPAI'S SPECIAL ABILITIES!

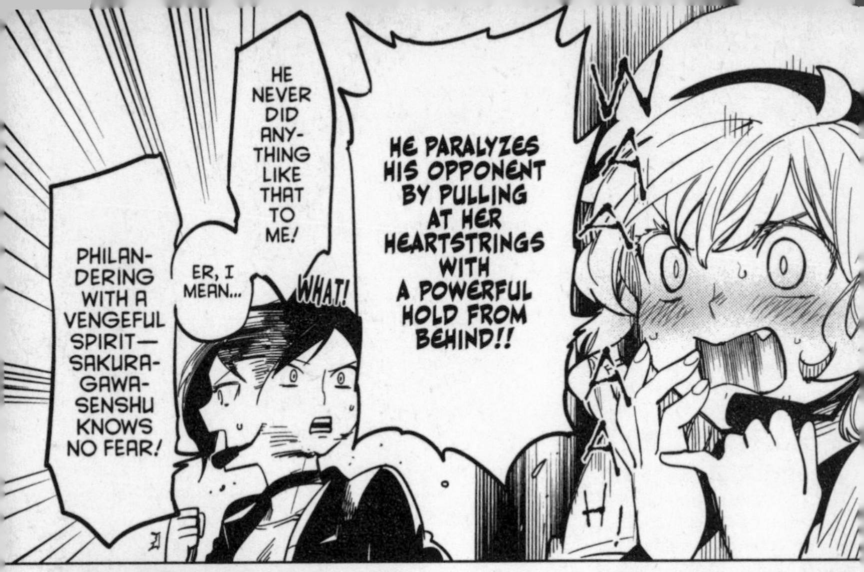
HE PARALYZES HIS OPPONENT BY PULLING AT HER HEARTSTRINGS WITH A POWERFUL HOLD FROM BEHIND!!
WHAT!
HE NEVER DID ANYTHING LIKE THAT TO ME!
ER, I MEAN...
PHILANDERING WITH A VENGEFUL SPIRIT—SAKURAGAWA-SENSHU KNOWS NO FEAR!

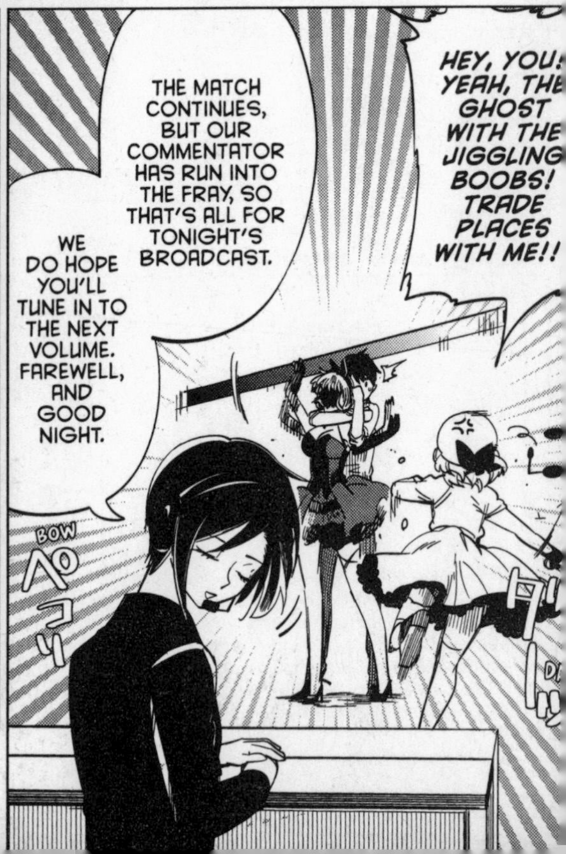
HEY, YOU! YEAH, THE GHOST WITH THE JIGGLING BOOBS! TRADE PLACES WITH ME!!
THE MATCH CONTINUES, BUT OUR COMMENTATOR HAS RUN INTO THE FRAY, SO THAT'S ALL FOR TONIGHT'S BROADCAST.
WE DO HOPE YOU'LL TUNE IN TO THE NEXT VOLUME. FAREWELL, AND GOOD NIGHT.
BOW

Thank you very much for picking up this manga. I hope you'll read the next volume, too!

Katase

- Staff -

Kuro Shima

Tonpu

Yamada

Yamamoto

- Editors -

O-kawa

T-da

(honorifics excluded)

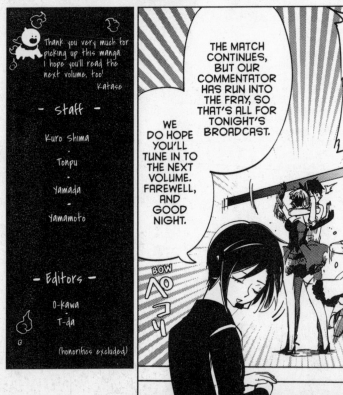

TRANSLATION NOTES

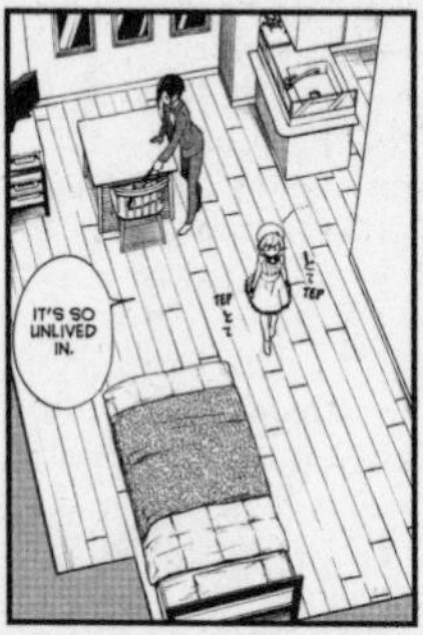
IT'S SO UNLIVED IN.
TEP TEP

As big as my bathroom, page 5

To give a clearer idea of the enormous size of Kotoko's home, when she says Saki's apartment is as big as her bathroom, she is referring specifically to the *toire*, or toilet room, containing only a toilet and no actual bathing facilities. In Japanese homes, bathtubs and showers are usually in a separate room.

Gravure idol, page 36

The short definition of "gravure idol" is a model who often wears skimpy clothing. The term comes from "rotogravure," which is a printing process that was used for magazines at the time these models first came into vogue. While they often pose provocatively, a gravure idol generally appeals to her audience with her playfulness or innocence.

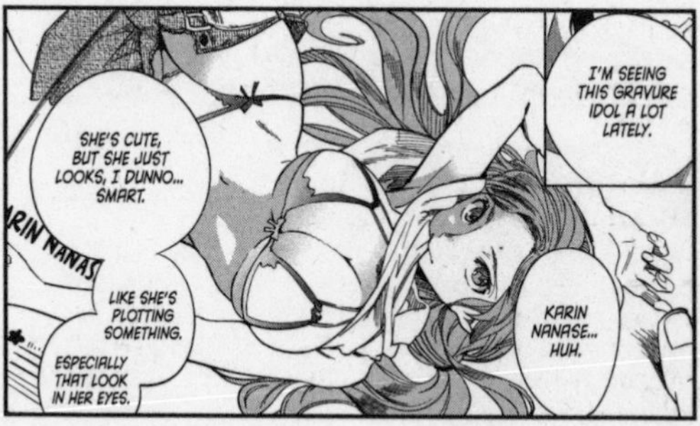
I'M SEEING THIS GRAVURE IDOL A LOT LATELY.
KARIN NANASE... HUH.
SHE'S CUTE, BUT SHE JUST LOOKS, I DUNNO... SMART.
KARIN NANAS
LIKE SHE'S PLOTTING SOMETHING.
ESPECIALLY THAT LOOK IN HER EYES.

Late-night serial drama, page 37-44

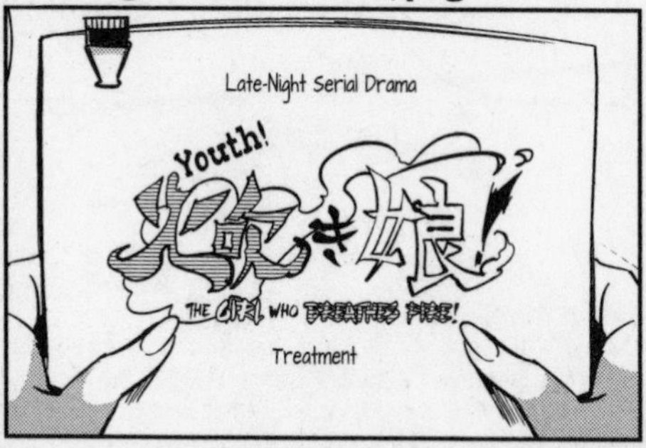
Late-Night Serial Drama
Youth!
火吹き娘!
THE GIRL WHO BREATHES FIRE!
Treatment

Like many places around the world, late-night television in Japan tends to have looser restrictions on what can be shown and has cheaper ad costs, allowing for more experimental and risqué programming. The adult nature and goofiness of a show like *"Youth! The Girl Who Breathes Fire!"* normally wouldn't be shown on public television during primetime hours, so they often have to be relegated to between the hours of 11 pm and 5 am, the hours for late-night programming (JP: *shinya bangumi*). Interestingly, shows like this were most prevalent in the 80s during Japan's "bubble era" but since the collapse of the economic bubble, Japanese television has become increasingly conservative and TV viewership has dropped considerably, so these types of programs aren't really seen much or are rather tame compared to what used to be shown.

Teikyô-me, page 40

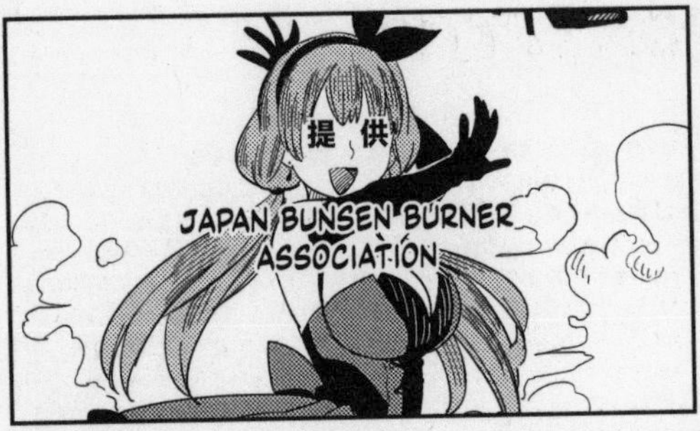
提 供
JAPAN BUNSEN BURNER ASSOCIATION

Most Japanese television programs have a brief moment before a commercial break to present the sponsors for the show being broadcast. When this happens, the kanji for "brought to you by" or "sponsor" (提供 or *teikyô*) is overlaid onto a freeze-frame from the show along with the sponsor's name as an announcer says something to the effect of "XX is brought to you by these sponsors." In recent years, people have spotted instances where the "sponsor" kanji has been laid perfectly over a character's eyes. This became a meme of sorts in Japan and there are people who also collect screen grabs of these funny scenes. These scenes have even become famous enough that some people suspect animation and production companies may be purposely setting up freeze-frames to create these *teikyô-me* (sponsor eyes). They are also known as *teikyô-megane* (sponsor glasses) or *teikyô-metsubushi* (sponsor blinders).

Koro-pok-guru, page 83

The Koro-pok-guru are a race of little people who live in northern Japan and are small enough to fit under a butterbur leaf, as pictured. They are part of the folklore of the Ainu indigenous people of Hokkaido and were on very friendly terms with humans, but were very shy, and although they would leave people gifts, they almost always did it under cover of night.

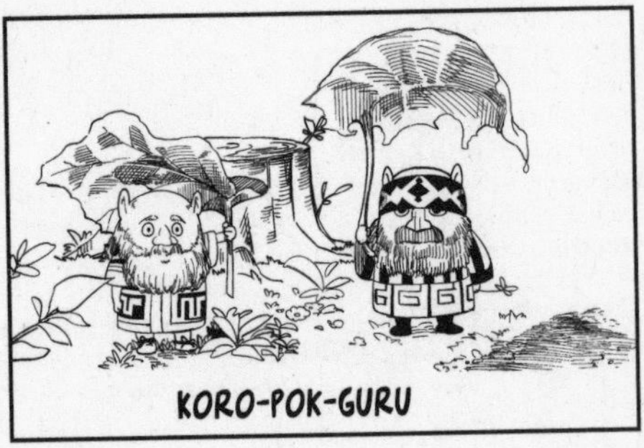
KORO-POK-GURU

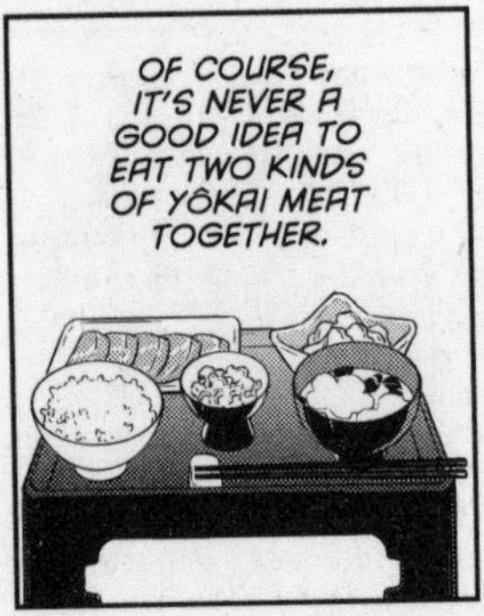
OF COURSE, IT'S NEVER A GOOD IDEA TO EAT TWO KINDS OF YÔKAI MEAT TOGETHER.

The Other Wight Meat, page 85

"Wight" is a word for supernatural creatures, like yôkai. The original Japanese title of this chapter is "The Other *Mazarimono*," or "blended thing," referring to the other type of yôkai meat that turned Kurô into what he is today.

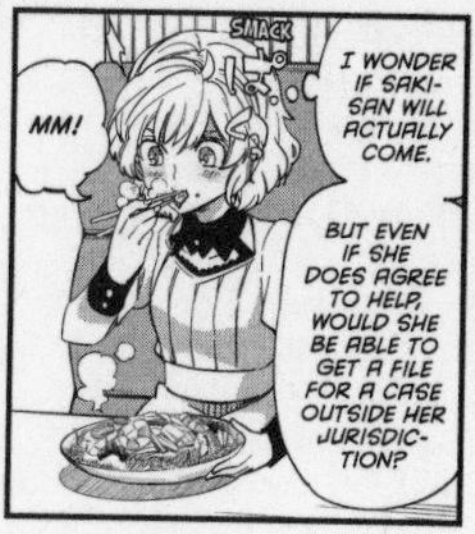
SMACK
I WONDER IF SAKI-SAN WILL ACTUALLY COME.
MM!
BUT EVEN IF SHE DOES AGREE TO HELP, WOULD SHE BE ABLE TO GET A FILE FOR A CASE OUTSIDE HER JURISDIC-TION?

Seafood kata yakisoba, page 105
This is a dish of fried noodles and seafood. The *kata* part means "hard," indicating that the noodles have been cooked until they are crispy.

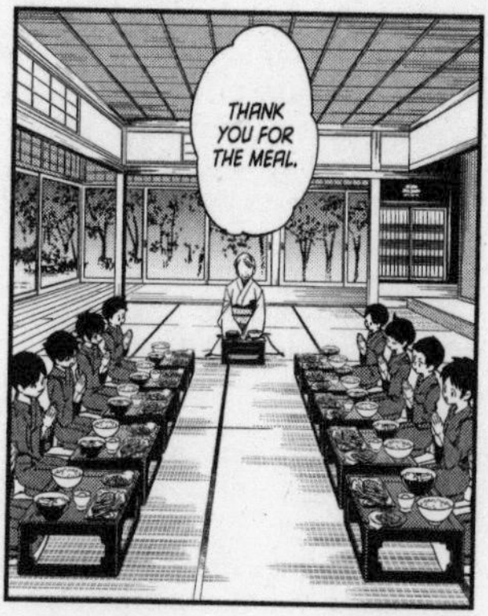
THANK YOU FOR THE MEAL.

Thank you for the meal, page 143
It is customary in Japan to say *itadakimasu* before eating, a phrase that means "I humbly partake." This generally considered to be a way of expressing gratitude to anyone or anything who played a role in putting this meal on the table.

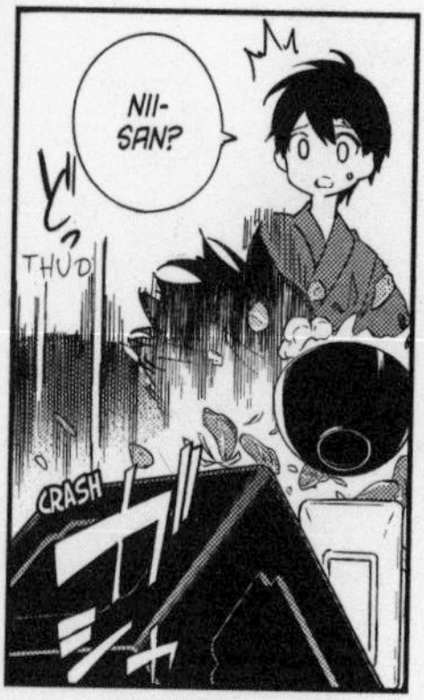
NII-SAN?
THUD
CRASH

***Nii-san*, page 144**
Nii-san literally means "older brother" and is used to address people who are the speaker's older brother, or people that the speaker considers to be brotherly figures, or as a polite way to address a young man when the speaker doesn't know the man's name. In this case, because Kurô is with his grandmother, it's likely that these boys are his brothers and/or cousins. Older sisters and girl cousins would be called *Nê-san*.

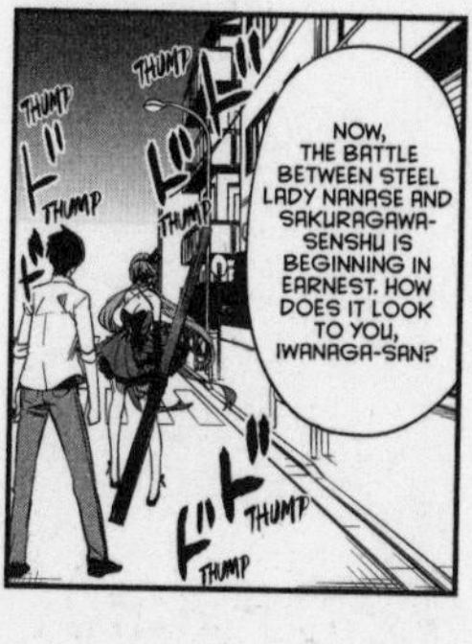
THUMP
THUMP
NOW, THE BATTLE BETWEEN STEEL LADY NANASE AND SAKURAGAWA-SENSHU IS BEGINNING IN EARNEST. HOW DOES IT LOOK TO YOU, IWANAGA-SAN?
THUMP
THUMP
THUMP
THUMP

***Senshu*, page 175**
Senshu is another title attached to people's names in order to show respect, like *sensei.* It is given to athletes, such as baseball players, soccer players, martial artists, and fighters in supernatural death matches.

IN/SPECTRE

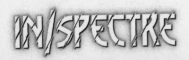

We're having sashimi tonight!

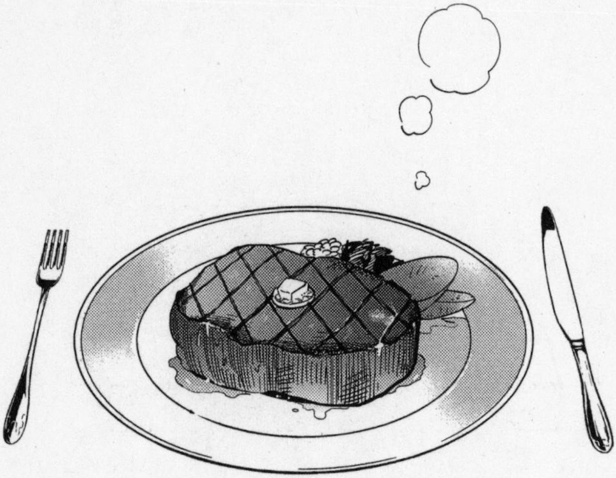

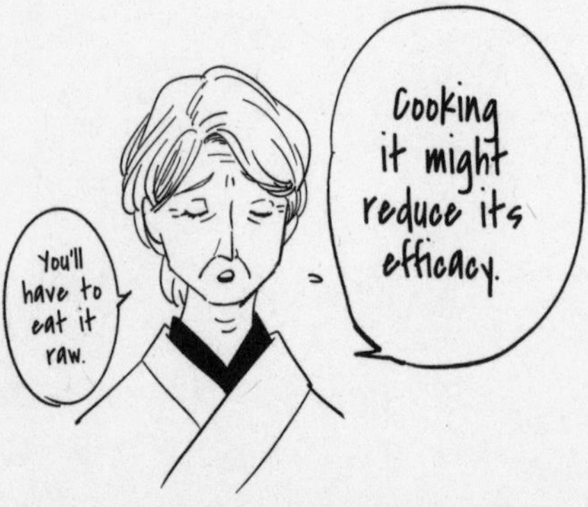
Cooking it might reduce its efficacy.
You'll have to eat it raw.

my Little monster

POSITES ATTRACT...MAYBE?

u Yoshida is feared as an unstable and violent "monster."
utani Shizuku is a grade-obsessed student with no friends.
e brings these two together to form the most unlikely pair. Haru
ly believes he's in love with Mizutani and she firmly believes
insane.

KC
KODANSHA
COMICS

SAY I LOVE YOU.

KC KODANSHA COMICS

Mei Tachibana has no friends — and says she doesn't need them

But everything changes when she accidentally roundhouse kicks the most popular boy in school! However, Yamato Kurosawa isn't angry in the slightest in fact, he thinks his ordinary life could use an unusual girl like Mei. But winnin Mei's trust will be a tough task. How long will she refuse to say, "I love you"?